What people are saying about *Realizing the Promise of Corporate Portals:*

"Terra and Gordon have managed to write a book that is unique in that it is equally valuable for professionals with business AND IT backgrounds. By clearly linking Corporate Portals and KM to business goals, the authors help organizations to justify why such projects should be implemented. The book relies on in-depth case studies that are presented in a very structured, objective, and pragmatic way. It is a must read for practitioners."

—**Juliano Benatti**, Head of Ericsson University,
Region Latin America

"Corporate portals are at the leading edge of knowledge management practice. Terra and Gordon's book provides valuable insight into this key area of business innovation. This book will be of interest to academics as well as practitioners. Anyone who is involved in developing or managing corporate KM initiatives will find many useful learnings in this book about portal solutions, their technical solutions, their performance metrics, and the organizational roles, strategies, and cultures that support successful KM-oriented portals."

—**Charles H. Davis, Ph.D.**, Professor, Management
of Technological Change, University of New Brunswick

"Corporate portals are key to knowledge management as well as a host of productivity improvements within and across enterprises. Anyone involved in developing a corporate portal will benefit from reading this book, but it will be particularly valuable for CEOs, without whose active support a comprehensive portal is impossible to create. The authors' emphasis on the human side of portals highlights critical organizational and cultural issues that are often overlooked. The case studies provide valuable guidance to the efforts required to create a portal and the benefits that it can deliver."

—**Rick Stuckey**, retired Accenture senior partner
responsible for Global KM

"This book should be a first read for managers of knowledge-intensive enterprises and a must read for IT professionals who implement Corporate Knowledge Portals. Cláudio Terra and Cindy Gordon provide excellent insights into the role and functions of CKPs. They provide an unusual understanding of how CKPs change the way business is conducted to improve enterprise performance. This understanding is crucial to ensure successful and effective portal implementations and has been missing from most books and articles."

—**Karl M. Wiig**, Chairman and CEO,
Knowledge Research Institute

REALIZING THE PROMISE OF CORPORATE PORTALS

REALIZING THE PROMISE OF CORPORATE PORTALS

LEVERAGING KNOWLEDGE FOR BUSINESS SUCCESS

José Cláudio Terra, Ph.D.
and
Cindy Gordon, Ph.D.

Routledge
Taylor & Francis Group

LONDON AND NEW YORK

First published by Butterworth-Heinemann

This edition published 2011 by Routledge
2 Park Square, Milton Park, Abingdon, Oxon OX14 4RN
711 Third Avenue, New York, NY 10017, USA

Routledge is an imprint of the Taylor & Francis Group, an informa business

Library of Congress Cataloging-in-Publication Data

Terra, José Cláudio.
    Realizing the promise of corporate portals : leveraging knowledge for business success
/ José Cláudio Terra and Cindy Gordon.
    p. cm.
    Includes bibliographical references and index.
    ISBN 0-7506-7593-4 (pbk. : alk. paper)
    1. Knowledge management. 2. Business enterprises—Computer networks.
    3. Information technology—Management. 4. Web portals. I. Gordon, Cindy. II. Title.

    HD30.2.T47 2002
    658.4'038—dc21

                                                                    2002074384

British Library Cataloguing-in-Publication Data
A catalogue record for this book is available from the British Library.

For Janine Dodge, my love, my wife, and my super editor! You were with me all the way during the course of this project, always pushing me forward. Thank you for that! I dedicate this book to our family!

My parents, Ruy and Neide, your love is a strong foundation.

Cindy, we made it! People who live around you are inspired by your collaborative leadership. It has been a pleasure working with you on this project!

José Cláudio Terra

Personal dedication to Perry Muhlbier, husband and friend, for his support during the research of our book. To my children, Jessica and Bryce, your inquisitive minds inspire the creative spirit for lifelong learning. Your patience and love fed my spirit. Thank you!

To my parents, Norma and Benny Gordon—thank you for your inspiration and confidence in creating a loving home environment filled with support and appreciation for lifelong learning. To my father who passed away on July 7, 2000—you will forever be in my heart.

Tremendous recognition for this book goes to Norma and J. B. Gordon whose life-long learning inspiration have helped my spirit soar with confidence during life's interesting pathways. Although my father died from cancer and will not be able to read this book on this earth, I know he will hear the words we cannot hear.

Dr. José Cláudio Terra, business colleague and friend: Your focused commitment and leadership for ensuring this book became a reality for both of us has created a level of trust and respect for you that I will treasure always. To our new possibilities in ensuring the world around us continues to learn how to implement capabilities for collaboration commerce; this is a legacy to leave our footprints in the sand together!

Cindy Gordon

CONTENTS

PREFACE

We wrote this book because corporate portals (CPs) and other Web-based solutions, when deployed with a strong knowledge management (KM) and users' perspective, can cause a major shift in the quality and speed of work in knowledge-intensive firms and, ultimately, in how enterprises function. Trillions of U.S. dollars have been invested in information technology (IT) to date, and there is finally a business solution that can seamlessly link data, information, knowledge, and people. A new world of connectivity has arrived: The CP is a new glue to support this fundamental business transformation and the rapid leverage of intellectual assets. The speed of businesses recognizing the importance of CPs is evidenced in the exploding growth of the software market. Over the next 2 to 4 years, the sales of CP software will triple, reaching between $5 and $10 billion or even more, depending on the forecaster and the definition of a CP. Anyways, a very large market!

The origins of CPs can be linked to consumer portals such as Yahoo!, Alta Vista, and Lycos. These gateways (portals) to the Internet demonstrate the value of providing people with an organized "view" into the diverse sources of disparate information on the Web. Portals started as a point of entry to the Internet and evolved to destinations by providing aggregation of third party (and more recently proprietary) content, functionality, and e-commerce.

The early movers, such as Yahoo!, became leaders by moving rapidly without losing focus on the ultimate needs of the consumer.

They continually rapidly integrate design, technology, applications, content, and services, while leveraging proprietary distribution and preexisting customer relationships. Successful portals have been adept at creating trust-based environments where content is relevant, accurate, and timely; communities thrive; and users engage in deeper relationships with the portal through personalization. The provision of a seamless, consistent, and personalized experience anywhere and anytime, along with the integration of different media assets delivered through a variety of devices, represents the current battleground for the leading portals.

People are increasingly multitasking, checking and receiving information from various sources and participating in projects that cross many geographic boundaries. Many professionals are also constantly connected, regardless of their physical location. In this scenario, it is no surprise that the "myxxxx.com anywhere, anytime, any device" concept, promoted by large mass-market portals, is making big strides into the corporate world. The CP is, in this respect, a natural evolution to the way most people are already getting connected and exchanging information in their personal lives.

Perhaps one of the most significant factors unique to CPs, unlike many other IT investments, is that CPs are being implemented to serve the needs of employees, communities, and even the extended networks that go beyond the walls of traditional organizations. CPs start squarely with the needs of a wide base of groups of end-users in mind (in many cases all employees of the organization; in other cases just some selected groups within and outside the organization):

- What do users need to know to perform their job functions?
- What knowledge sources do users already rely on or could rely on in the future?
- How will users access information and knowledge?
- Will the CP be intuitive for users?
- How will the CP support user skill development and decision making?

CPs represent an important advancement in collaboration software that can be used to develop and implement knowledge management initiatives. CPs are fundamentally changing how information and collaboration responsibilities are shared in an organization: from a narrow, functional, and uncoordinated focus to a broad, project, and collaborative approach. CPs integrate many features closely related to processes that can be important in the deployment of a KM strategy: personalization and search; access to information sources in a Web-friendly environment (from highly unstructured to highly structured digital data); internal and external information; communications and collaboration; ease of publishing; and access to a vast amount of data, information, and knowledge. CPs can be designed and deployed to support connections between people and knowledge or information sources (internally and externally). Thus, they can spark knowledge creation, the reuse of documented (explicit) knowledge, and the rapid mobilization of individuals who can apply their tacit knowledge to specific business situations, hence improving customer services and increasing innovation capabilities within an organization.

Although IT plays only an enabling role in KM efforts, we believe that it is important for organizations to understand the technology landscape so they can choose appropriate solutions that support KM projects. Today's new generation of CPs have become more sophisticated in terms of integrating a broad range of applications and tools, including content management systems, categorization and taxonomy tools, search engine tools, and collaboration online applications, among others. Collectively, these new capabilities can work to integrate and balance the structured flow of information and support knowledge creation within organizations with unprecedented speed of deployment and success.

We are convinced that many of these new CP solutions will have a significant impact on how organizations create, organize, access, and reutilize knowledge. This new generation of CPs has deep roots in the original solutions developed for the publishing, the media, and other business-to-consumer (e.g., auctions) industries. They are, however, also integrating many new Web-based solutions designed to foster higher levels of collaboration within and outside organizations.

This book, however, is not about how to select CP platforms, although even the more technically inclined will be better equipped to do so after reading it. Contrary to previous IT waves, CPs are being developed with a social-technical perspective underpinned by KM and community of practice theories. This book is about KM and the use of CPs for this purpose.

We feel strongly that CPs are rapidly becoming an essential corporate capability for competitive advantage. There are many examples (including the cases in this book) of how organizations are implementing CPs to improve and leverage their knowledge assets. CPs can be used to make it easy to rapidly identify assets and best practices within and outside an organization and to efficiently share these practices widely to help an organization achieve its strategic objectives. In this sense, CPs are becoming essential to support fast-paced and continuous innovation.

CPs are also becoming mandatory from a cost management point of view. They provide substantial productivity improvements, costs savings in IT and content management, and interesting opportunities for centralization of corporate services. They can also significantly help reduce the "reinvention of the wheel" syndrome. Finally, CPs are proving to be an important strategic tool for more rapidly integrating newly merged organizations and an essential tool for helping organizations to act as "one firm" regardless of site location.

With all these attributes, it is not surprising that a Delphi Survey (Fall 2000) of 300 IT and business managers from Fortune 500 companies, discovered that more than half the companies surveyed were introducing a CP. Another quarter indicated that they would follow suit in the next two years.[1] These numbers are in line with other market forecasts that consider CPs a very large and high growth market:

- The worldwide Enterprise Portal Software Market will increase from $1.46 billion in 2001 to $7.04 billion in 2005 (OVUM 2001 forecast).[2]
- The portal software market reached over $405 million in 2000, an increase of 128% compared to 1999. By 2003, this software market will reach $1.9 billion (Delphi research and forecast).[3]
- By 2004, more than 85% of Global 2000 organizations will be deploying enterprise portals (META Group forecast).[4]

We think that global companies are particularly likely to benefit from CP implementations, since employees could grow accustomed to seeing and analyzing the same information, regardless of whether in the head office or a small office thousands of miles away. In a way, CPs can help large organizations with multiple hierarchical layers and office locations behave a little more like a startup firm. One characteristic of startups (at least of the most successful ones) is that most employees operate within similar contexts, share similar information very fast, regardless of hierarchical level, and collaborate intensively. CPs cannot replicate this environment, but they can certainly help mitigate some of the problems of information-filtering that haunt bureaucratic chain-of-command organizations.

If a CP becomes an integral part of the daily life of every employee, then some of the nonhierarchical cultural aspects of the Internet may start having an impact on the evolution of an organization's structure and culture. Through a CP, organizations may be adopting a de facto Internet culture. On the Internet, a person's ideas and the frequency and clarity with which he or she communicates them are more important than how a person looks or stands in the hierarchical ladder. CPs create a level playing field in terms of access to information. Thus, it is possible to foresee that the implementation of CPs may lead to greater appreciation of employees' insights, creativity, and analytical capabilities. CP has been almost exclusively discussed by IT professionals with a strong IT perspective. It is high time all senior management joined in the discussion. This book brings a senior management and balanced (business, IT, Human Resources, etc.) perspective to an area we strongly believe will occupy a prominent space in the agenda of all forward-looking firms. This book is filled with many detailed examples of how organizations are leveraging CP technologies and also precursor Web-based technologies to improve the ability of knowledge workers to perform. We examine not only the key functional aspects of the technologies deployed but also many issues usually the domain of senior management: the important and active role that the leadership can play in a digital enterprise and the changes in organizational processes and structure that support key KM processes.

This is a book written for management and practitioners. We strive to balance real-life storytelling with our own hands-on experiences and that of the many collaborators who helped us along the way. It is not supposed to be a toolkit, since successful CP implementation does not for allow this kind of approach. Throughout the book, we frequently put on our academic hats and include carefully selected solid theoretical frameworks and scientific research to shed further insight into our learning. Practice without theory, although extremely important, tends to be difficult to generalize and usually strikes different learning chords from those provided by sound frameworks and conceptual models. On the other hand, theory without practice has no meaning in the business world. We chose a dialogue between practice and theory—and invite you to join us!

REFERENCES

1. Delphi Group Research Study. *Corporate Knowledge Portal.* Fall 2000.
2. OVUM analyst Angela Ashenden. *KMWorld.* July–August 2001, p. 9.
3. Delphi Group. Press release. May 16, 2001.
4. META Group. *Portal Market Segmentation: Part 2.* November 1, 2001.

ACKNOWLEDGMENTS

In one of the chapters of this book, we discuss the idea that knowledge and collaboration go hand in hand. In the case of this book, it is particularly true. Although we assume complete responsibility for the ideas in this book, we know very well that this project would not be possible without the support of an extensive learning network. We have, therefore, a number of people to thank.

Some old friends and a number of new ones have helped during important phases of this Project. Thank you

- Daniel Robinson and Janine Dodge, for your voluntary and excellent editing of many parts of this book.
- Rick Stuckey, retired Accenture senior partner responsible for Global KM, who reviewed important parts of the book and offered many interesting comments.
- Brian Detlor, David Brett, and Will Novosedlik, for the innovative contributions for the book.
- Nyla Ahmad and Kim Silk, for sharing ideas.
- Bryan Davis, for the many good corporate portal references.
- Nick Bontis, professor at McMaster University, for your support and interest at a critical stage of this project.
- Fábio Galízia, Marco Petruzzi, Jon Huggett, Fernando Pacheco, and Themis Assis Brasil, for helping us establishing important contacts to conduct this research.
- Flávio La Terza, Andrea Lopes, Paulo Lie, and Franscesco Cardi, for your help in the final formatting of this book.

- Fábio Tavares and the portal team at Balance Consulting for the tremendous support.

We are particularly grateful to the leading practitioners who shared their knowledge with us. Without your stories and support this project would not be possible. Thank you very much!

- ADC: John Beattie, Lynn Harrison, Cory Garlough, Shaun Hills, and Dan McMullen.
- Bain & Company: Steven Tallman, Mark Horwitch, Robert Armacost, Marco Petruzzi, and Jon Huggett.
- Bank of Montreal: Richard Livesley, Sasha Zupansky, and Dave Reddoch.
- Context Integration: Bruce Strong, Chuck McCann, Meg Salgado, and Karl Kutschke.
- Eli Lilly: Aaron Schacht and Vickie Nooe.
- Hill & Knowlton: Ted Graham and Nicole Doyle.
- Motorola: David Cox, Maureen Presner, and Tom Simon.
- Nortel Networks: Danny Murdock, Greg Kowal, Richard Martin, and Micky Verma.
- Serpro: José Alberto Cadais and Sylvio Bari Filho.
- Siemens: Michael Wagner, Beatriz Eguiluz Moreno, Monika Sengberg, Loraine Ricino, Fernando Stefano, Filipe Cassapo, and Sandro Melhoreto.
- Texaco: John Old, James Hughes, and John Gazouleas.
- Xerox: Danny Bobrow, Michel Boucher, John Burgess, Pricilla Douglas, Gary Lee, Thomas Ruddy, Jack Whalen, and Bernie Colligan.

Finally, we acknowledge the total support from our families during this journey. Thank you very much Janine Dodge and Perry Muhlbier, Jessica and Bryce.

FOREWORD

"Opportunities multiply as they are seized."—Sun Tzu

Turmoil in capital markets. The horrific events of 9/11. Fear of more terrorist acts, new forms of military conflict, and economic disruption. Enron, Andersen, WorldCom, and a crisis of confidence in business. Shareholders and consumers ratchet up scrutiny of corporate behavior and want greater business transparency. Ever higher customer expectations. We're riding a wave of rapid change and a much faster metabolism of commerce. So when will things get back to normal?

They are. This is the new normal. It involves bolstering backup and contingency plans, boosting security, building in more redundancy, and preparing for the worst. Companies need to manage costs, innovate business models, and be agile as never before. That's the easy part. The bigger challenge is building high performance vehicles to create customer and shareholder value in the toughest business environment that's ever existed.

I spend much of my time helping executives/companies develop effective business strategies. But increasingly I see management teams unable to convert their solid thinking into solid action by their entire workforce. It's clear that in the networked economy, despite powerful information and communication technologies—indeed, *because* of powerful information and communication technologies—it has become tougher for companies to make things happen.

There are a number of reasons for this. Under industrial capitalism, key corporate assets were physical plant and financial capital. No longer. Today, the most meaningful assets are knowledge assets and the most meaningful form of capital is human capital. Human capital comprises the skills, knowledge, intellect, creativity, and know-how of individuals in the company. In other words, it's the company's ability to create value for customers.

Companies today must attract and nurture knowledge workers and provide the environment for extraordinary thinking—for problem solving, executing complex business functions, and innovation. But it is much tougher to speed up today's knowledge workers than yesterday's factory workers. The latter involved issuing an edict and pushing a few buttons. The former requires sustaining a positive environment that motivates and nourishes the human mind, giving it the most critical raw material of all—abundant information.

To add to the managerial challenge, today's knowledge workers function within a corporate structure that is more difficult to control. In yesterday's hierarchical organization, with its multiple layers of management, accountability, and bureaucracy, information flow was vertical. But today's best companies are fluid and supple, with workers assigned to ad-hoc, interdisciplinary teams. They work on objectives that span multiple parts and levels of the organization, generating faster responses to changes in the business environment and customer demands. And while this corporate structure is clearly more effective, no one suggested it was easier to manage. Yesterday's yes/no decisions for managers and employees have become multiple choices with a dozen or more options.

The trend to distributed, empowered, and team-based enterprises creates an empowerment-control paradox. Of course, yesteryear's command and control hierarchies are obsolete. Firms need to distribute authority and decision making out and down into the firm—especially the front lines. We can't turn back the clock—the lumbering bureaucracies of the industrial age are no longer effective in a volatile, customer-centric world.

But this raises a crisis of control. On the surface, the culture of empowerment seems antithetical to effective management control and the execution of enterprise business strategies. If everyone is given enormous latitude, how can executives ensure that their company resources all march in the same direction?

Add to this the Internet—a deep, rich publicly available information infrastructure that grows relentlessly in functionality and bandwidth. Because the Internet slashes the cost of sharing knowledge, collaborating, and meshing business processes among corporations, smart companies—both old and new—focus on core competencies and partner or outsource to do the rest.

These teams of specialized firms (I call them business webs) prove more supple, innovative, cost-efficient, and profitable than their traditional, vertically integrated competitors. But, again, their complexity makes them harder to manage. Executives need new tools—including strategic concepts and analytical methods—to comprehend and exploit the unprecedented array of business architectures suddenly available.

The Internet's rise also changes dramatically the number and nature of business relationships. Historically such relationships were mostly internal to the corporation—an individual had a relationship with their boss, secretary, employees, project team, dotted-line relationships, and so on. Today relationships extend beyond the boundaries of the firm to customers, business partners, and others. Managing a soaring number of relationships is a skill required not just with senior managers, but most employees. And as many discover, it's hard to do.

All the while the pace of business quickens. Managers must make more difficult decisions in less time. Product development times collapse. A decade ago, automakers took five to six years to bring a new car to market. Now it's usually three years, sometimes less than two. Rather than stockpiling cars on dealer lots, automakers want to build a car within a week to a buyer's specifications and deliver it to their driveway. And since fussy buyers now consider a model's design stale after only a couple of years on the market, car companies regularly invent "limited editions" to help keep the product looking fresh. Producers of virtually all consumer goods and services face this twin threat of compressed development time and shorter shelf life.

Firms today also operate much more transparently and in a much more transparent environment. As information and communication technologies advance, companies can expect to hide virtually nothing from employees and outside organizations. Almost all decisions, from boardroom deliberations through to day-to-day purchases of supplies, now occur with somebody, somewhere (or more likely, many people in many places) looking over the company's shoulder.

CEOs are held accountable for all facets of their companies' behavior. This goes beyond signing off on financial statements. The "out of sight, out of mind" approach to low-cost offshore production is dead. If a company uses inputs produced by kids in sweat shops, everyone will know. As companies build their business webs, suppliers and partners are seen publicly as part of the enterprise. Innocuous products such as running shoes, lumber, chocolate bars, and cellular phones suddenly become politically charged. "The buck stops here" sign on the CEO's desk grows larger by the day.

An essential part of the solution is technology. Firms today need additional functionality and an integrated IT infrastructure to enable smooth, cost-effective execution. Unfortunately, traditional home-grown systems intended to be part of the solution are often part of the problem. The enterprise is locked into the technology of the past—islands of computing that aren't integrated and replicate the old organizational chart. Together they form an environment that is confusing, arduous to navigate, and doesn't provide the information and tools employees require to execute effectively.

Thankfully, new developments in systems help firms tackle the challenge of execution. Combined with new approaches to business processes and management, these developments hold tremendous promise for companies to achieve competitive advantage.

Web Services refer to new standards (such as XML) and innovations in software development that change the Web from primarily a publishing platform to a platform for distributed computing. With Web Services, applications work together regardless of where they reside or how they were implemented. This enables integration of applications and collaboration among people, profoundly improving how businesses functions are executed.

Knowledge Portals provide workers with a personalized desktop—giving them the information, knowledge, and resources they need to execute their jobs. Portals integrate both structured and unstructured data throughout an enterprise and beyond. Their design reflects a fundamental transformation of our view of enterprise information management, from a series of isolated tasks to the coordinated integration of knowledge.

There is no question that the corporate portal infrastructure and Web Services create profound changes in the deep structures of the corporation. They provide a window to creating a new business world and "context" for constituencies to interact.

Corporate portals enable companies and employees to cooperate and produce powerful new insights, knowledge, and connections. Organizations that have embarked on corporate portal implementations have learned that they can profoundly alter how work is conducted and intellectual capital is created, retained, and reused.

The authors excel at analyzing the interrelationship among business imperatives, technology, and human dimensions. This is valuable since many executives see the corporate portal as simply an Internet browser that extends their current Internet capabilities—and miss the fundamental richness of what a corporate portal server infrastructure does to restructure how content is created, used, and distributed across an enterprise and beyond.

Every organization concerned about customer service and employee relationships needs to view the corporate portal as a new possibility for creating economic value, customer value, shareholder value, employee value, and community value. Business strategy needs to ensure corporate portals and knowledge management foundations are a core competency.

Realizing the Promise of Corporate Portals provides a comprehensive view of the market landscape, case studies, and best practices and lessons learned. Read and profit.   *Don Tapscott*

REALIZING THE PROMISE OF CORPORATE PORTALS

1

INTRODUCTION

We begin this book with a peek into the near future!

We describe a series of scenes from an office that has a very advanced knowledge portal. All the interactions with this portal are through verbal exchanges and all our characters and companies are fictitious. We hope that the conversational tone of the story will help readers better imagine the enhanced work situations and the role that a knowledge portal can play.

K-Agent is the knowledge portal. It is a personalized knowledge portal that talks to people—it can answer questions, make suggestions, and connect people to one another. It can also alert, beam signals, display documents, and offer links to various knowledge sources.

SCENE 1

Characters:

K-Agent, the knowledge portal

Joe Armstrong, chief technology officer, Sigma Inc., Boston office

Susan Dodge, senior researcher, Sigma, Zurich office

Locations:

Joe's car

Joe's office

1

Context:

Sigma is a leading vendor of high-end engines for the aircraft and aeronautics industry.

Joe is the leading person in a product development project called Project Alpha.

Susan just joined another division of Sigma in Zurich, Switzerland.

Joe is driving to work early in the morning.

Joe: Good morning, K-Agent!

K-Agent: Good morning, Joe!

Joe: What is the relevant news related to project Alpha?

K-Agent: External news agencies are reporting that the director of R&D of Sigma's top competitor is leaving his company.

Joe: OK. Next.

K-Agent: A senior engineer named Susan Dodge just joined our Zurich office yesterday. She has experience that is highly relevant for Project Alpha.

Joe: Give me more details.

K-Agent: She worked for five years for Boeing in their new materials advanced lab as a senior researcher. Most recently, she was at Zurich University finishing her Ph.D. in Nuclear Engineering with a focus on the reuse of nuclear waste materials.

Joe: That is indeed interesting. Please try to book an introductory virtual meeting with Susan anytime on Friday morning.

K-Agent: Based on her online calendar, she is available for a meeting at 10:00 AM. I will book the time, wait for confirmation, and let you know.

Joe: OK. Anything else of interest? Perhaps on Susan's self-stated personal profile?

K-Agent: Yes, she loves golfing and spent a year here in Boston as an exchange student at MIT.

Joe: OK. Please send her a link and a password to the Executive Summary of Project Alpha.

K-Agent: OK.

Three hours later in Joe's office . . .

JOE: Did you hear from Susan?

K-AGENT: Yes. The meeting is confirmed for Friday at 10:00 AM. She left you a video message and also sent a number of related links to some of her previous papers. Do you want to see the message now?

JOE: No, thanks. I'll check it later. Please print all the documents she sent. I need to go now.

The above scene and subsequent scenes highlight key KM concepts and CP tools that are detailed, discussed, and exemplified throughout this book.

Key KM concepts, tools, and references in the book in scene 1:

In scene 1, the following topics were introduced:
Topics: Personalization, automatic notification, integrated external and internal information, expert locator, personal profiling, virtual collaboration.
These topics are particularly addressed in the following case studies:
Most relevant case studies: ADC, Bain & Company, Context Integration, Eli Lilly, Hill & Knowlton, and Texaco.

SCENE 2

Characters:

K-Agent, the knowledge portal
Joe Armstrong, chief technology officer, Sigma, Boston office
Mr. Nagano, project lead at SUMIMO, the firm's top client in Japan

Locations:

Joe's office
Joe's home

Context:

Joe finished the first draft of the product development strategy document and is looking forward to feedback.

At Joe's office . . .

JOE: Hi, K-Agent! The first draft of the product development strategy for Project Alpha is done now. Please publish it and notify the core team members and all other interested parties. Let them know that the deadline for feedback is 1 week from now and that I would appreciate one-to-one offline or online feedback.

K-AGENT: Before I do it, shall I include all the relevant links you used during this project?

JOE: Good idea! Please include links to the following references:
- Draft of main document.
- External and internal sources.
- Contact info for all the people who contributed to the draft.
- List of other internal and external experts.
- Video of digital prototype.

Next morning working from home . . .

JOE: Good morning, K-Agent! Any urgent messages?

K-AGENT: Yes. Mr. Nagano has already reviewed the draft, forwarded you his comments, and included a red flag in section C of the draft and also a list of external experts that can help with the issue.

JOE: Okay, let me have a quick look. I see his point! Can I see a list of top references for the last 2 years that are related to excessive heating in our front engines?

K-AGENT: Yes. I have the following two suggestions, in order of priority:
1. See the video and written discussions that occurred within the community of practice "Engines and Heating" between March 12 and April 15 of last year. There are relevant ideas, particularly those suggested by H-TECH, Sigma's partner and supplier, based in Toronto.
2. There are five relevant internal documents available at the K-portal, including a white paper that has been rated exceptional by the Advanced Lab. Three external sources are also highly recommended. I am printing the links to all documents, related personnel, and communities.

> Key KM concepts, tools, and references in the book in scene 2:
>
> Topics: Content management system, automatic notification, communities of practice (including third parties), recording of tacit knowledge, and advanced searching.
> Most relevant case studies: ADC, Bank of Montreal, Bain & Company, Context Integration, Eli Lilly, Eureka-Xerox, Hill & Knowlton, Serpro, Siemens, and Texaco.

SCENE 3

Characters:

K-Agent, the knowledge portal
Joe Armstrong, chief technology officer, Sigma, Boston office
Mark Cook, director of Marketing, Sigma, Boston office
Shawn Stewart, sales manager, East Coast USA, Sigma, New York office
David Adams, vice-president, Customer Services, Sigma, Boston office
Laura Alvarado, account director, CREATE Inc., Sigma's public relations partner
Chris Pringle, logistics manager, Sigma, Boston office

Locations:

Meeting room at Sigma's Boston office
Sigma's New York office, Shawn's location
Flight between Boston and London, Laura's location
Chris's home

Context:

Joe and Mark and two other members of the global marketing team are discussing ideas for an innovative booth for a next major trade show. They want to introduce Project Alpha to the trade press and potential customers.

In a boardroom in the Boston office . . .

MARK: Joe, I suggest we ask K-Agent to suggest a few people who could help us now. We are not making any progress and we need to present a few innovative ideas to the board early next week.

JOE: I agree. K-Agent, please show us some options. We need to contact others in our network who have had experience at the Le Bourget Air Trade Show in Paris. Please find who is available for a 30-minute brainstorm at 2:00 PM today.

K-AGENT: Here are my suggestions based on people's stated calendars and dynamic profiles (a list with each person's current title and relevant experience is highlighted on the screen):
1. Shawn is available and is on a very fast bandwidth connection.
2. David's calendar shows he is here in the office today.
3. Laura will be traveling by plane, but she is available to participate via text messages.
4. Chris's log-in information shows she is working from home today. She has asked, however, to be contacted only for critical or urgent issues.

JOE: Very well, K-Agent. Please invite Shawn and Laura only. I will walk over to David's office to invite him personally. No need to interrupt Chris, but please include the recording of the meeting in the project folder and notify her that it is there. I would like her input when she is less busy.

Key KM concepts, tools, and references in the book in scene 3:

Topics: Advanced searching, face-to-face and virtual meetings, instant messaging, integration of telecommuters and third parties, personal profiling.
Most relevant case studies: Context Integration, Nortel, Serpro, Siemens, and Texaco.

SCENE 4

Characters:

K-Agent, the knowledge portal
Joe Armstrong, chief technology officer, Sigma, Boston office
Alexa Sterling, senior quality assurance engineer, Sigma, Boston office

Location:

Joe's office

Context:

Joe is preparing for the semi-annual performance appraisal of his staff.

JOE: K-Agent, please give me the K-stats for Alexa for the last 6 months.

K-AGENT: Here they are:

- Her knowledge area in the portal had the ninth highest traffic volume when considering only the internal audience and the fourth highest volume when also considering external access by customers and partners.
- She had three documents or knowledge objects (KO) ranked in the Top 10 list for over 1 week and eight KOs in the Top 50 list.
- She was invited on average 3.4 times/week to participate in virtual meetings that were set up by other divisions and third parties (customers and partners). The Singapore and Japan offices, in particular, have asked her to join them in virtual meetings very frequently: 1.3 times/week.
- She has responded, on average, to two urgent virtual requests or questions/week. Her responses were considered excellent by 82% of individuals who asked the questions.
- She has been nominated by five other employees as a leading knowledge sharer.
- It is estimated by the knowledge brokers that the "best practices" she helped to document were reused elsewhere in the company at least five times with an annualized bottom-line impact of $10 million.

Joe, do you need more details?

JOE: No. These stats already offer enough evidence to support my initial evaluation. Alexa's leadership skills, knowledge creation, and knowledge sharing are having a very positive impact on the organization. Her knowledge objects and expertise are in high demand internally and externally and people are getting very good value from the interactions with her.

Key KM concepts, tools, and references in the book in scene 4:

Topics: Rewards and recognition for knowledge creation and knowledge sharing.
Most relevant case studies: Bain & Company, Context Integration, Siemens, and Texaco.

SCENE 5

Characters:

K-Agent, the knowledge portal

Jane Horwich, management trainee at Sigma

Location:

Jane's office

Context:

Jane just joined Sigma and K-Agent is helping her navigate in this new environment.

JANE: Hi, K-Agent. I have been told that you can help me to get up to speed.

K-AGENT: Yes, indeed. Do you want me to give you a few tips now?

JANE: Yes, go ahead! I have about half an hour before my next meeting.

K-AGENT: First of all, let me tell you that the K-Portal is there to serve you and help you make significant connections to

- Projects that it anticipates that you might be interested in.
- People and communities that share your interests and learning agenda.
- Corporate and external news, data, and information relevant to your work and personal life.

JANE: Great, what else?

K-AGENT: I will also alert you from time to time about online learning modules and objects closely related to your activities, projects, and career path. A complete list, however, of online and offline learning opportunities is permanently available at your own personal learning space within the K-Portal. Use them at your convenience.

JANE: Can I also contribute to the learning of others?

K-AGENT: Yes, you can. If you request, I can walk you through a number of easy to create e-learning templates. Also, any knowledge object (drafts, documents, drawings, and even conversations) that you create alone or with others can be automatically published within the K-Portal and shared as widely or narrowly as you wish.

JANE: How do I get started using the K-Portal?

K-Agent: Well . . . you already have started. Based on your resume, initial projects that you have been assigned to, and your stated expectations during the interview process, I preconfigured your professional profile. You can correct it at any time and also include personal interests. I will work with you and try to learn as much as possible about your interests. Based on your feedback, I will be constantly adjusting and improving my offers to you.

Key KM concepts, tools, and references in the book in scene 5:

Topics: E-learning, human capital, learning communities, personalization.
Most relevant case studies: Bank of Montreal, Bain & Company, Context Integration, and Eli Lilly.

Scene 6

Characters:

K-Agent, the knowledge portal

Joe Armstrong, chief technology officer, Sigma, Boston office

Wouter Van Basten, production manager, CENTRIX, Sigma's supplier, Indianapolis

Carlos Batista, MEX-TECH, Sigma's top Mexican client, Mexico City

Locations:

Joe's office

Wouter's office

Context:

Joe is in his office working on a board presentation when he sees a red flag on his screen.

Joe, Wouter, and Carlos have met virtually before.

Joe: K-Agent, what's up?

K-Agent: Wouter Van Basten, from CENTRIX, is requesting an urgent meeting.

JOE: Put him through on the video conferencing channel.

WOUTER: Hi, Joe! I gather you may be able to help me with "cooling systems" issues.

JOE: Hi, Wouter. I'll certainly try my best. What seems to be the problem?

WOUTER: MEX-TECH has requested that we modify the design of a few components on the FOX-100 engine. We think that this will affect the "cooling system." The order came directly to us, as usual, but K-Agent red-flagged me since these changes are to be made to the original design. The changes requested are available in the MEX-TECH section of the K-Portal. Why don't you have a look? According to our estimates, which are based on the needs of the entire supply chain, we need to decide on these changes within 1 week to meet the order's delivery deadline.

JOE: Thanks for the info. A quick look at the new proposed drawings available at the K-Portal leads me to believe there shouldn't be much of a problem—with only one minor exception. It seems like Carlos is available now for a conference call. If you are free for another 30 minutes, I can invite him to join us now and we can discuss this exception. I'm including some additional references and alternative designs in the K-Portal that we can consult during the conference.

WOUTER: Go ahead!

Key KM concepts, tools, and references in the book in scene 6:

Topics: Value chain integration, external K-Portal, distributed content management system.
Most relevant case studies: ADC, Context Integration, Eli Lilly, Hill & Knowlton, and Nortel.

Back to reality!

This fictitious story may seem like it's a long way into the future—probably because of the "conversations" with K-agent. Yet all of the KM concepts and solutions presented are already available for organizations through the implementation of sophisticated corporate portals and collaborative platforms as highlighted in each particular scene. Throughout this book we will be addressing a lot of those concepts in detail and show examples of how they are being put into practice. The main difference between current reality and the tale is the state of voice recognition technology (which is still limited to a few operations such as in-call centers), number of clicks, and how often one needs to type in. But even that is changing rapidly.

Like any good science fiction story, we believe that these scenes foretell what soon will become ordinary. We hope you agree after reading the rest of the book.

The book is divided in two parts:

- Part I includes review of concepts, literature, technologies, basic knowledge management (KM) processes, and the synthesis of the main lessons learned through the case studies and the authors' own experiences.
- Part II includes the 11 case studies about implementations of corporate portals (CP).

PART I: THE FOUNDATION

In keeping with a senior management approach, we begin Chapter 2 with a "big picture" discussion. We highlight some of the fundamental changes in business prompted by the Internet, increased levels of interoperability, and the rapid growth of knowledge-based business models. In particular, we focus on (1) the changing concepts of value chain and core competencies, (2) what is happening to information and knowledge flows within and beyond the walls of the enterprise, and (3) the emergence of new organization and business models. We demonstrate a strong link between the changes in the competitive environment and the adoption of corporate portals. Following this discussion, we delve into the corporate portal world. We examine the rationale behind the adoption of CPs in the corporate world. The chapter ends with an exploration of the key benefits an organization can realize by developing a robust CP.

Chapter 3 describes the critical components and architecture of a CP to help managers develop a comprehensive list of key functional requirements to select a CP solution. Key topics addressed include personalization, taxonomies, search, integration of data sources and software package applications, collaboration tools, and content management systems. In addition to examining these core functionalities, we examine the integration of stand-alone Internet applications based on an intellectual capital framework; that is, we look at possible software applications in terms of their impact on various sources of intellectual capital. Finally, we compare different levels of portal sophistication.

Our underlying conviction (further confirmed by the case studies) is that technology is only the tip of the iceberg: CP implementations require deep levels of leadership commitment that are visible and ongoing. Consequently, Chapter 4 explores a diverse range of perspectives on CPs and KM. We present our perspective on what is KM and examine key issues related to this emerging discipline. Topics include (1) differences between information and knowledge management, (2) human capital and e-learning, (3) communities of practice and online communities, and (4) organizational culture, trust, rewards, and incentives.

We also reflect on KM from both the strategic and tactical levels. The book, including the case studies, focuses primarily on the practical and tactical implementation level of a KM and CP initiative, that is, on the leadership, organizational, human resource, and information systems infrastructure requirements of CPs. However, by highlighting from the start the issues related to corporate strategy, we avoid committing the usual mistake of failing to link KM to the core business strategy and the sources of intellectual capital of a knowledge-based enterprise.

In Chapter 5, we introduce the key lessons learned from the 11 detailed cases from both a theoretical and a practical CP perspective. While we acknowledge that it is not easy (and often imprudent) to "amalgamate" lessons from different industries, contexts, technologies, and corporate intent in a useful manner, we strive to provide a summary of lessons learned and link them to relevant management theory and the concepts introduced in Chapters 2 through 4. For practical reasons, easy reference, and understanding, this chapter includes discussions and lessons from various perspectives: leadership, business, human resources, organization development, IT infrastructure, and so forth. The 12 key lessons are

1. Organizational alignment is the first priority.
2. Be clear about business case, value proposition, and metrics.
3. KM and CP require innovative rewards and recognition strategies.
4. Organizational change does not happen by chance.
5. Communicate, communicate, communicate!
6. New roles and responsibilities need to be clearly assigned.
7. Focus on users' needs.
8. Online communities require careful planning, infrastructure, and ongoing support.
9. Quality of content is more important than quantity of content.

10. The CP should reduce information overload and simplify access to information, templates, and expertise from within and outside an organization.
11. Give priority to the integration of IT applications.
12. Develop a due diligence process to select the CP platform.

In Chapter 6, we briefly review the links between knowledge management and innovation in light of the innovative practices depicted in the case studies. We also reiterate our strong conviction in the need for a holistic approach and what we believe should be the key visions driving CP implementation. Finally, we remind the readers about the "spirit of the frontier."

PART II: DETAILED CASE STUDIES

Chapters 7 through 17 include 11 detailed case studies of CP implementation. Throughout the book, we anchor our suggestions and theoretical frameworks on an extensive literature review, our own experience, and that of many other organizations. The case studies featured in the book use the power of storytelling, a key skill for leaders. Storytelling adds vivid, colorful, and contextualized tales to simplify complex subjects and make them more human, real, and applicable. Many practitioners from leading organizations share their CP implementation experiences, insights, lessons learned, frustrations, and hopes for the future. The cases are diverse in terms of scope and stage, size of organization (from large multinationals to strong local players), and different industry segments (professional services, communications and high tech, pharmaceutical, manufacturing, and so on).

The case studies were developed through a combination of face-to-face meetings and telephone interviews using a structured qualitative and quantitative inquiry guide. The research interview guide was based on an extensive search of the literature and personal experience as practitioners of KM and e-business. The organizations were selected because of the advanced stage in their CP implementations or their strong KM capabilities. In almost all cases, these were large global companies that had a strong need to share knowledge across offices situated in different corners of the world. The following organizations provided us the opportunity to understand their CP/KM projects and develop in-depth case studies: ADC Telecommunications, Bain & Company, Bank of Montreal, Brazil's Finance Ministry

IT Agency (SERPRO), Context Integration, Eli Lilly, Hill & Knowlton, Nortel, Siemens, Texaco, and Xerox.

In every case, we conducted a number of in-depth interviews with senior executives in charge of CP implementation. Many of these executives were KM leaders in their organizations. We did not, however, limit the interview process to KM leaders. More often than not, we also interviewed project managers, users (employees), and community leaders. In most cases, we interviewed three to six persons per organization. Frequently, we were also introduced to live demos of the CPs. A number of companies also shared their internal documentation related to the CP/KM efforts.

After an initial round of interviews, as researchers, we would prepare a first draft of the interview conclusions and submit it to the organization for further review, discussion, and refinement. This allowed us not only to correct any misinterpretations but to take the interviews to a deeper level of communication as interviewees were prompted to reflect on what they had learned. A number of those leaders told us that this exercise led them to pause for a moment and, through a dialogue with researchers, to rethink their overall goals, achievements, and lessons learned and to provide a learning case to reinforce the value of their CP/KM initiatives to support ongoing organizational learning practices.

Although the focus of our research was not on the issues of IT implementation, the understanding of the IT infrastructure provided us the necessary context to analyze the KM initiatives the CP supports. Indeed, as we found out through our interviews, the most important factors of success were related not to the choice of technology but the managerial practices and processes aimed at increasing knowledge flow in the organization.

Finally, it is important to mention that readers should not expect a recipe in the case studies. Rather, they should expect a collection of lessons learned that can help organizations approach their CP implementations with more strategic insight and understanding of the importance of specific context, and recognize that CPs are about fundamental organizational and business model changes.

PART I

THE
FOUNDATION

2

THE
NETWORKED
AND
KNOWLEDGE
ERA AND
CORPORATE
PORTALS

"We are not in the product business; we are in the knowledge business."
—Ralph Larsen, chairman, Johnson & Johnson[1]

"The Internet is simply a library, instant access to everything, good and bad. The Internet is the telephone, the Internet is a circle of friends, the Internet is billboards, the Internet is radio, the Internet is television, the Internet is books, the Internet is journals, the Internet is discussion in a bar, the Internet is a church bazaar. The Internet is anything. It's nothing but a medium."

—George Lundberg, editor-in-chief, Medscape[2] website

While the core of this book focuses on practical issues related to Web-enabled knowledge management (KM) implementations (from custom developed to very sophisticated corporate portal platforms), we think it is important to understand some of the "big picture" drivers of corporate portals and KM implementations. To facilitate such understanding, in this chapter, we discuss a number of important trends that are making corporate portals an essential tool to conduct business:

- The emergence of the Networked Era.
- The role of knowledge in business.
- New organization models in the Networked Era.

With this background in mind, we then link the discussion with the solutions provided by the corporate portal (CP) platforms in a section called The Role of Corporate Portals in the Networked Era.

THE EMERGENCE OF THE NETWORKED ERA

The explosive increase in the capacity and need for communication via the Internet is a significant milestone in human development. Throughout history, we have observed advances in the human capacity to communicate as a result of major innovations. Such innovations include the invention of writing, the Gutenberg printing press, the ability to circumnavigate the globe, the telegraph, and the satellite. The impact of the Internet on the human capacity to communicate is far-reaching: One-to-many and many-to-many communications have reached unprecedented and unanticipated levels.

We are just beginning to understand this new medium and how it is affecting human interaction and the development of communities and business models. The impact of community interaction can be expected to fundamentally alter organizational business models, as communities are growing organically and often without the knowledge of organizations. The net result? An absolutely exponential and, sometimes, chaotic pace of change. With online community interactions rapidly growing, corporate portals become a significant enabling infrastructure to support and sustain a more optimal flow of information and knowledge.

The Internet is sometimes incorrectly perceived to be about an increase in computer processing capacity (although it is starting to affect that as well, through the leverage of P2P platforms). However, the rapid acceleration of processing capacity has been occurring independent of the Internet. The Internet can be seen simply as a set of connectivity, interoperability, and presentation protocols that allows the efficient communication (by dividing information into small packages that maximize network flows and by establishing standard information about information tags) of

- People with people.
- People with machines.
- Machines with machines (of different origins, functions, and processing capacity).

The new technologies based on Internet standards are making it much easier for organizations to exchange data and for people to work collaboratively in synchronous and asynchronous modes, regardless of physical location. In addition to improved communication, the Internet allows for greater integration and coordination of both inter- and intracompany functions. It may not be long before client-server applications fade away, replaced by ubiquitous middleware that connects every workstation with multiple systems, server applications, and Web services in real time. All these components will be built to Internet industry standards[1] and run on any kind of platform or device (PC, cell phone, PDA).

This is a very different scenario from the mid-1990s. Indeed, a very different scenario from just a few years ago. This not to say that companies did not exchange data and information electronically. It was, however, a process dictated by the rule of power: The strongest link in a value chain would choose and impose its standards on everyone else—a far cry from the kind of global electronic markets that we currently see.

Now, we increasingly see the following business transformations accelerated by the common set of standards and deeper level of integration (in order of increasing complexity):

- *Cross-Activity Integration and Value Chain Integration.* The integration in a corporate portal of multiple internal activities through Web-enabled tools, such as customer relationship management (CRM), supply chain management (SCM), enterprise resource planning (ERP), many online collaboration and project management tools, the integration of entire value chains in specific industries from suppliers to customers, and the development of end-to-end solutions that fully integrate the ERP, SCM, and CRM applications of different companies in the value chain.
- *Virtual Organizations.* This is a concept similar to value chain integration, in the sense that many organizations are electronically linked to deliver products and services. However, virtual organizations are also characterized by a limited physical capital presence and coordination of the work of many virtual individual collaborators (who may never meet face to face).
- *e-Marketplaces.* The coordination of a multitude of servers from different organizations, enabling real-time transactions and the exchange of information. Many emerging models focus entirely on the exchange of information and knowledge services or expertise (we discuss a few examples later in this chapter).
- *Product Development.* The exchange of complex product models and deep collaboration among companies. The most advanced companies from almost every industry now leverage the Internet to work with different parties along the value chain to share information and knowledge, in real time, in their product development processes.

The Information Era allowed people to automate repetitive tasks and do things more quickly and efficiently. The Networked Era is evolving due to important advances in information technology, or IT (primarily, the growing connection between computers and the exponential growth in bandwidth capacity, which greatly improves the richness of human exchanges over long distances), and the increasing levels of inter- and intraenterprise collaboration required to create more knowledge-intensive products and services and that are changing the traditional boundaries of the firm.

The Networked Era also requires a better understanding of the new patterns of sociability as pointed out by Manuel Castell,[3] a well-known scholar and professor of sociology at Berkley. According to Castell, the Internet is changing the patterns of social interaction and creating a society characterized by increased *networked individualism*. This means that the Internet has greatly improved individuals' learning ability and freedom and capacity to increase their reach and create their own networks. Knowledge workers, in particular, are a lot less constrained by previous limits imposed by location or organizational boundaries. Castell puts forward the concept that *the network is the enterprise*,[3, p. 67] which takes the idea of a "network of enterprises" and an "internally networked enterprise" much further. In his view, the *network enterprise* is a *lean agency* of economic activity where business practice is performed in an ad hoc manner, depending on specific projects and ephemeral business demands.

The emergence of the Networked Era is also closely associated with the increased speed in life and business. When Microsoft launched Windows 95 globally in less than 24 hours, back in October 1995, this was seen as major event, not only in terms of the product itself but also in terms of the global approach of the launch. A few years later, this is still remarkable but not uncommon. Long gone are the days when corporations could launch their products in their home markets and slowly (in some cases, a decade or so later) move into new markets. In the high-tech sector, in particular, we now see global ambitions very early on from startups to large corporations. Everyone knows now that information and knowledge travel much faster in the Networked Era and knowledge can quickly lose its value if not fully leveraged.

As we see in the next sections and chapters, the successful deployment of CPs provide some of the initial building blocks toward the establishment of the *network enterprise* and the shared infrastructure for the development of business-to-consumer (B-to-C), business-to-business (B-to-B), and business-to-employees (B-to-E) applications and services. To fully leverage the new available infrastructure, however, many organizations need to revisit their current underlying managerial principles and give new emphasis to the proactive management of information and knowledge flow and collaboration. Internal and external corporate visions need to be aligned: This is not easy. New organization models based on reduced transaction and coordination costs are also emerging, allowing, at the same time, increased centralization and decentralization and increased control and empowerment.

It is hard to predict which change forces will win over time. However, based on our case studies, we can tell that many organizations are already making fundamental changes to improve how they collaborate both internally and externally.

In fact, we think that, although many facets of knowledge management are clearly not dependent on the Internet and Web applications, it is clear that the discipline and practice of KM benefit tremendously from the higher levels of connectivity brought by the Networked Era. Today, however, we are experiencing unprecedented challenges in terms of knowledge management. The challenges are driven by three forces in particular: the enormous volumes of information being created, stored, and distributed; the tremendous speed with which knowledge content changes; and the ongoing transformation of the workplace. Increasingly, to survive, organizations need to be more proactive in their support of knowledge creation and reuse. They also need more automated systems that can bring the right source of knowledge or information to the user—wherever that person is located—in a virtually instantaneous manner.

New communication and collaboration means are required to meet these demands. The Internet now plays a central role in accelerating and increasing communication. Less than a decade ago, for example, a multinational company that wanted to link thousands of employees around the world via a corporate network would have faced a prohibitive cost. Today, due to the ubiquity and pervasiveness of the Internet, this is an affordable and relatively simple task. The most recent technological advances also expand the bandwidth of distance communication. KM in the Networked Era has, therefore, a lot to do with using the power of the Internet to bring the sources of knowledge (codified or tacit) closer to where they are needed. In this respect, KM is about supporting and improving "meaningful connections" among knowledge sources regardless of their format.

THE ROLE OF KNOWLEDGE IN BUSINESS

At the same time as we are experiencing the rapid evolution of the emergence of the Networked Era, the portion of the population, particularly of developed nations, that works exclusively with diverse forms of knowledge continues to grow at a very fast pace. Although there is nothing new about knowledge resources playing a pivotal role in economic and human development, the speed with which knowledge and the number of knowledge workers are expanding is unprecedented. It has not always been this way. In a not too distant past, a firm's physical location and access to cheap labor, natural resources, and financial capital were of greater concern (in terms of competitive advantage) than the management of knowledge. Now, increasingly, there is little doubt that, to support and sustain growth, management must play a visible leadership role in managing knowledge assets. CPs, in their most elaborate deployments, as we will see, indeed rely on strong senior management visions such as Bain's Mark Horwitch, a senior VP, who sees KM and CPs at the heart of Bain's "new wave of innovation."

Much has been written already about the emergence of a Knowledge Society. We feel, therefore, no need to try to convince the readers. As a fact-based background, however, we have selected a few typical indicators that are usually used to support the view of the key role that knowledge is playing in our society and organizations. They are grouped in the following categories:

- *The New Economy.* Many studies show the rapid change in the composition of the GDP of developed economies and the increasing and pervasive role played by knowledge-based industries as opposed to traditional sectors:
  - The inflation-adjusted price of natural resource products fell almost 60% between the mid-1970s and the mid-1990s.[4] In most OECD countries, agriculture accounts for only between 1 and 3% of the GDP. The countries where agriculture has the smallest participation in the economy are the United Kingdom (0.9%), Germany (1.1%), and the United States (1.3%).[5]
  - The purchasing power of manufactured goods has fallen about 75% over the last 40 years, while the price of health and education products (knowledge products) has risen about three times as fast as inflation.[6]
  - IT investments account for close to $700 billion per year in the United States (7% of the GDP). As a percentage of total business investment, IT went from around 20% in 1990 to about 50% in 2001.[7]
- *Value of Intellectual Assets.* The value of organizations is increasingly tied to their intangible assets (R&D, patents, brands, customer and suppliers relationships, internal processes, human capital). Most efforts to date, however, to evaluate the individual contributions of these groups of intangibles are still very

rudimentary and open to debate. The market capitalization of an organization, in a way, includes all this, since it reflects the expected contribution provided by these intangibles working together with the tangible (hard) assets in terms of future earnings and cash flow. The difference between market value and book value can then be attributed to all these intangibles. Many studies show the increasing importance of intangibles across almost every industry:

- It has been estimated that, in 2000, the top 10 brands in the world had a combined value of $435 billion. The top three in the ranking were Coca-Cola ($72.5 billion), Microsoft ($70.2 billion), and IBM ($53.2 billion).[8]

- Arthur Andersen consultants Richard Boulton, Barry Libert, and Steve Samek compared the market to book value ratio of 3500 U.S. companies from 1978 to 1998. During this 20-year period, the ratio shot up from 1.1 to 3.6.[9]

- In the most knowledge-intensive industries, such as pharmaceuticals, beverages, media, business services, electronics, and IT products and services, the market value of companies is, on average, about three to four times the book value. In more traditional industries, such as automaking, mining, pulp and paper, and manufacturing, the differences between market and book value are much smaller.[10] Recent data from Fortune 50 companies are a good illustration of this point. The market to book value ratio on March 15, 2001, for some selected companies, grouped according to their knowledge intensity, were the following (calculations from Professors Baruch Lev and Marc Bothwell):[9]

Knowledge Based	Physical Asset Based
Pfizer (15.1)	Ford (2.9)
Coca-Cola (12.7)	Compaq (2.6)
Bristol Myers Squibb (12.5)	Alcoa (2.7)
General Electric and IBM (8.1)	Texaco (2.7)
Philip Morris (7.0)	Sears Roebuck (1.8)
Microsoft (6.9)	General Motors (1.6)

■ *The Innovation Imperative.* Knowledge, in its various formats, is the key ingredient to innovation. Innovation or the rate of innovation, however, can be much more easily measured than knowledge, which is a much more elusive concept. Many studies have linked rates of innovation to competitiveness and market leadership. For instance, Reichheld[11] studied 100 high-tech firms and found that products launched in the last five years accounted for 49.1% of total sales of market leaders. In contrast, new product launches accounted for only 10.7% of total sales for the group of companies with less than 30% of market share.

- *Profiting from Protected Knowledge.* The protection and leverage of knowledge are top priorities for corporations and governments in the developed world. Not only is it easily seen that intellectual property protection is one of the top items in many international global economic forums, it is also easily seen how patents and licensing have become one of the top business concerns over the last decade:
  - The number of worldwide patent applications has increased from 1 million in 1985 to about 7 million in 2000.[12]
  - U.S. licensing revenues from patents grew from $3 billion in 1980 to more than $100 billion in 2000.[13]
  - Export revenues from royalties and licensing, in the United States, increased from $16.6 billion in 1990 to $27.3 billion in 1996.[14]
  - IBM's annual revenues from patents is about $2 billion.[15]
  - A typical laptop computer includes between 500 and 5000 patents.[15]

- *The Knowledge Worker.* In developed economies, work in almost every industry is very rapidly becoming knowledge intensive. This represents a huge challenge to management, since the majority of our current enterprises were modeled on the basis of an industrial paradigm. Knowledge workers have very different needs and aspirations when compared to workers from the industrial age (discussed later). Some statistics highlight the speed of change:
  - The percentage of workers doing manual work in the United States fell from 70% in 1900 to 35% in 1950 to 15% in 2000.[16]
  - The top three professions in terms of forecasted growth in the United States for the period 1998–2008 are computer engineers (108%), computer support specialists (102%), and systems analysts (94%).[17]
  - An econometric study involving 29 countries showed that investment in education was responsible for 25% of economic growth.[18] It has also been shown that each additional

year of study in a country improves productivity by 8.5% in the industrial sector and 13% in the services sector.[19]

The knowledge worker needs to

- Balance personal and professional life.
- Avoid menial activities.
- Save time.
- Be productive and creative.
- Have access to knowledge sources at the point of need.
- Manage information overload.
- Work from anywhere.
- Collaborate with others from his or her own department or area, other departments or areas, and other enterprises.
- Keep in touch with others and with his or her own field of knowledge.
- Learn continuously.
- Take care of his or her own career.
- Be positively surprised.
- Be heard and recognized.

Knowledge and Collaboration

Knowledge and collaboration go hand in hand. Those who believe that the evolution of human knowledge is the result of geniuses and visionaries working in isolation are wrong. Exceptional talents have contributed significantly to the evolution of human knowledge; however, the world's greatest geniuses did not work alone. Recent studies reveal that the winners of Nobel Prizes are, for the most part, those scientists who most frequently participated in conferences, wrote articles together with others, and were always ready for an unexpected external stimulus to spark their creative impulses. However, do not be fooled into believing that collaboration necessarily means an absence of competition. For effective collaboration to occur, it is necessary for each individual or group collaborator to continually strive for new and improved levels of performance, thereby ensuring that the network of collaborators continues to find value and interest in individual or group contributions. In this sense, continuous improvement is very much part of collaboration.

An organization that is vertically structured and not capable of fostering an environment of intense collaboration with its customers, employees, suppliers, and partners has failed to understand the principal paradigm of the Knowledge Era: Organizations must compete and collaborate at the same time. Often, companies compete in certain markets and collaborate in others. *Collaboration capital* has become the new catchphrase in the most developed markets. The phrase refers to companies' ability to leverage the infrastructure of the Internet to increase revenues and profits by achieving large-scale, previously unattainable levels of collaboration and coordination, independent of geographic location. In this emerging model, everything begins with the needs of the customer and there is a strong sense of codependence. Activities and output emerge in function of an intense collaboration to optimize combined processes of the different parts and to stimulate the exchange of information, knowledge, resources, and people.

"The importance of collaboration is obvious," academics or someone with a clearly humanistic background might say. However, unfortunately, human collaboration within and across companies is not always present or effective in practice. Many companies and employees do not understand that collaboration has economic benefits, independent of benefits derived from moral principles or personal convictions. Without engaging in another realm of discussion, we can highlight international scholars, such as David Landes[20] and Francis Fukuyama,[21] who have clearly demonstrated that knowledge and wealth have sprung more often in societies where higher levels of collaboration and trust prevail. At the firm level, the linkage between competitive advantage and higher trust levels producing more interaction and tacit knowledge has been argued most convincingly by leading strategists C. Prahalad and G. Hamel.[22] Hence, in reading the rest of this book and working to implement and manage a CP, it is important to always keep in mind how different features of the CP affect the level of trust and, consequently, the levels of collaboration and knowledge creation.

Meaningful, trust-based collaboration is not simple, static, mechanical, linear, or wishy-washy. It requires strategic decision, aligned goals, monitoring systems, authenticity, respect for individual identities and cultural backgrounds, and maturity or training about dealing with conflict. If a humanistic view is not enough to convince organizations to develop more collaborative behaviors and orient themselves toward collective learning, then we hope that the need to innovate, become more competitive, and improve bottom-line results does the trick. The lessons and points of view of very senior executives from leading organizations, discussed here, are also a clear indication of the increasing correlation between collaboration, innovation, and knowledge creation.

Knowledge-Driven Alliances and Collaborative Product Development

Recent trends in knowledge-intensive sectors clearly point to higher levels of collaboration and the rapid growth of knowledge-driven alliances. Some data from the pharmaceutical sector, for instance, seems to confirm this changing mindset. This industry, with sales of almost $300 billion per year, outsources a large chunk of its R&D investments—more than $5 billion per year. The large drug firms have been going through major restructuring over the past few years and increasingly focus on what they know best and establishing strong knowledge and collaboration links with other complementary or specialized players in their network, through complex alliances and partnerships.[23] To be successful at these partnerships they need to learn how to standardize data and information, so they can be easily exchanged through Web-enabled applications. However, as Eli Lilly (the case profiled in Chapter 11) and GlaxoSmithkline[24] have also learned, collaboration starts at home. These companies are, therefore, making important investments to set up the digital infrastructure based on CPs and other Web-based tools that can be easily integrated into the portal (such as advanced search engines that can tap simultaneously into many disparate databases and internal and external sources of information).

Harvard professor Rosabeth Moss Kanter captured the visions about innovation management of senior executives of leading firms like Pfizer, DuPont, and GE. These CEO visions offer further insight into how even powerful organizations feel a strong need for intimate network connections to create and leverage knowledge:[25]

> We are also extending our reach beyond our corporate walls, to establish relationships with dozens of small organizations on the leading edge of research in such areas as viruses, bacteria, and certain genes. As big and talented as our corporate research team is, today's fast paced advances are too diverse and dynamic for any one organization to handle alone. (William Steere, Jr., Chairman and CEO, Pfizer, page 45)

> In the modern world, knowledge—not labour, raw materials, or capital—is the key resource. Communications networks, the means by which we obtain and share knowledge, are therefore critical determinants of success or failure. Unless researchers net-

work, they cannot create a product or bring it to market. At DuPont, we consider networks essential tools of innovation, and we encourage them in every way—including financially. DuPont supports more than 400 formal and informal networks, most of which operate by means of fax, e-mail, electronic bulletin boards, or groupware. These networks transfer technologies throughout the company, reach decisions on preferred suppliers, develop standards and guidelines, conduct training and development workshops, help establish collaborations, and avoid duplication of effort. (Dr. Joseph Miller, chief technology officer, DuPont, pages 79–80)

One challenge in relying on suppliers for certain technology is maintaining our touch with up-to-date technology. If we don't remain sophisticated enough to understand their technologies completely, we won't get the most out of our partnerships, and we can't be sure that the final product will meet the established specifications. Furthermore, by being on top of the latest technologies, we can contribute enormously to our suppliers' efforts. My staff and I work hard to make sure we take full advantage of the collective knowledge of our people. (Dr. Lewis S. Edelheit, senior vice president, General Electric Company, page 110)

Very few other companies, however, are as closely associated with the emergence of the Networked Era and establishing as many knowledge-driven alliances as Intel. Intel's example is also particularly important in the context of this book and CPs. After the initial automation of electronic exchanges involving demand forecasts, inventory, and changes in product configuration, Intel is focused on electronic collaboration related to product innovation. It is establishing unique IT collaboration standards to link suppliers and customers and creating "online spaces to communicate with suppliers, share documents and files and exchange messages, and track comments and corrections concerning product designs."[24]

The aircraft industry, too, offers good examples that support this forecast. Major aircraft manufacturers are working with their suppliers, partners, and customers to codevelop sophisticated planes. Depending on the project, tens or even hundreds of cross-organization teams work together across continents, electronically exchanging and interacting to develop project plans, designs, specs, and documentation. For example, Embraer, the fourth largest global aircraft manufacturer headquartered in Brazil, indicated during our research[26] that it is increasingly developing planes through risk-sharing partnerships with suppliers and partners. The company also increasingly relies on a robust and secure corporate portal that allows it to code-velop new plane projects, in real time, with partners across the globe. CPs are fundamentally changing how the company conducts business globally.

Finally, another example, from the food industry, is a good indicator that the use of Internet-based tools (or a CP) to improve collaboration in product development is not restricted to high-tech industries. A report, from early 2002, from the *Food Institute Daily,*[27] explains how Sainsbury, the United Kingdom's second largest grocer, was about to become one of the first grocers in the world to develop products on the Internet. The company was planning to achieve this by deploying a secure website (*ProductVine,* hosted by GlobalNetXchange, a B-to-B e-commerce exchange) that allowed everyone working on a project to share the same information and databases in real time anywhere in the world. The company expects this to greatly reduce the time it takes to introduce new products into the markeplace. This is critical for Sainsbury: In 2001 alone, it developed or improved the recipes of 2750 products.

E-Knowledge Marketplaces

Another interesting development related to the need for the optimization of knowledge exchanges and alliances is the rapid emergence of e-knowledge marketplaces. While knowledge-driven alliances have been traditionally linked to the strategies of corporations, the e-knowledge marketplaces are a direct result of the enabling power of the Internet in terms of finding, categorizing, providing connections, buying, and distributing knowledge-heavy services online.

Bryan Davis, president of the the Kaieteur Institute for Knowledge Management (www.kikm.org) in Toronto, Canada, has been mapping the emergence of this market for quite some time. (David Skyrme took this project even further in his book, *Capitalizing on Knowledge: From e-Business to k-Business,*[28, pp. 126–137] in which he provides a good discussion of these emerging knowledge business models and what it takes for them to succeed.)

According to Bryan, "e-Knowledge Marketplaces are ultimately on-line venues, where sellers of intellectual capital and intellectual property can be matched with potential buyers of such assets."[29]

Under the umbrella of e-Knowledge Marketplaces, he includes the following concepts or marketplaces: digital knowledge exchanges, knowledge networks, e-learning exchanges, knowledge trading, experts exchanges, e-lance intellectual capital exchanges, intellectual property markets, knowledge stores, knowledge auctions, idea exchanges, e-work exchanges, and talent markets.

Given this broad definition and the increasing need for individuals and organizations to capitalize on the value of their knowledge assets, it is no wonder that significant exchanges of money will flow through these virtual Knowledge Marketplaces. Several indicators and figures support the growth of this very large market:[29]

- New York research firm Datamonitor (www.datamonitor.com) estimates that direct information exchanges will be a $6 billion business by 2005.
- According to Content Intelligence Group, more than 10 million U.S. Web surfers had already paid for online content by mid-2001, including industry-specific business material, online database services, and premium music and news.[30]
- The U.S. education market is worth more than $700 billion per year. It includes K–12, postsecondary, and corporate training. Web-based solutions are being developed for each of these sub-markets.
- A number of new businesses are being founded on the premise that the Internet is a good vehicle through which to commercialize one's knowledge. Various services link buyers and sellers of advice. For instance, Keen, a portal that provides advice on a large number of topics (medical advice, tax advice, and the like) has already raised $109 million from the venture capital community. Its revenues for 2001 were forecast to reach $25 million. Some other companies in this field include HelloBrain, Askme, Yet2, Pl-x.com, Abuzz.com, and Knexa.
- The distinction between products and services is blurring. Many products include a service component and many services are being "productized" and marketed online. The cases of Ernst & Young and Andersen are worth mentioning. Both are "productizing" part of their knowledge and offering online advisory services, as evidenced by[28] www.globalbestpractices.com. This site, owned by Andersen, offers subscribers access to more than 20,000 pages of insight and tools that they claim to correspond to over 140 critical business processes.

In this age where knowledge is the key economic resource and collaboration is seen as a paramount skill for creating knowledge, it is interesting to note the parallels between knowledge-driven alliances and the emerging e-knowledge marketplaces. The two areas are converging significantly. Large corporations now depend a lot more on digital collaboration both internally and externally. Indeed, CPs implemented with a strong intellectual asset management perspective are becoming a tool for competitive advantage. The examples of Ernst & Young and Andersen, just cited, and the cases of Hill & Knowlton and Context Integration (described in Chapters 10 and 12) offer interesting evidence of how digital collaboration and leverage of internal and external digital assets are becoming a selling point for forward-looking organizations.

A few innovative organizations, such as Siemens, Serpro (from Brazil), and Context Integration—discussed later in the book—are adopting many of the e-knowledge open market concepts to reward their employees for their intellectual capital contributions. As knowledge alliances become even more granular and based on ad hoc relationships, it is possible to forecast that many creative ways will be developed to reward and share the benefits of collaborative intra- and interenterprise knowledge creation. Indeed, the lessons, technical infrastructure, and business models developed for the open market are now migrating into organizations. David Brett, CEO of Knexa, shares some interesting perspectives about this trend, based on the strategies of his own company and some interesting insights related to sound economic and management theories.

The Role of Corporate Knowledge Exchanges in the Evolution of CPs

David Brett

Is it "worth it" for an employee to inform a coworker that there is a better way to undertake a given task or is it "too much trouble"? Should an employee bring specific inefficiencies to the attention of management or would the "price" paid for speaking out be too dear in terms of time, recrimination, or lack of recognition? What "extra" benefit is conferred for sharing cost-cutting innovations? As articulated by Davenport and Prusak and others,[31] each transfer of knowledge from one individual in the firm to another constitutes an informal but significant economic transaction. Frequently based on reciprocity, agents in the market must keep score to determine whether or not a given transaction will maximize their own utility. In each case, the communication of discrete knowledge assets inside the organization involves economic issues of cost, price, imperfect information, information asymmetry, and supply and demand characteristics.

Corporate knowledge exchanges (CKEs) attempt to replicate inside the organization the vibrant marketplace dynamic that is characteristic of agora-style e-commerce business Webs. D. Tapscott, D. Ticoll, and A. Lowy define agora business Webs as self-organizing distributive networks where the participants are market players buying and selling goods using a price discovery system, such as eBay.[32] Most existing commercially available offerings (e.g., IntraKnexa, Askme, Organik, Infomarkets) have evolved from e-business strategies often referred to as "eBays for knowledge." CKEs usually retain many of the elements of P2P online auctions, such as rating systems for users, subjective feedback, treating knowledge objects as "listings" owned by participants, and giving exposure to "popular" objects and authors. In the CKE paradigm, organizational members are assumed to be quasi-arm's-length economic agents entering into discrete transactions or "exchanges" of explicit knowledge objects. Participants are not neutral units in the collective, accessing information "owned" by the firm; instead, CKEs posit a degree of individual ownership over their own knowledge assets, requiring specific pricing and payment. CKEs mirror to varying degrees the agoralike online free agent employment markets in aspects such as the posting and searching of resumes, skills matching capabilities, and the ability to build and advertise reputational information. The underlying assumption in CKE design and philosophy is that knowledge flows in markets and Web technologies can automate and improve certain aspects of these markets.

In this light, the role of CKEs in the evolution of CPs is best understood in the light of labor market economics and how Web technologies alter those markets. According to MIT economics professor David H. Autor, the Internet affects not only the way employers find employees, but also the way the work is carried out: "labor services—the actual work done by employees—may increasingly be delivered over the Internet rather than on-site."[33] Computer networks drastically lower the cost of publishing and accessing employee and employer information, resulting in a spectacular increase in the use of online job boards in recent years, yielding significant economic efficiency gains.[33] The ability to perform work remotely via networked computers also significantly reduces geographic constraints on employment. Lower job search costs for employees and employers enables greater ability to evaluate the market value of given levels of knowledge, skill, and experience. Simultaneously, the ability to perform work via the Internet lowers the cost of switching between employers and employees. These factors, according to labor market theory, result in overall productivity gains in the economy. Proponents of CKE strategies suggest that similar productivity gains can be realized inside the organization through application of comparable technologies.

Another element of the agora business Web paradigm is the ability to overcome imperfect and asymmetric information through reputation management systems. The collectible items that are the mainstay of eBay are very difficult to decisively evaluate without physical inspection, and significant risk is involved in proceeding with a transaction. As with résumés in the labor market, sellers of antiques can use embellishment, selective disclosure, and outright falsification of information to induce a sale. The cure for this information imbalance in both cases is ensuring the good reputation of the seller by receiving testimony from prior customers or employers. The eBay model involves individuals effectively building personal brand recognition through a simple but effective rating and review system. Similar reputation systems are used by public knowledge exchanges such as Knexa.com, Keen.com, Infomarkets.

com, and Intota.com. Personal reputation systems in the context of an exchange can be applied to internal markets as well.

The character of knowledge, however, introduces peculiar problems into markets for it. Unlike most tangible goods, knowledge goods are nonrivalrous, nonexcludable, nontransparent, and nonfungible. In other words, knowledge cannot be evaluated until it is revealed, cannot be withdrawn from use by the producer from the consumer, is not subject to exclusive use, and is not easily interchanged with other goods. Advice, for example, cannot be tested before it is given, cannot be withdrawn after it is given, and neither can the giver prevent the receiver from disseminating it to others, limiting rivalry for the possible resale of the advice. Digitized explicit knowledge is subject also to the ability of the Internet users to instantly replicate and globally disseminate it at no marginal cost. According to traditional economic theory, the price of any good with a marginal cost of zero should be zero.

The character of explicit knowledge as copyright intellectual property adds to the innate sense of ownership that authors have over their work, regardless of the contractual obligations implicit in employment. Some CKEs, such as IntraKnexa, have sought to overcome the potential resistance to the publishing of knowledge content in public databases by incorporating economic benefits directly into the technology. Standard economic units, on the other hand, do not easily value industrial property such as an invention. Complex due diligence and negotiating are typically involved in cases where employees are compensated for intellectual property (IP). However, CKEs can foster sharing of potential innovations by creating a "paper trail" that can help substantiate ownership by individual or team creators.

In summary, CKEs, like online auctions, incorporate many of the features of CPs, such as taxonomies, categorization schemes, document management features, search capability, data storage capacity, communities of practice, and common browser interfaces. Unlike CPs, however, the primary purpose of CKEs is not to point to preexisting knowledge stores but to elicit and capture new knowledge contributions and discover and publicize underutilized expertise. The presence of a market dynamic and focus on new knowledge discovery are attractive elements that will likely lead to CKE capabilities being incorporated into most CP offerings.

NEW ORGANIZATION MODELS IN THE NETWORKED ERA

Many scholars are forecasting that, through networking, we will experience the fast-changing role of large organizations and the emergence of how work will be performed in the 21st century in the same way that the industrial revolution defined work in the 20th century.[34] Despite constant news of mergers and acquisitions, the proportion of workers employed by a Fortune 500 company has fallen significantly in the last 25 years, from 1 in 5 to less than 1 in 10. Large organizations are clearly integrated far less vertically now than they were a generation ago.[34,35] Their primary role, as forecast by MIT and Harvard professors Malone and Laubacher, "will be to establish rules, standards, and cultures for network organizations operating partly within and partly outside their own boundaries."[34]

The competitive advantages achieved by companies that have learned to work collaboratively to leverage the power of networks can perhaps be best understood in terms of the business dynamics described by Michael Porter's seminal work, *The Competitive Advantage of Nations.* Porter drew attention to the learning environments of specialized micro-regions in which knowledge flows are intense among companies that collaborate and compete fiercely. Anna Lee Saxenian[35] further explores this concept in her book, *Regional Advantage.* She tells a compelling story about how the development of Silicon Valley was related to informal flows of collaboration and knowledge among firms, universities, and government. The Japanese *keiretsu* concept and the just-in-time production methods first developed by Toyota have been widely discussed and imitated with different levels of success throughout the world. In Europe, there are reports of an emerging new corporate structure: the "syndicates." Syndicates refer to associations of noncompeting, medium-sized manufacturers that unite to concentrate on core competencies (e.g., design) and to leverage market reach and other economies of scale (e.g., distribution), especially in foreign markets. The participants of the syndicate own shares of this supracompany and the syndicate also owns a share of each member's capital.[36]

The Internet, however, is definitely helping to take these concepts of association and networking to a much higher level. Unlike the more traditional symbiotic relationships discussed earlier, the new forms of networking are not constrained by geographical barriers, do not require cross-holdings of debt and equity, and the information flow between participants in the network goes far beyond the need to fulfill the existing production pipeline. In many cases, the exchanges of intangibles are the only relevant business exchanges among the players in the value-delivery network. In this new Networked Era, the participants that join the networks collaborate to deliver value for customers both in the short and long run and to jointly create new knowledge or develop new products.[32]

The case of Microsoft offers further evidence of how the Internet is forcing even dominant players toward more alliances and collaboration. Microsoft is one of the leading providers of Internet software and solutions to help companies connect with third parties. However, Microsoft itself has never been an "open source" company. Ironically, against its will, Microsoft has been forced to expand the role that partnerships play in its overall strategy. This is a strong testimony to the changing power of the Internet. A recent interview with Steve Ballmer, Microsoft CEO, indicated[37]

The Internet makes all of this more complicated. If it weren't for the Internet, we wouldn't be looking at MSN. We wouldn't have dot-net middleware. We had our partnering model pretty well taken care of, really, pre-Internet. It only involved Windows, Office, and a couple of servers. And then, darn—along came that Internet. It brought so many more people that we needed to touch—and with whom we needed to form partnerships in different ways.

The Internet has dramatically reduced coordination and transaction costs. It allows people and companies from different parts of the world to work together in real time and overcome the natural limits imposed by geographic distance. Real-time Web-based information flow improves efficiency by reducing the variability of information among employees scattered around the globe and among value chain players.[32] The Internet is also becoming by far the most important sales channel for many leading organizations, perhaps the most well-known of which are Dell and Cisco. To illustrate,

- Dell sold approximately 10 million built-to-order (BTO) computers through its Internet site in 2000, while turning over its inventory 52 times that year compared to Compaq's 13 and IBM's 10.[38]
- Over 80% of Cisco's total sales and 12% of all U.S. manufacturing transactions occurred through the Web in 1999.[39]

The companies that learn how to develop and orchestrate a healthy collaborative network are likely to be winners in the networked economy. A very recent McKinsey study found that companies, such as Cisco, eBay, Charles Schwab, and CNET, that have embraced the principles of a networked economy, are outperforming their peers in a number of indicators (during both boom and downturn times): market value per employee, revenue per employee, and market-to-book value ratio.[40]

Such success stories are not going unnoticed by business leaders. Recent surveys indicate that digitally integrating the value chain is one of the top concerns of senior management in leading firms. For example, in its 13th Annual Critical Issues of Information Systems Management Study, CSC (one of the leading consulting and IT service firms in North America) reported that 72% of high-technology executives rated electronically connecting to customers, suppliers, or partners as their top priority.[41] Another indicator of this shift toward integration is the very steep growth in the CRM and SCM software markets. Gartner, a research firm, forecasts that CRM software license revenues will grow from $4 billion in 2000 to about $16.1 billion in 2005, and SCM software revenues will grow from $1.9 billion to about $6.5 billion over this same period.[42]

We now discuss, in more detail, two of the emerging business and organizational models: virtual business organizations and value chain integration.

Virtual Business Organizations

In keeping with the forecasts about the changing power of networking, we are seeing the emergence of complete virtual business organizations. With specialists cropping up in practically every major business activity, from product design to delivery, it is now possible to pull together a virtual organization that employs only "best-of-breed," cost-effective contributors at each point. There are many examples of such virtual organizations, including

- *Reflect.com.* The concept of partnership is affecting even traditional consumer packaged goods companies like Procter and Gamble. P&G, in partnership with Silicon Valley investment capital companies, founded an Internet company based entirely on partnerships—with its consumers and product manufacturers. The company website, www.reflect.com, allows for the establishment of a relationship of trust with consumers: Consumers can personalize their site navigation experience and each of the products they wish to buy. The entire production and distribution of the products offered is contracted out to a large number of other companies and the emphasis on brand is significantly reduced. This marks a dramatic break with P&G's traditional "push" and mass production model, which has long been reinforced by the highest consumer advertising budgets in the world. Through the experimental Internet model, P&G is seeking to focus its efforts purely on R&D and the intermediation of relations between consumers and other companies in the production chain.

- *Nokia—Visor's Division.*[43] This division operates in the United States with only five employees. The company, including technical support, logistics, sales, marketing, and the like, contracts out almost every function.
- *Topsy Tail's.*[43] This is a fashion accessories company with annual sales of $80 million and only three employees. The company never "touches" the product. It contracts with third parties, including mold injection companies, packaging development agencies, and various functionally specific companies in the areas of logistics, customer service, distribution, and sales.
- *Zara—Clothing Business.*[3] The concept of the networking model in the clothing industry was first developed by Benetton. However, it has been taken to a much more sophisticated level by Zara, a Spanish company. Despite producing 12,000 new designs per year, sophisticated networks helps ensure that Zara's cycle from design to production and distribution is only 2 weeks. The company collects sales information with handheld devices at its (mainly) licensed chain of stores in 34 countries (end of 2000). The information is immediately transmitted to its design center, which is also electronically linked to its main plant and a number of local independent fabric factories.

No other business, however, exemplifies the new paradigm of virtual organizations better than the mass-market portals. Portals such as Yahoo!, Lycos, Excite, and Alta Vista started as gateways to the Internet and evolved to destinations by providing aggregation of third party content (and more recently proprietary content), functionality, and e-commerce. (Search engines accounted for 28% of all Internet advertising revenues in 2001 and the top 10 sites, including mainly portals, accounted for 77% of all Internet advertising revenues;[44] 60% of a typical online session includes visiting a portal.[45])

How did they accomplish this? The winners of mass-market portals were able to move quickly, without losing the focus on end-user needs. They were able to rapidly integrate design, technology, applications, and content, at the same time leveraging core competencies (e.g., directory building and interface design at Yahoo!), proprietary distribution (e.g., AOL), or preexisting customer relationships (MSN—Microsoft). They now pursue the provision of a seamless, consistent, and personalized experience anywhere and anytime, along with the integration of different media assets delivered through a variety of devices.

Regardless of their specific strategies, the leaders of these companies learned early that they needed a different mindset to operate in this business. No more: "Here's the solution, let's look for suppliers or distributors." In this new environment, achieving success requires superior skills at striking win-win partnerships with different players along the value chain. Many new features, applications and content areas require that all parties (software providers, content owners, distribution networks, managers of the relationship with customers) work collaboratively (and much more rapidly than in the past) to provide valuable user experiences. With the interconnection and instant measurement of results, the revenues or profits also had to be fairly distributed (or rapidly reconfigured) according to each partner's contribution to the overall success. Failure to do this means that the partnerships are not working to the benefit of all and that they risk rapidly becoming unproductive and ultimately doomed to disintegrate.

All these examples are still the exception to the rule. They point, however, to emerging business models that are very flexible and focused on the needs of the end customers. All the virtual business organizations are leveraging the new infrastructure provided by the Internet. Very important, they also rely on very innovative organizational and business models that require increased levels of trust and a deep understanding of the principles of community-driven relationships. As Francis Fukuyama noted,[21, pp. 25-26]

> The ability of companies to move from large hierarchies to flexible networks of smaller firms will depend, in other words, on the degree of trust and social capital present in the broader society.

Although the development of high-trust enterprises and societies has always been essential for economic growth, we argue throughout this book that the notion of trust is becoming far more important than it has ever been in the past, as knowledge and collaboration become the key drivers for value creation internally and in partnership with outside parties. The leverage of the full opportunities provided by CPs (especially in terms of virtual collaboration) clearly depends on trust . . . but more on that later.

Value Chain Integration

"Not that long ago, none of us doubted that vertical integration would provide the solution to any problem. If we needed new technology, we would create it ourselves. But in today's high-speed business environment, we know better. Today we develop technology for the sake of competitive advantage, but we no longer believe we need to be omnipotent. If we know that suppliers already own the technology we need, we don't bother wasting time and resources to duplicate their capabilities."
—Dr. Lewis S. Edelheit, senior vice president,
General Electric Company,[25, p. 109]

In the emerging Networked Era, the value proposition for the customer or end user forms the basis for the network. The ability of companies to better serve their end customers to succeed in their marketplace is becoming increasingly dependent on the infrastructure connectivity of customers, suppliers, partners, and distributors. Value chain integration should not be confused with outsourcing or supply chain integration. It is truly about integration of value and, in many cases, involves a high level of customization of products or services to address specific needs of end customers. Each participant in the value chain needs to provide superior value creation and strong partnership capabilities.[32]

Several studies have demonstrated that the majority of innovative ideas in companies originate with clients[25,46,47] or are refined particularly by "early adopters."[48] In the Networked Era, much effort is directed toward getting all the players in the network collaborating to quickly deliver innovative solutions that meet customer needs. In this new environment, customers are, indeed, as intrinsic a part of the value chain as any firm in the Web. They provide valuable real-time information that allows timely customization of products and services and important clues to the innovation process.

The automobile industry offers interesting examples of the move toward highly integrated and networked value chains. Once the epitome of vertically integrated organizations and champions of adversarial relationships with suppliers, the leading Western automakers are now becoming leading orchestrators of collaborative Webs. In Japan, the tight relationships of automakers and vendors through *keiretsus* are well known. *Keiretsus* have always involved cross-equity ownership arrangements, just-in-time coordination of production, general expertise exchanges, and high levels of collaboration in product development. Scared by the "Japanese invasion" of North America and Europe in the 1980s, Western automakers were obliged to make significant changes to improve their value chain management methods and principles. Just-in-time production coordination is now a lot more widespread, and the automakers are working hard to overcome the past adversarial relationships with suppliers. The numbers of suppliers have been radically reduced, and they no longer primarily deliver isolated parts. Instead, subsystems are jointly developed. The ability to provide innovative solutions and exchange knowledge has, clearly, become a very important criterion when selecting suppliers.

The kind of collaboration and value chain integration we talk about is very different from the outsourcing strategies that dominated the 1980s and early 1990s. It is not about shifting responsibility and inventory to others in the supply chain. It requires much higher levels of openness and visibility throughout the value chain, an ability to work in teams (permanent or ad hoc) that include members from different organizations, and the discipline to develop operating principles, budgets, metrics, and incentives that foster win-win relationships. On the technical side, value chain integration requires visionary IT leaders within organizations who can reshape the typical inward-looking and proprietary IT infrastructure into one that is highly flexible, open, scalable, and allows an easier setup of extended relationships.

In terms of software, value chain integration requires the integration of many, previously disparate, applications, such as SCM, ERP, CRM, and distributed content management systems. This will not be easy, as companies not long ago invested millions of dollars in a number of best-of-breed ERP, CRM, SCM, and even mainframe systems that do not necessarily integrate easily with each other. It is expected that most companies need to engage in the complex integration of these sorts of applications, particularly to identify and rank the most valuable (profitable) customers and serve them according to their sta-

---

India's Software Industry: From Cheap Outsourcing to Deep Value Chain Integration

India's software industry started as a cheap outsourcing alternative of low-level programming for companies in Europe and North America. Now, the industry is becoming more deeply (and virtually) and highly integrated in the product development efforts of large Western corporations. Consequently, India's software industry is one of the fastest growth areas in business worldwide. India's software exports have grown from $700 million in 1995 to $6.2 billion in 2000, and are expected to reach $50 billion in 2008.[49]

---

tus and preferences. Corporate portal platforms play an important role in this trend toward integration.

Although the technical side of the integration is not simple, its complexity pales in comparison to the other challenges companies face. These challenges include

- Redesigning processes and reorganizing different areas and functions within the firm.
- Partnering and sharing information and knowledge with inside and outside stakeholders.
- Making decisions about whether or not to pursue activities internally, to outsource, or to cooperate with another firm.
- Developing products cooperatively.
- Cross training of personnel.

More important though, it also requires traditional, hierarchical, bureaucratic, and vertically structured companies to make significant organizational changes in order to compete effectively and, in many cases, survive. Companies must look at themselves as open, social, and adaptive systems that are subject to a multitude of internal and external influences. Despite the growing importance of information systems—as repositories of an organization's knowledge—it is primarily people who, through effective collaboration, create, learn, retain, and transmit the knowledge that is most relevant for a company's success.

In the previous paragraph, we highlighted some of the challenges many companies will face transitioning to the Networked Era. Indeed, although this book focuses on the use of the Internet to further collaboration and KM, we will, more often than not, take a cautionary stand regarding the impact of the Internet. Scholar Francis Fukuyama's warning below highlights further the need for caution:[50]

> Trust does not reside in integrated circuits or fiber optics cables. Although it involves an exchange of information, trust is not reducible to information. A "virtual" firm can have abundant information coming through network wires about its suppliers and contractors. But if they are all crooks and frauds, dealing with them will remain a costly process involving complex contracts and time-consuming enforcement. Without trust, there will be a strong incentive to bring these activities in-house and restore the old hierarchies.

Clearly, one of the important challenges for traditional companies is that they already own large expanses of their value chains. For these firms, integrating for maximum customer value cannot happen until after they have *disintegrated*. In a world where the costs of collaboration and interaction are low, vertical integration cannot be sustained. Specialized niche players or smarter, faster competitors attack the weak parts of a firm's value proposition and marketing position. If the firm is not the absolute best at performing a function that can be bought elsewhere, it should not be doing it.

Many companies, however, are still fighting to win a game that no longer exists. Most of them continue to accept the assumptions and constraints of traditional economics and business strategy. They live by the catchphrase of self-reliance: "If you want something done right (and on time), do it yourself." Therefore, automobile manufacturers made their own parts; steel companies also owned mining companies; and many manufacturers had their own fleet of trucks. Given the high cost and risk of transacting business with others, self-reliance made good economic sense in the old economy. As with most management issues, the real question for the future is whether business leaders can change their mindsets and rethink the overriding logic of their relationship with the business environment and the value proposition of their own organizations.

The examples of competing Cisco and Nortel, which follow, are among the best examples to illustrate the concepts of advanced virtual value chain integration discussed here.

The Value Chain Integration Example at Cisco

Cisco, in particular, is a remarkable case of deep integration across the whole value chain. Its management of the value chain, highly leveraged by the Internet, includes not only the seamless flow of information and knowledge from customers to suppliers (and vice versa) but also various levels of partnership for product development and delivery of customer value. Cisco engages and coordinates the entire value chain, aligning and motivating all players from suppliers to distributors to better serve the end customer.[49] Cisco's executive vice president, Don Listwin, explains how Cisco has helped US West cut the costs of serving its asymmetrical digital subscriber line (ADSL) customers, by preconfiguring access devices for each individual US West customer. (Previously, US West was responsible for developing each configuration.) Cisco was able to achieve this by linking its own suppliers directly with US West's customers:

> Now, when US West places an order for Internet access devices through Cisco, our Web-based order form includes delivery to the end-consumer and the configuration of each device. The order enters our system and is transmitted to Celestica, the contract manufacturer in Florida who physically builds the box. Celestica does the required configuration, sticks on the waybill, and ships it directly to the customer via UPS. The knowledge about the end product—the UPS delivery information, the customer configuration, and the US West end of it—is all managed through the Internet. The box goes directly from point A to point B. Our return on invested capital is enormous because, at the end of the day, we take electronic cash for the execution of our intellectual property—by other people. And the higher your return on invested capital, the higher your price earnings ratio in the stock market. (page 106)

The Value Chain Integration Example at Nortel

Nortel, a relatively more traditional organization (as compared to Cisco) in the telecom industry, did not start with the same approach as Cisco. Nortel has, however, made major progress in its efforts to emulate some of Cisco's Internet-based integration strategies. In a recent interview with senior VPs Danny Murdock and Greg Kowal, we learned how Nortel's corporate portal is already playing a critical role in improving efficiencies and knowledge flow along Nortel's value chain. Nortel's CP builds on earlier supply chain management efforts. Its main goal, however, is no longer to help drive down supply costs but to deeply integrate into customers' processes and lock in customers' relationships through ease of use and rapid knowledge access to source solutions. Nortel's executives realize that this is much more valuable.

Nortel's current portal strategy is premised on the clear understanding by senior management that client relationships need to entail a much higher level of knowledge sharing and collaboration. The CP strategy also recognizes that Nortel's selling process is very complex: It involves codesigning and coplanning network solutions and deployment for a very wide range of products. Consequently, the CP strategy is heavily geared toward facilitating and fostering collaborative decision-making processes that involve product and knowledge communities both inside and outside Nortel. Not surprisingly, actual online ordering is just a small part of Nortel's CP solution.

In keeping with the strategies just outlined, Nortel's CP was designed to provide major customers (tier one) with a very personalized B-to-B collaboration that integrates the complete value chain: selling, planning, decision making, ordering, and fulfillment. The high level of personalization means that Nortel provides e-business solutions that directly plug into the customer's supply chain management needs and link all the way to Nortel's own suppliers. Nortel's suppliers have real-time access to orders, forecasts, and demand. In Greg Kowal's words: "It's not enough to have the customer plug into Nortel's supply chain. In fact, it is the other way around: Nortel needs to plug into their clients' supply chain solutions."

Through its CP, Nortel adds real value in a number of ways. The personalization and increased knowledge sharing enabled by its CP means that different individuals within the client company have different views of the portal, depending on their functions, and that Nortel's customers can use some of the same tools as Nortel's own engineers to configure their products. Thus, Nortel can become highly integrated into its customers' planning exercises, anticipating and helping to shape its needs. To ensure Nortel's CP continues to provide customers with accurate and up-to-date information, Nortel had to greatly improve its process to manage its internal content management infrastructure and assign accountability for key content process and maintenance roles for each area of the company. Since a lot of content is shared with customers, there is a strong incentive to keep it current. The Nortel experience, like that of other cases researched, demonstrates the organizational trend toward further integration of internal and external content areas.

Finally, it is important to highlight that all e-business solutions under the corporate portal umbrella are built on industry standards to facilitate integration with customers. They are also built organically around small cycles (about 6 months). The success of Nortel's implementation cycles is measured in terms of revenue, cost, and customer satisfaction. Other metrics include daily behavior of the site (number of orders, number of configurations online, etc.), and more important, the impact it has on the clients. For instance, one of Nortel's very large wireless customers moved from an EDI solution to the corporate portal/e-business solution, with the result that lead time was reduced from 9 weeks to 3 weeks and inventory levels were reduced by 40%.

The new organizational and knowledge-driven business models require important decisions in terms of adopting a technical infrastructure that can support increased levels of collaboration and leverage digital assets across a large number of stakeholders within and beyond of the walls of the organization. In the preceding pages, we discussed a number of trends that, from a strategic point of view, set the stage for a more specific discussion on corporate portals. We now proceed to that more specific, tactical exploration of the role played by CPs in the Networked Era.

THE ROLE OF CORPORATE PORTALS IN THE NETWORKED ERA

Millions of projects are under way globally to extend the boundaries and networks of firms through the use of corporate portals and other Internet-based technologies. Networking and e-business integration are affecting both small and large corporations, from traditional "bricks and mortar" enterprises to "new economy" organizations. A conversation with Marty Lippert, the global CIO of the Royal Bank of Canada (RBC), a tier-one Canadian financial institution, clearly reinforced our conviction that Internet-related investments are being fundamentally driven by their impact on the bottom line. Marty explained that RBC's 2001 corporate Information Technology budget was to focus about 70% on Internet-related initiatives, in contrast with previous corporate Internet budget expenditure of 30–40% of total IT budget. When asked why the significant budget increase, Marty replied:

> After years of customer intelligence research, we have learned that customer retention of Internet-based services is 30% greater than traditional modes of banking access. . . . We see that by integrating our Internet and intranets into a corporate portal around the customer, we can deepen our relationships and connections with our customers. New conversations emerge and as a result, our customer loyalty has consistently increased. There is profit in valuing customer connections and providing a corporate portal that easily navigates and personalizes the customer experience.

RBC's vision and insight about the value of digital integration both internally and externally are already helping to differentiate the organization and strengthen its brand. More important, the economics of this strategy make fundamental business sense.

CPs offer a powerful capability (and the required technical platform) for companies to embark on significant business model transformations to align the goals, motivations, and information context of all employees and the extended enterprise: customers, partners, and suppliers. If properly implemented and supported by trust-building managerial transformations, corporate portals may also establish the foundation and environment for the development of trust-based relationships, beyond the walls of the enterprise. The expected consequences of this vision may include faster innovation cycles, better learning environments, improved customer service, partner alignment, and finally higher revenues and reduced costs.

Internal Corporate Portals versus External Corporate Portals

Most of the cases and examples in this book concern the use of CPs to manage information and knowledge flow to foster meaningful connections within the boundaries of the organization. Although the technical platforms for both internal and external knowledge and content exchanges are rapidly migrating toward complete integration, mastery of the internal use of CPs is a prerequisite for any organization that aims to ultimately be fully integrated in the Networked Era in a much larger context. By learning, first, how to connect the collective intelligence of its employees, an organization prepares itself to engage in more sophisticated knowledge networks with extended communities. This was exactly what Martin Davis, program manager for Ford's ePortal project serving more than 175,000 employees, said: "You're not properly doing e-business unless you're doing it inside the company as well. It starts on the inside."[51]

By truly understanding the implications and major trends associated with the Networked Era, senior management can drive the implementation of CPs to provide a strong foundation for the leveraging of corporate intellectual assets both internally and externally. As David Skyrme, a leading KM author, said: "An important area of under-exploitation is that of converting an organization's internal knowledge assets into externally marketed knowledge-based products and services."[13] As noted previously and in the cases profiled in this book, the initial focus for deep knowledge collaboration is often internal. However, the emerging trend in visionary firms is to use CPs to integrate knowledge management and e-business to foster true collaboration commerce within an extended enterprise value chain framework.

CPs provide the essential e-business platform that allows the integration of information from disparate information sources, both internal and external. As valuable content is created, organized, and distributed, parts of it can be transferred from the internal corporate portal environment to external audiences, including customers, suppliers, and partners. Employees in a knowledge enterprise require effective tools, and a work environment that enables teamwork to effectively focus on customer needs. Organizations that create and structure CPs improve their knowledge assets.

Corporate Portals as the Single Point of Contact to All Information Sources and Relevant Daily Software Applications

With the complexity of providing a single point of contact for all information sources, the CP takes on the unprecedented role of universal integrator.[52] A CP should be viewed as a platform that allows flexible and, at the same time, very coordinated integration to a myriad of software applications. Some have gone so far as to call CPs the next generation of desktop computing, saying that portals will do for global knowledge work what the railroad did for the industrial revolution.[53] CPs are, indeed, an effective approach to seamlessly provide content and connections to data, information, people, partners, clients, and knowledge within and outside the organization. CPs may be used to completely change how information, activities, and responsibilities are shared in an organizational environment: from a narrow, functional, and uncoordinated focus to a broad, project, and coordinated approach. They can also be designed and deployed with the goal of generating connections among people and between people and information, thus sparking knowledge creation, innovation, and reuse of documented knowledge or locating people who can apply their tacit knowledge in specific business situations. CPs can be particularly relevant for people working on multiple projects and dealing with many complex situations that require multiple sources of information and opinions. They may make it easier for team members to share and see the same applications simultaneously even if not located in the same geographic area.

Information Overload and Corporate Portals

Information systems are useful only to the extent that the data, information and knowledge base that feed them are reliable, relevant, and timely. Information overload is a serious problem for organizations that can result in productivity declines (see the following list). CPs respond to the challenge of information overload and scarcity of time by providing sophisticated levels of personalization. Personalization deals with users' needs to quickly access information that is immediately relevant for their daily lives. For instance, based on a survey with its 22,000 employees, Johnson Controls reports that its CP has helped its employees save 1 hour per day.[54, p. 181] Instead of having to open many different windows and launch various applications every time employees turn on their workstation, CPs allow employees (and even outside partners) to predefine the applications (and the specific views, layouts, and priority levels) that will be opened up simultaneously each time. In this way, the many applications that the employees use frequently are just a click away. Our research demonstrates that a successful CP deployment makes life simpler for employees. As they continue to request for personalized information, "My Pages" will eventually become how people access their corporate know-how.

Here are signs of information overload:

- A University of California at Berkeley study showed that, by mid-2000,[55]
    - Already about 550 billion documents were on the Web (95% of them accessible to the public).

- Online information was growing at 7.3 million Web pages per day.
- The annual production of e-mail was 500 times greater than the annual production of Web pages.
- According to a study by the Institute for the Future, employees already receive, on average, 192 messages per day in the following forms: e-mail, letters, voice mail, books, magazines, and the like.[56]
- More than 1 million URLs were on Intel's Intranet in the first quarter of 2001.[57]
- In fall 2000, Angus Reid surveyed 200 physicians across Canada and found that 80% of them feel overwhelmed with the explosion of medical information they need to keep up-to-date: On average, they read 60 medical magazines and 58 peer-reviewed medical journals and attend 24 education events or symposiums per year.[58]
- A Gartner's survey showed that executives of North America corporations spend approximately 108 minutes a day just managing e-mail messages.[59] Other research points to a sixfold growth in the usage of e-mail in corporate America over the last 5 years.[60] And a different study reported that Americans sent about 100 million e-mail messages a day in 1994 and are expected to send close to 1.5 billion e-mail messages a day by 2002.[61]
- In many cases, Intranets have grown so fast that they have become unmanageable and inefficient. HP, for instance, before implementing a CP, had 4700 Intranet URLs.[54, p. 180]
- Worldwide digital storage services spending will grow from $682 million in 2001 to $10.7 billion in 2005 (IDC forecast).[62]
- Average digital storage capacity is growing at 50% a year (Forrester Research Inc.).[62]

In summary, in the Internet Age, CPs are a new and major cornerstone in the move toward pushing information and knowledge to where it is needed within and beyond the walls of the organization. It is also about the push for a common e-business platform (B to E, B to C, B to B, etc.) and deep integration in real time of many disparate Internet and other IT applications, content, and services. This represents a "seismic" change in the way information is presented and how the many back-end systems need to communicate with each other. Some are calling this new trend "collaborative commerce." In Chapter 4, we discuss, in much more detail, the key services and technical components of a robust corporate portal platform and other related software. Before that, however, in Chapter 3, we try to make even more evident the role that CPs can play in KM projects.

REFERENCES

1. Earl M. Every business is an IT business, FP Mastering. *National Post.* May 15, 2001.
2. Quoted in Sikes, A.C., Pearlman, E., eds. *Fast Forward.* New York: Morrow, 2000:3.
3. Castell, M. *The Internet Galaxy: Reflection on the Internet, Business and Society.* New York: Oxford University Press, 2001.
4. Thurow, L. *The Future of Capitalism: How Today's Economic Forces Shape Tomorrow's World.* New York: Penguin USA, 1997.
5. Eurostat; World Bank; CSO; BEA. *The Economist.* March 31, 2001:65.
6. The manufacturing paradox. *The Economist.* November 1, 2001.
7. The Conference Board, Bureau of Economic Analysis. iBiz. *PC Magazine.* July 21, 2001:7.
8. Interbrand/Citibank. *WPP Group plc Annual Report and Accounts.* 2000.
9. Stewart, T. The smartest U.S. companies. *Fortune.* April 16, 2001.
10. Morgan Stanley Capital International World Index. In: Sveiby K.E. *The New Organizational Wealth: Managing and Measuring Knowledge-Based Assets.* San Francisco: Berrett-Koehler Publishers, 1997.
11. Reichheld, F. The loyalty effect. *Harvard Business Review.* 1996.
12. World Intellectual Property Organization, available at www.wipo.org/ipstats/en/index.html.
13. Skyrme, D. New metrics: Does it all add up? In: Despres, C., Chauvel, D., eds. *Knowledge Horizons.* Boston: Butterworth-Heinemann, 2000:308.
14. Maskus, K. *Intellectual Property Rights in the Global Economy.* Washington, DC: Institute for International Economics, 2000:80.
15. Why high-tech firms can't afford to ignore patents. The Knowledge@Wharton Newsletter, http://knowledge.wharton.upenn.edu, December 19, 2001–January 15, 2002.
16. The new workforce. *The Economist.* November 1, 2001.
17. U.S. Bureau of Labor Statistics, 2001, available at www.bls.gov/emp/home.htm.

18. Psacharaopoulos, G. The contribution of education to economic growth. In: Kendrick J.W., ed. *International Comparisons of Productivity and Causes of Slowdown.* Cambridge, MA: Ballinger Publishing, 1984.
19. *The Economist.* September 1996:12.
20. Landes, D.S. *The Wealth and Poverty of Nations: Why Some Are Rich and Some Are Poor.* New York: W.W. Norton and Company, 1998.
21. Fukuyama, F. *Trust: The Social Virtues and the Creation of Prosperity.* New York; The Free Press, 1996.
22. Prahalad, C.K., Hamel, G. The core competence of the corporation. *Harvard Business Review.* 1990, 90, no. 3:79–91.
23. A survey of the pharmaceutical industry. *The Economist.* February 2, 1998.
24. McGee, M.K., Murphy, C. Collaboration is more than squeezing out supply-chain costs. Available at www.informationweek.com, December 10, 2001.
25. Kanter, R.M., Kao, J., Wiersema, F. *Innovation: Breakthrough Thinking at 3M, Du Pont, GE, Pfizer, and Rubbermaid.* New York: HarperBusiness, 1997.
26. Terra, J.C. Gestão do Conhecimento: o grande desafio empresarial. *Negocio Editora, segunda edição.* 2001:216–219.
27. Ipsos-NPD Grocery Digest. U.K.: Sainsbury to develop new food products on the Internet, bringing NPD to shelves quicker. January 24, 2002:8.
28. Skyrme, D.J. *Capitalizing on Knowledge: From e-Business to k-Business.* Boston: Butterworth-Heinemann, 2001.
29. Davis, B. e-Knowledge markets—the $ trillion opportunity, white-paper. The Kaieteur Institute for Knowledge Management, www.kikm.org, 2000.
30. Content for dollars. *PC Magazine.* August 2001:29.
31. Davenport, T.H., Prusak, L. *Working Knowledge: How Organizations Manage What They Know.* Boston: Harvard Business School Press, 1999.
32. Tapscott, D., Ticoll, D., Lowy, A. *Digital Capital: Harnessing the Power of Business Webs.* Boston: Harvard Business School Press, 2000.
33. Autor, David H. Wiring the labor market. *Journal of Economic Perspectives.* 15, no. 1(Winter 2001):25–40.
34. Malone, T.W., Laubacher, R.J. All change for the e-lance economy, FP Mastering. *National Post.* July 10, 2001.

35. Saxenian, A. *Regional Advantage: Culture and Competition in Silicon Valley and Route 128.* Cambridge, MA: Harvard University Press, 1996.
36. Will the corporation survive? *The Economist.* November 1, 2001.
37. Anders, G. Interview with Steve Ballmer: "Steve Ballmer's Big Moves." *Fast Company.* March 2001:148.
38. Venkatraman, N., Henderson, J.C. Business platforms for the 21st century. In: Marchand, D., Davenport, D., eds. *Mastering Information Management: Complete MBA Companion in Information Management.* Englewood Cliffs, NJ: Financial Times/Prentice-Hall, 2000:286–287.
39. Digital Economy 2000. U.S. Department of Commerce, June 2000, available at www.esa.doc.gov/de2000.pdf.
40. Häcki, R., Lighton, J. The future of the networked company. *The McKinsey Quarterly.* 2001, no. 3:26–39.
41. Computer Sciences Corporation. Press release. January 12, 2001.
42. iBiz stats. *PC Magazine.* July 2001.
43. Malone, T.W., Laubacher, R.J. The dawn of the e-lance economy. *Harvard Business Review.* September–October 1998:145–152.
44. Revenue report, a quarterly survey conducted by PriceWaterhouse Coopers. Internet Advertising Bureau, June 2002, available at www.iab.net.
45. The great portal payoff: matching Internet marketing to consumer behavior. Booz-Allen & Hamilton, 2000, available at www.bah.com.
46. Marquis, D.G., Myers, S. *Successful Industrial Innovations.* Washington, DC: National Science Foundation, 1969.
47. Von Hippel, E. Users as innovators. In: Rothberg, R.R., ed. *Corporate Strategy and Product Innovation.* New York: Free Press, 1981:239–251.
48. Chandler, A.D., Jr., Cortada, J.W. *A Nation Transformed by Information: How Information Has Shaped the United States from Colonial Times to the Present.* New York: Oxford University Press, 2000.
49. Nasscom. India software exports. *Financial Times.* February 21, 2001.
50. Fukuyama, F. *Trust: The Social Virtues and the Creation of Prosperity.* New York: The Free Press, 1996:25.
51. Kaplan S. Calling all workers. *CIO Magazine.* December 1, 2001.

52. Corporate Portal Architecture. *Delphi Research.* November 1999: 1–20.
53. Koulopoulos, T.M., Frapollo, C. *Smart Things to Know about Knowledge Management.* Mankato, MN: Capstone Press, 2000.
54. Digital doorways. *PC Magazine.* June 12, 2001:181.
55. Lyman, P., Varian, H. How much information? University of California, SIMS, research report, October 19, 2000. In: Castells, M. *The Internet Galaxy: Reflections on the Internet, Business and Society.* New York: Oxford University Press, 2001.
56. Davenport, T. Attention: the next information frontier, FP Mastering. *Financial Post.* May 29, 2001:M8.
57. Aneja, A., Rowan, C., Brooksby, B. Corporate Portal Framework for Transforming Content Chaos on Intranets, white paper available at www.intel.com.
58. Angus Reid. Information overload: What is it doing to physicians? Report 16, no. 3(May–June 21, 2001).
59. *PC Magazine.* June 26, 2001:64.
60. Chavez, J. E-mail blamed for wasted work time. Rogen International research results reported in: *Globe and Mail.* June 21, 2001:T2.
61. Kuitenbrouwer, P. Egads, we've got e-mail. *Financial Post.* October 18, 2001:FP 1.
62. Chu, S. Storage soars. *Globe and Mail.* June 21, 2001, page T1.

3

KNOWLEDGE
MANAGEMENT
IN THE
NETWORKED
ERA

"What Knowledge Management offers us is insight into aspects of management that we have failed to understand properly because of our failure to consider the nature and characteristics of knowledge."
—Robert M. Grant, professor of management, Georgetown University[1]

This chapter discusses a number of issues related to knowledge management in the Networked Era. The discussion serves to highlight the fact that KM is still an emerging and complex practice. The set of issues covered is quite extensive, but it is by no means comprehensive. There are many interpretations about what *knowledge management* means and just as many ideas about how to effectively maximize its potential power. At the end of this chapter, we provide a comprehensive KM agenda that maps many of the questions we found associated with KM in the management literature. A person's particular point of view is influenced by his or her work experience as well as his or her professional education, training, and functional responsibilities within an organization. The same applies to us. While we acknowledge the strong value of different perspectives (e.g., organizational learning theory, intellectual capital measurement, psychology, theory of the firm, to name a few), we also believe that to address all these issues would require significant analysis of corporate strategy, organizational, and learning theories and involve a level of complexity beyond the scope of a single book (and many have already been written on these topics).

Knowledge management is also not a complete novelty: The racks of clay tablets buried in the ruins of ancient Mesopotamian cities can be considered a form of KM effort. More than 2000 years ago, Aristotle also observed that power is derived from knowledge. Indeed, as far as we can look back, organizations have always had to choose a set of core competencies and develop a knowledge base to compete. Has much changed since then? Knowledge is more critical for competitive advantage than in any other time in history. Technologies, such as the Internet, have enabled businesses to leverage the collective intelligence of their enterprise. Organizations are redefining the role of employees and their work processes and how documents are managed.

In this chapter we focus on topics and aspects of KM that we found to be particularly important for the deployment of CPs: communities of practice, online communities and e-learning. We also engage in a discussion about the differences between information management (IM) and knowledge management, as it is very easy for projects that start with a KM purpose to become pure IM projects. Finally, we present some practical perspectives about dealing with the always critical goal of establishing a KM-friendly organizational culture.

Anyone participating in the field of KM should understand that

- KM is an emerging discipline.
- KM is necessarily complex in that it represents a shift from a focus on information to a focus on the individuals who not only use, but also create and own their pieces of knowledge (indeed, the majority of KM executives believe that the most challenging KM issues are people related, not technology or process related[2]).

- Many fields of theory (which may not have interacted in the past) contribute to the development of KM.
- There is no industry-standard definition or conceptual framework with which to align different professionals.
- Many management initiatives fall under the KM umbrella: The toughest thing is to develop a coherent, aligned, comprehensive, systemic, and systematic approach.
- It is important to understand that managing knowledge is not a new concept, just a newly framed one, enabled by recent technologies, media, devices, and techniques (in particular, those technologies that improve the management of unstructured data).
- It will take time for these new capabilities to fully evolve and the opportunities and impact they present to be fully understood.
- To date, most reports about linking KM investments with financial results have been anecdotal. However, some of the cases reported in this book (e.g., Siemens and Texaco) show emerging trends to quantify the bottom-line impact of specific KM efforts, and McKinsey & Company recently released the results of global research that establishes direct links between adoption of KM techniques and gains in market share value.[3]
- Given the current state of the KM discipline, large KM efforts may require high up-front investments in terms of developing alignment and understanding of the role and value of KM for both the organization and employees.

Whatever its form, format, or where it resides, companies are increasingly realizing that the knowledge resource has certainly become the key to establishing enduring, self-reinforcing competitive advantages. This realization, coupled with major advances in information technology, has led to the emergence of KM as a discipline or explicit concern for many organizations. KM, in its most current sense, may be thought of as the effort to improve an organization's ability to create new knowledge, leverage existing knowledge, protect strategic knowledge, and improve human and organizational performance through facilitated meaningful connections (with other people, documents, and communities). In practical terms, it means

- Making sure that an organization's most valuable knowledge (tacit or explicit) is more easily identifiable.
- Identifying, organizing, integrating, and disseminating both internal and external valuable knowledge.

- Helping and motivating holders of critical expertise to share their knowledge by making it easy for them to codify part of what they know and collaborate with others.
- Fostering higher levels of collaboration internally and with partners, suppliers, and customers.
- Implementing processes and management practices that improve the retention and protection of valuable knowledge.
- Making it easier for employees who share the same interests, learning goals, and business problems to find each other.
- Ensuring that those within an organization have access to the knowledge of the organization when, where, and in the form that they need it.
- And, perhaps most important, ensuring that an organization's employees are also capable, willing, rewarded, and motivated to share their knowledge.

In the context of such an understanding of KM, we elaborate further on the following topics that are particularly relevant for the successful deployments of CPs:

- Information management versus knowledge management.
- Organizational culture and knowledge management.
- Communities of practice.
- On-line communities.
- Human capital, the Internet, and e-learning.

Differences between Information and Knowledge Management

"Knowledge management does not begin and end with information technology."
—Anthony Wensley and Alison Verwijk-O'Sullivan[4]

Given that the Internet appears to be revolutionizing business across all sectors of the economy and the KM discipline is now beginning to truly benefit from dedicated Web-based technology solutions, this warning by Wensley and Verwijk-O'Sullivan might seem to be out of touch with reality. Indeed, theirs might be considered an almost humanistic and "soft" vision of today's "hard" business reality. However, it is very important to recognize that KM must necessarily go beyond the design of information systems or CPs. KM starts with a "knower," someone who has valuable knowledge and may be willing to share it with others. In this regard, KM does require a significant change in behavior in order to be effective. This is often *not* the case with traditional information management projects. Without the knowledge sharing, there is no KM. Second, increasing the richness and quality of available information sources and the interpretative capacity of employees is far more desirable than simply increasing the quantity of information available: Information per se can be meaningless and irrelevant without proper context and validation. Therefore, a main concern of KM (and traditionally not of information management) should be the provision of a context for and validation of available information. For example, basic information about the main information sources (especially unstructured information) should be enriched with additional details, including

- Who created the information.
- What is the background of the authors.
- Where and when was it created.
- How long will the information be relevant, valid, and accurate.
- Who validated the information.
- Who else might be interested or has similar knowledge.
- Where was it applied or proven to be useful.
- What other sources of information are closely related.
- How can we test some of the concepts (e.g., through templates and simulation).

Lessons from the Reengineering Fad of the 1990s

The innumerable reengineering efforts of the 1990s should serve as a warning for those involved with CP initiatives. For the most part, the implementation of these projects depended heavily on investments in information technology. (American companies invested close to $52 billion in reengineering projects by 1997. Of this total, $40 billion was related to information technology.)[5] Initially, there were reports of several success stories using this reengineering approach, principally with respect to reducing production or service cycle times, quality improvement, and cost reduction. However, later evaluations of these efforts have demonstrated that there were likely many more failures than successes.*[6] Indeed, several studies show that more than two-thirds of these reengineering projects did not achieve success.[5] The consulting company Arthur D. Little Inc. concluded that only 16% of companies were satisfied with the results of such projects.

Without a clear understanding of how knowledge is created or utilized by human beings and how certain design solutions affect the knowledge creation process, companies implementing CPs will almost certainly fall prey to the same traps that scuttled the reengineering fad. These major traps, according to leading critics of reengineering,[7,8] were

- Not considering the issues of past organizational learning in the form of the (tacit) knowledge of employees and future organizational learning in terms of the need for the company to be continually learning and adapting itself.
- Much less efficiency in knowledge-intensive activities where creativity and collaboration are much appreciated and where inputs and outputs are not well defined.
- An almost blind obsession with cost reduction, which meant that the human element of organizations and the need to change human behavior were forgotten.
- Losing strategic focus and automating processes that did not contribute to competing in the marketplace, thereby losing the capacity to innovate and use employees to create the future.
- Developing technology-intensive business process redesign solutions without understanding how knowledge and judgment are

---

*A rather recent study, involving 100 global electronics companies, conducted by Stanford University, the University of Augsberg, and the consulting company McKinsey corroborates these ideas. The study found that investments in information technology do not necessarily lead to better business performance:[6]

> The logic is clear and consistent: delegation reduced delays in getting management approval; dedicated assignments limit distractions; small team size minimizes time spent on coordination; and higher skill levels support the judgment needed for flexibility on schedule and late design changes. Building such capability, however, does not depend on substituting information technology and automation for people. In fact, the successful companies in our sample spend about 25% less on information technology and over 50% less on automation. Simpler business processes reduce companies' need for IT and automation. The key issue—for both leaders and laggards—is the development of the whole work force through enabling the delegation of responsibility, not the size of the investment in information technology.

related to such business processes and the willingness, or readiness, of organizations to change.

- Impeding lateral links and peer exchanges due to a single-minded focus on achieving longitudinal and cross-functional links and efficiency gains.
- Failing to consider the practical needs of employees, focusing instead on meeting process requirements. In John Seely Brown's and Paul Duguid's words, the reengineering movement failed to understand that "It is the practice of the people who work in [an] organization that brings process to life, and, indeed, life to process."[8]

Many recent studies pointed out that there is not much of a link between investments in IT and business performance or increased productivity. Interesting discussions about the lack of productivity growth in most industries in North America during the 1990s can be found in the study by R. J. Gordon.[9] Certainly, the true competitive advantage of companies is often incredibly hard to emulate, because it resides in the collective tacit knowledge that employees hold and not in any particular IT solution or business process. The collective tacit knowledge of employees includes a shared set of values, unspoken and uncodified common knowledge, communication patterns, and organizational routines that are heavily anchored in that joint experience.

In sum, by ignoring the human element of the organization, reengineering theories mistakenly assumed that investments in IT, streamlined business processes, and new business performance measurements would result in increased productivity. The outcomes of reengineering efforts demonstrate why it is critical that knowledge management strategy not be confused with information management strategy. Knowledge as an asset or resource, unlike information or data, is not easily understood, classified, shared, and measured. It can be invisible, intangible, and difficult to imitate. Expanding the knowledge base within an organization is not the same as expanding its information base. Expectations about the results of CP initiatives must be carefully considered accordingly. Indeed, the initial results of KM initiatives based primarily on information technology and almost void of human behavior considerations appear to be extremely disappointing.[6] A CP implementation may have very different degrees of a KM strategy behind it, depending on the desired outcome of the organization.

Tacit Knowledge

It is important to understand the limits of IT and CP tools at the out-set. The management and dissemination of codified knowledge can greatly benefit from the deployment of CPs. Understanding about their impact on decision making and the creation and dissemination of tacit knowledge is still in its infancy. In organizations, tacit knowledge is the personal knowledge used by members to perform their work and make sense of their world. It is acquired as individuals develop a feel for and capacity to make intuitive judgments about the successful execution of an activity through extensive experience doing that activity.

In 1966, the scientist who became a philosopher, Michael Polanyi, wrote the now classic "The Tacit Dimension," which laid the conceptual foundation for what has come to be known as *tacit knowledge*.[10] Polanyi introduced the theme of tacit knowledge with the phrase "we can know more than we can tell." By this phrase he meant that much of what we know cannot be verbalized or written in words. (More recently, Leonard-Barton added the following to Polanyi's definition: "We often know more than we realize."[11])

One implication of the concept of tacit knowledge is that, although CPs and other IT and Internet applications provide valuable collaboration tools and abundant information for employees, they will not ever entirely replace the role of intuition and face-to-face knowledge exchanges. The richness and depth of knowledge transfers and creation that occur during individuals' face-to-face encounters cannot be replicated by technology. (See the Microsoft case, which follows.) Personal encounters trigger many cues that help individuals to learn, including body language, tone of voice, facial expression, and hand gestures. It is clear, therefore, that when planning the deployment of CPs, KM leaders need to develop a solid understanding of the extent to which specific applications can point to holders of tacit knowledge. CPs should, therefore, be designed with two key objectives in mind: to make it as easy as possible for users to find experts with whom to dialogue personally and to foster and support the development of communities of practice among users.

Microsoft—The Importance of Personal Contact

In their extensive study about product development practices at Microsoft, researchers Cusumano and Selby conclude:[12]

We also suspect that learning may be easier at Microsoft than at larger firms that spread out critical operations around the globe. As discussed in other chapters, Microsoft has located nearly all its product development groups at the Redmond, Washington, headquarters. Despite extensive reliance on electronic mail, Gates and other managers have also insisted that people be close enough physically to solve problems face-to-face. It is our observation that much of the learning which goes on at Microsoft does take place informally—in conversations in the innumerable corridors, as well as in individual offices, over lunch tables, in retreats, and in more casual settings.

CPs can certainly help improve and increase the connections among people and often may lead to connections that would not occur without the tool. However, connections are, of course, only the first step in the knowledge-creation or -sharing process. To go to the next level, people must be willing to cooperate and the right incentives and rewards need to be in place. Individuals also need the time and budget to eventually meet face to face (or at least use bandwidth-rich communication media, such as teleconferencing) to develop more personal relationships that facilitate the knowledge exchange and ensure cooperation toward the same goals.

Despite the increasing importance of and investments in information technology (IT) and information systems, we strongly believe that organizations should be very careful not to confuse KM with IM projects. IM projects have very specific technical goals, timelines, data flow designs, and sometimes, a detailed end state. They are usually focused on maintaining the integrity of data and the policies and strategies to distribute information. Such projects necessarily assume a mechanistic view of the organization.

Ideally, the term *KM project* should never be used as if it pertained to the same category as an IT or IM project. KM projects should take a holistic or organic view of the enterprise and encompass different initiatives in many areas: certainly in IT, but also in human resources, organizational design, internal communications, and so forth. KM is more closely associated with the "act of managing" than IM. In this sense, KM is never ending. It is defined by the identification of people's expertise and the interplay of people with people (tacit-knowledge sharing) and people with information systems (two-way road of knowledge capture, reuse, and re-creation). Given that they depend highly on people's previous knowledge, motivation, and willingness to create, act, share, and codify their own individual knowledge, KM processes are a lot more complex than IT or IM projects. However, KM depends increasingly on the support of a solid IT infrastructure. This dependence is particularly evident in large, geographically dispersed organizations with significant numbers of knowledge workers who are constantly creating, applying, and storing information.

It is our opinion that KM projects need to be a lot more value driven than traditional IT and IM projects. Whereas the success of IT and IM projects is often judged based on technical achievements (in addition to cost and timeline considerations), the success of KM projects has less to do with technical achievements and more to do with changes in behavior or actions derived from connections or learning opportunities that the projects facilitated. In general, therefore, CP and IT solutions should be considered as distinct from KM projects but also as key enablers of greater levels of collaboration and knowledge sharing.

ORGANIZATIONAL CULTURE AND KNOWLEDGE MANAGEMENT

"If we learn anything from the history of economic development, it is that culture makes all the difference. Yet culture, in the sense of inner values and attitudes that guide a population, frightens scholars. It has a sulfuric odor of race and inheritance, an air of immutability. In thoughtful moments, economists and social scientists recognize that this is not true, and indeed salute examples of cultural change for the better while deploring changes for the worse. But applauding or deploring implies the passivity of the viewer—an inability to use knowledge to shape people and things."
—David S. Landes[13]

The topics of culture and organizational values are frequently associated with the "soft" side of the business world. Consequently, many business managers relegate them to a secondary level of importance. The relevance of these topics in the Knowledge Era and for the implementation of CPs should, however, attract the increased attention of management. As we will see in detail in the chapters ahead and, particularly, in the case studies, successful CP implementation depends on a number of actions aimed at changing the norms, values, and motivations of employees. We now review some of the underlying definitions, concepts, and practices related to organizational culture and KM to bear in mind when analyzing CP implementation issues in the next chapters.

First, we believe that organizational culture can best be understood as constituting the norms and values that help members interpret events and determine what behavior is appropriate or inappropriate. Norms and values help provide order, meaning, and an identity to organizations. As such, an organization's norms and values act as elements of communication and consensus. They also express and facilitate power relations and levels of collaboration. In a sense, the norms and values of an organization can be regarded as an internal system of control. Cultural norms and values can lead to a high degree of conformity. At the same time, they can provide members a feeling of significant autonomy. In this way, they are much more effective than formal systems of control, which create a permanent feeling of external constraint and can really work only for activities that are easily monitored (such as the output of manual work). This is a very important observation, since the notion of autonomy is not usually associated with the idea of "control systems." Consequently, this understanding of the "control" role played by culture may be counterintuitive to many managers.

Yet the concept of autonomy is probably a key pillar of KM and, to a large degree, of successful CP implementation. The fact is that knowledge, as KM guru David Snowden points out, can only be volunteered.[14] He argues (and we agree) that, to tap into the full knowledge contribution potential of employees, organizations need to rethink the reward structures, organizational forms, and management attitudes that shape voluntary behavior and their corporate culture.

Despite the tremendous impact of corporate culture on the ultimate success of companies and information-management projects, most books about e-business implementations dismiss it outright or point to the need for change to a more "knowledge-sharing culture." Rarely does one see discussions on how to effectively and proactively change a corporate culture in the context of these kinds of projects. As the quote at the beginning of this section by David S. Landes suggested, it would appear that the notion of changing a corporate culture frightens many people.

The creation and shaping of a knowledge-sharing culture depends heavily on the detailed attention and visible support of a devoted and committed leadership. In particular, an organization's leaders can help change existing norms and values and foster a knowledge-sharing and innovative culture by

■ Ensuring that the company's policies and norms for accepted and rewarded behavior and work processes are carefully laid out to reflect desired knowledge-sharing outcomes.

- Leading by example (using the information systems to share information and knowledge with subordinates or sharing knowledge through active mentoring of younger employees).
- Promoting knowledge sharing as a company value (for example, by frequently mentioning this topic in speeches and public statements and giving public recognition to people who make important contributions to the company's knowledge base or share important knowledge with other employees).
- Giving incentives for employees to foster networks outside the company (to help avoid the Not-Invented Here syndrome).
- Creating positions dedicated to the management of knowledge, such as chief knowledge officers (more on these new positions in Chapter 5).
- Requiring that employees write down "the lessons learned" (or have postmortem brainstorm sessions) after all important tasks or projects, and "calling managers" who do not enforce these requirements while rewarding those who do.
- Establishing human resource policies in line with the goal of knowledge sharing (e.g., emphasizing team-player qualities during hiring, avoiding the promotion of employees who do not share, and promoting office exchanges—moving people around, providing time and resources for team dynamics and knowledge-sharing training—techniques frequently used, for instance, by McKinsey & Company).
- Modifying reward systems (such as bonuses and formal recognition policies or prizes) to encourage knowledge sharing: "The trick is to catch someone doing something right and to reward it on the spot."[15]

Developing Trust

Knowledge-sharing is closely related to the concept of developing trust. People do not voluntarily share what they know with colleagues, bosses, partners, and organizations that they do not trust. Yet, it would appear that overall trust levels in many large organizations, at least in North America (in other places it could be much lower), is quite low. A recent survey, reported by John Izzo and Pam Withers, shows "that only 37% of employees rate the level of honesty in their workplaces as high or very high; and that only 14% agree that people trust each other."[16] No wonder so many KM efforts have failed miserably in the recent past.

Sociological and economic research and experiments repeatedly demonstrate that people tend to have less trust in individuals who do not share the same values and are of another race, country, or culture, or who have few friends in common.[17-20] This is an important issue for knowledge-based multinationals that require cooperation and the free-flow of knowledge among people from offices across the globe. For years, organizations have been trying to mitigate against the difficulty of building trust across cultures by periodically moving people to different offices and countries and by providing many employees with, among other things, diversity and cultural-sensitivity courses. (Sony, for instance, makes this kind of training mandatory in many offices.) A CP will not solve this problem, but as a type of global information and knowledge system for an organization, it can certainly help. A number of cases discussed in this book demonstrate how CP implementations can become an important tool for shortening distances and improving the transparency of information flows between previously separate offices, even during mergers and acquisitions.

It is clear that the degree of trust in organizations, and even in different departments or offices within large organizations, varies widely. An organization's degree of trust is rooted in its history, myths, and set of prevailing values. It develops over time and is not easily increased. However, it can be very easily reduced or even totally lost by visible and unexpected acts, such as massive layoffs. Philosopher Joseph Heath, for instance, has used very strong words to show how the untrustworthy behavior of a few can have a significant impact on everyone else's behavior. In his words:[21, p. 67]

> People who defect from the co-operative arrangement leave behind a visible sign of the defection—their garbage. This visible sign has the effect of undermining trust—the belief that others are going to play by the rules. And without this belief, no one can be confident that doing the "right thing" will not leave them open to exploitation by others.

This asymmetric nature of trust (hard to increase, easy to lose) and its fundamental importance for building a knowledge-sharing and, to a large degree, a more innovative risk-taking organization means that organization leaders (and KM leaders, in particular) should tread carefully and make trust building a significant part of an organization's agenda. This concept of the relationship between risk-taking and trust is particularly important in fast-paced, high-tech industries since it has been argued that only in risky situations is trust a relevant factor.[22] Next, we highlight a few examples from the literature of how culture and trust levels can be transformed through diligent, careful practices, both within the context of an organization and between organizations.

The case of GE, although highly publicized, is worth revisiting for a specific point that may not always catch the attention of the distracted reader of other writing about this organization. GE and its fabled CEO, Jack Welch, provide a very interesting example of how a massive organization worked very hard to change some aspects of its culture (toward higher degrees of trust and knowledge sharing) and put the Internet at the center stage of its corporate strategy. A few examples highlight the kinds of efforts being promoted at this organization:

- Welch has been an Internet evangelist within GE. He used the Internet to bring the company leadership closer to the front line and to increase the prevailing levels of trust and knowledge sharing. More specifically, for example, he now insists that the minutes of top management meetings are made available via its internal portal to the hundreds of thousands of employees in the company almost as soon as the meetings are finished.[23]
- Welch also made a concerted effort to encourage management to share "many anecdotal stories and give incentives" to help employees adopt the "e-way" culture. The following quote, from an interview in *The Economist*, describes the systematic efforts made to change elements of the corporate culture at GE:[24]

Today, all of GE's big divisions run their own web marketplaces, both for internal and external use. Three initiatives—"e-buy"; "e-sell"; and "e-make"—are digitizing the main functions of running the conglomerate, saving money, reaching customers faster and using Internet technology to extend the focus on quality that was the driving-force of Mr. Welch's previous passion, six-sigma manufacturing. The greatest hurdle has not been technology, but culture. Sales staff, worried that they might be destroying their jobs, had to be offered bonuses for helping customers to use GE websites to order. Managers had to watch carefully for reprobate employees using "parallel paths" (the telephone, for instance, or walking to a store) to order supplies, say, or to arrange travel. Some offices even closed their mail rooms for all but one day a week (and that only for the incorrigible legal department), to stop employees from using regular post. Others locked their printer rooms, except for occasional days when bosses would station themselves at the door and demand from those who came through an explanation for their sad inability to shake old paper habits.

KAO, one of Japan's largest chemical companies, was identified by leading KM authors Nonaka and Takeuchi as a company that has particularly well-developed knowledge-creating processes and practices. In the context of this section, we extract the following passage from their book, *The Knowledge-Creating Company*, that highlights KAO's efforts toward building a knowledge-sharing, trusting organization:[25, p. 172]

> To ensure free access to information, computer systems have been introduced throughout the KAO organization, with all information being filed in a central database. Through this system, anyone at KAO can tap into databases included in the sales system, the distribution information system, and the total information network from any office in Japan. The unique feature of this system is that any member, no matter what his or her position or what section she or he belongs to within the business system, has full access to the database (except for a limited amount of personnel information). In other words, anyone can get access to the rich base of explicit knowledge that exists within the business system at any time and from any office.

Trust-Building Efforts among Different Organizations

As discussed in Chapter 2, trust, collaboration, and knowledge creation are closely interrelated. Not surprising, then, trust-building efforts are also being actively deployed by organizations engaged in successful knowledge-creation activities with third parties (suppliers, partners, universities, etc.). A recent study at Michigan State University demonstrated that trust (not technology) is at the core of successful company-supplier integration. It identified, for instance, that the top three factors leading to successful supplier integration in product development are[26]

1. Including supplier employees as members of, or participants in, the buyer's project team.

2. Making active use of direct cross-functional, intercompany communication.
3. Shared education and training between the two companies (buyer and supplier).

Another example comes from research conducted by W. W. Powell, a leading management author. In the late 1990s, he carried out a comprehensive study of how knowledge is transferred between large pharmaceutical companies and biotech firms of various sizes. The study highlighted the importance of personal contact among employees of the different companies to increase the levels of trust. He summarizes his conclusions:[27]

> In all these activities, there is a persistent tension between those activities done informally and on an ad hoc basis and those efforts that are more formalized and structured. Clearly, there are trade-offs with both approaches. The insight appreciated by only a minority of the firms that we have had contact with is that developing routines for the transmission of information and experience does not necessarily entail formalization. Information can be conveyed routinely through informal means. While formal repositories and powerful task forces can be useful, they are too often not a forum in which outside input is allowed. Building routines for regular contact without formalization allows for the possibility that participants not only contribute ideas, they will take lessons learned and spread them in unexpected and unobtrusive ways.

Conclusion

Management literature is increasingly questioning one of the traditional pillars of the bureaucratic organization: impersonal relationships among employees. The importance of building deeper, more meaningful and trusting relationships among employees to develop more creative and innovative environments is currently being strongly advocated by influential authors in North America and Europe.[28,29] The literature also shows that learning and creativity depend mainly on intrinsically motivated people who are eager to learn through social and trust-based interactions, open to discussion, and willing to change their mental frameworks. Interesting discussions on learning and creativity related to the way people interact can be found in the several works.[11,30-32]

In the absence of a relationship of trust between a company and its employees, it is difficult to imagine that employees will be compelled to share their knowledge with one another. People are also very unlikely to share their own personal lessons (including mistakes) if an organization does not allow for and encourage a sufficient level of risk taking and failure. There is little point in companies investing heavily in information technology systems (such as a CP) if these systems are regarded, by the majority of employees, as simply another way for management to increase its control on employees' intellectual capital output or to broadcast information with limited transparency and access rights. In summary, CP projects may facilitate access to general internal and external information, but they will be transformed into tools that increase the stock and flow of very valuable knowledge within a company only if its employees are willing to share their knowledge and trust the organization.

In this section, we highlight a number of ways that organizations can work toward a more knowledge-sharing culture. The detailed case studies and Chapter 5 provide more ideas and practical actions that should be taken when implementing a CP. As we will see, the battle to instill a knowledge-sharing culture requires initiatives at many different levels. It is a battle that needs to be won day after day.

COMMUNITIES OF PRACTICE

In the face of the tremendous challenge of fostering knowledge sharing within and across companies, we need to discuss a concept that precedes the Web and CPs but also greatly benefits from these technologies: communities of practice (CoPs). The concept of communities of practice, originally coined by the organizational theorists Wenger and Snyder,[33] is one of the hottest topics in the KM literature. CoPs consist of people who are informally, as well as contextually, bound by a shared interest in learning and applying a common practice. CoP members may be part of the same department, belong to different areas of a company, or even to different companies and institutions. Members may create semi-open "clubs," where membership is based on relations of high trust and the contribution each person brings to the community or network. Another important distinction between CoPs and teams or task forces is that membership is usually voluntary or self-selected, which means that, although open in most cases, true membership only occurs if the individual actually participates in the CoP at a minimum through active, attentive "listening."

The term *community of practice* refers to the ways in which people naturally work together and associate with others. It acknowledges and celebrates the power of informal communities of peers, their creativity and resourcefulness in solving problems, and their ability to invent better, easier ways to meet their commitments. What holds CoP members together is a common sense of purpose, the needs of individuals to connect with others who share similar experiences or learning goals, and ultimately, each member's real need to know what the other members know.[34]

The most interesting CoPs are those bound (and motivated) by common challenges, interests, or specific problems. Communication tends to be ample and includes topics not necessarily directly related to the task or work projects at hand. Unlike teams or task forces, CoP members may or may not have participated in projects together. Encounters may or may not be regular, in fixed locations, or have structured agendas. They may be real or virtual encounters. CoPs can be ephemeral or last for a long time. In either case, they go through a life cycle of activity and varying numbers of members.

As such, they can bring together people who would otherwise never meet. Thus, when CPs are designed to help these communities to thrive, employees can tap even more effectively into the pool of knowledge (and practical business solutions) traditionally exchanged only among individuals who have the opportunity to work side by side or in frequent formal and informal personal encounters.

The circulation of knowledge happens more effectively when people work together in the tightly focused groups of CoPs. However, unfortunately, it has also been demonstrated that knowledge shared within a particular CoP quite often does not get shared beyond the members of the CoP. Dorothy Leonard Barton studied the impact of communities on knowledge sharing and shows how isolated communities tend to get stuck in ruts, with core competencies turning into core rigidities. Her research found that external cultural stimuli are needed to help propel a CoP's or organization's corporate culture forward. Without these external stimuli, it is very easy for CoPs to be blinded by the boundaries of their own limited view. By linking diverse communities with different belief systems and evaluative practices in a cohesive meld, organizations can challenge the narrow belief systems of each individual community and ensure that knowledge is moved around.

There is also a growing recognition that people "wear different and changing hats" as they go about doing their jobs, moving from project to project, and working within or beyond the borders of the organization. This means that people may participate in various different communities with different levels of intensity. They may be leaders in some, belong to the most active group in others, or simply join in different CoPs, from time to time, to find out what is happening. A well-designed CP acknowledges this natural human behavior and makes it easier for employees to learn about new communities, keep abreast of activities, and seamlessly check in and out of their communities of choice. The ability to organize, capture, and disseminate the knowledge of particular CoPs throughout an organization is at the core of successful KM efforts. Increasingly, a company's ability to survive and outperform others requires the continuous linking of distinct CoPs and the synthesis of collective and organizational knowledge.

The growing imperative of generating new knowledge and innovating quickly makes the concept and practice of communities increasingly more relevant, since it has been shown that innovation and knowledge creation tend to occur more often when employees are "well connected" both inside and outside the organization. Therefore, organizations have a deep interest in motivating employees to participate in CoPs. However, as with many things in life, there has to be a quid pro quo; that is, employees also need to see the benefits for themselves in participating in CoPs. This is something, for instance, that John Old, CKO of Texaco, found out after extensive internal research on the practices and results of Texaco's CoPs. He discovered that Texaco's most successful communities involved a strong "what is in it for me?" factor. In this age, where continuous learning is mandatory and people are bombarded with irrelevant messages and information, CoPs may provide employees trustworthy and focused learning environments and the opportunity to connect with other individuals with similar interests, projects, challenges, and motivations. All these are career-enhancing opportunities and should be well communicated during the launch of CoPs, be they integrated or not into a major CP implementation. We summarize the benefits for employees:

- Learning from experts and peers.
- Developing a sense of identity and belonging (sometimes, in a faceless organization).
- Improving ties with colleagues from other locations and organizations.
- Developing broader perspectives of the organization and environment.

- Developing long-term personal networks.
- Getting recognition for specific skills and knowledge not directly related to their main job description.
- Improving self-esteem.
- Rapidly identifying key knowledge sources, stakeholders, and current organizational priorities, especially new employees.
- The ideal space for self-realization and pursuit of personal passions.

Organizations, in a similar fashion, can greatly benefit from CoPs. By supporting or institutionalizing strategically relevant CoPs, firms can codify chunks of the knowledge carried by employees and, more important, promote focused organizational learning and innovation. It is a well-known fact that meaningful connections take individuals to levels of creativity well beyond what they would reach in isolation. Learning is a social act.[34] In their groundbreaking studies, Wenger and Snyder identified the many ways communities add value to organizations.[33] They

- Help drive strategy.
- Start new lines of business.
- Solve problems quickly.
- Transfer best practices.
- Develop professional skills.
- Help the company recruit and retain talent.

Based on our own research and case studies, we would add the following types of contributions. They

- Win new businesses more quickly.
- Better serve existing clients.
- Develop stronger relationships with clients.
- Facilitate integration of acquired companies and in post-merger efforts.
- Reduce cross-functional and cross-location cultural barriers.
- Improve organizations' social capital.
- Reduce costs.
- And, finally, may play a significant role in merger and acquisition activities.

Organizations that are knowledge intensive, such as consulting companies (like McKinsey, Bain, and Accenture, for example), have been fostering the development of global CoPs for a long time. Most organizations, however, have yet to pay close attention to CoPs. This is starting to change. Recently, a number of leading organizations (for example, Xerox, World Bank, IBM, HP, Siemens, Shell, and Texaco) started to recognize the contribution such networks can make toward the creation and diffusion of knowledge and started to formally support CoPs. According to the research firm Gartner, by 2004, formally supported CoPs will be prevalent in more than 50% of Fortune 500 enterprises.[35]

How do these organizations stimulate the development of CoPs? By

- Providing resources (content, time, and money) for people in different physical locations to meet.
- Accepting the informal legitimacy of CoPs.
- Promoting and sharing the practical results achieved by such CoPs.
- Communicating that this type of activity is welcome by institutionalizing the networks (whether they are formal or informal) into the company values.
- Valuing individual participation and initiative.
- Creating an infrastructure that helps facilitate communication among members.
- Supporting the creation of new roles aimed exclusively at fostering and maintaining these initiatives (so-called knowledge brokers or moderators).

ONLINE COMMUNITIES

Experiences with online communities, such as AOL, Compuserv, WELL, and Listserv, pre-date the Web. Some people, including sociologist and University of California professor Manuel Castell, suggested,[36] "The origins of online communities were very close to the counter-cultural movements and alternative ways of life emerging in the aftermath of the 1960s." Since the Web, however, they have become a mainstream fixture for focused files, information, and knowledge exchanges. These communities cross the boundaries of organizations, countries, age groups, and profit and nonprofit organizations. As we examine the long history (in Internet time) of both not-for-profit and commercial online communities, a few themes dominate the discussions. In our opinion, the most important are core groups and expanding general public participation.

Participation in online communities, although very large, is unevenly distributed: The heavy users tend to be more technically inclined professionals (Linux and Apache communities, for example) and younger people who grew up with chats, instant messaging, and peer-to-peer (P2P) tools. These groups of users are much more comfortable with the rules of engagement of this kind of community. They are more skilled at using the tools available, and they understand the culture and "netiquette" better. There are strong signs, however, that a growing number of less Web-savvy users are engaging in online communities. For example, a report by Pew Internet and American Life Project (October 2001) showed that 84% of U.S. Internet users subscribe to online e-mail groups. More important and more closely related to the concept of communities is that 49% of such users say that they subscribed to the online communities to create and maintain relationships with others in the group.

The Role of Core Groups and Moderators

The discussion forums of mass-market portals and niche content sites and pre-Web experiences with distribution lists, newsgroups, and bulletin boards clearly demonstrate the importance of having moderators (or a highly engaged core group of people) dedicated to the community and engaged in the promotion of knowledge sharing among members. Without such individuals, online communities can easily and quickly lose their focus, with discussions becoming increasingly unproductive.

The Commercial Value of Online Communities

AOL and other community-based sites can credit a great deal of their initial success to the work of thousands of volunteer community leaders who kept online discussions current, exciting, and relevant. Mass-market portals, in general, recognized early on the value of helping communities develop and of supporting many chat and discussion areas. They realized that communities, especially targeted communities, could become a source of very interesting and low-cost targeted content. This is important, since content development is an expensive proposition that very few companies can afford (this is also the case within organizations).

A number of other successful commercial ventures on the Web have been founded or rely very heavily on the exchange of trusted information and the knowledge of community participants. Abuzz, AskMe, eBay, epinions, MySimmon, Edmunds, Keen, and Motley Fool are examples of such ventures. A very recent article by McKinsey & Company,[37] "The Case for On-Line Communities," based on a joint study with Jupiter Media Metrix, shows that these communities create significant value to both B-to-C and B-to-B sites. Community contributors and participants are much more likely to stay longer, visit more often, and transact more heavily. Some large organizations, such as Sun and Cisco, learned the value of fostering and supporting the growth of electronic users' group forums (another type of community) with infrastructure and expertise. The lessons learned from all these types of online communities can certainly be applied to more internally focused KM initiatives.

Online Participation and Sociability

Contrary to common perception, Manuel Castell highlighted that the majority of scholarly studies show that an increase in people's participation in virtual communities and the use of Internet does not result in reduced sociability or fewer face-to-face contacts with other people. In fact, many studies have shown how, in a number of specific situations, these virtual communities have led to more vigorous social interactions. In Castell's words,[36, p. 131]

> Individuals build their networks, on-line and off-line, on the basis of their interests, values, affinities, and projects. Because of the flexibility and communicating power of the Internet, on-line social interaction plays an increasing role in social organization as a whole. On-line networks, when they stabilize in their practice, may build communities, different from physical communities, but not necessarily less intense or less effective in binding and mobilizing.

Promoting and Supporting Online Communities in a Corporate Environment

The 1990s saw the growth in collaborative work supported by LAN (local area networks) and WAN (wide area networks) in many large organizations (the next section lists some of the key lessons from research on computer-supported cooperative work). Since the Web, however, online collaboration has reached a much wider scale within and outside the business world. Collaboration and community building applications are, indeed, becoming a key component of any major CP implementation. They can increase the ability of employees, especially from different locations, to develop stronger bonds and a sense of community. In Chapter 5, we summarize the lessons learned and practices of leading organizations that are leveraging online communities in their CP implementations.

Lessons from Computer-Supported Cooperative Work

Brian Detlor*

Computer-supported cooperative work (CSCW) is a field of research concerned with the development and use of software to help groups increase their competence in working together. Since the mid-1980s, CSCW researchers have explored various ways in which organizational structure and culture affect the adoption and use of groupware and how groupware, in turn, influences the organizational context itself. By viewing corporate portals as a new form of groupware and not merely as a Web-based information dissemination tool, portal designers can leverage insights gleaned from the CSCW literature:

1. *Ensure That Everyone Benefits.* A mistake learned from the introduction of early groupware systems in organizations was that building groupware that satisfied the information needs of a subset of employees was detrimental to the overall adoption and use of the system. To be successful, groupware requires a critical mass of users. Corporate portals should follow suit. Designers should provide sufficient information resources and functions that address the needs and uses of a broad cross-section of employees. Further, designers need to build features into portal designs that respect people's social position within the firm and limit social repercussions that may result from use of the system. For example, in earlier implementations of groupware technology, junior employees often had difficulty negotiating the assignment of work to more senior colleagues via this medium, and some employees

---

*Dr. Detlor is an assistant professor at the Michael G. DeGroote School of Business, McMaster University, Hamilton, Ontario, Canada.

felt uneasy with their work becoming "visible" to others online, as it made them feel scrutinized and vulnerable.

2. *Create Incentives for Use.* Contrary to popular belief, users do not flock to a new groupware system simply because they should or because the designers are excited about it. The same lesson applies to portals. Employees need encouragement. To start, they should be educated on the benefits of this new technology and trained on how to navigate the portal interface. Preferably, this should be done on a continual basis and not only once during portal launch. In addition, employees need rewards to encourage use of the system. This could be done in a variety of ways. Some companies offer giveaways such as freebies and earned points, run contests, or profile key users and departments. As the CSCW literature points out, incentives are key to groupware adoption and use. Collaboration and information sharing are not "natural" ways for people to work, especially in competitive organizational cultures that emphasize and reward individual contributions through job advancement, cash incentives, and other such perks. A change in mindset from traditional ways of working is required to support user collaboration and the adoption of new concepts such as writing down one's ideas for everyone to see. Incentives can help in this regard.

3. *Promote Multiple Perspectives.* Much of the CSCW literature reports on the demise of groupware system use when management curtails open discourse and dialogue. CSCW researchers advocate that organizations benefit from this technology when the company accepts the ideas of collaboration and group sharing. This means not only tolerating but also promoting electronic interactions in groupware that induce people to talk more frankly and equally. Management should not adopt a critical and punitive attitude toward open dialogue nor attempt to curtail discussions made by more innovative employees. Therefore, in terms of portal design, organizations should steer away from enforcing adherence to "deemed" interface standards or regulating portal content. To CSCW researchers, this mentality stifles collaboration and, ultimately, buy-in to the system. The argument is that portal users will be reluctant to post Web pages if the company requires Web pages to adhere to a standard look and feel, if their con-

tent has to be altered to match a corporate viewpoint, or if users are not free to engage in open dialogue in chat rooms and discussion sessions.

4. *Understand Current Work Practice.* Any new form of groupware will change the way work gets done. For instance, the introduction of a corporate portal could significantly change patterns of information sharing through the increased exchange of formal and informal information across the enterprise; in the past, such communication was often restricted by physical proximity and social acquaintance. To handle such change, the CSCW literature emphasizes the need for developers, researchers, and practitioners of groupware to anticipate how new technology will be received in the workplace prior to implementation. This can be done by understanding current work practice and social interaction and using these insights to build features and functions in portal design that minimize disruption in social processes, such as violation of social taboos, threats against existing political structures, or demotivation of crucial users.

5. *Get Users Involved in Design.* To minimize possible user rejection, CSCW researchers laud the active inclusion and participation of users in the design of groupware systems. Participatory design (PD), an offshoot of CSCW, advocates the heightened role of users in design, turning the traditional designer-user relationship on its head. Here, users are experts in design and designers are technical consultants. Key conditions for successful PD projects are that the project makes a difference to participants, implementation of the results seems likely, and it is fun to participate. Two often-cited benefits of engaging users in design are the development of systems to better match user needs and heightened user trust and acceptance of the system. Corporate portals, as firmwide groupware systems, can benefit from such an approach.

HUMAN CAPITAL, THE INTERNET, AND E-LEARNING

The Internet and CPs already play an important role in the management of human capital. They affect how people get hired, how their careers evolve (new digital connections and projects in other locations are certainly changing many employees' career tracks), how they learn, and even, to a certain extent, how employees get paid. The emerging incentive schemes, based on employees' digital behavior and contributions, are discussed in Chapter 5 and a few of the case studies.

Hiring is probably one of the areas most affected by Web-based solutions. The rapid development of recruiting sites is certainly creating a more efficient job market. Companies can now tap into a much wider skills pool, and likewise, individuals are now able to more easily find job opportunities, especially those outside their place of residence. The Internet is also being used to prescreen candidates through online tests, thereby reducing hiring costs, improving matching of skills and company needs, and reducing the unproductive time of candidates and recruiters. Although we know of no research that studied the effects of this greater allocation efficiency, we suspect it has likely increased the productivity of the workforce. Indeed, online recruiting is clearly one of the success categories of the new generation of online businesses. In 2000, only three "dot coms" sponsored or were able to afford TV ads during the fabled, extremely expensive Super Bowl game in the United States. Two of the three were online recruiting companies: Monster.com and Hotjobs.com (acquired recently by Yahoo!). In 2001, Hotjobs.com was advertised again during the Super Bowl.

In the case of large corporations, online recruiting also means improved mobility for knowledge workers. Jobs may be posted online for internal or external audiences to peruse, and the creation of databases of online resumes more easily matches organizations' needs with employees' skills and experience. It should come as no surprise then that leading corporations such as Cisco already consider the Internet to be their leading recruiting vehicle. Even as early as 1999, two-thirds of Cisco's hires were recruited via Internet, reducing the recruiting cycle (from initial contact to the close of the deal) by 60%—from 113 days in 1996 to 45 days in 1999.[38] Other Global 500 companies are quickly following Cisco's steps. According to iLogos Research, in 1998, only 29% of these companies had an active "corporate web site focused on recruiting"; in 2001, this practice had been adopted by 88% of Global 500 companies.[39]

Human capital theory suggests that training, whether formal or on the job, enhances worker productivity and leads to higher wages and better performance of the firm. (According to a 1997 research by the American Association for Training and Development, based on a sample of publicly traded companies, training expenditures are related to company performance. The companies in the sample that had higher training expenditures per employee also showed higher average net sales and profit per employee.[40]) This theory seems to be widely accepted by most companies, at least in the United States. The budget for corporate training has been increasing constantly in recent years. It grew 24% from 1993 to 1998 to reach the formidable amount of $62.5 billion in 1998.[40] According to IDC, a leading IT research and consulting company, e-learning is growing at an even faster rate. It is forecast to grow from $2.2 billion in 2000 to about $12 billion in 2004,[41] a more than fivefold increase. Training prepares new workers and enhances the skills of existing workers. Leading companies, however, are shifting to a broader interpretation of human capital: from a paradigm of training to one of human performance. Consequently, the fusion between the goals of KM and e-learning is growing. Several emerging questions substitute for the paternalistic model of the past:

- How do we unlock the process of self-learning?
- How do we turn learning into a collective process?
- Is it possible to increase individuals' creative and self-learning capacities through training?
- What types of training are effective? Should companies "train" or "facilitate learning"?
- How do we integrate e-learning into a company's processes?
- How do we deliver e-learning to employees as they need it to perform?
- How do we customize e-learning modules to fit the profile of each individual?
- How do we push e-learning modules at the time of need?

It seems apparent to us that the leading companies are shifting from a training paradigm to a learning paradigm. Companies are recognizing that they can no longer centrally determine what skills and competencies each area or employee must develop or must apply at different times to serve clients' needs. In the emerging paradigm, it is the responsibility of companies to provide the necessary resources for learning (content, time, and money) and to create an environment that stimulates and promotes values related to personal growth and on-the-job training. It is up to individuals (ideally with the help of their mentors) to identify their own learning needs and determine when, how, and where to satisfy those needs.

The sharing of knowledge—be it internal or external, formal or informal—appears to be a principal organizational challenge facing companies in the new paradigm. Forward-looking organizations are, therefore, deploying CPs with a strong view toward enabling self-learning. The focus is now on accelerating learning and managing talent. The growth of online courses is clear evidence of the need for individuals to assume greater responsibility for their own learning. It is also another indicator that new knowledge must be acquired ever more quickly and continuously, and in ways that are adapted to the fast-changing challenges facing individual employees, project teams, and organizations. In this respect, it is clear that e-learning should not be seen exclusively as a training strategy. As Tom Kelly, head of the Internet Learning Solutions Group from Cisco, puts it: "E-learning is about information, communications, education, *and* training."[42, p. 501]

The growth in the deployment of e-learning is also being driven by the ability of e-learning to[41]

- Reduce overall training costs.
- Reduce time away from the job.
- Be highly scalable and reach an unlimited number of employees regardless of physical location.
- Accelerate the delivery of training when large number of individuals need to be trained.
- Be linked to a supporting learning community.
- Be easily personalized to meet user needs.
- Allow employees to learn at their own pace and in response to their own business needs.
- Occur anytime.

With so many benefits, it is not surprising that many large organizations are fully embracing e-learning:

- General Motors recently announced a partnership with Unext, one of the pioneer organizations in online education. GM plans to offer upper-level education courses to all of its 88,000 white-collar workers in the United States.[44]

- The Royal Bank of Canada recently launched an online professional tool and made it available to all of its 42,000 employees. The program offers more than 2700 online activities. Courses can be customized and information about new products and processes is pushed simultaneously to all employees, thereby integrating individual career training with ongoing job demands. Most important, RBC is providing its employees with time during regular working hours for professional development.[45]

- Bain & Company developed and made available to all consultants, regardless of seniority level, over 170 e-learning modules. The content for these modules was provided entirely by Bain's own senior consultants by means of easy-to-use e-learning authoring tools that include multimedia, simulation, and other advanced technical resources. It started as a separate initiative from KM. Now it is completely integrated.

- Yahoo! Broadcast Services works with companies such as PriceWaterhouseCoopers, Texas Instruments, and Cisco to provide the infrastructure and expertise to deliver live and on-demand streaming training sessions and seminars on various topics for employees, partners, and customers scattered around the globe.

- At Intel's "Corporate University" almost all training is preceded, intermingled, or followed up by an interactive, online learning experience that includes self-tutoring and very active online learning communities. Cal Stevens, head of Intel's Corporate University, is a strong believer that "traditional training functions that adopt a content-focused, knowledge-dispensing, didactic approach to corporate education often fail." In his opinion, training has to seamlessly blend with the business (and customer needs) and each individual's own needs. It is also strongly linked to KM initiatives. In his words, "Learning Is Intellectual Capital Development." Therefore, the key strategic decision is where an organization needs to develop its intellectual capital.[46]

- Cisco is not only a big promoter, but also an intensive user of e-learning coupled with portal/KM strategies. The company is using e-learning to raise the competence level of its employees, distributors, resellers, and clients. Its learning portal can be personalized to specific needs of individuals in the extended enterprise and includes learning objects and modules, such as online learning, live class schedules, white papers, Powerpoint presentations, recommended books and videos, online mentors available 24 hours a day, collaboration tools, video-on-demand, simulations, etc.[42]

Undoubtedly, the Internet is changing the goals and methods companies use to help employees learn. Large organizations, such as Intel, AT&T, Dell, Accenture, GM, IBM, Lucent, and Merrill Lynch, are reducing their investment in centralized training centers. They reserve those centers and "corporate universities" for more specialized training and training that requires high levels of interaction among employees. For example, team- and culture-building training continues to be done at centralized corporate centers. On the other hand, courses that are more introductory or focused on "plain" information sharing are moved to the Web environment. Training centers are also increasingly using resources available on the Web, through a CP, to supplement their programs. By integrating an organization's CP in training sessions, employees become familiar and trained with the same KM tools they have access to at their offices (the Bank of Montreal and Bain & Company cases presented in Part II offer further details of these types of training strategies).

When designing a corporate learning strategy and the training components of a CP, it is very important not to lose sight of the social aspect of learning. People learn primarily from, through, and with others. Hence, technology can and should be used, whenever possible, to (1) provide access to experts and company experience and history, (2) allow group training, and (3) most important, facilitate personal contacts with other employees or outsiders experiencing similar learning challenges. A firm sign of the importance of the social aspects of learning is the trend toward including many KM-related technologies, such as synchronous and asynchronous collaborative tools, in the latest e-learning platforms provided by IBM's MindSpan, Saba, and Click2learn.[47]

As a concluding note to this section, we stress our strong belief that, in the Networked and Knowledge Eras, firms will no longer "hire" people, they will form partnerships with them—sometimes (and increasingly) only for a few days or for the duration of a project. We see an increasing number of "free agents" in the marketplace. In this new environment, a core role of organizations will be to provide an environment where employees ("partners") can learn continuously, participate in interesting projects, and expand their own intellectual assets. Employees, on the other hand, will be increasingly expected to contribute not only to short-term tasks, projects, and results but also to the growth of the organization's intellectual capital. As a reference point, it is interesting to see how McKinsey & Company, a leading knowledge organization, describes the kind of behavior that leads to a successful career with the firm:[48]

> How People Succeed: McKinsey develops leaders through a single, rigorous evaluation process used worldwide. We don't evaluate leadership based on revenue generation, billable hours, or new client development. Instead, we look at what impact consultants have on their clients, how they develop other people, and how they contribute to the firm's knowledge. Our best people become partners, leading consulting teams, participating in every phase of engagements, coaching and mentoring colleagues, and contributing to knowledge.

CPs so far are not "the solution" for this new emerging "social contract" between employers and employees. They do provide, however, important tools to help employees fulfill learning and networking goals and, most important, to participate in interesting projects (regardless of their location) and get recognition for their contributions. This is likely to produce more skilled, motivated, and committed employees. Finally, through the CP, employers should also increase the value of their intellectual capital through the partial codification of their employee's tacit knowledge and overall leverage of employees' own intellectual capital.

We introduced, in this chapter, some of the main KM topics and concepts that we believe are important for the deployment of CPs. Many of the discussions are based on a mix of practical experience, field research, and to a large extent, a review of the literature. In this process, we anticipate some of the lessons and perspectives that we acquired during our field research. In Chapters 5, 6, and 7, we delve much deeper into the field research and present many more practical details and ideas that leading KM global leaders have shared with us. Before that, however, we introduce the readers to the "CP basics" in Chapter 4. In this coming chapter, we discuss the core services and technologies being developed or offered by the most important software vendors and, frequently, found in CP deployments.

A Comprehensive Knowledge Management Agenda

KM should be closely linked with an organization's corporate and business strategy. Only knowledge that supports unique value propositions and core competencies is really worth pursuing and protecting. Unfortunately, various surveys[49] completed in the late 1990s with hundreds of companies from the United States and Europe demonstrate that this link is rarely established in most KM efforts (we, however, were able to identify a good number of excellent cases where this is well established; in many of the cases later detailed in this book, the CP was implemented only after clear business goals and priorities had been established). This brings us to suggest that KM necessarily involves two intertwined levels of action: strategic and tactical. In organizations where KM is well structured the actions in these two levels should be coherent and aimed at bringing coordination to the tasks of identifying, creating, organizing, sharing, disseminating, and using the sources of knowledge available for the organization.

Strategic Level
This is a more analytical level of action and should have a top-management perspective. It should be focused on determining what types of knowledge provide a competitive edge and how the organization will acquire, develop, or maintain such knowledge advantages. Typical questions related to the strategic level include the following:

- How should a company's existing knowledge and intangible assets be mapped? Which of its assets are truly relevant for gaining or maintaining its competitive advantage? Which KM initiatives should hold high priority?
- Will the company pursue an aggressive and innovative knowledge strategy or will it adopt a more tactical and conservative ("follower") strategy?
- What are the most important areas or processes where knowledge is created and used in the organization?
  - In these critical areas or processes, does strategic knowledge reside predominantly in peoples' heads or is it documented? Are the most relevant documents composed of unstructured or structured data?
  - Where can the key expertise and skills be found that are related to the company's core competencies?
- What are the organization's sources of external knowledge? How can they be acquired? At what speed?
  - How can people with the necessary competencies, skills, and attitudes be attracted, selected, and retained?

- Which alliances should hold highest priority? How can the company be made more open to external knowledge? How can the flow of knowledge, insights, and ideas coming from clients, partners, suppliers, and the community at large be captured and amplified?
- How can an organization protect its most unique intellectual capital? Where does it reside? With a few individuals? In the collective working practices? Is it mostly documented?
  - How should the organization avoid the loss of strategic knowledge, when a few individuals or groups leave?
  - How should the organization prevent competitors and other external parties from copying or having access to proprietary knowledge (e.g., through the use of trade secrets, patents, or copyrights)?
  - Where should efforts be made to partially codify existing tacit knowledge?
- How can knowledge be used to increase profit?
- Toward what kind of new business opportunities can the existing knowledge be applied?
- How can customers tap into the organization's knowledge (and appreciate its value)?
- What are the best measures of intellectual capital?
  - How are they linked to the company strategy?
  - Which systems should be put in place to measure them?
  - How often should they be measured?

Tactical Level

Once the key decisions and strategies are formulated, companies need to implement the organizational processes, human resource policies, and IT infrastructures that support the chosen strategic directions. Typical questions and issues related to the tactical level include the following on organizational processes and human resource policies:

- How can an organization increase the speed and quality of knowledge generated internally?
  - How can a balance between team and individual work and between multidisciplinary work and individual specialization be achieved and maintained?
  - How can the process of making employees' tacit knowledge explicit be facilitated and encouraged?

- How can a company's collective knowledge be made accessible to employees when they need it?
- Which knowledge-transfer mechanisms should be put in place to get new employees "up to speed" very quickly?

■ How can an organization improve knowledge sharing and knowledge reuse?

- How do organizations change the common practice of controlling information as a key strategy for building power?
- What level of employee participation in decision making is required? Which employees participate in what decisions?
- What kind of formal and periodical knowledge-transfer mechanisms should be implemented (e.g., meetings, project "postmortems," status reports, offsite meetings)?
- How can the organization create socialization opportunities for employees to informally share relevant information and experiences?
- Which natural, informal communities that already create and share relevant knowledge should be more formally recognized and supported?

■ How should knowledge sharing be encouraged and rewarded?

- How can knowledge hoarding be discouraged?
- How can KM be made relevant for employees' own self-interest?
- How can new employees learn from old employees and vice versa?

■ What kind of organizational structure provides the best balance among knowledge creation, knowledge application, and knowledge dissemination?

- How should job descriptions be changed to support the KM effort?
- Should dedicated KM-related positions be created?
- How can the organization foster the development of mentor-apprentice relationships?

■ How can the organization promote a set of values and attitudes that lead to more innovation, risk taking, and knowledge creation?

- What systems, policies, and processes should be implemented to support behavior related to stimulating creativity and learning?
- What kinds of employees should be hired and promoted?
- What kind of training should they be provided? What kinds of creativity-enhancing techniques should be fostered?
- Which management practices point to more employee empowerment through knowledge?

- How can the organization make sure that ideas are not ignored but turned into valuable new products and services?
- What should an organization do to uncover existing knowledge (tacit and explicit) and put it to use?
- How can an organization's physical layout be modified to promote more serendipity, collaboration, and knowledge sharing?
- Who are the key employees that should be retained in the organization? How can this be achieved?
- How can the organization capture part of the knowledge of its experts (through codification or expert interviewing techniques)?
- How do inputs (information and knowledge flow coming from outside the organization) play an important part in knowledge creation and reuse in areas or processes that are strategic?

Some information technology issues include these:

- How can IT be used to help automate the monitoring of relevant external information and improve the inflow of knowledge from the outside?
- How can IT be used to transform data into valuable information (e.g., through data mining)?
- How can IT be used to support timely decision making (from top-management reports to decision support systems and work flow)?
- How can IT be used to reduce time devoted to menial activities?
- How can the investments in information and communication technology be used to improve decision making and not simply accelerate the flow of information?
- How can IT increase access to information and at the same time reduce "information overload"?
- How can IT be used to increase the conversion of tacit knowledge into explicit knowledge?
- How can IT be used to help locate experts and people with specific knowledge?
- How can IT be used to improve the reuse of (tacit or explicit) knowledge where it can have the most impact?
- How can IT be employed to support collaborative work?
- How can IT be used to extend the boundaries of the firm?
- How can IT help to better serve customers?
- How can IT support collaborative and rich information exchanges with customers, partners, and suppliers?
- How can IT be used to leverage valuable content—to repackage, add value, and offer to different audiences?

REFERENCES

1. Grant, R. Shifts in the world economy: The drivers of knowledge management. In: Despres, C., Chauvel, D., eds. *Knowledge Horizons*. Boston: Butterworth-Heinemann, 2000:39.
2. Skyrme, D.J. *Capitalizing on Knowledge: From e-Business to k-Business*. Boston: Butterworth-Heinemann, 2001:17.
3. Kluge, J., Stein, W., Licht, T. *Knowledge Unplugged*. New York: Palgrave, 2001.
4. Wensley, A., Verwijk-O'Sullivan, A. Tools for knowledge management. In: Despres, C., Chauvel, D., eds. *Knowledge Horizons*. Boston: Butterworth-Heinemann, 2000:114.
5. Tapscott, D. *Digital Economy: Promise and Peril in the Age of Networked Intelligence*. New York: McGraw-Hill, 1996.
6. Hope, J., Hope, T. *Competing in the Third Wave: The Ten Key Management Issues of the Information Age*. Boston: Harvard Business School Press, 1997.
7. Hamel, G., Prahalad, C.K. *Competing for the Future*. Boston: Harvard Business School Press, 1994.
8. Brown, J.S., Duguid, P. *The Social Life of Information*. Boston: Harvard Business School Press, 2000.
9. Gordon, R.J. Does the "New Economy" measure up to the great inventions of the past? National Bureau of Economic Research, working paper 7833, 2000.
10. Polanyi, M. The tacit dimension. In: Prusak, L., ed. *Knowledge in Organizations*. Boston: Butterworth-Heinemann, 1997.
11. Leonard-Barton, D. *Wellsprings of Knowledge: Building and Sustaining the Sources of Innovation*. Boston: Harvard Business School Press, 1995.
12. Cusumano, M.A., Selby, R.W. *Microsoft Secrets*. New York: The Free Press, 1995:329.
13. Landes, D.S. *The Wealth and Poverty of Nations: Why Some Are Rich and Some Are Poor*. New York: W.W. Norton & Company, 1998:516.
14. Snowden, D. The social ecology of knowledge management. In: Despres, C., Chauvel, D., eds. *Knowledge Horizons*. Boston: Butterworth-Heinemann, 2000:308.
15. O'Reilly, C. Corporations, culture and commitment: motivation and social control in organizations. *California Management Review*. Summer 1999:9–25.
16. Withers, P. *CMA Management*. October 2001:24.

17. Jones, G., George, J. The experience and evolution of trust: Implications for cooperation and teamwork. *Academy of Management Review*. 1998;23;no. 3:531–546.
18. Clark, K., Serfon, M. The sequential prisoner's dilemma: Evidence on reciprocation. *Economic Journal*. January 2001.
19. Fukuyama, F. *Trust: The Social Virtues and the Creation of Prosperity*. New York: Penguin Books, 1995.
20. Glaeser, E., Laibson, D., Scheinkman, J., Soutter, C. Measuring trust. *Quarterly Journal of Economics*. August 2000.
21. Heath, J. *The Efficient Society: Why Canada Is as Close to Utopia as It Gets*. Toronto: Viking/Penguin, 2001:67.
22. Das, T.K., Teng, B. Between trust and control: Developing confidence in partner cooperation in alliances. *Academy of Management Review*. 1998;23;no. 3:491–512.
23. Welch, J. A administração depois da Internet. *HSM Management*. September–October 2000;no. 22:6–12.
24. E-strategy brief: GE. *The Economist*. May 19, 2001:76.
25. Nonaka, I., Takeuchi, H. *The Knowledge-Creating Company: How Japanese Companies Create the Dynamics of Innovation*. New York: Oxford University Press, 1995:172.
26. Bidault, F., Nihitila, J. ESI and the role of trust in the information age, FP Mastering. *National Post*. June 26, 2001.
27. Powell, W.W. Learning from collaboration: Knowledge and networks in the biotechnology and pharmaceutical industries. *California Management Review*. Spring 1998;40;no. 3:228–240.
28. Pinchot, E., Pinchot, G. The end of bureaucracy and the rise of the intelligent organization. In: Myers, P.S., ed. *Knowledge Management and Organizational Design*. Boston: Butterworth-Heinemann, 1996.
29. Zarifian, P. *Travail et Communication: Essai sociologique sur le travail dans la grande entreprise industrielle*. Paris: PUF, 1996.
30. Amabile, T.M. How to kill creativity. *Harvard Business Review*. September–October 1998:77–87.
31. Argyris, C. Double loop learning in organizations. *Harvard Business Review*. September–October 1977:115–125.
32. Schein, E.H. On dialogue, culture, and organizational learning. *Organizational Dynamics*. Autumn 1993:40–51.
33✓ Wenger, E.C., Snyder, W.M. Communities of practice: The organizational frontier. *Harvard Business Review*. January–February 2000:139-145.
34. Brown, J.S., Duguid, P. Organizational learning and communities-

of-practice: Toward a unified view of working, learning and innovation. *Organization Science.* 1991;2:40–57.
35. GartnerGroup. Communities: Broad-reaching business value.
GartnerGroup Publication no. COM-13-9032, July 3, 2001.
36. Castells, M. *The Internet Galaxy: Reflections on the Internet,
Business and Society.* New York: Oxford University Press, 2001.
37. Brown, S., Tilton, A., Woodside, D. The case for on-line communities. *The McKinsey Quarterly.* 2002;no. 1, Web exclusive,
http://www.mckinseyquarterly.com.
38. Axelrod, B., Handfield, H., Welsh, T. *War for Talent.* Cambridge, MA: Harvard Business School Press, 2001:85.
39. iLogos Research. *CMA Management.* October 2001:58.
40. Rosenberg, M. *E-Learning: Strategies for Delivering Knowledge in the Digital Age.* New York: McGraw-Hill, 2001:6.
41. Lamont, J. KM and e-learning: A growing partnership. *KMWorld.*
July–August 2001:10.
42. Galagan, P. Mission e-possible: The Cisco e-learning story. In:
Rossett, A. (ed). *The ASTD E-Learning Handbook.* New York:
McGraw-Hill, 2002.
43. Neilson, G.L., Pasternack, B., Viscio, A. Up the (e) organization! A seven-dimension model for the centerless enterprise.
Strategy and Business [Booz-Allen & Hamilton]. First quarter
2000;18:52–61.
44. GM offers on-line business courses. *Globe and Mail.* April 11,
2001.
45. Bank site offers e-training 24/7. *Globe and Mail.* January 17,
2001:B16.
46. Stevens, C. From bland to blend: Intellectual capital development
and blended learning. Presentation at the Fifth World Congress
on Intellectual Capital, Hamilton, Ontario, Canada, January 16–
18, 2002.
47. Barron, T. A smarter Frankenstein: The merging of e-learning
and knowledge management. *Learning Circuits—ASTD,* www.
learningcircuits.org/aug2000/barron.html
48. McKinsey website: http://www.mckinsey.com/firm/people/, September 27, 2001.
49. Zack, M.H. Developing a knowledge strategy. *California Management Review.* Spring 1999:41;no. 3:125–146.

4

KEY SERVICES OF A CORPORATE PORTAL PLATFORM

The promise offered by corporate portals to capture and share knowledge is very compelling, especially for the knowledge-based enterprise. CPs can become a means by which companies overcome some of the key challenges they face managing information in a pre-Web and preportal corporate environment. These challenges include

- Incompatible proprietary file formats or platforms.
- Information accessed through many different methods, including client software, Web browsers, specific applications, individual hard disks.

- Information published in a very disorganized way.
- Individuals unable to easily publish information for enterprise-wide viewing.
- Many different methods for searching and accessing information.
- Nontechnical users highly dependent on the IT department to generate reports or obtain information.
- Inability to distribute information widely and beyond the walls of the organization.
- Expensive, nonintuitive, or even nonexistent viewing tools.
- Lack of effective online collaboration tools.
- Expensive proprietary architectures that are hard to integrate with different information types or sources.
- Overlapping systems with complex and different user interfaces (many without a browser-based interface).
- Outdated desktop-centered view of IT applications.

Similar to mass-market portals, CPs provide a format that requires limited technological expertise and comparatively little training from end-users. The Web is a very intuitive platform. This type of interaction is quite different from the traditional relationship between end-users and pre-Web sophisticated IT tools. In the pre-Web environment, information gathering and interpretation required an "army of analysts and programmers." Most people, for example, do not know how to query a database residing in a mainframe. However, with the Web tools, searching for information can be almost as easy as A, B, C. By facilitating the development and management of the sources of intellectual and network capital, CPs may well prove to be the next "killer" Internet application. CPs allow the nontechnical person to easily access (without the direct help of IT experts) the "wells of information and knowledge" existing inside and outside an organization.

There is no standard specification about which services a CP platform should include (we make references to *services* because this is what matters for end-users and administrators). At the end of 2001, numerous software vendors provide portal solutions (from very large software companies to startups). Indeed, because of the modular nature of standard Internet development, many companies provide CP solutions by integrating the products from a number of software vendors. Consequently, the description of a CP platform we provide in this chapter is not based on any standard vendor solution, but rather our understanding of the overall software market direction and typical

CP services provided by leading vendors. We are also aware that technology is changing fast in this area and many new solutions will emerge in the next few years. The choice of an integrated portal solution or building your own from "best-of-breed" components depends on a number of factors (e.g., existing legacy systems, speed requirements, budget, IT skills). This is not something addressed in this book.

A number of key software services are typically integrated in a CP architecture (see Figure 4-1):

■ The presentation and personalization service defines how the users see and customize the information delivered or accessed via the portal. The most intuitive solutions being offered allow users to access information in more relevant, context-centric environments. This is key for knowledge management efforts.

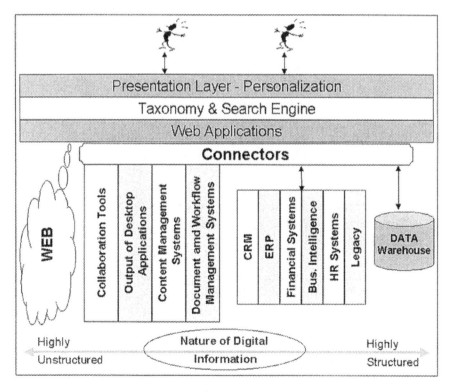

Figure 4-1
Key Services and Components of CP Architecture

- The search service determines how easy it is for users to find relevant information based on a set of search criteria. This core functionality has improved significantly over the last few years, with a number of KM-focused developments (a number of examples are provided later in this chapter). At the same time that it evolved to integrate various different information sources, it also became much more sophisticated, intuitive, and adaptable to different organization needs.

- While many Web applications were developed to leverage the Web (often based on B-to-C examples), many Internet front-ends were developed for legacy systems that maintain their legacy architecture. Sophisticated portal platform solutions provide a number of resources that make it easy to seamlessly integrate both sorts of applications. In the case of more traditional systems, the integration, at the presentation layer, is facilitated by standard application program interfaces (APIs) developed by the portal vendors or the user community. APIs that allow access to structured (data warehouses, ERP, CRM, etc.) and unstructured information (Web, desktop applications, content management systems, etc.) are called *connectors, Web parts, gadgets*, and the like.

In summary, CPs provide cost-effective solutions to increase the efficiency of many information management and organizational processes. We focus, however, on how CPs affect the key processes involved in KM. With this in mind, we highlight the recent developments that help employees to

- Find relevant information and knowledge sources.
- Codify and publish their knowledge.
- Collaborate online.

In addition to examining these three core functionalities, we also examine the integration of stand-alone Internet applications related to KM, based on an intellectual capital framework, and present a table comparing different levels of portal sophistication.

FINDING RELEVANT INFORMATION AND KNOWLEDGE SOURCES

A well-implemented CP simplifies access to information and knowledge and highlights important internal and external knowledge sources that are relevant for specific audiences. It reduces the difficulty of searching complex networks and disparate online data sources, improving return on investment by enabling smarter decision making and providing such benefits as increased productivity, better customer service, and reduced personnel costs. CPs may help companies save employees' time and provide them with focused, accurate, and relevant information and sources of knowledge. This is very relevant in the knowledge economy, where time and attention are among the scarcest and most precious resources to manage.

Access to Structured Data through Corporate Portals

CPs are the latest solution for an ongoing trend in business toward making information more easily accessible to management, employees, external partners, and customers. Prior to the Internet, much of the focus was on the deployment of enterprise information systems (EIS). These efforts were very expensive and aimed at helping a few managers find answers and information about the performance of firms, based primarily on historical structured data. However, due to the high cost and complex and specific nature (historical content) of most of these systems, very few employees were allowed or qualified to use them—typically only senior management had access—reducing their collaboration value. Few employees with access had the time or necessary training to properly learn how to use these systems (often requiring knowledge of SQL programming language). More important, usage was further impeded because the interface and navigation tools of these early systems were not nearly as intuitive as the Web-based tools currently available. The technical and economical barriers remained important obstacles. Finally, the hierarchical and bureaucratic view prevalent in many organizations did not help increase accessibility to organization information and knowledge.

Unlike EISs, CPs allow a diverse spectrum of employees and interested parties (customers, suppliers, bankers, vendors, etc.) access to predefined and prescheduled information as well as to customize and develop ad hoc reports, all without the help of the Information Technology Department. Another key advantage is that the CP, through XML, allows data and information to integrate supply chains without complex programming. The most advanced CPs make it easy to leverage business intelligence (BI; sophisticated statistical analysis software with user-friendly front-ends) and data-warehousing solutions to allow employees to customize their access to company information.

These customized reports can be based on preparameterized value ranges and formats or newly designed in toto, based on employees' personalized formats or views and sophisticated queries and data mining. The recent and rapid migration of traditional BI/ERP software to the Web environment demonstrates the importance placed on helping a large number of employees and third parties use and interpret the results from these applications. It is high time that companies start to see the results from the huge volume of money already invested in these applications. The BI and data-warehousing market, for instance, is growing at 50% per year and sales are expected to reach $113 billion by 2002.[1]

This trend is in line with one of the core management practices supported by the KM literature: ease of access to information and analysis of business results from multiple perspectives. BI and ERP systems with a CP front-end no longer require end-users to know a query language to define how they want to analyze the data. These types of systems allow for Web-based analysis and facilitate employees' understanding of the correlation between the many variables that affect a business. The Internet also allows for the collection of a tremendous volume of data and provides a cheap way to divulge results and receive comments from different areas within an organization. The hyperlinking property of the Net can be extremely useful by allowing users to drill down to easily access the sources of the information.

It must be stressed that, in most cases, CP platforms provide integration of these systems discussed only at the interface or publishing level, through APIs. Often, when applications are integrated at the portal, only small pieces are initially integrated (e.g., reports from the ERP system). CP platforms do not guarantee the integrity of data across many applications (they still search the data from as many data sources and systems as are available in the organization). This is an important issue. Enterprise application integration (EAI) continues to be an important underlying IT concern, beyond the choice of a CP platform.

Access to Unstructured Data through Corporate Portals

In addition to allowing access to Web-based reports from structured data (e.g., data warehouses, BI software packages) and transactional information (e.g., ERP, self-service HR applications), CPs provide employees, partners, and clients, a Web-based interface to access all types of unstructured information. Relevant types of information include e-mail, Web pages, the output of MS office applications, and information contained in collaborative applications (e.g., scheduling, online forums). It is also a logical directory of the corporate intranets.

Indeed, a significant portion of the most relevant and strategic information in organizations, however, is unstructured information that, before the Web-based applications, was hard to publish widely and even harder to find. This is changing in a CP environment. To understand how employees can more easily and efficiently find this kind of information, it is necessary to examine collaboration technology developments in categorization and taxonomy, search engines, and personalization engines.

Categorization and Taxonomy

To simplify searches and navigation and assign responsibility for collecting, assessing, organizing, purging, archiving, and providing user assistance, organizations need to develop information structures and categories that make sense to that firm's businesses and the communities using the system. Regardless of the power of the search engine deployed and the number of functionalities implemented, an organization must deal with the issue of categorizing and organizing information. Categorization adds fundamental indexing information to documents to make it easier to find them later on. Taxonomies are high-level rules for organizing and classifying information. Although very relevant for the Web environment, the discipline of taxonomy is not new. It has always been at the core of library science. However, it has become even more important as the volume of information to be organized grows exponentially and new software tools for automatic categorization emerge and improve rapidly.

Taxonomies are also necessary to tag (information about the information) the documents created. The tagging is an important step to ensure that search engines find required documents and for the distribution of documents based on personalization rules. Metadata, the information about information and a core feature of HTML and XML files, is at the center of the Internet revolution. It provides the necessary context for information, making documents easily located by search engines regardless of any previous information as to their physical location. Metadata also plays an important role by allowing different documents to be logically grouped together. The capture of metadata should ideally occur right after content creation. Increasingly, this occurs through a combination of automatic (typically author, name, date, etc.) and manual processes (keywords, category, etc.). The higher value metadata is usually that provided by the authors themselves and includes detailed description of the document (e.g., summary, context of creation, purpose, contributing authors, etc.).

The taxonomy should make it intuitive for employees to browse for specific information and "bump" into related but not anticipated topics or categories. This is better explained if we imagine a user scanning the titles on the shelf of a well-organized library, but in multiple dimensions and much faster. Employees should find common names, categorizations, and signals that are familiar to them. In this respect, the online experience should not be much different from the offline experience (except that the offline does not allow for multiple dimensions or views). Good taxonomies also make it much easier to search for documents by allowing searches to be conducted based on various criteria (e.g., author, date, file format, knowledge domain, etc.). There is, however, no scientific way to find out whether the chosen taxonomy really works. There are a few rules of thumb (such as categories with too many or too few documents will probably not work), but ultimately, the users need to tell us whether it makes sense or not (can they find the required information with only a few clicks?).

Taxonomies and categorizations are usually hierarchical. However, new forms that are more visual, for instance, spatial or hyperbolic trees, are becoming more common, as provided by Antartic.ca or The-Brain. Information architects, with the close help of "content area owners," are usually responsible for defining the taxonomy employed in each organization. In some cases, they use automatic classification tools, such as those provided by Semio's SemioMap or Verity, to simplify or speed up processing. (Classification tools are algorithms that provide clusters of documents based on statistical or semantic proximity rules.) Some CPs also import the category hierarchies from existing applications, such as ERP or CRM. This can make the transition to a Web environment easier for users already familiar with the existing applications. Ultimately, the true test of any taxonomy is the efficiency it provides the group of users it was designed for: Are the users able to find meaningful and relevant information in a time-efficient manner?

Some of the challenges to creating and maintaining a working taxonomy come about because

- The most important categories are not always obvious and ambiguity is part of the game.
- Automated categorization based on frequency of words may not provide good results. Some new software solutions allow auto-

matic recategorization of schemas based on user feedback. Preferably, building a taxonomy should start with some inputs developed jointly by content "owners" or domain experts and information architects. In many cases, this is an important collaboration because many experts are not too concerned about how knowledge is organized and classified in CPs. The experts already have their "own" particular ways of finding what they need; the novices need help understanding a specific domain (how it is organized and related to other domains).

- Tagging can be a labor-intensive process—it requires cooperation among content creators (new tools aim to minimize most of the manual input by automatically generating standard tag information, such as author and time of creation).
- There is no universal right or wrong: Different people develop different taxonomies. Consequently, it helps to create multiple ways (categories) to find the same information.
- Who maintains the integrity of the taxonomy as it grows over time?

Although in many cases external system integrators or Web development firms are responsible for developing the initial taxonomy, it is clear that the ongoing maintenance of information architecture requires many new assigned responsibilities and the use of sophisticated tools to automate most of the classification effort.

Search Engines

Almost everyone who uses the Internet is somewhat familiar with search engines. Indeed, statistics show that hundreds of millions of people use search engines daily. Consumer search engine leaders, such as Google and Altavista, reported over 100 million searches per day by mid-2001. This does not mean that people are actually finding exactly what they need, as fast as they should. In addition, in a corporate setting, employees do not have time to just "surf" the Web and the search results. They also need to search, not only Web pages, but across a number of disparate sources of information, including structured databases and very unstructured information sources (e.g., desktop applications such as e-mail, word documents, intranets).

If one objective of KM and CPs is to make it easier for people with a need to know to find relevant information and knowledge sources, then search engines are an important enabling tool. The goal of a search engine is to provide relevant results (not the highest number of results) for a query, in the least amount of time. However, in many cases, users need assistance defining exactly what they want. Documents also frequently refer to similar subjects using different terms in varied levels of depth. This may generate results that are not very precise (too many, very few results, or irrelevant ranking). Finally, it is important to note that different people search in different ways, according to many factors, such as

- Characteristics and capabilities of specific search engines.
- Preference for navigation or search.
- Level of experience with search engines.
- Previous knowledge of the domain, related domains, or specific subject.
- Personality: intuitive or analytic.

To respond to these individual circumstances and the exponential growth in the amount of information and types of data and knowledge sources, there have been very interesting advances in search mechanisms over the last few years. Many search options, features, and levels of sophistication are now available. They include the following (from the most common to the more sophisticated or specific):

- Keyword and exact phrase searches are available in most search engines, which list results based on the occurrence of chosen words or phrases. These types of search engines have been used extensively in libraries and allow for users to target their search to specific areas of documents, such as the title, keywords, and author. Such search engines now often include URL and existing links as well.
- Boolean searches return results based on the use of logical operators such as AND, OR, and NOT.
- Bayesian inferencing searches present results based on the frequency with which the chosen words appear in each document.
- Concept searches return results in which the most relevant documents shown may not necessarily contain the chosen keywords. This is because the search mechanism looks for additional words that are related to the chosen keywords based on a thesaurus or statistical approach.
- In context searches, certain engines can be calibrated to understand the searchers' context and show search results accordingly. This is useful when words can have very different meanings, de-

pending on context (e.g., the word *SAP* can mean "the fluid of a plant" or refer to the ERP software company SAP).

- Natural language searches use a type of search engine exemplified by AskJeeves in the consumer market. This natural language-based software allows users to post queries using plain English (or any other language). More sophisticated solutions, however, are being developed, which include agents that mimic real, intelligent human conversations (as provided by MangoMoon). A typical example the question "Where can I find information about supermarket chains in Canada?"
- Knowledge-based searches use search engines closely related to the natural language search engines. Such engines can automatically build structured cases that let users tap into previous responses to similar questions. These engines learn every time a new interactive Q&A session occurs. If the search engine does not find the appropriate answer, it can be programmed to direct the user to talk to a person who will try to answer the question (this is being deployed particularly in call centers).
- Popularity-based searches automatically change the ranking of links that are displayed, based on various types of algorithms that aim to evaluate users' own perspectives of the document or site. It may, for instance, consider the number of times that previous users have checked the link or information source or how many other users link to that specific site (the popular site google.com uses this technology). It may also display documents based on users' direct and proactive evaluation of the document or site.
- Collaborative filtering searches are based on the idea that individuals that share similar interests will also find similar documents relevant. Amazon's suggestions of books ("People who bought X also bought Y") exemplify this type of search mechanism.
- Affinity searches are similar to collaborative filtering searches. However, they take the idea of linking people and documents even further. They discover many levels of commonality among different kinds of documents, based on the people who write, read, or update them. They can be particularly useful for very large organizations that want to link people with similar interests and competencies.
- Visual mapping searches allow users to see the results of their searches in a more graphic manner. Documents are aggregated and linked according to categorization algorithms that allow users to easily navigate through clusters of related information.

- Case-based-reasoning searches allow users to find cases that have similar (typical in service centers) patterns of problems or solutions. The idea behind them is "find me other cases like this one . . ."
- Peer-to-peer searches allow searches within a self-selected community without the need of any centralized document index. The emerging enterprise solutions are based on the consumer models originally developed by companies such as Napster and Gnutella.
- Personalized agents have strong dynamic learning capabilities based on each user's pattern of searches and choices of documents. Advanced agents combine concept and context search concepts (discussed previously) to build relevant users' profiles.

The process of selecting a specific search engine solution depends largely on the specific needs of the organization and complexity and size of information sources that need to be searched. Search engines can range tremendously in price. Standard searching and indexing solutions can be fairly inexpensive. On the other hand, complete and sophisticated search solutions for large enterprises can cost millions of dollars in software licenses, hardware, and consulting and development costs. It may also require a number of months to perform the required custom developments and calibrate the engine to meet the needs of the organization. Although the decision about the search engine is an important issue in CP deployment, it does not mean that it should be bundled with the CP platform. More often than not, we see companies choosing the "best-of-breed" approach.

Finally, not until employees start finding the most relevant information available at the top of the search results can one say that the implementation process is successful. Indeed, search engines depend on heuristic algorithms that need to evolve with the business needs of each firm, and their optimal use can be achieved only through ongoing maintenance (indexing, reindexing, purging, etc.). In addition to choosing from among this core set of search approaches, firms must address many other issues related to search engines and their integration into a CP solution. We highlight next some of the most interesting search functionalities related to KM and some of performance and back-end issues.

Notification:

- Users or administrators can schedule routine spiders and crawlers.

- The search engine can be programmed to crawl information sources regularly and generate results to specific groups.
- The engine allows exception-based notification (e.g., sales are down by 20%).
- Users are notified whenever a new document is added to the knowledge base or created by another person in the organization.
- The user can define where (e-mail, pager, phone, etc.) and how frequently (daily, weekly, instantaneously) he or she wants to be notified.

Search process and interface:

- The search engine lets users choose which sources to search (folders, Web, databases).
- It is possible to save search results and share these results (e.g., via e-mail) with other people in the organization.
- The search engine caches results for faster access.
- The search engine includes heuristic capabilities allowing users to drill down and narrow the results incrementally.
- Users can search simultaneously for categories and attributes of such categories.
- The search engine learns with each interaction with users. It asks the users whether the results were accurate and relevant and builds the response into the system.
- Search results can be personalized according to skill, role, or access level of users.
- The search engine provides "clues" to related topics.
- The search engine automatically corrects spelling mistakes.
- The search engine automatically searches for synonyms.
- The search engine groups search results based on predefined categories or even instantly created directories (e.g., as provided by the Northern Light engine).
- Users can see the results through various different views of the data.
- The search engine allows multilanguage searches; that is, users can specify that they want to see the results in only a specific language or group of languages (and to exclude specific languages from the results).
- The search engine of search engines (metasearch) sends query to multiple search engines and integrates the results.

Engine performance and back-end issues:

- It is possible to integrate the search engine with business intelligence applications.
- It allows the searching of XML tags and attributes.
- The indexer and search mechanisms allow users to define criteria or search models for indexing and searching.
- It is possible to search multimedia documents that have not been manually tagged before (e.g., as provided by Convera).
- It includes an automatic categorization engine.
- For speed and accuracy reasons, the engine allows simultaneous searches across distributed databases and entire documents at once.
- It may crawl the intranet or extranet and save the retrieved documents for faster display (e.g., Google).

Searching the E-Mail Repository

E-mail management, cataloging, organization, and distribution in a Web-based environment are of particular interest to organizations. E-mails and their attachments are becoming the main source of team-based communications (including, in many cases, exchanges with clients). Consequently, they are also a key repository of corporate memory. Given the nature of the content and the informal style of communication in this medium, capturing this flow for further usage is also an important move toward registering and partially reusing tacit knowledge. A number of software providers have paid attention to the amazing volumes of information that companies generate via e-mail and have developed interesting KM-focused solutions to mine this repository. Among the leading players we can cite are Tacit, eManage, eRoom, and Intraspect. These vendors provide solutions to effectively search this repository and automatically categorize e-mail around client engagements, internal projects, specific technologies, or any other business rule specific to the organization. The cases of Hill & Knowlton and Texaco described in Chapter 5 are good examples of large global corporations that learned the benefits of incorporating a solid e-mail search and management system focused on KM.

Personalization Engines

The CP, in its various facets and applications, has to make sense for each individual and be clearly linked to specific business processes and goals. It must not be only about information sharing, since information overload can have a very negative impact on employees' creativity and productivity. Most people, especially those working in fast-paced wired environments, are increasingly swamped with irrelevant information, reinforcing the time-starved reality of most organizations today. If CPs are to be successful and become a fundamental tool for employees' work, they need to allow employees, regardless of location and means of access, to personalize their access to the vast volumes of information and assets stored in the company's disparate databases and digital formats. Ideally, CPs should allow employees to seamlessly explore, in the same browser window, information generated internally and externally.

Personalization, or content-tailoring, of specific applications or individual customer experiences based on implicit and explicit data and information should minimize browsing efforts. The most advanced sites combine personalization defined by the users and the system or administrators. In the first approach, the content and display of the site depend on choices made by the user. The second approach can be simple or sophisticated. The simple, most common approach is to have the site personalized (or customized) by Web administrators, according to the employee's profile (role, location, or access rights). The more sophisticated system approach includes dynamic personalization or personalization "on the fly." This refers to personalization based on a number of sources of accumulated or real-time information, including the navigation path, device used for access, current location of user, and available bandwidth. The personalization engines use such information to make intelligent predictions about users' preferences and display content based on individuals' stated preferences, employees' roles and location, and behavior during visits to the portal.

Since personalization can have various levels of sophistication (and very different price tags), companies should decide early on which elements and pieces of content should be permanent to specific groups of users and which ones can be personalized. Ideally, employees should also have "roles" assigned them, regarding the use of the CP and a predefined personalization given when they join the company. Over time, employees can then truly personalize their CP experience, but this practice allows new employees to, at least, start with information and links relevant and directly related to their initial tasks and responsibilities. It also allows companies to better evaluate what levels and areas of personalization have the greatest impact on employee performance, collaboration, and use of existing information and knowledge sources.

Sophisticated, high-end portals usually have interesting personalization features. The most advanced ones include:

- They provide a high level of customization: layout, color, fonts, etc.
- Many elements of the page can be changed: A large number of colors are available and they allow high levels of customization to match the brand needs.
- They make it easy for users to drag and resize the windows.
- New page templates can be easily created through wizards requiring no programming skills.
- They support personalization based on a combination of attributes: roles, business rules, navigation patterns, collaborative filtering, and time- and event-based targeting.
- They personalize the way information is displayed according to the access device or bandwidth.
- They provide easy synchronization with major wireless and PDA standards and devices.
- Employees' personal profiles can be shared across all applications.

Personalization and Mass-Market Portals

Personalization, to the extent deployed by Excite, Yahoo!, or MSN, requires that pages be dynamically formed for each user in a faultless, time-efficient manner. It also requires a Universal Registration System (URS) that allows users to tap into the same personalized experience regardless of point of access (narrowband site, broadband site, different language sites, wireless, PDAs). This was not, until recently, by any means an easy accomplishment.

Once users are convinced that your company can provide an interesting value proposition, most will gladly register and personalize their experiences. Indeed, they may provide an increasing volume of personal information through such services as address books. Securing this kind of a relationship with consumers certainly provides competitive advantages: It increases users' switching costs in terms of time and personal commitment, inhibiting them from visiting and registering with competitors. An increasingly close relationship with users must be developed step by step. It is maintained by constantly improving users' experience and nurturing a high degree of trust.

Codifying and Publishing Knowledge—
Content Management Systems

An important goal of any CP solution or KM initiative should be to empower employees to easily access information and knowledge in a timely and effective manner for the targeted group or even the whole enterprise and its customers. Hence, content management systems (CMSs), associated with a CP implementation, represent a significant opportunity and challenge for organizations and consultants in the KM field. The processes related to CMSs are closely associated to those of KM. These processes include the creation, publishing, reuse, and storage of content (or information). In that respect, good CMSs can play a very important role by making it much easier for knowledge holders to codify and distribute part of their knowledge and information sources. This is, of course, very relevant for experts who tend to be bombarded with the same questions repeatedly.

Regardless of specific KM goals, CMSs are also becoming a very practical necessity in large-scale Web deployments, where thousands of pages share common elements (e.g., corporate logo). It is very difficult to maintain the integrity of Web pages and links, in general, without the use of robust CMSs. In a Web-publishing environment, single pages may consist of hundreds of individual sources, links, gifs, or images, all shared in separate files.

CMSs, although initially developed for large online publishing operations, clearly are knowledge-sharing tools and should be treated as such in a corporate environment. The most advanced CMSs allow for the seamless and dynamic integration of very structured data (from back-office systems) and unstructured data (entered by individuals within and beyond the enterprise). They can also be deeply integrated with electronic work-flow applications and other collaboration and project-management tools. A standard CMS process generally involves the following steps: (1) document creation; (2) document review; (3) indexing, addition of metadata and quality assurance; (4) publishing; (5) periodical review; and (6) document archiving or deletion. They are depicted in Figure 4-2.

CMS deployments can play a critical role in the implementation of CPs. They provide the technical infrastructure and core processes that ensure that correct, updated, and timely content is available for those who need it. Although straightforward at a conceptual level, the CMS platforms can be quite different in terms of their many

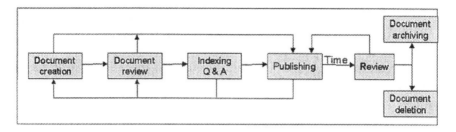

Figure 4-2
Standard CMS Framework

technical features (and are starting to include some features of traditional document management systems). Some of the features found in the most advanced CMS solutions include, but are not limited to, the following lists.

Design and authoring features:

- There are very few layout and design limitations.
- Content is separated from format.
- They include graphical and intuitive tools to build a work flow.
- They allow users not only to post information and content but also customize the interface of their postings.
- They make it easy for nontechnical people to continue to work with their desktop applications.
- They include sophisticated tools for template development.
- They automatically include standardized metadata.
- They allow the creation of XML-based documents by users with no knowledge of XML.
- They make it easy for users to organize, classify, and cross-reference content being publishing.
- They allow users to easily associate search terms (keywords) to their created content.
- They support the publishing of many content file types (e.g., audio, video, image, presentations, HTML code, Java components, ZIP files for download).
- They allow content creators to include priority levels on the documents that are going to be published or distributed to selected groups.

Rule-setting features:

- They allow easy changes of rules for authoring, editing, approval, publishing, and removal of content.
- Ordinary users can easily define or change the publishing review process.
- Individual employees or Webmasters can easily manage roles and access rights.
- They allow both public and privately controlled publishing (i.e., the users control who has access to their published pages).

Version and system administration control guidelines:

- They provide many options for version control.
- They allow the addition of comments to revised documents.
- Prebuilt interfaces are easily modified.
- They allow a view of the "change history" of any given item that has been published.
- They automatically generate attributes associated with each published document (creation date, creator, document size, new item indicator, updated item indicator, etc.).
- They make it easy to define roles—who may deposit, read, edit, publish, archive, or delete a document or page.
- They offer many prebuilt choices in terms of deletion or purging policies.
- They provide tools and reports for easy monitoring of the system.
- They include e-mail alerts for administrators.
- They allow roll-back of published items, if necessary.
- They provide fully auditable archives.

In addition to these core operational features, a number of other considerations should be made before deciding on a specific CMS solution. Many of those are highly technical. In the lists that follow, we selected a few questions that IT managers should be asking.

Architecture and management:

- Does the CMS include separate servers for development, staging, and production?
- Does it include one global, robust repository? Does it also allow the creation of federated or clustered repositories?

- Does it provide redundancy solutions in case a repository is lost or offline?
- To what level of granularity can the content be saved in the repository? Are these levels easily configurable by the users? Are these chunks of content easily reassembled and redeployed?
- Does it make it simple to repurpose and recombine content for new uses and multichannel delivery?
- Is it XML based? Which other standards does it support?
- Does it integrate well with leading CP platforms, databases (Oracle, Sybase, SQL, Informix, etc.), legacy applications, Web servers, application servers, and commerce servers? Does it provide prebuilt adapters for these integrations?
- Does it support the integration of suppliers and partners into a content management process required to deliver real-time e-business solutions?
- Does it include caching?
- Does it make it easy to back up files?

The importance of CMS for the KM process is reflected in the very fast growth of this market. According to the Yankee Group, sales of content management software are forecasted to grow from $900 million in 2000 to $3 billion in 2004. Strategy Partner's forecast puts the number for 2004 at $3 billion on a pessimistic scenario and $13 billion on an optimistic scenario. In light of these forecasts, it is no surprise that we are currently seeing a very large number of vendors in the marketplace. These vendors range from small ASP solution providers to enterprise-class solutions.

The rapid growth of the CMS market and the convergence of the functionality of these systems with those of more traditional document management systems (DMSs) are probably signs that these ideas about knowledge supply chains will soon become a reality for a considerable number of organizations. A robust CMS is also a fundamental component of any CP solution. The CMS can be part or even the "root" of the system or a third-party solution easily integrated into the CP solution.

Collaborating Online

The Internet provides both synchronous and asynchronous opportunities for individuals to meet; share information, knowledge, and opinions; make presentations; and collaborate on real-time decisions.

Synchronous tools, such as voting online, electronic meeting systems, electronic whiteboards, conferencing, and chat tools, allow two or more people to work together simultaneously, whether in the same place or at different places. These tools enhance collaboration and make meetings more effective. Asynchronous tools permit people to work together at different times (e-mail, discussion databases, knowledge repositories, document and content management systems, and work-flow tools). Asynchronous tools are particularly helpful for people who have busy schedules and participate in multiple projects. With asynchronous tools, it does not matter when or where a person is working; the tools replace meetings and may make them unnecessary for certain types of collaborations. Each type of tool has its place and timing during the life cycle of a project or virtual relationships.

Some of the most sophisticated digital workplace tools provide a seamless integration of structured and unstructured data and information, voice, and synchronous and asynchronous groupware tools. They also provide easy ways for companies to track the history of previous project developments and team dynamics (not only the project results). In this way, these tools help codify part of the tacit knowledge developed in any organization and increase indirect collaboration.

Although discussion databases, such as Lotus Notes, have proven a useful solution for large enterprises, the integration of the discipline of traditional work-flow programs with the friendliness of content management systems is drawing a lot of attention now in the KM field. A number of new software solutions are helping knowledge sharing become "an integral part of the work processes themselves— not an add-on frill that can safely be ignored,"[2] as recently emphasized by Bill Gates in *Business @ the Speed of Thought*. This need for discipline in managing knowledge was also one of the core ideas about KM that Paul Haskins, AVP e-business of Alcatel, shared with us: "KM processes need the same discipline as the traditional supply chain processes. Companies should build knowledge supply chains."[3]

We are seeing a convergence of collaboration tools from four different software fields (see Figure 4-3):

- The first two groups include the Web-based discussion and communications tools and the content management systems. Both have their origins in the Web. The first ones are a common feature of many mass-market portals, and CMSs are the cornerstone of any site with high-volume publication needs. Both tools are now recognized as very valuable for KM initiatives and digital

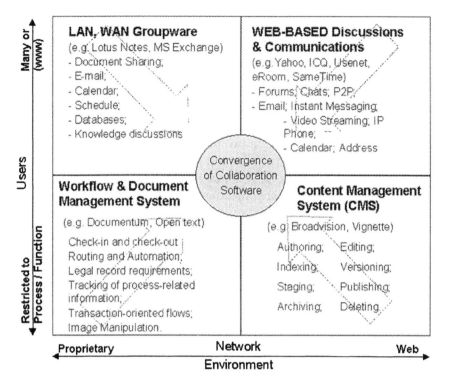

Figure 4-3
Convergence of Collaboration Tools

workplaces. Many CP solutions already come or easily integrate with a set of Web-based discussion and communications tools and a CMS solution.

■ Most companies, however, still have collaboration software tools that are not Web based. Such software can be included in two broad categories: LAN and WAN groupware, work-flow, and document management systems. These traditional systems are now developing a Web interface and, in some cases, being totally rebuilt on standard Internet architectures.

Ultimately, the selection of a particular collaboration tool to be integrated into a CP implementation depends on many factors, including the existence of and dependence on collaboration tools (e.g., widespread use of Lotus Notes) and the required new functionality or type of knowledge that needs to be shared (structured or unstructured, project based or function based, internal or external). We discuss now, in more the detail, the Web-based tools.

Web-Based Discussion, Communications, and Community Tools

It is clear that many of the tools now implemented at the enterprise level have their roots in the consumer sites, in particular large-scale portals, that provided Web-based discussion, communications, and community tools. In fact, some software vendors now tapping into the enterprise market still have those mass-market portals as their flagship clients. Other software solutions were developed specifically for the corporate market: from low-end standard Internet solutions for small companies to robust enterprise-level solutions. Some of the most recent solutions are leveraging peer-to-peer (P2P) platforms (decentralized collaborations platforms that may not include a Web server) that include wireless applications to keep members constantly connected to the community.

Many software players are in this nascent market. Some tools are already being widely deployed, especially for large organizations (e.g., Web conferencing), while others (e.g., P2P) are being tested by more innovative firms. Ultimately, especially for organizations that have a strong understanding of KM principles, these tools provide a technical foundation to foster the development of communities of practice (as per the concepts elaborated originally by Etienne Wenger and the practical examples of online communities discussed in the previous chapter). In essence, as many of these tools (e.g., Tomoye) are integrated and customized to specific organizational environments (based on a number of choices such as best-of-breed or suite solutions), a set of functionalites related to five core areas has emerged:

1. Synchronous and asynchronous online discussions capabilities:
   - Threaded discussion databases.
   - Discussion threads shown according to user profile or choices.
   - E-mail and digests.
   - Chats and instant messaging.
   - Ability to work offline (users can download the collaboration files to their PCs).
   - Ability to target questions to groups or subgroups.

- Ability to easily set up group, subgroup, or private interaction environment.
- Electronic meeting places with advanced presentation features: Web tours, whiteboards, conferences, etc.
- Audio and video streaming.
- Instant polling and rating features.
- Anonymous postings.
- Ability for mobile and remote users to participate.

2. User identification capabilities:
   - Manual or automatic profiling of individuals (by moderators or users).
   - Knowledge-mapping and affinity-building tools to help people who share interests to meet.
   - Ability for users to digitally express their moods and feelings through icons.
   - Ability to easily assign and modify different roles for individuals of the community (e.g., administrator, moderator, core member, affiliate member).
   - Tools for recognizing different levels of participation and for users to develop their individual digital reputations.
   - Ability to create members' directories and subdirectories.
   - Ability for both administrators and individual users to define access rights to other members of the community.
   - Ability to personalize some elements of each group or community (e.g., images, color, layout).

3. Knowledge-base repositories:
   - Ability to easily upload, distribute, and archive all kinds of document formats (even for non-IT individuals), in a way, including many of the advanced features of CMSs. These features were discussed in detail in the earlier CMS section.
   - Ability to cross-reference documents into multiple topics so they can be accessed from different sources.
   - Direct link between documents and authors' profiles and contact information.
   - Ability to check same applications simultaneously (apps sharing); for instance, project plans, business intelligence, ERP.
   - Searchable databases of discussions and previous Q&A sessions.
   - Integrated search with the ability to search based on a number of criteria: author, date, subject, subgroups, or the like.

- Automatic grouping of search results according to topics or types of files.
4. Events management:
   - Invitation according to role or choices.
   - Notification according to role or choices.
   - Calendar.
   - Schedule.
   - Inclusion of new members and groups.
   - Site statistics (stats by users, location, topic, contributions, etc.).
5. Administration tools:
   - Ability to manage without knowledge or programming skills.
   - Ability to easily conduct online surveys.
   - Ability to establish groups and communities that extend beyond the firewall.
   - Ability to operate without client software.
   - Ability to set up different levels and areas of site management.
   - Ability to set up different access levels and so forth.

Finally, it must be said that, to customize and deploy collaborative software solutions, it is very important to understand the actual work practices of the targeted groups within the organization. That usually includes a deep analysis of the formal and informal work processes, the physical context, and how information and knowledge are exchanged both tacitly and explicitly. The initial step to achieve this is to ask the people doing the work. However, sometimes it is necessary to observe people at work because they are not able to explain how the work actually gets done and which information sources they really use.

INTEGRATION OF STAND-ALONE APPLICATIONS RELATED TO KNOWLEDGE MANAGEMENT

In Chapter 3, we highlighted many of the broad issues related to KM. We do not tackle all of them in this book. We have, however, developed a framework that links and categorizes the enabling tools to specific KM facets that are the core sources of intellectual capital (IC) in an enterprise. The facets are divided into the internal source of IC, which include leadership capital, social capital, structural capital, and human capital and the external source of IC, its network capital.

Many KM objectives and corresponding Internet applications should be integrated under a corporate portal. Consequently, we developed a conceptual model of CPs around these sources of intellectual capital (see Figure 4-4). This model highlights the concept that the CP should be developed with an eye to understanding the main sources of wealth in a knowledge-based enterprise.

Internal sources:

- *Leadership capital.* The intangible value that an active leadership team may deliver to an organization is its leadership capital. More than anything else, the role played by leadership may explain why some companies succeed while others with similar

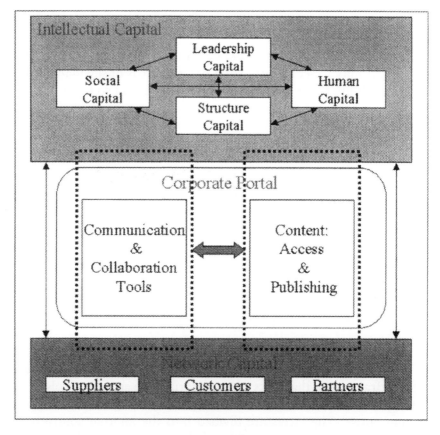

Figure 4-4
Conceptual Model for the Relationship between CPs and KM (developed with recognition of the earlier contributions and theoretical framework models by KM thought leaders: Hubert St. Onge, Debra Amidon, Leif Edvinson, Karl Eric Svieby, Nick Bontis)

material conditions (finance, contracts, technology) fail. In our rapidly changing environment, an organization's leadership sets the tone for the employees' commitment to value creation, innovation, knowledge sharing, risk-taking attitudes, and the like. The Internet can be used in many innovative ways to further these objectives.

- *Social capital.* The exchanges individuals have in an organization form its social capital. The overall health of these exchanges has a huge impact on establishing a knowledge-creating environment. The social capital is affected by a number of issues, such as the frequency, content, tone, and channels of communication chosen by individuals, small groups, and the organization as a whole. Numerous tools converge to help foster both online and offline knowledge exchange.

- *Structural capital.* An organization's ability to effectively create and produce knowledge is affected by its structural capital. It consists of everything that remains in the organization when knowledge workers go home:[4] the organization's physical assets. These assets usually include information systems (databases, customer files), work group tools for collaboration (manuals, documents, software), and business processes. Most IT-related KM efforts traditionally concentrated on structural capital. Codifying, storing, retrieving, tabulating, mining, and distributing are some actions usually associated with the management of these sources of IC.

- *Human capital.* In knowledge-based enterprises, it is a well-accepted fact that a large portion of an organization's wealth walks home every day: its human capital. Activities related to the proactive management of employees or influencing the full cycle of an individual's life within an organization pertain to this domain. Such activities range from hiring, training, project allocation, evaluation and promotion, and termination. Many Internet applications have been developed in the last few years to help make this critical knowledge resource more productive and ensure individuals' alignment with corporate needs.

The external source is the organization's *network capital* or value-chain capital. The focus on customers is often referred to in the IC and KM literature as *customer capital*, which can be defined as the effective leverage of information, knowledge, and experience in the acquisition, development, and retention of a profitable customer portfolio.

The most common customer capital measures include customer satisfaction (service designed and delivered to meet customer targets) and customer loyalty (retention, repeat business, and referrals). In line with our previous discussions about the Networked Era, we believe that it is preferable to use a broader definition that also includes partners and suppliers in the value creation process.

Mapping and classifying the different KM-enabling Internet applications are important to help companies prioritize their Internet-based and CP projects (Which application should be integrated into the CP?). Figures 4-5 and 4-6 provide a large number of interrelated key KM objectives and software applications (tools).

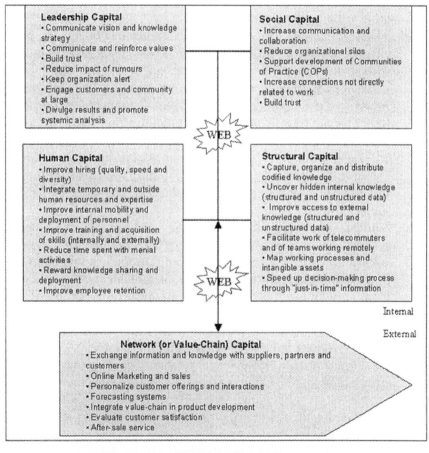

Figure 4-5
KM Objectives and Sources of Intellectual Capital

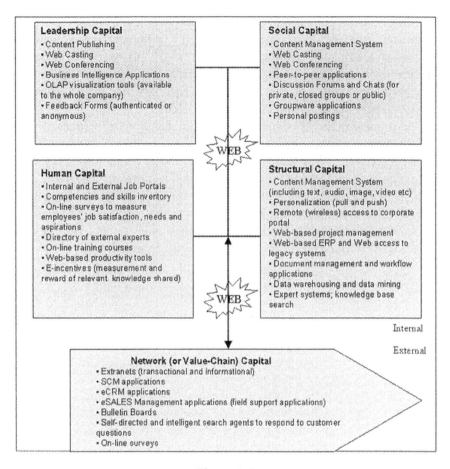

Figure 4-6
Corporate Portal Tools and Sources of Intellectual Capital

Figures 4-5 and 4-6 make it clear that no single package software provides the answer for the KM challenge. Although recent CP platform advances and integration are welcome, it is clear that KM can touch almost every single digital point of the organization, which is why it is hard to have "the" software solution. As usual, the dominant software companies strive to provide a one-stop solution. To do that, they try to integrate as many pieces of the puzzle as possible. In the end, organizations make their choices based on many factors: business impact, existing in-house platforms, balancing the benefits of different solutions with the required levels, custom-code development, interoperability, ease of maintenance, need for in-house versus external technical teams, price, and so forth. This book's primary goal is not to recommend specific software but to provide detailed information that can help companies to determine solid requirements for the selection of CP platforms that meet their specific needs.

As we see by the list of objectives and tools listed in Figures 4-5 and 4-6, Internet applications can be used in a number of ways to foster KM objectives. We argue, however, that implementing this complete list requires a committed organization and leadership. Therefore, as a first step in building the necessary thrust, those in charge of the project should lead soul-searching discussions with the top levels of management to decide which Internet applications will attract the required support in terms of resources, time, and visible signals.

CP and the Brand

Will Novosedlik*

To many people brand is still defined as the image projected by an enterprise. But, as technology makes companies more transparent to customers, suppliers, employees, and partners, the value of the brand rests increasingly on the strength of relationships.

These relationships are built on an exchange of value in the form of information and knowledge. Managing that exchange redefines the brand, because in this scenario, rather than wrapping the brand as an image around the enterprise, companies wrap the brand as an experience around customers, suppliers, employees, and partners.

This requires an expanded definition of organizational brand management. No longer just a marketing function focused on the control of intended messages, brand management must now consider all contact points between an enterprise and its stakeholders as potential contributors to the growth of the brand. This approach demands collaboration and a shared understanding of the role everyone has to play in fulfilling the brand promise.

In a global enterprise, this is a daunting challenge, but it is one to which the CP is well suited. For instance, by facilitating the frequency, content, and tone of individual exchanges across an enterprise, the CP weaves employees' shared values into patterns of behavior that then collectively reflect the purpose of the brand. A companywide understanding of the brand and how it affects each component of the value chain facilitates a consistent brand experience at all contact points.

Keeping the brand front and center in the minds of employees is a key role for any CP, and a key ingredient of leadership capital. The consulting firm of Bain and Company, for example, reports that its "culture" modules are among the most visited pages on its intranet. They lie at the "mythic core" of the company and, as such, play an important emotional role in motivating employee performance. They also play a team-building role: They encourage collaboration toward a common purpose. They remind employees why they work there.

In the realm of structural capital, the CP provides a valuable platform for brand asset management. As companies grow globally,

---

*Will Novosedlik is an expert in brand development and evaluation. He is currently the branding practice leader at Taxi, a leading advertising agency in Canada. He has written many articles about branding and the Internet and is frequently invited to speak at conferences throughout North America.

they must balance consistent delivery of the brand experience with sensitivity to local context. To deliver shareholder value, consumer goods giant Coca-Cola, for instance, is struggling to make what was once a monolithic superbrand relevant to different cultures around the world. Its success will depend on its ability to respond to input from local operatives on a timely basis.

Local operatives not only need access to key brand properties but to guidelines that govern the elasticity of their usage, so that they can "translate" the brand into a culturally appropriate experience. The CP empowers local offices by facilitating dialogue with other offices and giving more information to local brand managers. This results in a greater sense of empowerment for the local office and more control for the head office because they can stay in touch constantly.

The brand's personality is reflected not just in its communications but also in the hiring, training, evaluation, promotion, and termination of employees. An enterprise that values its human capital will use the CP to effectively manage employee life cycles and improve retention. Thus, the CP becomes an agent of internal brand loyalty.

The CP perhaps plays its most important brand-building role in the realm of network capital. Using the collective knowledge and experience of the enterprise to drive the consideration, conversion, and retention of customers, suppliers, partners, and employees is the ultimate goal of any contemporary brand. The CP, by allowing more fluid links among these groups, increases the likelihood of satisfaction and loyalty. The more you know about your customer or supplier, the better equipped you are to meet its needs. The more access you have to the collective knowledge of the enterprise, the more quickly and authoritatively you can solve problems. Ultimately, that translates into a positive brand experience, which builds trust, repeat business, and the likelihood of referrals.

This is what Marty Lippert, CIO of RBC Financial Group, was referring to in Chapter 2. When he spoke of integrating the Internet and intranets into a corporate portal around customers in order to deepen RBC's relationships with them, he was talking about how the CP wraps the brand around the customer. It may be possible to achieve this without a CP if your enterprise is local. But if your company is spread across markets, countries, and industry segments, creating and maintaining a consistent brand experience across all contact points is less and less possible without it.

LEVELS OF CORPORATE PORTALS

In terms of levels of sophistication of interface, functionality, and back-end systems' architecture, CPs represent a major advance over basic intranets. They go well beyond what intranets have been able to offer:

- They provide a core IT infrastructure that allow organizations to streamline their information management, integrate disparate applications, and leverage their digital assets to serve different audiences internally and externally.
- They make it easier for employees to find information and knowledge sources regardless of which system holds them.
- The user need not open many different windows.
- Employees need not learn the intricacies and complexities of many different systems and ask to be admitted (get a password) to use each one.
- Employees do not have to deal with various types of non-user-friendly interfaces. CPs provide a common interface (look and feel) that makes it easier to find information.
- Employees may not even be bound by location to access information and perform their tasks.
- They make it easy to combine internal and external content.
- They clearly reduce information overload by providing information that is filtered, categorized, targeted, and personalized.
- They provide very advanced search mechanisms that allow users to quickly find relevant information and people with related knowledge.
- They make it easier for employees to publish their content to an enterprisewide audience or to a very targeted segment or community within and beyond the walls of the organization.
- They make it easier for employees to multitask.
- They embed core business processes with relevant knowledge sources based on individuals' roles.
- They can be configured to facilitate one-to-one, one-to-many, and many-to-many communications and collaboration.
- They may reduce desktop support and client software costs by hosting applications in a central server.

It is clear, however, that different people have different ideas of what can be considered a portal. To distinguish between a simple intranet and a sophisticated portal, we developed Table 4-1.

As corporate portal technology evolves and becomes a mainstream application (which we forecast for the next couple of years), a deep understanding of collaboration from a strategic and human perspective will separate the organizations that thrive in the Networked Era from those that struggle because they are rigidly attached to old patterns of organizing work and establishing relationships with clients, partners, and suppliers. In the next chapter, we focus on the still emergent KM field. We include some of our own perspectives, especially as they relate to the strategic and human aspects of KM, while acknowledging some of the groundbreaking insights of authors making fundamental contributions to this management domain.

Table 4-1   *Levels of Corporate Portals*

Features	*Intranet*	*Basic CP*	*Advanced CP*
Organization and management	Usually decentralized (proliferation of URLs): very labor-intensive, low skill level required	Centralized management (unification of URLs): easy management of group and users' rights, requires separate database to install	Highly coordinated multiple levels of Web-based management: very easy (intuitive wizards) to set up different levels of management; easy to analyze log of all events within the CP
Personalization	None	Limited: basic users' preferences and based on stationary location	Advanced: full control of layout and colors, role based, dynamic, on the fly, and triggered by device, users' current location, or bandwidth

Table 4-1   *Levels of Corporate Portals (continued)*

Features	Intranet	Basic CP	Advanced CP
Search	Basic spider	Enhanced search: full text, Boolean, Bayesian, concept, natural language, popularity; provides notification; searches unstructured and structured documents	Advanced searches: collaborative and affinity searches (links individuals to subjects), unified internal and external WWW results, multimedia file searches
Taxonomy	Only top level hierarchy and many uncategorized documents	Many category levels highly hyperlinked, automated categorization; well-organized directory	Other forms of categorization (e.g. spatial, hyperbolic trees); advanced thesaurus
Collaboration tools	Not integrated with CP	Integrated at the notification level only, but links to e-mail, online threaded discussions; project-management software; calendar and scheduling	Deeply integrated within the CP window, no need to launch native application; includes instant messaging and electronic meeting places
Content management system	Not available	Available on a limited basis: cumbersome process for uploading documents, supports document versioning and routing	Widely available: automated tagging of documents, little effort required by users for further categorization and targeted distribution, process, and work-flow features

continues

Table 4-1   *Levels of Corporate Portals (continued)*

Features	Intranet	Basic CP	Advanced CP
Measurement tools	Separate software	Integrated software	Integrated and easily customizable, real-time surveys
Integration of internal applications (ERP, CRM, etc.)	Rare	Few and integration at the interface or reports level only: applications run on the Web server	Many and deep integrations of data sources: communication among APIs, integration of mainframe and legacy systems, applications run on a separate server
Integration of external applications and data sources	None	Few and at the front-end only	Integration of many content and data sources: same platform for B2E, B2B, and B2C applications, XML integration*
Development environment	Basic Internet standards: HTML, DHTML, JAVA, JSP, etc.	Requires high level of programming skills: not easily customizable	Provides turnkey solutions easily customizable: supports object-oriented development

*To learn more about XML, check the following sites: www.xml.org and www.ebXML.org.

Table 4-1 *Levels of Corporate Portals (continued)*

Features	Intranet	Basic CP	Advanced CP
Systems architecture and performance	Basic Web server based on Internet standards: integrated software applications require lots of custom development	Multitiered architecture: clear separation of presentation and applications layer, integrates easily with most databases and runs on the most popular operating systems	Supports XML-based, wireless and P2P applications and robust integrated solutions for Internet, intranet, and extranet applications, highly scalable, offers caching and load balancing, APIs run on separate servers
Security	Standard firewall	Supports all standard authentication and security protocols out of the box	Supports high-level encryption and customized solutions, single sign-on

REFERENCES

1. Davenport, T., Harris, J., DeLong, D., Jacobson, A. Data to knowledge to results. *California Management Review.* 43, no. 2(Winter 2001):117.
2. Gates, W. H. (with C. Hemingway). *Business @ the Speed of Thought: Using a Digital Nervous System.* New York: Warner Books, 1999:240.
3. Interview at Alcatel offices in Kanata, Canada, on June 13, 2001.
4. Edvinsson, L., Malone, M. *Intellectual Capital: Realizing Your Company's True Value by Finding Its Hidden Roots.* New York: HarperCollins, 1997.

5

IMPLEMENTING CORPORATE PORTALS: KEY LESSONS

As we examined the detailed case studies from our research (presented in Part II), a number of trends and general lessons emerged. They are discussed here in light of the most current general management and knowledge management theories presented in the preceding chapters. While we believe that the "structuring exercise" developed in this chapter can be very useful for those initiating or revisiting a major CP implementation, we have a strong appreciation for the importance of context- and strategy-driven CP implementations. The detailed case studies in the next part, therefore, also provide specific background, driving factors, and corporate goals for each of the organizations researched. Although implementing a CP is not "rocket science," it is important to make sure that all the key business, organizational, and human elements are taken into consideration, something by no means simple.

The key lessons for CP implementation that we identified and explore are

- Organizational alignment should be priority 1.
- Be clear about the business case, value proposition, and metrics.
- Innovative rewards and recognition strategies are critical.
- Organizational change does not happen by chance.
- Communicate, communicate, communicate!
- New roles and responsibilities need to be clearly assigned.
- Focus on users' needs: Get to know your different audiences.
- Online communities require careful planning, infrastructure, and ongoing support.
- Quality of content is more important than quantity of content.
- The CP should reduce information overload and simplify access to information, templates, and expertise from within and outside an organization.
- Set priorities on the integration of IT applications.
- Develop a careful due-diligence process to select the CP platform.

LESSON 1. ORGANIZATIONAL ALIGNMENT SHOULD BE PRIORITY 1

The most significant learning from the case research was the unifying recognition of the need to focus on the vision and corporate alignment. A vision is needed to communicate the strategic intentions of the portal and make sure the value and importance are shared at every level in an organization. An important underpinning is clearly defining how people's behavior will have to change to fulfill the vision. One needs a great deal of clarity to think through in terms of how an organization wants to change its culture, working habits, and processes, and the business benefits that will result. In all our case studies, a senior executive champion was actively involved—and without this alignment and support in place, organizations are best off *not* to deploy a corporate portal, as this type of solution deployment cuts across too many organizational areas.

A few examples:

- At Bain, the CP initiative was driven by the chief operating officer throughout all implementation stages; senior partners were aligned to the vision and held accountable with specific performance metrics.

- At Motorola, a senior business line executive and its global CIO have joint responsibility for the corporate portal improvements and monitoring the CP journey integrated with its e-commerce initiatives.
- At Nortel Networks, John Roth, the prior CEO, was actively involved in promoting the vision for unified communication, internally and externally, and actively supported online collaboration strategies.
- At Serpro, direct and visible involvement came from the president, and a large number of senior executives went through KM immersion courses to develop alignment.
- At Siemens, a global KM community was founded with the support of its global CIO and a corporate knowledge office was created. This global community is not only permanently virtually linked but also meets periodically, drawing as many as 300 people from around the world to KM summits.

Ultimately, the development of a CP should serve the business goals of an organization. This may seem obvious; however, it is easier said than done. Many IT-related projects end up being led and implemented by people whose main objectives are to "get things rolling" (there is nothing wrong with that, if the ultimate vision and business reasons are not forgotten). As the Internet and the most recent advances in IT make connecting people and information a rather easy proposition, a key challenge for senior management is to help the organization focus the KM efforts in the areas where it will have the greatest competitive advantage impact. Management plays an important role in making sure that the CP links the appropriate internal and external sources of information and knowledge with the appropriate groups within the organization who will benefit from the efforts.

Key stakeholders' (users, line management, IT personnel) perspectives should be considered from the outset. There is no universal blueprint that management can use to direct the development of its corporate portals. However, by clearly linking the CP development to the sources of company intellectual wealth, senior management plays an important guiding role for the development teams.

It's also very important that the senior management's commitment be translated into appropriate levels of support. This includes providing long-term resources, budget, and time to develop sound IT applications and corresponding new processes and management policies.

Senior management should become champions, or at least obvious sponsors, of the CP effort and a knowledge-creation and -sharing culture. If such support and commitment are adequately communicated to the organization, the chances of success are likely to increase dramatically. Generally, problems with CPs and IT/KM implementations arise due to a lack of long-term planning, clear definition of priorities, and attention to the required changes in behavior and success metrics. IT projects that are half-implemented or not operationally and organizationally supported do not produce half of the benefits. Truncated projects usually become a waste of money and energy and foster skepticism.

Governing Corporate Portals

Brian Detlor *

A variety of styles and approaches can be used to govern the way corporate portals are managed and developed in organizations. For the most part, many firms concentrate on tangible concerns, such as the look and feel of the portal interface and the type and format of portal content. These are important facets, but they are not the only ones. Equally important are the less tangible concerns surrounding portal design. Thomas Davenport, IT guru and leading academic, outlines several "softer" areas where corporations need to concentrate to improve the deployment and use of information technology for knowledge work. In *Information Ecology: Managing the Information and Knowledge Environment* (New York: Oxford University Press, 1997), Davenport recognizes the impact of elements such as information politics, information staff, and the information behavior and culture of the firm on the degree to which firmwide information systems are adopted and used.

---

*Brian Detlor is an assistant professor of Information Systems at the Michael G. DeGroote School of Business in Hamilton, Ontario, Canada. Dr. Detlor specializes in research on portals, electronic government, e-shopping, and intelligent agents. He is the coauthor with Chun Wei and Don Turnbull of *Web Work: Information Seeking and Knowledge Work on the World Wide Web* (Waltham, MA: Kluwer Academic Press, 2000).

- *Information politics* involves the power information provides and the governance responsibilities for its management and use.
- *Information staff* refers to the people in the firm needed to provide and interpret information to others in the organization; these include both technology specialists and information content professionals.
- *Information culture* comprises a firm's information behaviors and determines how much those involved value information, share it across organizational boundaries, disclose it internally and externally, and capitalize on it in their businesses.
- *Information behaviors* include information sharing, which requires the removal of various political, emotional, and technological barriers to encourage the exchange of information between organizational participants; handling information overload, which requires information filtering and engagement (i.e., the communication of information in compelling ways to encourage the recognition and use of the right information); and dealing with multiple information meanings, which requires consensus and cooperation among organizational workers if multiple meanings need to be controlled.

These factors apply equally to corporate portals. An independent case study research investigation by Detlor (*Internet Research*, 11, no. 4:286–295) provides empirical evidence of how these factors affect the design, adoption, and use of an organization's corporate portal.

In terms of information politics, the study's data showed that control over content and the financial purse strings of a corporate portal led to a final design that better matched the information needs and uses of controlling stakeholder groups while isolating user communities, who lacked influence over the portal's content and budget.

With respect to information staff, a perceived slowness or inability to respond to user demands by information technology and content specialists was shown to negatively affect end-user system acceptance and utilization.

In terms of the information culture of the firm, many subfactors were shown to influence system use. Distrust of fellow users, a low capacity to filter information, too much control, lack of accessibility, or an unawareness of portal features and functions all were shown to result in a decline of or resistance to use of these systems.

From the study's findings, several recommendations can be made on ways to govern portal development to improve their adoption and use across the firm:

- Establish a democratic steering committee composed of various stakeholders to oversee the development and implementation of a portal solution to promote a design that better addresses the requirements of a diverse user population and balances tensions between stakeholder groups.
- Gain support of upper management to promote the use and direction of corporate portals and the provision of an underlying infrastructure to support their development and roll-out.
- Streamline the system development process to ensure that speedy modification and enhancement of portals are made.
- Loosen control over technical standards and information content to encourage greater user acceptance of these systems.
- Market and train organizational workers on a corporate portal's functionality and strategic importance to help showcase the system's potential, facilitate a more accurate perception of the features available for use, and instill greater interest in use of this technology by employees.

Lesson 2. Be Clear about the Business Case, Value Proposition, and Metrics

Based on our own experience and the case studies presented in this book, we are convinced that KM applications, and CPs in particular, may produce very high returns on investment. This is not to say that it is easily accomplished, since it requires action in many different areas (culture, leadership, reward, user satisfaction) not traditionally in the realm of IT projects. Our conviction comes about because

- Knowledge and intellectual assets are increasingly the most valuable assets of organizations.
- Compared to more traditional IT applications, Web-based KM applications are relatively easy, fast, and cheap to deploy.
- When important human connections are made and significant knowledge reused, the increase in profits can be very large, since

marginal development costs to develop the solution may be minimal.

- CPs are becoming "must-have" tools for any organization competing in knowledge-intensive and fast-changing industries.

Senior executives are increasingly concerned about the return on investment (ROI) on IT-related projects. However, measuring return on CP investments may pose a significant challenge. The establishment of a strict causal relationship between investments on CPs and the gained results is not always possible (and if it leads to a narrow understanding of its impact, not even desirable). Indeed, the more strategic in nature such investments and objectives are, the harder it is to measure their overall impact. It is one challenge to try to measure the impact of a CP implementation on the performance of customer service representatives. It is a completely different challenge to evaluate how a CP project has helped shape the direction, product development, or level of innovation of an organization. Finally, as previously discussed in Chapter 3, the results will, in general, also depend on behavioral changes.

Another way of looking at this and justifying such investments is to try to imagine work without such tools when they have become the norm at leading offices and companies. This is particularly true when most competitors are adopting them. In these circumstances, it is also helpful to ask the cost of not developing or applying such cutting-edge communications, collaboration tools, and information systems. (Has anyone ever seen an ROI analysis for investments in an advanced telephone system or e-mail system?) Clearly, CPs are becoming an essential piece of IT infrastructure in many medium- and large-sized organizations, especially those with important e-business plans or that are knowledge and document heavy. Consequently, measuring the ROI requires a good understanding of the many benefits across a vast number of applications and services that are enabled or better deployed through the CP infrastructure.

A clear focus on the needs of clients may also help everyone to see the benefits of the CP. CPs can be built with a strong orientation toward developing a stronger, real-time collaboration environment with clients. A good test of the value of the portal is when everyone, from senior management to new hires, can immediately see the benefits of the portal and how it can help the company win more business and better serve existing clients. It is also interesting to ask questions such as "What is the value of cutting product development time by a couple of months?" For the auto or pharmaceutical industries, for example, the answer is probably that the value is very high and, if achieved, justifies the CP budget many times over. In fact, the impact of CP implementations is likely to vary significantly from industry to industry. Companies in the information- and knowledge-intensive sectors (e.g., consulting, pharmaceutical, etc.) stand to benefit more than companies in the commodity or unskilled-labor-intensive sectors (e.g., textile manufacturing).

The bottom line is that the kind of business case/value proposition that can be elaborated to support the development of a CP project is not as straightforward as a typical business case to support investments in tangible assets such as new plants, machines, or offices. Although it is not easy to develop specific metrics and frameworks for measuring CP investments, most executives know that sooner or later they must provide evidence that CP investments have been or will be worthwhile.

In our research, the development of the CPs usually followed a higher-order strategic goal (e.g., provide better solutions for customers, improve integration of newly acquired companies, get new employees up to speed faster, improve overall collaboration, document and standardize best practices, codify tacit knowledge) and was supported, to a great extent, by senior management's initial "leap of faith." In most cases, however, soon after the CP was implemented, firms started to develop a number of indicators and "proxies" to prove the value of the investment and monitor progress and improve users' experience continuously.

We believe, however, that, in most cases, a more structured analysis, which combines quantitative and qualitative data and operational and strategic goals, is needed. Not having a specific financial goal is very different from not having very clear goals. A strong business case tries to show how the CP helps improve typical business metrics (e.g., increased revenues, acquisition of new clients, cost reduction, quality improvement) and detailed descriptions and scenarios of how:

- Work is expected to be conducted.
- Information is created, gathered, disseminated, and used.
- People separated geographically can collaborate and work together.
- Meaningful connections are made.
- Non-value-added activities are eliminated.
- Suppliers, partners, and customers benefit.
- Learning changes.

Although we recognize, once more, the risks involved in trying to synthesize lessons from case studies of KM and CP projects, we must keep in mind that these organizations had very similar primary goals in their CP projects. This is particularly evident in Table 5-1, which tabulates the explicit objectives these organizations had when conducting their CP projects. By asking company leaders to answer a structured questionnaire, it became clear that these organizations were looking at their CP projects primarily to achieve the following objectives:

- Improve overall knowledge sharing.
- Increase collaboration among different functions and locations of the organization.
- Support the development of communities of practice.
- Facilitate search of previously developed knowledge.

Table 5-1   *Comparison of KM Goals*

Question	Primary	Secondary	Not Relevant
Communication tool (top down and bottom up)			
Improve communication of vision and knowledge strategy	4	6	2
Improve communication of company values	3	7	2
Keep organization alert	5	6	1
Engage customers and community at large	5	6	1
Divulge results more broadly and promote systemic analysis	7	5	0
Facilitate bottom-up communications	6	5	1
Make it easy for employees to suggest improvements to management	4	4	4
Push information and knowledge to employees			
Capture, organize, and distribute codified knowledge (e.g., database access)	8	4	0
Improve access to external sources of information and knowledge	5	6	1
Improve decision making	6	5	1
Empower front-line employees	10	1	1

Table 5-1 *Comparison of KM Goals (continued)*

Question	Primary	Secondary	Not Relevant
Improve reuse of knowledge			
Develop expertise maps (uncover existing knowledge)	7	5	0
Map and measure intangible assets	2	6	2
Facilitate search of previously developed knowledge	11	1	0
Foster collaboration			
Increase collaboration among different functions of the organization	12	0	0
Increase collaboration among different locations of the organization	11	1	0
Improve overall knowledge sharing	12	0	0
Support the development of communities of practice	11	1	0
Increase connections not related to work	1	8	3
Improve human capital management			
Improve hiring	1	2	9
Improve internal mobility and deployment of existing employees	3	7	2
Integrate temporary and outside human resources and expertise	2	2	8
Improve training and acquisition of skills	5	6	1
Get new employees up to speed very quickly	10	2	0
Reduce time spent on menial activities	7	2	3
Improve employee retention	2	8	2
Facilitate work and integration of telecommuters	1	6	5
Improve relationships (external stakeholders and increase information flow)			
Improve information exchange with suppliers, partners and customers	4	7	1
Capture customer information	6	2	4
Improve customer satisfaction	7	4	1
Reduce sales costs	4	7	1
Reduce customer service costs	5	5	2

Note: The numbers in the table represent the number of times a goal was agreed to be primary, secondary, or not relevant.

- Get new employees up to speed very quickly.
- Empower front-line employees.

A number of other objectives were also present in the cases, but they were not as prevalent as in these.

Some of the goals are more easily quantifiable than others. Although we focused our research on the KM-related benefits of a CP implementation, we clearly recognized and, in fact, found out that a number of other interesting productivity, cost-reduction, and strategic benefits could be achieved through a CP implementation as well. Ultimately, CP implementations should be considered successful if they achieve a combination of quantitative, semi-quantitative, and qualitative goals.

Quantitative (The more easily quantifiable metrics may not be the reason why a CP is implemented, but as we learned through experience and research, they may be the ones that help executives get their CP project budgets approved. Although in none of our cases was this the reason why organizations developed their CPs, we think understanding how CPs can rapidly help "pay the bill" is important. These metrics are usually associated more with cost reduction than improved collaboration and use of organization knowledge.) metrics could include

- Reduced costs due to centralization of certain operations to lower-cost locations.
- Reduced clerical work (e.g., fewer secretaries).
- Reduced Web management and custom development costs.
- Reduced publishing, communication, and physical distribution costs.
- Reduced duplication of documents.
- Reduced costs with other systems that become redundant.
- Reduced costs of administrative tasks (expense reports, health claims).
- Reduced use of e-mail with heavy attachments (reduced network and storage costs) and "broadcast" e-mails.
- Less paper flows in the office and between the company and third parties (suppliers, partners, and customers).
- Reduced cost of Web-enabling back-end applications.
- Reduced costs of integrating externally developed Web services.
- Reduced costs of systems integration.

- Reduced telecommunications costs (phone bills and private networks).
- Reduced travel expenses.
- Reduced sales costs.
- Reduced customer service costs (self-service applications and content available through the external portal).

Semi-quantitative (These benefits are usually associated with gains in productivity through easier and faster access to information and knowledge sources. Depending on the scope of CP implementation, it may also include employees' access to learning and career opportunities whose results are also not always easily translated into financial metrics. Last, but not least, also included in this category are metrics linked to increased revenue or sales derived from access to specific knowledge sources. These metrics are usually obtained through surveys or anecdotal evidence.) metrics include
Productivity:

- Reduced time spent looking for information or locating an expert (measured through surveys).
- Reduced time to upload (publish) and distribute documents (measurement through surveys).
- Reduced time to train employees (especially getting new employees up to speed [anecdotal evidence]).
- Reduced time spent in menial activities (measured through surveys).
- Reduced time spent preparing sales proposals.

Satisfaction indexes:

- Better working conditions for telecommuters and employees on the road (anecdotal).
- Improved employees' morale (measured through surveys).
- Employee satisfaction with CP (usually measured through surveys, discussed later, with detailed questions to evaluate users' perspective).
- Improved internal mobility and deployment of existing employees (anecdotal).
- Increased sales (usually measured through anecdotes).
- Improved satisfaction among suppliers, partners, and customers (usually measured through surveys).

Improved use of knowledge assets:

- Usage of CP by employees (measurement easily automated in the portal).
- Growth in number and reuse of documents and knowledge objects (measurement easily automated in the portal).
- Number of responses obtained through knowledge exchange mechanisms, such as questions and answers (measurement easily automated in the portal).
- Reuse of "best practices" (usually measured through direct reports from users).
- Increased use of external information and knowledge sources, competitive intelligence disseminated more broadly.
- Growth of online communities of practice (indirectly measured through growth in online activity).

Qualitative (In knowledge-intensive organizations, many of the most important results will be intangible. They will be very hard to measure or even directly link to the CP implementation, since knowledge-creation and product and services innovation are the result of many factors that go beyond the CP implementation and, often, show results only in the medium to long term. Consequently, at present, the truly qualitative impact of CPs can be evaluated best through anecdotal evidence and user surveys. A good sign that senior management is behind the portal deployment is when the "business case" is strongly supported by these more intangible but often very strategic goals.) metrics include

- More knowledge creation and innovation.
- Faster product development.
- Better use of existing company knowledge, reduced reinvention of the wheel.
- Reduced knowledge hoarding and individual files.
- Improved company communications (especially among different areas, hierarchical levels, and locations).
- Improved access to information, legacy applications, and knowledge by all employees.
- Empowered front-line, better and faster decision making.

- More collaboration among employees from different locations.
- Improved integration with previously remote office locations.
- Improved information, knowledge flow, and collaboration with external parties (customers, partners, suppliers).
- Faster integration of acquired companies.
- Protection of corporate knowledge.

The old saying "if you can't measure it, you can't manage it" holds true with CP implementation. What was interesting in most of our case studies is the number of companies that developed and deployed a CP without a solid business case (Bain & Company being an important exception). More often a leap of faith surrounded the CP deployment. In many of our cases, the CEO or COO simply believed a corporate portal that could capture business practices and skill sets throughout the company was as essential to a business as chairs and computers.

This aside, we do not deny the need for measurement. We believe that organizations that are serious about KM will develop detailed business cases—even if most metrics are not financial. Indeed, most leading companies developing portals with a focus on knowledge management, include metrics and proxies to help management "measure" the usage of the system (e.g., growth in traffic, contributions, questions), the key knowledge sources (e.g., documents frequently sourced, patterns of high usage, contributors by business area), and the changes in users' (including employees, customers, partners, etc.) satisfaction levels. These metrics may not always reveal the quality of the knowledge exchanges, but they certainly provide clues that an attentive and astute management team can use to further investigate and evaluate more qualitative results. The metrics also provide important signals to the employees about the kind of behavior the company expects of them.

Finally, it is important that measurements are reviewed openly by the organization and business line executives in real time in order to help them collect business intelligence and develop alternative strategies to keep the CP on course. Ultimately, the reinforced support and alignment built out of the collection of success stories from corporate officers, line executives, management, and employees will validate the investment and make the CP an integral part of an organization's modus operandi.

LESSON 3. INNOVATIVE REWARDS AND RECOGNITION STRATEGIES ARE CRITICAL

"All human beings believe they have a certain inherent worth or dignity. When that worth is not recognized adequately by others, they feel anger; when they do not live up to others' evaluation, they feel shame; and when they are evaluated appropriately, they feel pride. The desire for recognition is an extraordinarily powerful part of the human psyche."
—Francis Fukuyama[1]

CPs can certainly help improve the connections among people. Often they help foster connections that would not occur in the absence of the CP support environment. Of course, connections, especially electronic connections, are only the first step in the knowledge-creation or -sharing process. To ensure that knowledge is actually exchanged, people need to cooperate with one another. A well-planned, carefully executed incentives and rewards strategy can go a very long way toward encouraging people to cooperate. Our research suggests that this type of strategy is critical for successful CP deployment.

However, relating a reward and recognition program to KM efforts is very difficult. It requires clearly identifying specific behaviors that can impede or reinforce knowledge sharing and determining how to affect these. Fundamentally, the issue is how to convince people that knowledge sharing can be valuable for them personally. For many people, this notion is contrary to what their personal experience has led them to believe. The prevailing logic of most organization cultures has long been based on the idea that "knowledge is power—my power." In addition, it is critical to understand that most people have very busy and increasingly hectic schedules. Consequently, it is natural to expect that many employees will frequently ask themselves: "Why should I contribute? It is hard enough as is to find time to focus on client demands, and time is precious. Why should I also then have to worry about sharing what I know? Besides, everyone knows that knowledge is power. My knowledge is my edge for moving ahead. Why should I share?"

Because of this, we think it is extremely important to reward the new heroes and discourage the dissenters. Companies that tried only monetary incentives, however, found these approaches, on their own, were not enough to sustain the motivation of employees. Our research reinforced our view that the companies that had the most success with their CP initiatives concentrated on recognizing employees for their frequent contribution of valuable knowledge by flagging the contributions most frequently used by employees and the employees voted by colleagues as best in class. Often the peer-to-peer recognition strategies were more successful than "trinkets."

Successful practices involving awards and formal dinners with senior executives to recognize knowledge innovations, with company plaques to display on their walls, as used by Bain, were also strong strategies to support employees and develop pride in people for their inspiring behaviors. This strategy, of course, is not very different from awards given in more traditional knowledge- (R&D departments of large organizations) and creativity- (advertising industry) intensive organizations. Such organizations learned a long time ago that "awards" can play a significant motivational role, and they use this strategy extensively to reward top contributors and innovators. Now these tactics need to be applied to motivate a much wider audience and different types of knowledge workers.

Having said that, even in the most nonhierarchical and knowledge-sharing cultures, the introduction of direct recognition and financial rewards to people who contribute to the knowledge base of the organization has proven to be productive (see the Siemens and Context Integration cases). More than the actual benefits derived from the financial rewards, we think this demonstrates the power and importance of giving explicit and visible recognition and rewards for sharing knowledge.

Balancing the individual-focused reward strategies with more group-based incentives, many of the most successful CP implementations developed strategies to recognize the leaders of regional offices or specific departments of the organization for their leadership in KM and creating a serious annual recognition process. While some developed clearly stated core values for knowledge sharing, others used existing core values and evolved principles or behavioral competencies to recognize and reward appropriate behavior. The more advanced organizations ensured that their performance appraisal processes created a feedback loop on leadership activities related to knowledge sharing and that everyone was accountable for creating best practices to achieve global high performance. Consistently, senior executive leadership and leading by example were imperative for any organizational CP initiative to succeed.

Siemens, Bain, and Context Integration provide good examples of these thoughts. They implemented metrics that help create a healthy competitive environment for ideas and knowledge-sharing behavior. In this environment, different offices and departments are clearly reminded that they cannot be "free riders." They also need to contribute to the knowledge base of the organization. Knowledge sharing and codification are becoming essential parts of everyone's job. Therefore, not engaging in these activities is, increasingly, being seen as not fulfilling one's core obligation to the organization. In the information-overloaded world, capturing employees' attention and interest could be the ultimate sign that a specific area of the company is turning out relevant, value-laden content. According to John Dolan, senior CP leader at Allied Irish Bank, this is taken to heart by many business executives, who can get very competitive about the kind of traffic their areas of the CP are getting.

It is important to highlight that many of the interesting stories that have a business impact are not captured by standard CP usage metrics. In many cases, such as Hill & Knowlton, Bain & Company, Siemens, and Texaco, the KM teams have a system and personnel in place to capture these anecdotes and publicize them. They make sure, through regular e-mail and postings in the portals, that these success stories do not go unnoticed. There is a strong belief that these actions are an important part of the recognition program and help foster the attitudes and motivation in everyone else required to make the most of the KM tools and increase participation.

Finally, in organizations with a knowledge-hoarding culture, employees are afraid to pose questions that may show their lack of knowledge in specific areas. They also tend to not share work in progress. This is a huge problem in organizations, with no immediate solution. However, in leading organizations such as Siemens and Context Integration, senior management sends clear signals that this is not appropriate behavior. In fact, people are being rewarded for asking questions and everyone has access to every project, as it is being developed.

Lesson 4. Organizational Change Does Not Happen by Chance

Developing new reward and recognition strategies is an important but not sufficient driver for change. Despite the importance of a CP implementation, many companies continue to fail with large-scale change efforts, which require a balance of sophisticated technology, new processes, and human capital strategies to support change efforts.

With KM programs more often failing than succeeding, what lessons can be learned to help practitioners successfully wrap change around management strategies that offer insightful yet practical advice?

An important change management alignment strategy is to clearly know where your journey begins and where it is heading. Too often organizations do not take the time to identify the gaps between their current and desired cultures. It is helpful to use symbols, images, and stories as powerful ways both to understand the current environment and project a compelling new future. Nortel and Eli Lilly spent a great deal of time and effort framing their current state and mapping the major projects required to meet that state. There are helpful communication approaches, in particular use of color-coding schemes against project types and deliverable status, to rapidly communicate progress being made.

Another important area to define clearly throughout all stages of any large-scale change program is ensuring that senior executives have the courage and understand the importance of sponsoring a CP initiative. Gaining an active commitment of the full senior management team and direct reports from it is required. Senior leadership must be engaged to lead by example and to release key staff members to help work on culture change initiatives. Developing a scorecard on each executive and his or her visible commitments is an important sponsorship-planning requirement. In the early stages of deploying a corporate portal, it is not necessary to have active involvement from all members of the senior executive team, as CPs typically start in a pilot area that has immediate value benefits, then future rollouts are planned. Having the project actively sponsored by a CEO, COO, or CFO is important though, as future deployments will cut across organizational boundaries; and for continued investment support, the most senior executives need to actively nurture and support the CP deployment.

In the majority of our case studies, the core project teams enlisted active stakeholder support and fostered regular communication with them. Few, however, invested the quality time to develop more formalized change management stakeholder mapping techniques, which can be very useful to evaluate the readiness for change across multiple stakeholder groups. These approaches are very helpful in communicating back to senior sponsors the current change-support environment, but this is difficult for internal project teams to do, given the tremendous political risks in positioning a senior executive squarely in a resister quadrant. This is why we recommend that, in some cases, internal project teams also augment their delivery resources with external consultants to enhance the effectiveness of their change management delivery.

An important early alignment strategy is to ensure that the reasons for the change, in terms of business context and rationale for changing the culture, are clearly understood. Creating dissatisfaction with the status quo and a sense of urgency for the change are important implementation levers for senior executives to focus on. Driving shortened timeframes, focusing on scaling one valuable business process area, such as Human Resources, for intelligent self-service applications like in Nortel Networks, or streamlining R&D product communications, such as in ADC, demonstrates early successes.

Another important way of showing support for these initiatives is to use the very best people—at all levels and from all functions—to demonstrate how serious you are about the cultural change. Such people become symbols and change agents; and if they are well respected by their peers and known for results, the speed of the change effort improves significantly.

The death of many large-scale programs occurs when there is a lack of focus on the demonstrated benefits early in the program. Developing tangible symbols to support the emerging culture, like pillars that people can see mature over time, is important to planning. The symbols can be as simple as this: stage one, all senior corporate communication will be delivered via the CP; stage two, all HR processes will be implemented in a self-serve mode; stage three, one centralized content publishing environment will be set up to manage all document and corporate portal knowledge transfers; stage four, the business units will have automated work-flow processes linking their tier one customers and suppliers to a collaborative product planning environment. Each stage can be marked using tangible change symbols to indicate an early stage to the mature form so, as every victory is completed, the organizational roadmap of success is visible to the entire organization. Consistency in journey management frameworks is a powerful change tool; even though not complex, the power of visible, tangible symbols to align cultural awareness and understanding is often forgotten.

Storytelling is another powerful way of communicating change initiatives. As Harvard Professor Howard Gardner says, "Leadership involves the creation of powerful narratives . . . that are much more than mission statements or messages." They are actual stories where there are goals and obstacles, where good and bad things can happen along the way, and where the people involved feel part of an enterprise that's trying to end up in a better place. We have told stories since the beginning of time. They are the narratives of life, spanning the centuries and connecting the generations. They are the vessels in which we carry our shared adventures and most precious memories.

Storytelling encompasses virtually every facet of human endeavor. This ancient tradition is at the heart of human experience, and it is just as vital today, just as much a thread of our social fabric, as ever before. Though organizations have been telling stories unconsciously, it is not until recently that the people in these organizations have realized that they are sharing their information and knowledge in a natural way, storytelling. (The Xerox-Eureka case offers a good example of the relation between storytelling and the creation and sharing of knowledge.) People already share stories in their organizations, but they do not call it storytelling. They may call it sharing examples, using case studies, or having conversation. But by learning an awareness of how to make their story more effective, they can use the story for its fullest potential. The KM leadership at Hill & Knowlton, Texaco, and Siemens, for instance, is constantly digging for inspiring KM stories to communicate to a broad audience through a number of offline and online venues: KM summits, KM communities, broadcast e-mail, highlights in the home page of the CP.

Inevitably, there will be peaks and valleys in the CP deployment. People change constantly in an organization; hence, broad stakeholder strategies deep into multiple pockets in an organization are required to be resilient to the natural life flows in an organization. It is important to appreciate that changing culture takes a long time—it is not revolutionary process but evolutionary, with no definite end point. If a culture does not have a propensity to share knowledge, the number of change management interventions has to be carefully orchestrated with relentless executive attention. We must ensure enough time to implement and scale a large CP and the commitment to complete it. Cultural change is a process, not an event.

A risk in many change efforts, and CP deployments are no exception, is forgetting that communication is a two-way learning process: listening and responding. Not only is it important to understand and communicate why the change is required, but it is even more important to explain how employees can contribute to supporting the change. This can be done by setting up interactive focus groups, online presentations, best practice collaboration rooms, community of practice structures, surveys, and the like. Given the particular importance of this topic in CP implementations, the following section focuses exclusively on communication strategies.

LESSON 5. COMMUNICATE, COMMUNICATE, COMMUNICATE!

Successful change is not done to people but implemented through people. Developing communication strategies to convince people of what they stand to gain, while recognizing what they perceive they lose is important. Often people fear that, with new technology solutions, their job becomes more complicated or that information streams of "junk" cascade upon them like an uncontrollable flood. So easing their fears—talking about them and providing employees concrete scenarios or guided tours—is important to helping employees visualize the future. Learning maps and storyboards help people visualize the future. Rapid prototyping is a frequently used visualization approach in our case research.

We learned that launching CP and KM tools requires important behavior changes and dedicated champions. In various successful cases, such as Texaco, ADC, Siemens, and Serpro, we saw concerted effort by the KM teams and champions from other areas. Indeed, our research and experience suggest that multidisciplinary teams are extremely important for successful KM implementation. In the cases in this book, we saw multidisciplinary teams working together, not only to develop the infrastructure, but also to publicize, train, and motivate people throughout the organization. They worked with employees in general but also with a number of early adopters and communities that helped disseminate concepts and remind other employees.

It is also important to develop a good branding and communications plan. Many of the organizations in our research gave the CP a personality and an easy-to-remember name. From the cases in this book and other examples:

IAN (intellectual asset network), Context Integration.

MAX, Motorola.

ELVIS, Eli Lilly.

Sharenet, Siemens.

K-Village, Mobistar.

IWIN (I want information now), Charles Schwab.

World, Cable & Wireless.
InSight, Gillette.

In some of the most successful cases, the rollout and key improvements (new functionality or added content areas) in the CP were also preceded by significant internal communication, including posters, newsletters, communication booths, local training sessions and gatherings (with the presence of senior management), and e-mail communications.

During the periods of strong internal communication, the number of users and volume of traffic in the portal usually grew very rapidly in the cases we studied. This is very important, since if critical mass is not created very rapidly, most users never bother to use or feel motivated to contribute to the CP. Employees at all levels need to embrace the KM concepts and the new Web tools that support them. Also, contrary to many other IT initiatives, CPs cannot be successful without the "buy-in" at many levels of management and various divisions. Consequently, companies that developed enterprisewide CP initiatives took this advice to heart and provided substantive training for many layers of their management team.

It is also critical not to forget to communicate the benefits of the CP to employees—what's in it for them? More often than not, however, organizations forget that and communicate only the benefits for the organization. This is not an effective approach to introducing the CP and KM in general. KM and CP initiatives have important benefits for participating employees, and this should be promoted as well. CPs, for instance, help employees better execute their jobs and find new opportunities for personal and professional growth. By strongly participating in knowledge exchange activities, employees can be rewarded with better and more visible recognition within the company, new learning and networking opportunities, and ultimately, more opportunities to participate in interesting projects that rely on their accumulated knowledge.

As shown by our research (Bank of Montreal and Serpro cases, in particular), CP implementation is fundamentally a change management issue, not a technology issue. In almost every implementation, both the stick and the carrot approaches were used to highlight the importance of the corporate portal initiative and the need for behavior change. The stick aspect was usually related to the strong participation of senior management, which frequently reminded other management levels about the importance of contributing to the knowledge base and having employees start using the CP. Various carrot approaches were usually employed, including prizes (e.g., Siemens, Hill & Knowlton), bonuses (e.g., Bain, Context Integration), and highlighting the achievements of top knowledge contributors (e.g., Bain, Texaco, Hill & Knowlton).

As we know quite well, the Web can be a daunting challenge for many senior executives (who has not heard a story about executives that use the Internet only through their assistants?). The transformation power of this technology requires, however, deep understanding, if not of its technical elements, at least of its applications and implications for organizations. Successful leaders wisely embrace the Internet (without being mesmerized by it) to further the knowledge strategies of their organizations and to exercise their leadership even more deeply and more frequently. They also are highly involved in the decisions related to the application of this technology to improve the KM processes.

Therefore, if a CP is to focus on KM, it should start by providing a means for effective communication between top management and all employees. This may also convey a powerful symbolic message to the organization: "information need not follow traditional hierarchical levels." In line with this purpose, corporate video streaming is already a significant business. Many large multinational companies, including Ford, Cisco, Apple, and Microsoft, already extensively use video streaming to communicate with all employees (and external stakeholders) around the world. Many suppliers of production facilities are emerging. Yahoo! is a key player in this market, with various large multinationals (such as Ford and PriceWaterhouse) as clients. The CP can also provide all employees a history of top management communications with the rest of the company and a way for all employees to give feedback and speak to top management. The CP solution also provides a high level of customization of the message and instantaneous delivery, based on employee roles or defined personalization preferences.

These are small technological challenges that require, however, a high-level commitment by top management. This can, if properly managed, lead to higher degrees of transparency and trust. It can, on the other hand, backfire if the employees view it with cynicism and mistrust. Again, it is not about the technical challenge but how one uses it, and the cultural context plays a significant role in determining employees' "absorption capacity" for sending and receiving new knowledge freely. This may sound like a simple Internet application, but do not forget that a few years ago it would have been nearly impossible (or very expensive) to have a CEO communicate frequently and directly with entire organizations spread across the globe.

LESSON 6. NEW ROLES AND RESPONSIBILITIES NEED TO BE CLEARLY ASSIGNED

"The CEO's role in raising a company's corporate IQ is to establish an atmosphere that promotes knowledge-sharing and collaboration, to prioritize the areas in which knowledge-sharing is most valuable, to provide the digital tools that make knowledge-sharing possible, and to reward people for contributing to a full flow of information."

—Bill Gates[2]

A wide-reaching CP implementation is bound to affect how most employees and even third parties conduct their jobs, process and create information, and collaborate with people from other locations. Many new roles and responsibilities directly involved with the CP, however, need to be specifically created or assigned within the organization. Having a KM leader is certainly a good first step. When large-scale CPs are implemented, however, many other functions related to new processes should be anticipated in the planning process. In fact, many companies report a significant number of professionals dedicated solely to content publishing or knowledge management (not necessarily new employees but existing ones with redefined job descriptions). This trend has been led by firms in the business service sector (consulting, auditing, advertising, public relations, legal services) but is rapidly spreading to companies in other sectors, such as pharmaceuticals, telecom, consumer packaged goods, manufacturing.

Knowledge Management Leaders

Recognizing the challenge of KM, many companies, such as those highlighted in our case studies, are creating centralized functions such as the "knowledge manager" or "knowledge director." This new function requires a person with both soft and hard skills, such as those related to implementing an organization culture and developing a facilitating infrastructure (primarily by leveraging recent information technology investments and advances). In practice, the new function is being integrated into organizations in one of three different ways:

1. As an independent area at the top management level.

2. As a function associated with the Human Resources area.
3. As a function associated with the information technology area.

The best results appear to come from the first alternative, which requires people with a fairly well-rounded and diverse background, including experience with information technology, strategy, human resources administration, and finance.[3] Indeed, we agree with Davenport and Prusak,[4] who think that the CKO is a very important position that includes many of the following responsibilities:

■ Lead and advocate for the definition of knowledge areas the company should focus on and strive to measure the value of specific knowledge bases.
■ Establish an adequate technical infrastructure and processes geared to knowledge creation and use.
■ Manage the relationship with external providers of information and knowledge, such as database companies.
■ Lead and manage other professional knowledge managers within the organization.

To understand the difference between the role of a CKO and a traditional CIO, it is important to understand the differences between KM and Information Management (as discussed in Chapter 3). As much as the importance of information management to KM cannot be denied, it is critical, as demonstrated by cases such as Eli Lilly and Bank of Montreal, to explain to all stakeholders the differences between KM and Information Management. The CKO and the KM teams need to get involved in a number of projects, in addition to improving information management. They also participate in a number of projects related to the "softer-side" organizational issues, such as training, revamping rewards programs, and fostering a more KM-friendly culture and a more collaborative work environment, which may extend even to suppliers, customers, and partners. KM teams also frequently focus on identifying subject matter experts, connecting them through communities, and to some extent, codifying and embedding parts of these experts' tacit knowledge in specific processes.

In one of our interviews, we obtained this job description for the knowledge management director of one of the largest consulting companies in the world. Working together with the top management of the company and in close collaboration with other executives in the areas of information technology, information services, and training, this professional had the following responsibilities:

- Determine the priorities of the company and activities for
  - Capturing and disseminating knowledge and internal know-how.
  - Facilitating the access of the consultants (employees) to external knowledge.
  - Promoting the creation and use of the proprietary intellectual capital.
- Develop and maintain standards for identifying and focusing on the types and sources of knowledge that should be captured, codified, and disseminated.
- Develop processes, specifications, and formats for the inclusion of individual knowledge in the database of the company (intranet).
- Work in close collaboration with the information technology area, to define the hardware and software infrastructure that will facilitate the implementation of knowledge management.
- Develop the necessary changes in processes and the organization, including incentive and control mechanisms that permit greater effectiveness of the knowledge management.
- Develop and implement the necessary support and training programs.
- Maintain the organization informed about the direction of and activities related to knowledge management.

Knowledge Practice Leaders

To create organizational knowledge certainly needs intellectual leadership or mentoring. That concept should translate to the CP environment; content areas should have designated champions within the firm. Depending on specific situations, this could be a full-time job or a key responsibility of a group of individuals. Whatever the tools, these champions (usually domain experts, not professionals from the IT department) need to make sure that the existing content is accurate, relevant, and frequently updated. They should also be the "energizers"—introducing new employees or relevant stakeholders to the tools and content area and tenaciously prompting colleagues across the firm to use the system and share their knowledge and lessons learned. Richard McDermott, for instance, when discussing the role of communities in knowledge creation, highlights the roles of community coordinators:[5, p. 114]

> Community coordinators are usually a well-respected member of the community. Their primary role is to keep the community alive, connecting members with each other, helping the community focus on important issues, and bringing in new ideas when the community starts to lose energy. . . . They use their knowledge of the discipline to judge what is important, groundbreaking, and useful and to enrich information by summarizing, combining, contrasting, and integrating it.

The case of Ernst & Young is also quite interesting.[4] The knowledge manager roles for each area of expertise are filled by consultants that cycle in and out of these roles for periods of 1–2 years. In this way, the company maintains a good level of dialogue between consultants in the front line and the KM infrastructure and, thereby, keeps the repositories of each practice relevant, updated, and organized around the specific needs of the ultimate users.

Knowledge Brokers Play an Important Role

Although some employees may understand that one of their responsibilities within the organization is to codify part of the intellectual capital (most employees, however, do not even think about that at all), it is very easy for this responsibility to take a backseat as employees worry about their daily tasks. In view of this situation, in a number of the leading organizations surveyed, knowledge brokers are the keepers of the "knowledge codifying process." They make sure that employees do not forget to codify relevant knowledge-sharing elements of their projects, activities, and tasks. (The very active role played by these professionals at the Bain and Context Integration is particularly interesting.)

The knowledge brokers are also key resources for employees who need a human introduction to an organization's core intellectual assets in specific knowledge domains. The experience of many organizations has shown that users highly appreciate the role played by knowledge brokers. They add a human dimension to the CP. This is similar to the traditional experience of call centers. Clients appreciate the option of having many points of contact. Some gladly use self-service information tools, while others feel a lot more comfortable with the idea that "someone is listening." Finally, knowledge brokers play an important role in organizing and keeping the online information up-to-date and focused on strategic issues.

Roles and Responsibilities Associated with the Publishing Process

"Do not trust the maintenance of content areas to junior resources that do not really understand the business or judge the relevance of content."
—Paul Haskins, Alcatel

Making it easy for content creators is certainly very important, but assigning clear responsibilities forms the building blocks of any content management system's successful implementation (the publishing process). Developing and having an extensive and powerful IT infrastructure is of no use if the available content is inaccurate, outdated, misleading, or irrelevant to improving employees' ability to perform. Unfortunately, based on our experience and interviews, such a situation is not unusual in many companies' intranets. To avoid these problems, organizations need to be as disciplined about the publishing process as much as they are about their manufacturing or customer services processes. The following questions illustrate some of the most typical new responsibilities that need to be assigned early on and that are directly associated with any publishing process:

- What content is strategically relevant and should be made available for employees, customers, and outside partners?
- Who has the right to actually create content?
- Who has the right to remove content?
- Who is responsible for approving publishing the content?
- Which areas of the CP have no restrictions either for content publishing or access? Which ones require passwords?

In addition to these process considerations, it is important to highlight that knowledge-intensive firms are becoming more and more like media companies. This means that content publishing is increasingly becoming a core skill and responsibility of not only Communications Departments but also of many knowledge workers and, ultimately, senior executives. Indeed, "virtual publishing models" have emerged in very large organizations, such as Nortel, Motorola, and Allied Irish Bank. They usually consist of a core dedicated team that sets editorial and technology standards and coordinates a wide team of publishers scattered across different departments, business units, and locations.

Research Professionals and Information Architects

Although CP solutions provide many automation features, organizations should not dismiss the critical role that editors, librarians, information architects, and designers will continue to have. As discussed before, KM requires that online investments be accompanied by offline investments. It is fairly easy to be overly impressed with the power of the Web and forget about the fundamental role played by human intelligence to convert information into knowledge.

Developing and keeping the information architecture relevant is a cornerstone of a sound CP strategy. This requires skilled personnel specialized in this function. Often, large corporations do not have these professionals in-house. As the Web and CPs become more prevalent, we hope this will change, as these professionals need to work in tandem with the leaders of the KM strategy within the firms. Not only are these professionals the most qualified for developing taxonomies, labeling, and navigational elements, they are in the best position to help IT professionals develop effective tagging of information, or "information about information." New content formats such as XML, for instance, allow information about each piece of content that is created: author, date of creation, format, category, functional description, and the like. Well-designed CPs, which include the possibility of distributed content creation, take these design issues very seriously, since this will allow not only appropriate publishing, but also easier search and reuse of such content.

Companies that lead the pack have always paid substantial attention to the role of librarians and information or research analysts. In the Web environment, they continue to do so, despite massive investments in information technology. These same professionals are now, sometimes, called *information architects* and are playing a greater role in companies' successes. They understand the shift in paradigm provided by the Internet: On the one hand, users have significantly more autonomy; on the other hand, they can be easily "burned" with information overload. In successful CP implementations, such professionals are involved from the start, to ensure that the user experience and needs are reflected in the information architecture and design of new Web-based systems and that only relevant, accurate information is pushed toward users. They are also the ones in partnership with business-unit leaders, making important choices in terms of which topics are included and how deeply they are covered. Companies such as the progressive and innovative Owens-Corning, for instance, have deeply understood these changes. They have outsourced some of the traditional librarian functions and changed the title of their library to the knowledge resource center. Librarians' primary role now is much broader; they are focused on the information and knowledge needs of employees, regardless of the medium or physical location.[4]

The Librarians Fight Back![6]

The U.S. Library of Congress initiated a very large project to bring together the power of technology and knowledgeable librarians to help users worldwide to find answers to their research questions, 24 hours a day, 7 days a week. A pilot project started in the summer of 2000—the full service is to be rolled out in 2002—with the cooperation and interconnection of hundreds of libraries around the world. This project is called the Collaborative Digital Reference Service (CDRS). The service uses new technologies to provide the best answers in the best context, by taking advantage of not only the millions of Internet resources but also the many more millions of resources that are not online, held by libraries. CDRS supports libraries by providing them additional choices for the services they offer their end-users. Libraries can assist their users by connecting to the CDRS to send questions that are best answered by the expert staff and collections of CDRS member-institutions around the world. Local, regional, national, and global, the library tradition of value-added service will be the CDRS hallmark. The service will use a database of member profiles to ensure that questions are distributed to the best member to provide the best answers in a timely fashion. A request manager processes and a database manages the flow and tracking of questions and answers. Many questions and answers are available in an archive database, maintaining full confidentiality, which also serves as a resource node on the CDRS network.

LESSON 7. FOCUS ON USERS' NEEDS: GET TO KNOW YOUR DIFFERENT AUDIENCES

It is very important to take users' perspectives into consideration throughout development. CPs are successful when both senior management and the most junior people in the organization or front-line employees find them essential to performing their daily routines. The needs of content creators should also be addressed: style guides and templates and lower-level technical denominators should make life easy for those who want to enter data and information into the organization's knowledge repository. To make the navigation easy, clear, and intuitive, an early decision should be the taxonomy (as discussed in Chapter 4).

The simplicity of the CP environment for user traction is fundamental for success. A number of initiatives can be undertaken in a CP program. Examples include making it very easy to post information (from a technical and process perspective); setting up quality controls and categorization to be completed automatically; setting up environments for people to establish rules for handling each posted document (who can read, edit, etc.); providing tools, such as efficient and target e-mail alerts linked to public folders; and other news prompts to real-time learning. Investing design time on simplification for valuable knowledge sources and working with end-users to understand further their unique personal or community requirements are more valuable to execution than posting a wealth of content that no one uses.

If people start finding ways around the CP or if the CP makes life more complicated than an offline alternative, the implementation does not achieve its goals. (How often do we learn about stories of employees that do not trust the "system" and keep parallel communication outlets and information sources?) Again, a CP is not useful when people cannot find or achieve what they want very easily. If other general information systems are in place (including more primitive intranets), try to use as much as possible the same nomenclature, taxonomy, and navigation. Many people, especially the most senior management, lack the time or patience to learn many changes. Irritated users could be a deterrent to fast wide adoption.

Ideally, users should use a minimal number of "clicks" and strolling to find the information they need. Hyperlinking should provide different paths for users to find the same information. The graphical design and layout should be clean (not crowded) and convey the overall tone of the company's brand position or support the identity of the specific community toward whom it is geared. Regardless of the application or component being implemented, it is highly advisable to get input from users and content creators very early on. Prototyping and usability tests are commonplace in the software industry. They can have a tremendous impact on the functionality and intuitiveness of the CP. CPs are not about putting every available piece of information and data on the Web. They should aim to make life easier, not more complex. People who have been responsible for developing sites (especially portals) have learned many lessons over the last few years.

Even if we suppose that employees have ample access to data sources, that the publishing process is in place and widely understood, and that employees are motivated to publish their learning, working processes, and sources of reliable information, it is still possible that the accumulated information and data have little value for the end-user. It is not unusual for large organizations, in their push to document and codify the knowledge of their employees, to end up creating information junkyards.[5, p. 104] To be valuable, the information on a CP must be focused clearly on satisfying users' needs. This requires paying attention to such things as format, language, background information, level of detail, timing of publishing, frequency and access to authors, and so forth. In large organizations, this also means that a great deal of attention needs to be paid to the different segments, or user groups, which may have distinct skills, interests, needs, and responsibilities.

To survive and thrive, commercially driven Internet portals must strive to deeply know their users and their use of the site, in order to continually improve the users' experience. Improvements may include, for example, dropping or enhancing content areas, integrating and hyperlinking different site areas, and pushing specific content according to one's profile. In contrast to commercially driven portals, it is unusual to find organizations that continuously improve their CPs based on the employees' satisfaction and the use of sophisticated tracking mechanisms (e.g., online surveys, log analysis, and data mining tools), using measurements that provide understanding about the ways in which different areas or segments of the CP are used. As the price of these tools becomes more accessible and CPs become more pervasive and an integral part of employees' working lives, we expect this lack of deep commitment to continuous measurement and improvement to change dramatically.

In summary, organizations in many fields need to develop the knowledge and skills traditionally reserved for media companies that deal with large audiences. This is especially true for large organizations, where business success depends ultimately on communicating and catering to the functional and emotional perspectives of thousands of employees and other external constituencies.

Given that knowledge management and successful CP implementation necessarily involve human motivation and action (as opposed to automation IT projects), companies should pursue their CP projects in tandem with efforts to train employees to best use the tools being released. Since the intangible benefits of a CP are often not easily measured in the short term, it is important that companies focus on "early wins" before moving on to new applications. The software industry, and in many cases companies' own IT departments, will strive to make companies believe that there is an urgent need to deploy all the "bells and whistles" as soon as possible. However, it is very important to remember that the technical challenges, although not trivial, pale in comparison with the need to have employees trained to properly use the new systems and change any existing destructive behavior regarding knowledge hoarding.

One area, for instance, where training is of utmost importance is content publishing. Although, the most sophisticated CMSs have many features that allow most employees to continue to work with their usual desktop applications (Word, Power Point, etc.), most employees do not have well-developed Web-publishing skills. Even professional writers, used to print, are finding the transition to the Web not an easy experience. This is not to say that everyone needs to learn HTML or another Web-publishing language. The Web, however, requires specific approaches regarding how text, design, and images are applied. At Allied Irish Bank, for instance, a strong emphasis is placed on training the staff to learn how to write for the Web, not the actual programming language but the style, length, and so on.

Finally, to really take users' perspectives into account, organizations must begin asking themselves a number of questions about their CPs. The list that follows, although incomplete, provides a good sample of questions about CPs that we believe should be posed frequently to employees to evaluate the users' perspective.

Usage:

- Do you check the CP daily and frequently?
- Is the CP the most important desktop application for you to perform your job?
- Is the CP your main source of documented information?
- In how many internal and external online communities do you participate?

Ease of use:

- Is the CP easy to navigate? Is it intuitive?

- Do you think your specific needs were taken into consideration in its design?
- Do you find documents or information on people mostly through search or through navigation?
- Does the CP operate at a good speed? Do you ever feel frustrated by its technical performance?
- Do you feel properly trained to maximize the features and applications available at the CP?
- Do you find the process of publishing content in the CP easy and transparent?

Quality and usefulness of content and applications:

- Does the CP help you find relevant, useful information?
- Do you feel the CP provides a good balance between internal and external sources of relevant information?
- Do you feel the CP provides a good balance between departmental, local office, and general corporate information?
- What areas of the CP do you find the most useful?
- Do the documents available through the CP present the right level of detail to be useful?
- Are the document sources properly identified?
- Do you find the information available in the CP accurate and up-to-date?
- Have you ever found duplicated, contradictory information in the CP?
- Are you notified of important information in a timely manner?
- What kind of information that you use frequently is unavailable or hard to find through the CP?
- What would you like to find in the CP that you are not finding yet?

Employees' contributions and commitments:

- Have you ever contributed or posted any information to the CP?
- Are your contributions to the CP (or knowledge repository) automatically accounted for?
- Do you feel others are using your contributions?
- Do you find it easy to upload and post relevant information that can be accessed through the CP?

- Do you feel other employees are committed to using the CP to share their knowledge?
- Do you feel senior management participates, uses, and supports the CP?
- Have you made suggestions about improving the CP? Is there a clear online channel to do so? Have you gotten any response?

Impact on establishing meaningful connections:

- Do you feel you have enough contextual or background information on other people (employees or third parties) before connecting with them?
- Has any other employee ever found you through the CP?

Impact on work:

- Do you feel the content of the CP is particularly relevant to your work?
- Are you receiving more relevant external information that affects your work?
- Do you feel better informed about what is happening in different parts of the organization?
- Has the CP helped you cut time spent on menial activities or looking for information?
- Has the CP helped you find other employees who helped you in your activities? Is it one of the most important sources for finding experts?

Impact on learning:

- Is the CP an important source of learning for you?
- Are the learning tools in the CP relevant to your career goals?
- Are the learning tools and content presented in a format that facilitates learning?

Ultimately, the true test of a CP is whether employees use the system and find that it provides them tools and information to help them do their jobs better. The tools for measuring usage are already very sophisticated after years of measuring the audience of client-facing Internet sites. As noted in a previous section on the users' perspective, the actual usefulness of a CP can be tracked through semi-quantitative surveys with users. The case of Alcatel is illustrative. Alcatel devotes significant resources to usage measurement and frequently applies the following four methodologies to gauge results:

1. *Transactional* (site statistics). It uses Accrue software to measure things such as page views, length of sessions, and most visited content areas.
2. *User modes.* It analyzes how different groups of users interact with the site on an ongoing basis.
3. *Satisfaction measurements.* It uses both online surveys and interactive real-time tools that pop up during users' sessions, depending on a set of predefined behaviors.
4. *In-depth free-flow interviews with groups of users.*

Like Alcatel, companies should aim to constantly measure user satisfaction and the value users get out of the corporate portal. Only in this way can companies be assured that they will reap all the benefits CPs can offer. Indeed, CP implementations never end. Once the initial rollout is finished, the planning for the next phase should be set in motion. This is not the nature of the technology but the business environment. CPs require constant improvement, based on changing business circumstances, reconfiguration of work arrangements, and user feedback.

LESSON 8. ONLINE COMMUNITIES REQUIRE CAREFUL PLANNING, INFRASTRUCTURE, AND ONGOING SUPPORT

With CPs and other integrated Web-based collaboration tools, the sophistication, user-friendliness, and mobility capabilities of online communities have been taken to a much higher level. This is not going unnoticed by leading knowledge-focused organizations. Various CP implementations are strongly leveraging communities of practice (CoPs) concepts such as ADC, Bain & Company, Eli Lilly, Siemens, Shell, and the World Bank. Our research found that, often when CoPs, and more specifically online communities, become an important KM strategy, KM leaders can work with either existing informal communities or communities purposely formed under the strong leadership of a few engaged domain experts. In general, successful CoPs relied on the following strategies:

- *Develop the rules of engagement for the community.* Moving to an online community is like moving to any new environment: People need to learn the rules of participation, the "netiquette" of the community (e.g., when and how to contribute). The leader(s) of the community should curb any activity that runs against these predetermined principles or does not belong within the context of the community (Context Integration, for instance, has a prominent section in its CP about appropriate behavior called Social Contract; Siemens has something very similar, Quality Guidelines). Indeed, it is clear that many organizations need to extend existing traditional "team dynamics training" to include "rules for online collaboration." In a way, virtual meetings and collaboration need as much attention as offline meetings and collaboration. Offline meetings can become unproductive due to a lack of planning or the poor collaboration skills of participants. The same can happen with online communities. Because of this, a number of new startup organizations provide training services on online meetings.

- *Allow both centralized and decentralized community creation.* Organizations deploying CPs may take two complementary approaches to integrate CoPs in a CP environment: They can provide predefined community environments (with targeted content, list of individuals, collaboration tools, and so forth) that are carefully, strategically, and centrally planned or they can provide the tools that allow like-minded individuals to easily set up their own communities. ADC, Eli Lilly, and Hill & Knowlton, for instance, adopted both strategies. They created a few core communities that were strategic (based on existing core competencies or target industries), such as the Health Community in Hill & Knowlton, and also implemented solutions that allow communities to be easily set up. At Hill & Knowlton, for instance, communities can be created by linking e-mail and messages in real time and distributing them to folders according to users' own interests (users can direct their messages and preselect topics they are interested in). At ADC, they provide "plug and use" capabilities that allow almost anyone to quickly set up communities with applications such as calendars, discussion forums, whiteboards, and notification.

- *Develop expertise maps and make sure users' profiles are updated.* Expertise maps may include databases with lists and descriptions of the competencies of individuals within or outside the organization. New tools can, for instance, mine unstructured information sources, such as e-mail to help locate experts or employees who are interested in a particular topic (Texaco uses this). Ultimately, these tools facilitate the sharing of tacit knowledge and the development of communities by allowing people to more quickly find and establish personal contact with one another. Thus, firms are clearly documenting subject matter expertise, where such expertise lies, how to reach out to the experts, what knowledge they have. The ability to rapidly talk to an expert, supported by the knowledge infrastructure of codified knowledge, can create a strong intellectual asset base for these companies. Detailed, accurate, updated, and meaningful profiles of users help spark connections and create the required level of trust among participants. People tend to collaborate more with others if the relationships become somewhat more personal. In some cases, it may even include photos and personal information such as hobbies (this is the case, for instance, at ADC, Eli Lilly, and Texaco).

- *Recognize different levels of participation.* The recognition and identification of the different levels of contribution (both quantitative and qualitative) of each individual are of particular importance to knowledge-exchange communities. Bain & Company and Hill & Knowlton are among the leading corporations that include features highlighting top contributions to their CPs.

- *Keep the users motivated.* Motivation involves alerting users of events, reminding them of the benefits of the community and the rules of engagement, and inviting those who are absent to contribute if they feel their participation could elevate the level of discussions. It is particularly important to greet, coach, and get new members up to speed. In the online environment, it is quite easy to have newcomers to come, check in a few times, and then never show up again.

- *Lead by example.* Frequent participation by community leaders in the activities of the community (especially if the leader is also a domain expert) certainly prompts higher levels of participation by members of the community at large. Bain & Company's successful CP implementation is attributed, to a great extent, to the many hours that its most senior partners dedicated, not only to planning the project, but also to contributing content.

- *Establish a sense of identity for the community.* A sense of identity can be created through the establishment of a clear purpose and specific goals and objectives for the community, as well as through the development and fostering of a sense of history for the community. Let new members know how the community got started, who was involved in the beginning. It is also important to create a strong messaging and branding effort (with adequate visual cues). This plays a critical role in reminding members of their affiliation and promoting the goals and values of the community. The discussion on branding the CP is particularly related to this concept of identity.
- *Promote the achievements of the community.* Savvy community leaders clearly understand that, in knowledge-creating or -sharing communities, participation depends highly on voluntary participation and members can only be inspired, not forced, to participate. Consequently, promoting the achievements of the community (online or offline) ignites existing members and acts as advertisements for potential participants who have not already joined the community. At Texaco's General Engineering Department, the leaders of the Best Practices–KM community take this task seriously. The community achievements (usually stories on how the sharing of best practices has saved the company millions of dollars) are easily found on the community intranet and heavily promoted through the company's newsletters, leaflets, internal magazines, and the like.
- *Create special events.* Schedule online and offline "gathering" events. These events create important milestones and a good reason for people to assemble and establish synchronous communications. Many communities also bring special guests from time to time to increase participation and attract new members. Siemens learned this lesson. After realizing that the "chat" functionality within its CP was hardly used, it started promoting worldwide events with senior executives and leading experts.
- *Monitor activity and satisfaction level.* Active leaders keep good statistics about the participation level of users, areas of the content most searched and visited, and frequency of contributions. They also conduct, from time to time, offline and online surveys to understand the needs and levels of satisfaction of members. With these kinds of data at hand, they can direct their actions to the root causes of occasional problems or diminishing participation. We increasingly see close monitoring in leading organizations that

implement CPs (e.g., ADC, Bain & Company, Context Integration, Siemens).

Based on these recommendations, it is clear that developing online communities and CoPs requires organizational support and careful planning of both the underlying technology and the supporting processes and roles. Given all these requirements and precedents for the development of successful online communities, it is no surprise that many communities start very small and grow organically. It is clear that it takes both technology and a dedicated group of individuals (leaders and a core group of active participants) to spur growth. An implication for organizations embarking on a CP initiative is that they should focus on communities and knowledge areas they are sure will have a significant competitive impact. Once initial success is achieved, rollout to the rest of the organization should be easier.

Lesson 9. Quality of Content Is More Important than Quantity of Content

If a CP is to focus on knowledge flow, it is very important that people trust the information they receive; otherwise, users quickly disregard the tool. One remarkable thing about the most successful CP implementations is their stringent focus on quality. In large organizations, in particular, collaborative portals can easily become a "dump" and quickly lose credibility if employees do not trust the information available in the system. It is very important, then, to develop a number of practices and policies focused on keeping only high-quality references within the CP. A few good strategies that we uncovered are the following:

- The rollout of the CP should progress steadily but carefully. It is important to develop a content strategy, before doing any development work.
- No CP implementation should proceed without a good understanding of how employees conduct their work and when and how they look for other sources of knowledge. The best way to do this is to focus on the key strategic business processes and knowledge domains before doing any development work. By asking the right questions, one can more easily understand the core knowledge sources: What is explicit? What is tacit? Is it internal or external? This, as we learned from our case studies,

results in less time and money spent on costly reworks and sets of portal taxonomies and structures. Finally, it is critical to develop a clear sense of priority: In large organizations, the impact of a CP implementation and the relevant sources of content can vary dramatically among different groups of employees.

- There should be a validation process so employees can trust the content accessed via the CP.
- Regardless of whether content is added to the knowledge base of a small CoP or published more widely for the organization or third parties (customers, partners, etc.), a validation process should be in place. Organizations such as Bain, Siemens, Context Integration, and Xerox developed well-marked paths to have new content (formal documents, tips, even recordings of discussion forums) to be reviewed by respected, trusted experts or committees.
- Build a content-capture process that is simple and useful.
- The success of a CP and of KM in general depends significantly more on the willingness and quality of knowledge creators and contributors than on knowledge seekers. A good part of the planning process in successful CP implementations was spent on developing guidelines and templates that made it very easy for all knowledge contributors to publish content online. Time is a scarce resource for knowledge workers, so streamlining and simplifying knowledge-capture processes was a key criterion for success.
- Timing is critical. Some of the most advanced companies realized that perfect timing adds significant value to knowledge. To be successful in highly competitive environments and better serve customers, employees need to be able to tap the organizational knowledge very rapidly. In some cases, it might be a matter of hours; in other circumstances, the requests may be treated as routine learning. This might be a straightforward concept, but most companies pay little attention to how perfect timing improves the quality of content. Perfect timing is achieved through a combination of personalized notification, quick content management processes, and the ability of employees to direct their requests for help according to different levels of priority (see the Context Integration case).
- Attention also needs to be given to information that employees cannot find on the CP.
- In addition to conducting periodical surveys, interviews, and focus groups, leading organizations such as Bain & Company

and Microsoft also monitor the searched terms frequently to develop a content strategy that meets changing employees' needs. According to Gytis Barzdukas, group product manager of Share-Point Portal Server at Microsoft, this review includes a biweekly formal meeting where senior managers and directors from different areas of Microsoft come together to set priorities for the ongoing development of Microsoft's own internal CP.

- Easy feedback mechanisms guarantee continuous improvement of content.
- Many teams in charge of CP implementations realized early on that knowledge grows as it is applied or reused. Also, available content may not always be 100% right. Consequently these companies developed easy mechanisms for employees to add comments to posted information on CPs. At Bain & Company and Mobistar, every page published on the CP has a direct link for feedback back to authors or content owners. By these mechanisms, users can easily add value to the original documents, keep the knowledge base updated and relevant, and quickly exclude references that have low value.
- Weed out bad content.
- As the cases of Nortel and Bank of Montreal showed, migrating to a centralized content is a tremendous challenge in large organizations. Many of these organizations are faced with the proliferation of intranet websites and other KM applications that, until recently, were managed with high degrees of autonomy. However, the centralization process, in addition to making access much easier, can also be used to reduce content duplication (at Motorola, they talked about 50% reduction in content volume; at Cable & Wireless, Robert Nuttall, VP of Internal Communications, said in a recent conference that the company got rid of 75% of "bad" content after implementing a centralized CP), weed out outdated content, and stimulate the standardization of processes based on best practices (see the Bank of Montreal case).

LESSON 10. THE CORPORATE PORTAL SHOULD REDUCE INFORMATION OVERLOAD AND SIMPLIFY ACCESS TO INFORMATION, TEMPLATES, AND EXPERTISE FROM WITHIN AND OUTSIDE AN ORGANIZATION

Many of the organizations in our study conducted a number of surveys with employees to understand what kind of information they actually needed to perform their jobs before engaging in a broader CP initiative. Particularly in large organizations, which depend highly on structured processes, employees are not concerned about high-level strategic information. They want, first and foremost, information and knowledge to simplify their job. Besides, information overload is a significant problem in almost every organization. The ability to speed up information exchange via e-mail, Internet portals, and other channel sources continues to be a productivity challenge in organizations. Finding pathways to simplify employee and customer communication processes, via CPs, is a powerful mode for productivity and organizational reach effectiveness. Our research demonstrates that a successful CP deployment makes life simpler for employees. As employees continue to request personalized information, "My Pages" will eventually become how people access their corporate know-how.

To reduce overload, many CPs allow employees to preselect the newsletters or notices they really want and reduce e-mail broadcasting (employees' self-defense mechanism of copying as many people as possible on e-mail). By posting information or questions via CPs, employees receive feedback or responses according to other peoples' expertise, interest, and availability. Many companies, however, do not yet focus on individual personalization, as in the case of mass-market portals. Instead, they focus on "communities," as a kind of prepersonalization. This strategy is chosen because employees might not use the portal as much if they need to understand all the data sources and "gadgets" that would make sense for them.

Many companies have learned that search engines can be a red herring. People tend not to use search very often; therefore it is important to make sure the directory is really good. It is also important to install notification services that are community related to draw peoples' attention to the portal: "We know that you are part of this community and that you are interested in this content. It has been updated." It is important to understand how employees conduct their work and when and how they look for other sources of knowledge. It is advisable to do a careful "audit" of each business process and knowledge domain before doing any development work. The result of the audit process becomes a set of portal taxonomies and structures that closely fit an organization's business and users' needs. It also means less time and money spent on costly reworks.

Codification efforts may also become actionable platforms. Employees who want to reuse the codified knowledge benefit from finding automated links to people, information, and templates at each step in the process. Some of the most interesting CPs include a number of actionable and knowledge-rich work flows. For example, the Bank of Montreal focuses its efforts on sales and some critical business processes, linking knowledge access throughout the work process exchange steps to support learning and ongoing knowledge creation and capture. Bain & Company, on the other hand, includes a number of simulation applications that include workable templates consultants can immediately apply to their cases.

LESSON 11. SET PRIORITIES FOR THE INTEGRATION OF INFORMATION TECHNOLOGY APPLICATIONS

It is particularly important to learn how to set priorities. Large corporations have so many content areas and applications that can be built into the portal that it can become unproductive and overwhelming if they are launched at the same time. Our advice is to focus initially on a combination of applications that the employees really want and those that deliver the highest business impact and get immediate senior management attention.

The other critical aspect related to the implementation of CPs is locking the scope for each phase of development. Scope "creep," or frequent changes to scope, is usually the result of poor gathering of requirements and unclear business goals. Although the most recent CP platforms (as offered by SAP Portals, IBM, Oracle, Plumtree, Viador, or Microsoft) make large-scale, simultaneous rollouts of a number of applications easier, organizations must be careful to not lose sight of the human aspects and ultimate business goals they set for the project in the first place. As argued elsewhere in this book, IT investments are not necessarily related to better business performance. Do not rush the process.

By following this strategy, organizations also are likely to minimize their IT expenses. Despite the sophistication of many CPs, they do not have to be costly. There is no major secret to keeping CP costs in check. The keys are to concentrate on functionality that really adds value to the business; avoid costly "bells and whistles"; leverage existing data, systems, and infrastructure; and roll out applications incrementally. In many cases, as we learned with Bank of Montreal, the KM team has even discovered opportunities to further leverage existing applications for improved collaboration and knowledge sharing.

It is particularly important to focus on specific audiences and specific clusters of content that have depth or are considered strategic. Most organizations in our research proceeded with small launches, and only after careful analysis of how work is conducted and how knowledge is shared and created. All were intensely focused on developing solutions that immediately added value and created "stickiness," to return end-users to the environment.

We also learned that, in KM-related efforts, rapid development and proof of concept are more effective than "big picture" projects. The Internet environment, with its underlying open architecture and standards, allows the rapid development of proof of concepts and implementation of modular solutions. This, in turn, allows for fast tangible results and increased support and visibility for KM initiatives. While, as in the cases of Bank of Montreal and Eli Lilly, the implementation teams believe that infrastructure and carefully designed solutions are critical to long-term sustainability, their primary focus is on the generation of value to the enterprise and speed to market.

Lesson 12. Develop a Due Diligence Process to Select the Corporate Portal Platform

KM-related and CP technology is changing rapidly and there are still too many players in this market (see Appendix A), so it is important to conduct a detailed product and company analysis. After all, corporate portals are becoming a core platform (or piece of IT infrastructure) for the "digitalization" of organizations. As with many other IT choices, it is clear that the cost/benefit ratio also plays a key role. The prices of the portal platforms are not necessarily easy to compare, however, because different vendors use different schemes to charge for the software. Some charge license fees based on the number of users or seats, others on the number of servers, and a few based on site traffic. In addition to the initial costs, it is important to develop a sense for the costs of associated hardware and annual maintenance. Consequently, to have a clear picture of the evolution of costs, it is important to elaborate a few forecasts, based on company-specific expected usage of the portal.

In addition to the key features related to presentation, personalization, search, taxonomy, content management, and online communities (discussed in the previous chapter), many technical criteria can be used to select a CP platform. Based on the review of the software market at the end of 2001, in Appendix B, we provide a fairly long list of technical questions that can be useful when selecting a CP platform. The questions are organized around the following seven categories:

1. Integration of applications and components.
2. Development environment.
3. Management, maintenance, and monitoring.
4. Systems architecture.
5. Performance.
6. Security.
7. Vendor's future and platform evolution.

In the end, organizations should develop their own requirement lists, group them into a number of categories, and judge which ones are most relevant. They should then compare vendors' offerings and prices against the selected criteria. Table 5-2 provides a simple yet

Table 5-2 *Illustrative Framework for Selecting CP Platforms*

Criteria for Selection	Importance	Vendor A	Vendor B	Vendor C
Advanced personalization	Very high	Y	N	P
Integration of outlook (e-mail)	High	Y	P	N
Easy integration with existing CRM application	High	P	Y	P
Ability to search unstructured documents	Medium	Y	P	N
Easy integration with existing document management system	Medium	Y	Y	N
Highly scalable	Medium	P	Y	P
Advanced application for measuring and reporting traffic and usage of portal	Medium	Y	P	P
Low level of custom development	Low	N	Y	Y
Quality and number of system integrators supporting the platform	Low	N	Y	Y

Y, meets the needs; P, partially meets the needs; N, does not meet the needs.

good framework for the selection of a vendor's platform (the criteria, values, and list of vendors are only illustrative). A final suggestion is that, after the initial list of vendors is narrowed down to just a few, and if time and budget allow, ask vendors for prototypes (despite similar claims from vendors, the differences in response time and overall delivery can vary greatly).

CONCLUDING NOTE

These twelve lessons clearly demonstrate that, while CPs may provide significant benefits to organizations, they require much more than technology to succeed. By providing powerful tools that can significantly affect how information and knowledge flow within and across organizations, CPs are bound to profoundly alter existing power structures, the use and ownership of intellectual capital, and ultimately, an organization's business model. Therefore, we strongly recommend that anyone leading CP efforts make sure that the human, cultural, and social aspects are taken into consideration from the outset. The cases described in Part II of this book provide further examples of how these issues have been addressed by leading organizations.

REFERENCES

1. Fukuyama, F. *Trust: The Social Virtues and the Creation of Prosperity.* New York: The Free Press, 1996:358.
2. Gates, W.H. (with C. Hemingway). *Business @ the Speed of Thought: Using a Digital Nervous System.* New York: Warner Books, 1999:260.
3. Davenport, T. Putting the "I" in information technology, FP Mastering. *National Post.* May 15, 2001.
4. Davenport, T, Pusak, L. *Working Knowledge: How Organizations Manage What They Know.* Boston: Harvard Business School Press, 1998.
5. McDermott, R. Why information technology inspired but cannot deliver knowledge management. *California Management Review.* 41, no. 4(Summer 1999).
6. Available at http://www.loc.gov/rr/digiref, June 22, 2001.

6

CONCLUDING REMARKS

We began this book with a quick peek into the future and explored a number of emerging organizational and business models by leading companies. We now return to the beginning of our personal journey writing this book—the innovative practices of the organizations profiled in this book. We believe that the case stories described throughout this book (particularly in Part II) provide a unique contribution to business management, as they are grounded in the practice of innovative organizations. The cases are current and, at the same time, forward looking. If you skipped a few of the previous chapters and delved directly into the case studies, we don't blame you. This book was not written to be read, necessarily, in the sequence defined by us. In fact, we expect you to have moved back and forth between theory and practice. We believe learning is a multidimensional experience and not meant to be a linear—this was the approach of our book.

Innovation involves the transformation of a knowledge-based idea and turns it into action. Knowledge is the core DNA of innovation. Without knowledge, innovation is not fostered. Innovation and knowledge transformation can be in the form of a new marketable product or service, a new or improved business process, or a new method of social service. As Theodore Levitt of the *Harvard Business Review* stated, "Innovation is the vital spark of all man-made change, improvement and progress." Too often, however, this resource is irretrievably squandered, threatening the financial viability of our organizations as well as the health and well-being of employees, customers, suppliers, and community members.

Embarking on an enterprise of CP initiative takes courage; the journey is broad and crosses many organizational boundaries and barriers of resistance. To be successful takes focused leadership as the prevailing guiding light and important changes in processes (new activities, policies, metrics), organizational structures (new jobs, roles, and rewards), and people's dimensions (skills, behavior, and motivations). Throughout this book, we describe the experiences of a number of Fortune 500 and mid-sized companies. Their personal stories reveal rich insights and lessons learned for others to learn from.

Like many business strategists, we could rapidly define a few business models or frameworks to shine a path for our readers. However, such an approach would mean we are clairvoyants, who know who our readers are and how KM and CP solutions should be implemented in their unique contexts. A key lesson of this book is that managing knowledge capabilities requires a deep understanding of corporate strategy, work practices, sources of information and knowledge, relevant technologies, and the learning and motivational factors of different stakeholder groups within the enterprise. In summary, an effective KM and CP strategy requires that organizations make a focused effort to understand how "knowledge" capability affects their processes, business models, and people within their enterprises.

We believe it is difficult to remain competitive in industries that demand rapid cycles of knowledge creation, diffusion, and usage without highly advanced digital collaboration tools. We describe a number of these tools in the preceding chapters, particularly Chapter 4. In the cases ahead, readers can learn how leading organizations apply Web-based collaboration tools (and, in a number of cases, sophisticated corporate portal technologies) for effective leverage of their corporate know-how.

An indirect and important consequence of the speed of knowledge flow is that organizations better recognize (and measure) the contribution of different organization areas, both internally and for clients. We observed how internally driven KM practices can modify organizational and business models, particularly when enterprises successfully articulate an integrated approach for the development of their B-to-E, B-to-C, and B-to-B corporate portals. As discussed in this book, the technologies that support corporate portals have evolved dramatically over the last few years. However, successful CP implementation requires much more than technology. Organizations will not see a noticeable improvement of their competitive edge until senior management realizes that KM and CP projects produce significant results only when there is clear organizational alignment, the governance of the portal is treated as a strategic issue, a strong focus is placed on the quality and validation of information, processes and rewards are continually reviewed and modified, and the employees and external stakeholders willfully collaborate and experience "personalized value" to enrich online interactions to solve business and personal needs.

Many key lessons were learned throughout the case stories and interview research. Perhaps the compelling factors to take away from this book are a few key messages:

1. The meaning of *context* formed by interactions between the organization and the outside world is very important to understand how knowledge flow and innovation occur. While it may appear obvious that employees, customers, suppliers, and competitors interact daily in one form or another, the opportunity to develop streamlined ways of connecting and simplifying business processes to enhance business collaboration—hence, increasing knowledge flow—has never been more important in the Networked Era.

2. We already stressed leadership and the importance for visible signs throughout a CP implementation. In the majority of cases, the leaders could see the possibilities of how the future would unfold as a result of having a CP. They were willing to put business strategies in place to help identify opportunities to pave a path for future success. They reached actively into their organizations to empower the people and removed roadblocks to ensure the vision imperative would become a reality.

3. Organization culture is perhaps the biggest playing field to either enable or inhibit CPs. Organizations that are empowering, flexible, cope with ambiguity, encourage risk taking, support and nurture knowledge sharing, celebrate success, foster collaboration across the enterprise, and encourage innovation have a healthier organizational climate to be more innovative and successful with CPs.

4. We cannot emphasize enough that the soul of knowledge flow resides in *people*. Nothing happens without people—they are the

unique personality and DNA of an organization. Their collective beliefs, behaviors, and relationship networks enable day-to-day execution. Organizations implementing CPs need to focus squarely on the needs of the different stakeholder groups throughout the enterprise to be successful.

This book strives to highlight the need and value of a social-technical approach for implementing CPs. A balanced approach to business strategy, people, technology, and organizational considerations is demonstrated throughout the case stories. However, each company's experiences with CPs have different strengths and context. Some have a very conceptual foundation; others demonstrate the use of advanced technologies; while still others are valuable not for what they have achieved to date but for the visions championed by their leaders.

Due to the incredible advances in Internet-based collaborative technologies and the growing impact of the knowledge resource, we are seeing significant transformations in organizational and business models. The companies highlighted in this book recognize that they are, with different degrees of success and emphasis, at the frontier where Internet-based technologies, knowledge management, and new collaborative business models meet. They may not have yet implemented a sophisticated corporate portal infrastructure, but all have shown a deep understanding of the power of a central digital system to facilitate access to information and knowledge exchange.

We hope, as you read this book, you are inspired by the "spirit of the frontier." At the frontier, there are no established rules, clearly marked paths, or perfect solutions. The best one can do is to learn how to use intuition calibrated by previous experiences, learn quickly from others, and venture onto a few paths that few have traveled before.

The organizations depicted have this spirit of the frontier. We believe they are not only creating value for their shareholders through advanced KM processes and use of CP technologies but help to improve the practice of KM, the emerging, sometimes controversial, but clearly indispensable discipline of the Networked and Knowledge Era.

PART II

DETAILED CASE STUDIES

7

ADC Telecommunications Inc., the Broadband Company

CP/KM Experts

John Beattie, VP information services
Lynn Harrison, director of corporate applications
Cory Garlough, director, knowledge management and training

Shaun Hills, knowledge broker for the iPoint Community
Dan McMullen, applications manager

Background

ADC Telecommunications is a leading global supplier of equipment
and software for telecommunications, cable television, broadcast,
wireless, and enterprise networks. The company was founded in 1935
in Eden Prairie, Minnesota, where it still has its corporate headquarters. The company has annual sales exceeding $2 billion, close to
14,000 employees worldwide, and market capitalization of $6 billion,
in July 2001. ADC has sales, manufacturing, and development offices
in more than 35 countries and sells to over 130 countries. ADC's
main manufacturing facilities are located in the United States, Scot-
land, Mexico, and China.

ADC serves its customers through two main business units: the
Broadband Infrastructure and Access (BIA) and Integrated Solutions
(IS) organizations. These two organizations service all types of broadband communications providers, through a combination of equipment, software, and professional services. The company has recently
focused on the following four technologies: DSL, IP cable, optics, and
software. Its portfolio also includes fiber, copper and wireless connectivity products, and systems integration services.

The software division of the Integrated Solutions organization led
the development of the corporate portal.

The Catalyst, Goals, and Driving Factors

The direction to implement a corporate portal came straight from
Larry Ford, president of the Integrated Solutions organization. Larry
had prior exposure to corporate portals, as he used to work with
Information Advantage, a corporate portal provider, prior to that
company being acquired by Sterling Software. Larry had a clear
vision of the value of corporate portals and their potential "business
reach." He requested a very quick implementation. Given the urgency
of the request, Lynn Harrison took only 1 week to find out who the
key CP vendors were and rapidly decided to go with Plumtree Software, Inc. The main reasons for her decision were that Plumtree had
the highest mind share in the industry and its customer service was
very responsive.

The only other collaboration solutions available in the software division, at the time, included the intranet, Lotus/Domino databases, and discussion solutions. The company president, however, wanted a new platform that would allow stronger collaboration among employees, especially in the R&D department, and provide global access to the knowledge base of recently acquired companies.

In addition to these initial reasons, the ADC portal implementation had a number of primary and secondary goals (specified P, primary goal; S, secondary goal; or N, not relevant).

Communication tool (top down and bottom up):

(P) Improve communication of vision and knowledge strategy.

(N) Improve communication of company values.

(P) Keep the organization alert.

(S) Engage customers and community at large.

(S) Divulge results more broadly and promote systemic analysis.

(P) Facilitate bottom-up communication.

(N) Make it easy for employees to suggest improvements to management.

Push information and knowledge to employees:

(P) Capture, organize, and distribute codified knowledge (e.g., database access).

(P) Improve access to external sources of information and knowledge.

(S) Improve decision making.

(N) Empower front-line employees.

Improve reuse of knowledge:

(S) Develop expertise maps (uncover existing knowledge).

(N) Map and measure intangible assets.

(P) Facilitate search of previously developed knowledge.

Foster collaboration:

(P) Increase collaboration among different functions of the organization.

(P) Increase collaboration among different locations of the organization.

(P) Improve overall knowledge sharing.

(P) Support the development of communities of practice.

(N) Increase connections not related to work.

Improve human capital management:

(N) Improve hiring.

(N) Improve internal mobility and deployment of existing employees.

(N) Integrate temporary and outside human resources and expertise.

(N) Improve training and acquisition of skills.

(S) Get new employees up to speed very quickly.

(N) Reduce time spent on menial activities.

(N) Improve employee retention.

(N) Facilitate work and integration of telecommuters.

Improve relationship with external stakeholders and increase information flow:

(S) Improve information exchange with suppliers, partners, and customers.

(N) Capture customer information.

(S) Improve customer satisfaction.

(S) Reduce sales costs.

(N) Reduce customer service costs.

ORGANIZATIONAL SUPPORT

In addition to the initial mandate established by the president, the implementation of the portal relied on a number of senior executives who agreed to sponsor the initiative and become "content owners" of specific areas of the site. Human Resources was the first area that made the commitment. In Lynn's words, "We never had sponsorship problems from the top." In reality, since the portal implementation started, the company has been suffering from a severe downturn in the telecom market with a significant reduction in personnel, so the company leadership has focused its energy mostly on other projects. In this scenario, the portal implementation is moving forward through the initiative of the CP leaders at the divisional level, in the ISG Software organization.

John Beattie, VP information services, has more than 20 years of IT experience and always has been interested in collaborative software. His early interests began in deploying e-mail solutions at Amoco and working with Lotus Notes. Cory Garlough, director of knowledge management and training, has experience in the development of online tools for sales training, which led to an academic and practical interest in KM. Lynn, director of corporate applications, has a strong software development background and is a driving force behind the portal implementation. She is in charge of tools, processes, and culture-related aspects. This is the core team. It is supported by an extended team that maintains specific areas of the sites across the regions and departments. This extended team includes another five or six people in the Eden Prairie headquarters. Lynn's own team dedicated to collaboration solutions includes another four people (one Web master, one developer, one business analyst, and one person in charge of the document management system—more on this system later). The most successful communities, such as R&D and her (the HR community), have dedicated significant effort to the evolution and management of the portal.

Implementation Journey

Phase 1 (July 2000): Mandate, Product Selection, and Implementation of Global Pilot Project

- Selection of product took 1 week. Implementation of first pilot version took only 2 weeks.
- It involved 50 users over 2 months, from five global locations: Brisbane, Australia; Galway, Ireland; Edmonton and Toronto, Canada; and Minnetonka, Minnesota.
- Software administrators were trained for 3 full days.
- HR was the functional area that "owned" this first rollout.
- The initial portal focused on establishing an organized taxonomy and creating the links to existing content that people care a lot about (including the Internet, document management systems, HTML, and discussion databases).

- The project team tested the performance of the system and paid very close attention to the statistics that showed which areas of the site were really popular.

Phase 2 (September 2000): Global Rollout of Plumtree Corporate Portal 3.5

- The system went live with 3000 users but did not force the portal as the default page in browsers.
- The new version included some key crawlers for the intranets and document management system.
- A number of Plumtree Gadget Web Services linking to back-end applications were deployed.
- An internal marketing campaign was put in place.
- The project leaders were looking for buy-in for the project, not forced acceptance by the users. Unfortunately not many people paid attention: Most employees continued to go directly to their usual intranet pages.

Phase 3 (February 2001): Global Rollout of Plumtree Corporate Portal 4.0

- The key new feature was the creation of communities of practice areas (eHR, Product Development, Sales, etc.) and the profile system, late in the summer.
- The buy-in policy was changed and the intranet home pages started to migrate into portal communities. Users were forced to go through the portal to reach previous content in the intranets.
- The company started promoting the use of the portal more heavily, including offline communications (e.g., posters) marking key improvements of the portal (new functionality or added content). During those periods of strong internal communications, the volume of traffic in the site grew very rapidly.
- By June 2001, traffic reached 10,000 hits/day.
- The plan is to shut down the intranet home pages, as soon as all communities are integrated into the portal.

CORPORATE PORTAL ENVIRONMENT

The ADC corporate portal home page (shown in Figure 7-1) is the gateway to a number of different applications and communities. It in-

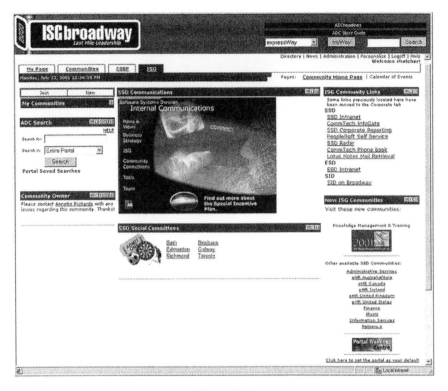

Figure 7-1
ADC Corporate Portal Home Page

cludes a section dedicated to communications from senior management, basic search functionality, e-learning applications, access to collaboration databases, Domino-Document Management Systems, a yellow page application, various community pages, and a personalized section called "My Pages."

A Verity search engine currently powers the portal. The engine crawls all applications and databases that are linked to the portal. The user can restrict the search to specific portal sections.

Plumtree is the corporate portal solution that has been adopted. The portal architecture (Figure 7-2) is quite straightforward. It includes one server for development and multiple servers for production. For performance reasons, users' browsers still connect to local servers for accessing more "heavy-duty" content and applications, such as the Domino-Document Management Systems (DMS) that are replicated in every location. The centralized portal Web server links and calls other key centralized servers: an Oracle database, a job server for crawling

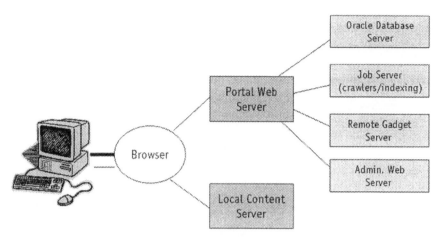

Figure 7-2
Portal Technical Architecture (Source: ADC)

and indexing documents, a remote gadget server, and a separate administration server.

Through the portal, most employees can access two other important repositories/KM tools based on a Lotus/Domino platform, a document management system, and discussion databases:

- The DMS has been widely adopted in the software organization and is tied to the full cycle of the sales process, from statement of work, contract, specific code development, and so forth. According to Lynn, "there's a lot of cut and paste" or in KM words, "knowledge reuse." By the end of August 2001, it included over 20,000 documents with nearly 2000 new documents being added every month.

- The collaboration application includes more than 100 databases. These databases are Web-accessible and can, therefore, be used by Exchange users as well. Those databases vary from very technical community discussion groups to more personal bulletin-board databases.

The cornerstone of the portal and the main attraction for employees revolve around the communities that have been created. The R&D community, called iPoint, and the HR community, called her, are the most visited ones (see below). The eHR community has, in fact, been split into various eHR communities, focused on specific locations (e.g., Canada, Ireland, etc.). Both communities had strong support from their functional leaders.

The iPoint community is strongly supported by senior R&D managers. Indeed, a core group of three people working full time and two working part time has been designated to act as knowledge organizers, knowledge brokers, and coaches of R&D personnel. Although this group uploads the content (within 24 hours, if required), the R&D personnel are responsible for keeping the content up-to-date and maintaining the overall accuracy and relevance of specific content areas. This team also makes sure that *all* employees, even those from other areas of the company, receive quick personal responses if they do not find the required information at the iPoint site (Figure 7-3). In particular, for a subset of users (from Sales and application consultant teams), a structured feedback application is available. This application, called iPointExpert, allows rapid responses to very detailed questions. According to Shaun Hills, who is responsible for the implementation and

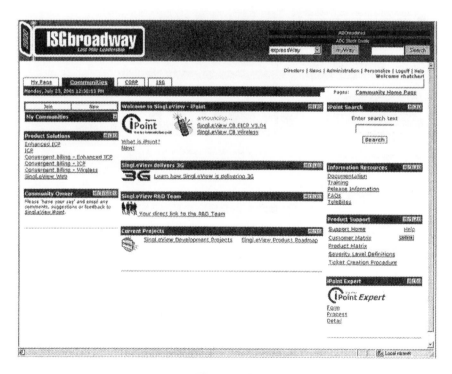

Figure 7-3
iPoint Community

management of the application, this is a good example of how, despite the enhanced technical platform, the "human factor" strongly affects the knowledge transfer process.

The eHR community has an enthusiastic leader in the person of Annette Richards, who works in close coordination with Lynn Harrison. Another person who has contributed to the development of this community is Cory Garlough. Not only is he a strong believer in KM but also an early adopter of online training. The eHR community (Figure 7-4) includes Gadget Web Services for automated self-services applications (e.g., benefits, vacation, and travel) and a number of other content areas associated with the improvement of human talent. For instance, it includes a section for new employees to learn about ADC and get up to speed more quickly and another one on training opportunities. Because of different laws and country-specific HR policies, the eHR community is customized for each different location where the software organization has offices.

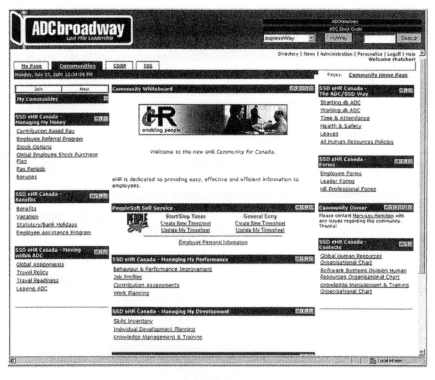

Figure 7-4
eHR Community

Through a specially developed application, the Profile Systems, employees are also encouraged to keep their skills inventory up-to-date. As in the case of the iPoint community, the eHR community has a prominent section for employees to ask questions and send feedback. Questions are answered very quickly, so employees know that they are interacting with a live community.

METRICS

The KM team believes that the value of collaboration cannot be measured by simple statistics. The attitude at ADC is refreshing, as the CP champions believe "it requires a leap of faith." Their efforts are justified, based on the anecdotal evidence of how people find and use information and connect with other people. The team documents success stories, as these help create the organizational memory to introduce new employees to the value and convert the late adopters. These stories can ripple through the organization, creating new conversations and, in time, becoming folklore, reinforcing that the sustaining belief system is aligned.

Ultimately, ADC's senior leadership is more interested in how the portal influences the flow of knowledge in the organization and creates new value for executing business outcomes.

This is not to say that they are not paying close attention to who are the users and who rarely checks the portal. They also have daily detailed information on which content areas and applications are popular and which ones are not. Lynn, particularly, is interested in this information. Based on it, she discusses new development or training needs. The Plumtree platform provides a few Gadget Web Services to collect standard metrics such as top publications, top gadgets, top folders, top crawlers, least popular, number of hits, and so on. ADC developed a few other Gadget Web Services for measurement (such as the ones for measuring individual and location participation).

KEY LESSONS LEARNED

Despite its recency, many lessons can be learned from the ADC implementation.

Lesson 1. Focus on Passionate Early Adopters

Start the implementation in areas of the company where people are most passionate about it. At ADC, R&D was the key area top management focused on, but the portal and communities implementation started in HR and other areas where strong supporters were found. In Lynn's words, "Find the communities and keep them interested."

Lesson 2. Strike a Balance between Applications That Employees Really Want and Those the Organization Needs

To drive employees to the portal environment, it is important to focus on the applications they want, such as the profile system, and those they need frequently, such as "time entry" applications. This makes the rollout of the portal friendlier and immediately useful for employees.

Lesson 3. Include a Human Dimension to the Functioning of Communities

The experience of the R&D community has shown that users highly appreciate the role played by knowledge brokers. They add a human dimension to the portal. This is similar to the traditional experience of call centers. Clients appreciate the option of having many points of contact. Some gladly use self-service information tools, while others feel a lot more comfortable with the idea that "someone is listening."

Lesson 4. Search Engines Can Be a Red Herring

People tend not to use search very often; therefore, it is important to make sure the directory is really good. It is also important to install notification services that are community related, to draw employees' attention to the portal: "We know that you are part of this community and that you are interested in this content. It has been updated." Many employees tend to go directly to their community's page. This has reinforced a core idea the CP team espouses: "The value of communities of practice."

Lesson 5. "My Pages" Will Eventually Become How People Get Their Information

Full personalization is installed and anyone can fully personalize his or her pages. The team, however, has not promoted this functionality to employees. Instead, they focus on the "communities" as a kind of pre-personalization. This strategy was chosen because employees might not have used the portal as much if they needed to understand all the data sources and Gadget Web Services that would make sense for them.

Lesson 6. The Culture Is the "Big" Thing

Although ADC is a high-tech company with many savvy Internet users and developers, the project leaders found it necessary to pay a lot of attention to training both users and employees responsible for maintenance of specific content areas. According to Lynn, "The implementation is really plug and play to do the basics. A knowledge-sharing culture is the big thing."

Lesson 7. The Portal Already Helps Reduce Silos in the Organization

Not only do users find the information they need more easily, but they are also "running into" information from others areas. Shaun Hills, the "knowledge broker" from the R&D community, told us that he has often heard from a few employees in R&D that, since the portal implementation, they know more about the projects and activities of other groups within their own department.

Lesson 8. Promote the Portal

In tandem with the internal communications department, Lynn made sure that, when significant new content sections or applications were linked or uploaded to the portal, an offline and online internal campaign promoted the change. Users usually respond with increased traffic to the portal.

Lesson 9. Make the Transition to the Portal as Familiar as Possible

If other general information systems are in place (including more primitive intranets), try as much as possible to use the same nomenclature, taxonomy, and navigation. Many people, especially the most senior management, may not have the time or patience to learn many changes. Irritated users could be a deterrent to fast, wide adoption. Lynn says that she learned that "People are passionate about their tools in the software world." Consequently, the portal implementation team left the content development and publication processes un-changed. They focused, instead, on changing how people get to the in-formation to maximize initial buy-in and efficiency.

Lesson 10. Pay Attention to the Operational Performance of the Portal

The company made maintaining high-speed access to the portal's con-tent and applications a priority. In addition to replicating some content in local servers (e.g., content from the document management system), the team in charge of the portal also modified the portal when it recog-nized that not all "gadgets" on the portal (e.g., a clock-time image and a stock ticker) needed to be streaming continuously and that several banners on the portal reduced the speed of access considerably. The plan is to replicate some of the "gadgets" on local servers in the future. All these initiatives demonstrate the company's focus on addressing the needs of the user and the functionality of the portal (as opposed to adding more "bells and whistles" or containing additional marginal costs). The team is clearly conscious that mediocre performance of the portal can alienate a significant percentage of users.

Lesson 11. Be Ready to Motivate and Help People, Principally Those Responsible for Updating the Content of the Portal

The implementation team believes that it should have held far more training (and persuasion) sessions with front-line employees and man-agers. In particular, they feel that, during these sessions, they should communicate more effectively about how the portal benefits employ-ees. In hindsight, it is clear to them that not all areas in the company are used to publishing and accessing information on the intranet. Consequently, a few communities and individuals responsible for spe-cific content areas on the portal did not fully appreciate the need to keep their information up-to-date. To prevent and overcome these problems, it is important for CP implementation teams to pay close attention to the frequency with which the content of different areas is updated, to help people understand the functionality of the portal from the very beginning, and to create an environment of tighter dis-cipline when it comes to content publishing.

Lesson 12. The Ability to Easily Create Decentralized Communities Is a Very Important Feature

It is important to ensure that even users with limited IT knowledge can easily and quickly create their own communities and include features such as links, calendar, document files, notification signals, whiteboards, discussion forums, and task lists. Plug and use features, which are specifically designed to make it simple for people to create online communities, are essential tools for encouraging online collaboration.

Future Directions

In the very near future, due to current budget restrictions, the company will focus on incremental improvements of the portal. One priority is to implement the publication feature of the portal, so employees can sign up to be notified whenever new documents that meet their selection criteria are added to the portal. This could include documents from the portal itself, the Web, or other linked systems, such as the document management system or Lotus Notes databases. The company is also discussing the possibility of adding e-incentives. The e-incentives would depend on employees' contributions to the growth of "valuable" documents to the many databases linked to the portal. The e-incentives may be exchanged, for example, for stock options.

The KM leaders at ADC also believe that automated tools for mapping tacit knowledge are likely to be more effective at uncovering knowledge existing in employees' heads than voluntary skill inventory tools that need direct input from each employee. The experience so far with applications where each employee needs to proactively update his or her profile has not been very successful. In Lynn's words, "Many people have uploaded a lot about their personal hobbies but have not yet explained what they do in the job." The software organization is currently evaluating software provided by AskMe and Tacit.

Lynn also feels that, for the portal to be even more successful, ADC must implement a lot more Gadget Web Services linking to back-end systems, such as SAP. Both issues are in the agenda for the future, and she believes that they may have a significant impact on use of the portal. The ultimate goal is to reach a point where anything one needs will be found through the portal. Many native applications will coexist with the portal for a long time, but the portal will be the gateway to all relevant information and back-end applications. The other key long-term goal is to integrate partners and customers through the portal. This is done presently only through specially set up extranets for a few partners. The initiative will probably be driven initially by the training department, which already uses an online application, such as SameTime from Lotus, for training. Over time, the idea is to integrate the KM applications with all back-end and e-business applications, developing a collaborative e-commerce platform. This is still in its infancy, but Lynn Harrison is already participating in some corporate forums where these ideas are being discussed.

The portal will certainly expand to the manufacturing division as well and likely need new kinds of solutions, such as kiosks, since most employees at this other division (with close to 9000 employees) have no computer access.

Asked about more long-term future initiatives, Lynn agrees that there still are far more complex applications to operationalize and integrate into the portal than the currently deployed initiatives. She also agrees that, as the confidence and value of the corporate portal extend into the ADC enterprise, the opportunity to champion more complex and value-laden business processes is the direction for exploration and value creation.

CLOSING PERSPECTIVES

Lynn feels that the CP implementation has been fairly successful. The cost/benefit ratio has indeed been positive, and there are many anecdotes about new connections being made and employees able to find information more easily. The project has been embraced particularly by the more technical staff and developers who are more used to the Web/portal environment. As more applications geared toward senior management (such as the existing digital dashboard) migrate to the portal, Lynn feels that usage among these people will also go up.

8

BAIN &
COMPANY

CP/KM EXPERTS

Steven Tallman, vice president of global operations, U.K. office

Mark Horwitch, vice president and director, head of Bain's KM consulting practice, Chicago office

Robert Armacost, internal director of KM, Boston office

BACKGROUND

Bain & Company (Bain) is a leading management-consulting firm founded in 1973. The firm currently has more than 2,800 consultants working in 28 offices across six continents. Bain's business mission is "to make companies more valuable and convert strategy and action into economic performance." The firm offers expertise in a number of industries, including conglomerates, consumer products, financial services, etc. and functional areas, including strategy, e-commerce strategy, customers, and growth.

THE CATALYST, GOALS, AND DRIVING FACTORS

Bain has been an early adopter of KM and demonstrated strong KM leadership. Its awareness of KM started in the early 1980s, when the firm created a KM function, the Experience Center. All client presentations were captured in a database, which was searchable from a mainframe computer by a staff of librarians. With momentum from consultants for increased knowledge source content, in 1992, Bain built its first desktop application, BRAVA (Bain resource archive for value addition). Although BRAVA helped increase knowledge sharing, by the mid-1990s, Bain knew that, to continue as a leader, it needed to extend its learning and knowledge systems to the next level, utilizing Web-oriented technology solutions to make it easier for consultants to locate the most knowledgeable colleagues, the newest codified insights, and the most relevant and updated industry data. In summary, Bain's KM support systems were far from being cutting edge in the mid-1990s: It did not leverage the power of the latest Web-enabled KM tools.

Hence, in 1997, Internet technology solutions were deployed to support Bain's KM client delivery support services. A critical viewpoint shaping the KM deployment strategies was that Bain's senior leadership embraced training and KM as essential for success in today's increasingly competitive environment, an environment where clients are more demanding and sophisticated everywhere. Over the last few years, especially in fast-paced high-tech areas, industry cycles have become shorter, which makes it critical for consultants to tap into Bain's knowledge real-time as it is created, regardless of location.

Training has always been a highly structured core activity at Bain. Tom Tierney, Bain's former managing director, was a strong advocate for learning initiatives. At Bain, Training, IT, Intellectual Property Management, and KM all report to Steven Tallman, Bain's VP of global operations. Ultimately, KM evolved in close synchronization with the evolution of training, which has helped ensure that such training is well designed for rapid learning and rapid access, both value levers to the success Bain has achieved in its KM efforts.

However, Steven Tallman took on the role of spearheading Bain's global Training and KM strategy to convince other Bain partners that they were not fully leveraging the "knowledge of the firm." With sponsorship from other senior Bain talent, Mark Horwitch, a senior VP, and Robert Armacost, a former senior manager consultant, and

Tallman formed a core change leadership team to champion Bain's KM strategy and execution efforts. Mark's words were very emphatic: "KM is not just a tool or a flash silver bullet; it's at the heart of Bain's next wave of innovation." In his view, KM is not a system but a set of good business practices that play a key role in the delivery of strategic business goals.

This view is that KM should be a core concern of the chief executive's own agenda, which seems to be the case at Bain. In 1998, Tom Tierney, then Bain's worldwide managing director, made building a KM system one of the firm's top three strategic priorities. This is still the case with current managing director, John Donahoe. This is not to say that Bain's board (the Policy Committee) signed a blank check to Steven and Mark back in 1998. They had to "earn their budget" by convincing very fact-based senior consultants that it made good business sense. To achieve that, they not only set out on an "evangelizing" journey, they built a strong business case, pinpointing the constraints to case-team success from not having the right data, information, and access to experts at the right time (again, P is primary goal; S, secondary goal; N, not relevant).

Communication tools (top down and bottom up):

(N) Improve communication of vision and knowledge strategy.

(S) Improve communication of company values.

(S) Keep the organization alert.

(S) Engage customers and community at large.

(P) Divulge results more broadly and promote systemic analysis.

(N) Facilitate bottom-up communications.

(N) Make it easy for employees to suggest improvements to management.

Push information and knowledge to employees:

(P) Capture, organize, and distribute codified knowledge (e.g., database access).

(P) Improve access to external sources of information and knowledge.

(N) Improve decision making.

(P) Empower front-line employees.

Improve reuse of knowledge:

(P) Develop expertise maps (uncover existing knowledge).

(S) Map and measure intangible assets.

(P) Facilitate search of previously developed knowledge.

Foster collaboration:

(P) Increase collaboration among different functions of the organization.

(P) Increase collaboration among different locations of the organization.

(P) Improve overall knowledge sharing.

(P) Support the development of communities of practice.

(S) Increase connections not related to work.

Improve human capital management:

(N) Improve hiring.

(N) Improve internal mobility and deployment of existing employees.

(N) Integrate temporary and outside human resources and expertise.

(P) Improve training and acquisition of skills.

(P) Get new employees up to speed very quickly.

(S) Reduce time spent on menial activities.

(S) Improve employee retention.

(N) Facilitate work and integration of telecommuters.

Improve relationships with external stakeholders and increase information flow:

(S) Improve information exchange with suppliers, partners, and customers.

(N) Capture customer information.

(S) Improve customer satisfaction.

(S) Reduce sales costs.

(S) Reduce customer service costs.

IMPLEMENTATION JOURNEY

1973–1983: Word of mouth, one-on-one training.
1983–1993: Experience Center, local training programs.
1993–1999: BRAVA, global training programs.
1998–1999: Bain Virtual University (BVU 1.0 and 2.0).
2000: KM application: Global Experience Center (GXC 1.0).
2002: GXC 2.0.
2002: My Bain.com (new corporate intranet).

TRAINING AND KNOWLEDGE MANAGEMENT

Knowledge management at Bain is closely linked to training efforts and programs. The ultimate goal of both KM and training is to prepare consultants to do more effective client work. Since most of Bain's projects involve customized solutions, knowledge reuse is not about providing off-the-shelf solutions, but about consultants with a strong foundation in core business concepts and general industry knowledge that allows them to better leverage their own analytical and creative capabilities. It is also about a continuous effort to facilitate the transmission of tacit knowledge from more experienced consultants to more junior consultants and from "owners" of specific expertise to seekers of such experience or skills.

Although training and KM are becoming highly interwoven, a few differences keep the two efforts from becoming one:

- Training tends to be significantly more structured than KM: As consultants move up in their consulting careers, they participate in a number of training programs carefully designed to give them the skills and knowledge they need to succeed. Consequently, as consultants develop, increasing weight is given to training project management skills, overall office management, coaching, and selling skills.
- Training modules are usually more perennial than KM applications (documents in the KM databases tend to get outdated more quickly and people leave the firm).
- A lot of training, even online, is focused on the development of consultants' soft skills (leadership, teamwork, client relationships, selling, etc.) and the transmission of Bain's corporate values.

Although Bain has no explicit cultural values on knowledge sharing, its core value as "one global firm" reinforces the value of sharing and transferring knowledge rapidly to meet client requirements. Highly responsive behaviors exist at Bain, so when a consultant reaches out for support, the cultural expectation is that support will be returned rapidly with "value." Another key supporting KM core value of the firm is continuous learning, which reinforces the value of knowledge stretch and sharing to achieve business goals. The core values of "one global firm" and " continuous learning" are continually reinforced in KM communication initiatives to foster alignment.

Moving Training and Knowledge Management Online

Training at Bain, prior to the online environment, usually involved a combination of one-to-one coaching and local and global training programs. Bain Virtual University (BVU), a complete Web-based learning environment, was introduced in 1998. By the summer of 2001, more than 170 modules were available to all employees across the globe. Although the traditional training methods remain in place, the BVU has changed many of them.

Like other leading consulting firms, Bain always had some form of knowledge management. KM is at the core of successful consulting firms. It plays an important role in making each consultant perform "smarter" than if he or she acted and learned alone. It is no surprise that many of the best practices, concepts, and vocabulary used today in the KM literature (mentoring, communities of practice, reuse of codified knowledge, etc.) evolved from the consulting firms. The Web, however, introduced many new opportunities to accelerate knowledge flow, provide targeted knowledge (tacit or explicit) for those who seek it, and make it much easier for knowledge owners to distribute it more widely.

Since 1993, Bain has had an online environment for sharing codified knowledge. Bain's first online initiative was BRAVA. The BRAVA initiative was an important step toward accelerating knowledge flow. However, it did not leverage the power of the Web and had a limited number of applications (cases, clients, and internal people information). BRAVA also had very little human support on content. This started changing in 1999, when a new KM initiative was organized. In 2000, Bain launched its state-of-the-art KM platform, the Global Experience Center (GXC).

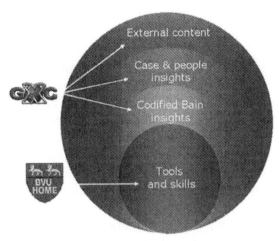

External content
- Top outside sources/content
- Major research databases

Case & people insights
- High-level insights on projects
- Used to "create conversations" (tacit knowledge)

Codified Bain insights
- Insights and approaches for Capabilities and Industries
- Shorter "shelf life"
- Heavy ongoing investment

Tools and skills
- Common set of global tools/skills
- Integrated over career lifetime
- Long "shelf life," with heavy investments to update

Figure 8-1
Bain's GXC and BVU (Source: Bain & Company)

Both BVU and GXC were developed in-house in a relatively short period of time (each in less than 1 year). One reason the GXC was successful was that the implementation scope started with four of the firm's most important industries and four of the most important capabilities, to demonstrate value creation and impact early in the deployment of the new KM capabilities.

In the GXC, each application is maintained and branded as its own area in Bain's CP environment. The design of these two complementary areas, however, makes it very easy for consultants to jump from one application to the other. Certain applications, such as search and peer finder, in particular, can show integrated links and search results. Figure 8-1 helps explain how Bain looks at the role and areas of BVU and GXC. Next, BVU and GXC are discussed separately in more detail.

Bain Virtual University

The BVU Environment

BVU's design takes into consideration that individuals have different learning styles. Modules are presented in a variety of formats, including Web-based Power Point presentations, hands-on exercises (computer-based training, CBT), multimedia courses, and templates that can be used in real-life projects. There is a "training on demand" philosophy. This design also makes extensive use of hyperlinking, which enables consultants to easily move between different parts of a particular module, complete modules, and even offline references, such as related books. In summary, the Bain training design creates a very integrated approach to learning.

BVU includes courses tailored for every level of consultant, from recent junior hires through partners who need to hone specific client relationship skills. All consultants have full access, anytime, anywhere to the complete library of modules. This total access approach to BVU helps convey a very open, transparent environment and pushes the responsibility for learning to the consultants. Bain's philosophy is that the consultants themselves know best when they can and want to acquire skills: at the beginning of a new case, during slack times, after performance review.

Bain integrated offline training with the online environments of BVU. According to Steven Tallman, the primary goal of BVU was not to reduce training costs but improve the skills of consultants and the efficiency of their training. There have been only minimal reductions in the time consultants spend in offline training programs. However, some innovative ideas have been developed to improve synergies between on- and offline training. For example, consultants are now usually required to take some preparatory BVU courses before attending offline-training sessions. In addition, consultants take online tests before and after attending offline-training programs. Test results are available only to that consultant and the training department, which uses the results as a way to measure the effectiveness of both the online modules and offline courses.

The Development of BVU Content

With a large number of proprietary frameworks, concepts, and culture-specific modules, the success of BVU has relied enormously on the voluntary participation of Bain's own consultants. According to Steven, more than 10% of the worldwide staff contributed to the development of the courses, logging more than 16,000 hours on content development and review, focus groups, testing, and the like. (This contribution is certainly worth far more than the approximate $1 million spent on the actual software and IT development.) Module authors, contributors, and reviewers are clearly identified at the beginning of each module. Indeed, participating in the development of a module is regarded as a way for consultants to gain prestige and credibility within the organization.

Of particular interest in terms of KM is that considerable effort was spent developing the "culture" modules of BVU. These modules play an important role in creating the myths, folklore, and attitudes that help shape their core value of being "one firm" across the world. There are 75 videos in this area of BVU alone. The culture modules are among the most popular modules. Included are presentations and stories told by a large number of the most senior partners at Bain. They present Bain's history, mission, core values, and visions about what it takes to achieve great results and build extraordinary teams. New hires, in particular, tend to spend a lot of time watching these videos. As existing management literature shows, there is no effective KM without close attention to the "soft" and cultural issues. The collection of "culture" modules demonstrates that Bain's BVU architects were well aware of this.

Another interesting aspect related to new hires is that most of the initial content in BVU was developed with a focus on this group of consultants. The approach reinforced their implementation philosophy of not trying to be everything to everyone. The strategy employed was to have valuable content (100 modules that every new person needs) "growing with the class"; that is, the growth in the volume and topics of content would meet the career growth needs of this group. This allowed Bain not only to have a more focused approach but also to leverage the initial energy, openness, and interest for Internet applications in this group. Business fundamentals, such as "Bain Speak," "Core Analytics," and "Basic Communication Tools," were some of the early modules deployed. Over time, Bain introduced additional modules aimed at senior consultants.

Employee Use of BVU
Employees can search for modules on BVU according to a number of criteria: alphabetical, type of toolkit, type of course, and format (standard Power Point–like presentations, video presentations, interactive training, templates). A number of courses can also be downloaded for offline training and greater speed. To better illustrate this, a selection of BVU's screenshot samples is presented in Figures 8-2 through 8-5: an alphabetical module list, a standard presentation, a video module, and interactive computer-based training.

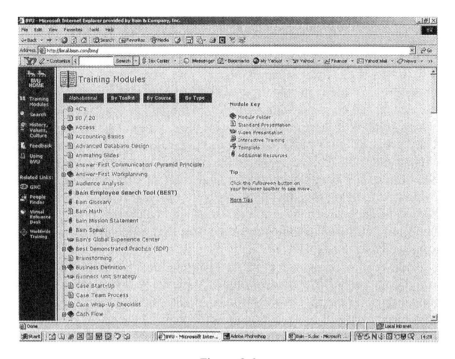

Figure 8-2
*BVU Training Modules Listed in Alphabetical Order
(Source: Bain & Company)*

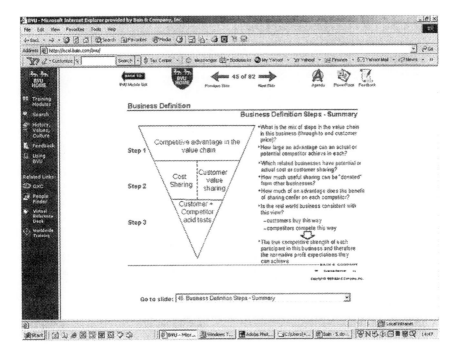

Figure 8-3
BVU Standard Presentation Module (Source: Bain & Company)

BVU Video Module

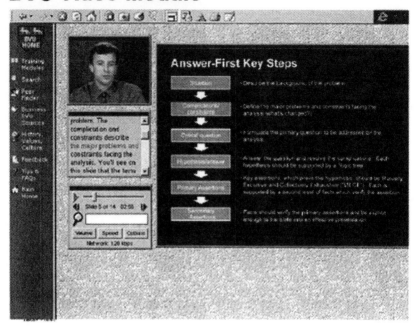

Figure 8-4
BVU Video Module (Source: Bain & Company)

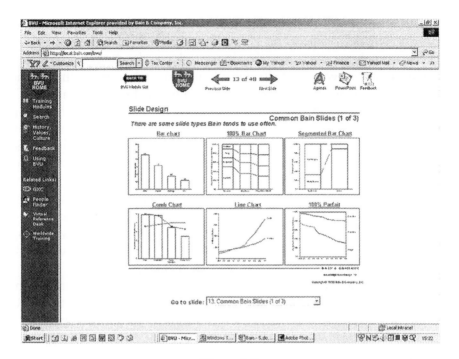

Figure 8-5
BVU Computer-Based Training (Source: Bain & Company)

BVU's architects clearly understood that most learning still occurs during human connections. Therefore, a special search mechanism, Peerfinder (Figure 8-6), was developed to be used in both the BVU and GXC environments to help consultants to find peers with specific knowledge. This is, indeed, the most used tool in both BVU and GXC. Consultants can use Peerfinder to look for other consultants based on a number of categories of experience: industry, study type and tool, and technique (e.g., experience curve) employed. It also includes the possibility of limiting the search based on the location and level of the consultant.

Steven believes that this last feature is particularly important, because it reduces "expert overload" by allowing consultants who have simple questions to look for peers at their level, thereby helping ensure that only very complex questions are asked of more experienced consultants (usually senior managers and partners).

One final feature of BVU and GXC warrants particular mention: the feedback application (Figure 8-7). Every document in the BVU and GXC environments has a direct link to a feedback application.

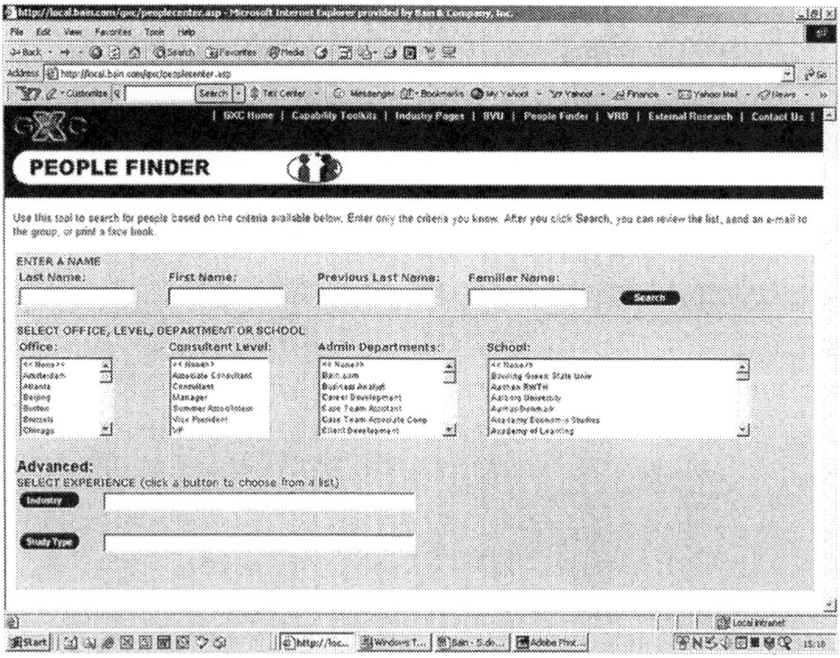

Figure 8-6
BVU and GXC Peerfinder (Source: Bain & Company)

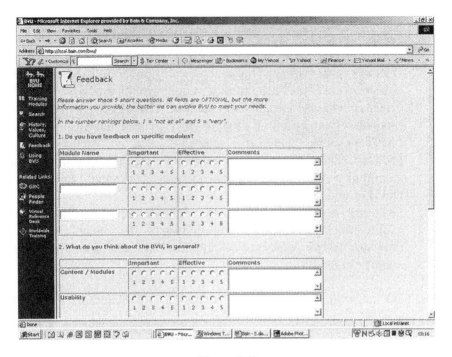

Figure 8-7
BVU Feedback Application (Source: Bain & Company)

This application allows consultants to evaluate complete modules and send commentary about specific parts of a document or module. Consultants may choose to identify themselves or provide feedback anonymously. Most choose to identify themselves. Evaluations of complete modules follow a more structured questionnaire given to consultants to fill out periodically. Documents that receive a high number of positive feedback are more likely to be ranked higher in search results.

Global Experience Center

The GXC can be seen as a CP organized around five core sources of knowledge for Bain's client work:

1. *Tools.* These are proprietary and nonproprietary frameworks, concepts, templates, and other tools that can be applied across a number of projects.

2. *Capabilities.* This is a repository of Bain's proprietary insights across all its key "study types" of client work (e.g., cost reduction, mergers and acquisitions (M&A), growth strategy).
3. *Industry information.* This source of organized information per industry combines both internal and external sources.
4. *Case, client, and people information.* This is Bain's improved repository (as compared to BRAVA's) of information on previous client work. Client information is "sanitized" by knowledge brokers (client names are removed and data disguised) to allow a companywide view, and the repository is designed to facilitate tacit knowledge sharing.
5. *External research.* Such research includes access to high-value subscription databases as well as links to top business sources that have been preselected or suggested by the research department or consultants.

The GXC was built on top of an existing IT infrastructure as shown in Figure 8-8.

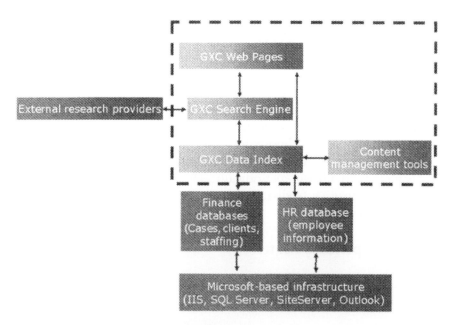

Figure 8-8
GXC IT Architecture (Source: Bain & Company)

Searching for Knowledge

All these core knowledge sources can be easily accessed through the use of an integrated search mechanism that allows users to preselect specific areas of interest (see Figure 8-9 of GXC search page). It also seamlessly integrates external research and offers unlimited access to all consultants worldwide. One of the biggest challenges of most search mechanisms is helping the users, especially novices, narrow down the scope of their search. Bain's KM team responded to this challenge by having the content area "owners" (usually practice experts) and the KM team put significant effort into categorizing the existing documents and developing a comprehensive thesaurus. Thus, GXC users are offered additional keyword suggestions to reduce the scope of their search or to find related terms and documents.

The GXC search mechanism also helps users by displaying more relevant documents first. The order that documents are displayed in

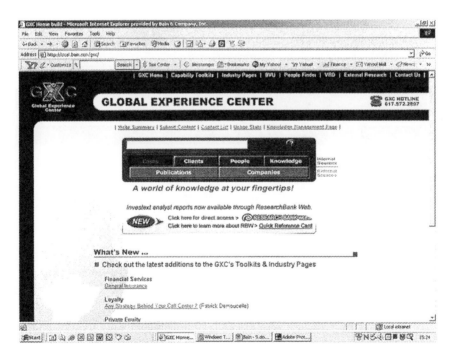

Figure 8-9
GXC Home and Search Page (Source: Bain & Company)

on the results page is influenced by a couple of weighting factors (different types of content have different weighting factors):

- Prevalence of existing keywords.
- Date of the documents.
- Experts' points of view tend to rise to the top of the page.
- The proximity of the office that produced the document (the closer it is to the consultant's office, the higher the ranking).

Browsing for Knowledge
Search, as many in the KM field have learned, is just one way of finding relevant information. The other is through effective browsing. However, effective browsing can happen only when users have some idea of what they are looking for and when a site's taxonomy and organization are relevant. The screenshots of an e-commerce toolkit page and a consumer product page (Figures 8-10 and 8-11) exemplify how a great deal of GXC's success can be attributed to the careful clustering of relevant and updated information and the direct contact

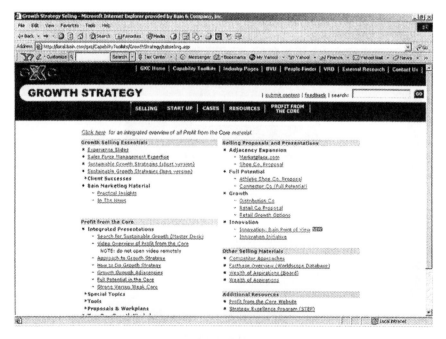

Figure 8-10
GXC Example Toolkit (Source: Bain & Company)

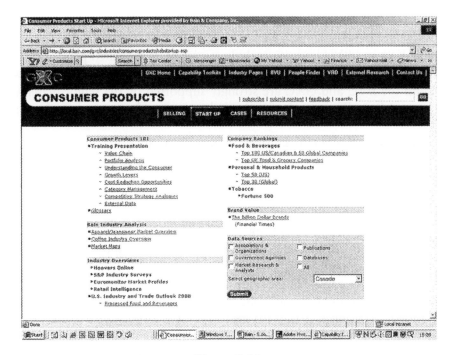

Figure 8-11
GXC Example Industry Analysis, Consumer Products
(Source: Bain & Company)

it offers to practice leaders. GXC's clusters of information provide newcomers with enough of a knowledge body to get them started on specific projects. More experienced consultants also find some of the most recent announcements and studies posted in these "clusters." The responsibility for maintaining these pages is usually divided among members of the KM team and leading practice experts (usually senior consultants).

The GXC now has 14 industry pages and 15 capability toolkits, covering the full range of internal and external knowledge that teams need when getting started on a topic.

The pages and toolkits are organized not only to cluster information in a simple way but also to tailor relevant material for the needs of specific users. The Selling tab, for example, is intended to be used by VPs and managers when selling projects. The startup tab is for case teams to use during the first couple weeks on the case, when they need to get up to speed.

Organizational Support

The KM and BVU budgets, including salaries of dedicated personnel, IT infrastructure, and expenses, is less than 1% of Bain's overall revenues. Both the BVU and GXC are strongly supported by the senior management at Bain. This support has been demonstrated in a number of ways:

- Reinforcement of cultural expectations in KM, in which John Donahoe, Bain's current managing director, consistently reminds consultants of the importance of contributing to KM.
- Adequate funding for the development and maintenance of state-of-the-art applications.
- Personal involvement and encouragement of companywide participation in the development of many BVU and GXC modules and documents.
- The direct responsibility of many senior partners for the quality of the content in the GXC in their practice areas (both industry and capability focused). Not only are the partners supposed to support the offline activities and projects of their practice areas, but they are also required to assume a senior content leadership role to ensure the GXC practice toolkits are populated with the most useful and relevant content.
- Support for the creation of a formal KM organization, including a KM director and 10 knowledge brokers. Each local office also has a knowledge officer, a senior consulting staff member responsible for local KM on a part-time basis.
- A professional standards manager in every office, who has annual responsibility for reviewing the local office case submissions to ensure codes of client confidentiality (i.e., cleansing names of companies) and the like meet the internal audit standards; this reinforces an intellectual asset management process to the KM infrastructure and the importance of our knowledge assets.
- An annual conference with all knowledge brokers and knowledge officers. Knowledge brokers meet more frequently.

Knowledge Brokers

The knowledge brokers are dispersed around the globe and are usually responsible for a specific region and a specific knowledge area. These individuals, although not consultants themselves but often with a general business education or information science background, were selected based on their first-rate skills in research, information analysis, and written and verbal communication.

Bain's most important knowledge assets are created during client projects. Knowledge brokers play an important role in the knowledge capture process. They are immediately notified when a new project in their domain starts and work closely with the project managers to capture new insights at agreed-on milestones (start, client presentations, wrap-up). The knowledge brokers also alert team members of relevant documents, people, and knowledge that may be useful for particular projects.

They also play an important role in the codification process. In addition, to make sure that teams follow required codification guidelines, they extract key insights (tacit knowledge) by interviewing managers at the beginning and end of a case, using questions such as "What did you learn that is applicable to other industries?" Throughout the interviews, the brokers work to identify categories of learning that can be assembled for the GXC. They also have direct responsibilities for adding data sources, identifying Bain's experts, and editing, upgrading graphics, reformatting, and packaging codified content (produced by consultants) for GXC. Figure 8-12 summarizes the case team knowledge process that knowledge brokers facilitate.

Case Team Knowledge Process

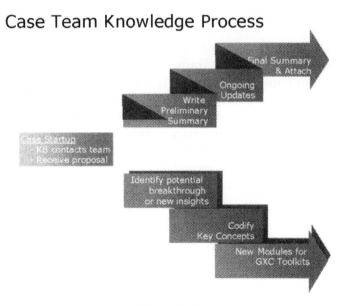

Figure 8-12
Case Team Knowledge Process (Source: Bain & Company)

METRICS AND USER SATISFACTION

Bain understands that metrics are meaningful only if they are clearly linked to help the organization achieve its business goals. In Bain's case the KM initiative has the following explicit goals:

- Create a useful everyday tool.
- Help sell work in half the time (cut proposal development time).
- Make case startups 30–50% faster.
- Help teams deliver greater value creation to clients.

To gauge its success, Bain's KM team uses a number of "proxies" (they know that it is almost impossible to measure a direct bottom-line impact) and evaluation techniques. Given that both BVU and GXC are Web based, designing tools to measure site traffic and activity by office and content area was not very difficult. In addition to these basic metrics, the KM team also

- Evaluates which search terms are not finding any matches.
- Relies on document- and module-specific feedback from the consultants.
- Conducts periodic surveys to gauge the level of satisfaction of consultants with the various areas of the sites.

Overall, the outcomes of the "measurable" proxies suggest that Bain is on the right track. Traffic on Bain's CP (BVU and GXC) has grown continuously. By mid-2001, BVU and GXC combined were getting more than 500,000 hits per month (or more than 4.5 million hits since launch) and the average consultant was tapping into BVU alone around 50 times per month. Fewer and fewer searches were resulting in no relevant matches and surveys showed that 98% of consultants were either satisfied or extremely satisfied with GXC. Through informal surveys, the KM team believes that partners now build proposals in 30% less time and that the case team process is at least 30% faster.

These are remarkable results, given the critical nature of the user base: top-notch consultants with very high-level expectations. As mentioned earlier, the ultimate goal of Bain's CP is to have better-performing consultants. The KM leadership team knows that establishing a direct link is often not possible. The already mentioned proxies and anecdotes of how the CP has helped in specific project situations provide the best indirect solutions to determining the success of Bain's KM initiatives.

INCENTIVES, REWARDS, AND RECOGNITION

Bain's consultants pride themselves on delivering measurable results for their clients. As we saw, they try to apply the same "fact-based" rules to measure the impact of their internal KM initiatives. In a similar fashion, they make a clear effort to link the compensation of Bain consultants to their efforts in building the firm's intellectual assets.

This is not to say that consultants (especially more junior ones) have their pay directly linked to their contributions to the KM repositories (even though the contributions are highlighted in performance reviews). This is becoming increasingly important, however, for more senior consultants. The team managers are gauged on their compliance with completed case summaries and on how much their work draws out new industry insights. Office heads' compensation is tied to similar measures. In the case of the most senior partners, specific contributions already make up part of their bonus. Many partners are responsible for the quality of the information on their practice areas' GXC sites. They are also expected to contribute at least one meaningful piece of new content per year (usually not related to specific cases—often insights on a specific industry or functional capability).

The KM team also developed a number of creative tools and incentives to help shape behavior. These go well beyond direct links to individuals' pay. They include required actions and a number of initiatives to create a "healthy" competitive environment for intellectual asset creation and codification:

- There's a stronger focus on the performance of individual offices. One metric to track is the percentage of case summaries written within 2 months of the end of the project. The current target is to have 85% of summaries written in this period. Many offices are already reaching the 100% mark. Those offices that lag behind are quickly reminded, by the most senior partners, of their obligations to the firm.
- Every 6 months, a KM recognition award (an honorary plaque for Outstanding KM Leadership) is given for outstanding performance to one large and one small office. The recognition involves

some extra money for the offices to take consultants to "fun" out-of-the-office activities. Some local offices have also created their "own" rewards and recognition for teams and individuals.

- The most valuable form of recognition based on their consulting survey feedback is that the contributors appreciate having their contributions recognized and most frequently used content is a reinforcement of value contribution to help the firm be "one global firm."

BAIN'S EXTRANET

Another initiative that exists at Bain and that can, to a certain extent, be related to KM is the extranet. Bain uses eRoom as a platform to connect with clients and keep all stakeholders abreast of project developments. So far, eRoom is not widely deployed and is instead a "niche product"; it tends to be used when cases involve multiple offices, clients with various geographic locations, and in projects that require constant and detailed exchanges among different teams (e.g., process redesign). In more traditional strategy cases, the extranet plays a less critical role. It acts more like a virtual library of milestone presentations where clients' senior executives can easily find past documentation. Occasionally, it is also used to download some of Bain's codified knowledge assets to clients.

All and all, this is still seen, primarily, as a team collaboration and file management tool and not a core platform for Bain's KM strategy. This is not to say that Bain does not recognize the value of distributing codified knowledge through this channel. In fact, a conscious decision was made to stick to its core value proposition; that is, sell customized, innovative solutions and not packaged knowledge solutions.

KEY LESSONS LEARNED

Lesson 1. KM Initiatives Benefit Tremendously When There Is Personal Participation and Strong Commitment from Senior Management

At Bain, support was provided not only in terms of budget and resources but also the personal and direct participation of senior management in the development of the CP. Senior partners dedicated much time producing content and evaluating the evolution of the portals. This level of participation sends a clear message to the rest of the organization about the quality of contributions and commitment that are expected.

Lesson 2. Initiate CPs with Areas That Directly Impact the Business Results

A lot of momentum was achieved by focusing on applications that would help Bain sell more and become more productive. This generated a lot of energy and goodwill for the CP across all partner levels and offices. Web enabling of routine, back-end applications might have been easier to implement but would have had minimal business impact and generated far less interest. Bain's basic philosophy for capturing knowledge was to build a system that was flexible for a specific user group. In other words, by focusing on high leverage areas first (i.e., largest industry segments within Bain and working with leader-oriented change models), their traction success achieved early adoption momentum as the focus was always on critical-path value creation rather than conquering too broad a spectrum of customer requirements and attempting to execute all at once. In other words, avoid the "elephant sandwich" or "world hunger approach" to have more rapid impact.

Lesson 3. Develop a Content Strategy before Doing Any Development Work

It is important to understand how employees conduct their work and when and how they look for other sources of knowledge. Steven recommends a careful "audit" of each business process and knowledge domain before doing any development work. It is also very important to develop a clear understanding of the knowledge sources: What is explicit? What is tacit? Is it internal or external? For Bain, the end result of the audit process was less time and money spent on costly reworks and set of portal taxonomies and structures that was familiar and closely fit Bain's business and users' needs.

Lesson 4. Build a Content Capture Process That Is Appropriate

The success of a CP and of KM in general depends significantly more on the willingness and quality of knowledge creators and contributors than on knowledge seekers. A good part of the planning process at Bain was spent developing templates that made it very easy for knowledge contributors to publish content online. Time is a scarce resource for consulting professionals; hence streamlining and simplifying knowledge capture processes was a key criterion for success.

Lesson 5. Quality Is More Important Than Quantity

If a CP is to focus on knowledge flow, it is very important that people trust the information they receive; otherwise, users quickly disregard the tool. Bain made it very easy for consultants to give feedback about the information they found on BVU and GXC. Consultants are invited to give feedback at the page level or about the overall importance and effectiveness of modules, documents, and specific applications. The feedback mechanisms and frequent surveys of users allow the KM team to quickly correct mistakes or address missing points. Particular attention is also given to information that consultants are unable to find on the CP: Searched terms are periodically monitored to develop a content strategy that meets changing consultant needs.

Lesson 6. Make Authors' Contributions Highly Visible and Use Both "Sticks and Carrots" as Incentives

Knowledge creators and contributors to the online environment need to be clearly recognized. Documents on both BVU and GXC clearly state the names of the contributors, including primary and secondary authors, as well as reviewers. Additionally, a general e-mail message is periodically sent to all consultants highlighting the "top 20" most used documents in the portal environment. This top 20 list serves not only to direct consultants to those documents most useful to their peers but, by listing the author and office, gives additional prestige to the documents' authors. Given that a core characteristic is their desire for recognition of Bain's consultants (or high-end strategy consultants in general), this visible recognition leads to a healthy competitive environment, where a large proportion of consultants are motivated to be among the leading contributors to the KM effort.

Lesson 7. Modular and Meaningful Launches Tend to Be More Effective

Closely related to a content strategy is the idea of modularity. The Internet itself is a very modular network that allows pieces of content and applications to be seamlessly integrated into existing solutions. Bain took advantage of that. Not only did it focus on specific audiences (and, according to Steven, will continue to do so) but on specific clusters of content that had depth or were considered strategic enough to justify the creation of a training module or a section within GXC. For instance, GXC launched with specific content areas for only four industry verticals and five core capabilities. Over time, other industry and capability content areas were added.

Lesson 8. IT Need Not Be Costly

Despite its sophistication, the deployment of Bain's CP was not costly. The firm spent less than $2 million in software licenses and "coding" costs. For Bain, a few additional project sales and the improved quality of case results already guarantee a high return on this investment. There is no major secret to keeping CP costs in check. The keys are to concentrate on functionality that really adds value to the business, avoid costly "bells and whistles," leverage existing data and systems, and roll out applications incrementally. An important lesson was not to implement Web applications just because it is easy to do so. For instance, Bain could have easily added chats, instant messaging, and discussions forums. However, after careful analysis of how work is conducted and how knowledge is shared and created, the KM team decided that it was not the right time to implement these tools.

Lesson 9. Knowledge Brokers Play an Important Role

Although consultants may understand that one of their responsibilities with the firm is to codify part of the intellectual capital created during client engagements, it is very easy for this responsibility to take a "backseat" as consultants move from project to project. At Bain, knowledge brokers are the keepers of the "knowledge codifying process": They make sure that consultants (especially project managers) do not forget to codify relevant knowledge-sharing elements of their projects. This occurs at various milestones (start, presentations, wrap-up) during projects. The knowledge brokers are also key resources for consultants who need a human introduction to Bain's core capabilities in specific knowledge domains. Finally, they play an important role in organizing and keeping the online information up-to-date.

Lesson 10. Librarian and Researcher Roles Are Changing

As consultants find it increasingly easier to search for codified information and experts online, the role of librarians and research professionals within the firm is changing. These professionals are rapidly abandoning some of the more menial research activities and focusing on higher-level tasks, such as finding relevant information sources, updating taxonomies, keeping track of new advances in research-related technologies, developing vertical expertise in different areas, and so forth.

FUTURE DIRECTIONS

Bain is currently working in version 2.0 of GXC (to be released by the end of 2002). After extensive surveys and interviews, the company developed a plan that will include but is not limited to the following improvements:

- Improve the interface design and the integration of external research.
- Make searches more accurate and relevant (by improving the search algorithm and eliciting constant feedback from consultants through a star-rating system like Amazon's).
- Improve the Peerfinder search tool by including new search criteria. Given the large number of consultants worldwide, it was determined that it was also important to improve relevancy ranking for people searches.
- Add tools that help partners sell projects more easily.
- Integrate the BVU and GXC (there will be no distinction from an interface point of view). Because the BVU is geared toward more junior consultants, it will be more seamlessly integrated with other GXC tools used more often by this level of consultants. In fact, a key change to the next GXC version is a clearer division in the environments for junior and senior consultants (from managers to partners). This change is not geared toward restricting access to information but to enable finding appropriate information more quickly (e.g., junior consultants do not need to look for proposals, while this is an important part of the partners' job).
- As with many other KM databases that grow very quickly, Bain has learned that content duplication and outdated information

can become a problem. A content audit was done, and as a result, the new GXC 2.0 version will streamline some content areas and improve others.

■ Have a single point of access to all external research sources (with some value-added intelligence), since consultants reported that these searches were too complex and buried in many hard-to-find sources and databases.

Bain is rethinking how work is performed at the team level to make teams and individuals more efficient and to facilitate the knowledge capture process. This may include more sophisticated Web-based tools (potentially like eRoom) that provide strong document management system capabilities to improve the teams' internal document work flow and make the capture process at the end of each case a simpler process.

Steven Tallman's CP vision for Bain is to offer a single global home page: My Bain. My Bain would be designed with 50% of the real estate completely personalized by the consultants and 50% centrally controlled with information pushed to consultants based on their office location. Such an enhanced CP would allow consultants to build personal "dashboards," integrating all their communication tools, interesting news feeds, and updated Bain content with areas of professional interest as well as personal feeds such as weather. This application is scheduled to be launched in the second half of 2002 and represents a major step in improving personal productivity. Given Bain's initial experience and success building BVU and GXC, Steven thinks that most of this new project can be developed internally with standard Internet tools and programming languages.

CLOSING THOUGHTS

The case of Bain offers interesting insights about KM- and CP-oriented projects. Bain's experience appears to support the two main schools of thought in the KM literature: the information school and the behavioral school. It is clear that the deployment of Bain's CP significantly improved the speed and accuracy of knowledge flow in the firm. It is also evident, however, that the IT investment would not have succeeded to the extent it did if Bain did not already have a KM-friendly culture and did not create new incentives and rewards (and also requirements) to shape consultants' behavior toward more intellectual asset creation and codification. Consultants' values and attitudes were clearly demonstrated by the very high levels of participation in the development, rollout, and maintenance of the CP tools. Their openness to learning irrespective of hierarchy is also reinforced by the design and access structure of their CP, which promotes tremendous vision for "empowered learning for employees." Finally, three of Bain's core explicit values are clearly revealed in the design and practices related to the deployment of BVU and GXC: a continuous learning environment, one firm, and focus on client services and results.

9

BANK OF MONTREAL

CP/KM EXPERTS

Richard Livesley, senior manager, knowledge management

Sasha Zupansky, Sr., business architect, knowledge management

Dave Reddoch, senior manager, intranet communication, project leader for the My Bank®* project

BACKGROUND

Founded in 1817, the Bank of Montreal is Canada's first bank and one of the largest financial institutions in North America. The bank offers clients a broad range of financial products and services across Canada and in the United States, both directly and through its Chicago-based subsidiary, Harris Bank, a major U.S. Midwest financial services provider, and BMO Nesbitt Burns, one of Canada's largest full-service investment firms.

---

*My Bank® is a registered trademark of the Bank of Montreal.

With average assets of $246 billion and more than 33,000 employees, the bank has diversified activities concentrated in retail banking, wealth management, and corporate and investment banking. The Bank of Montreal group of companies is made up of three client groups:

- Personal and commercial client group (P&CCG).
- Private client group (PCG).
- Investment banking group (IBG).

Emfisys®,* the technology and e-business group, provides information technology planning, strategy, and development services, together with transaction processing, North American cash management, and real estate operations for the Bank of Montreal group of companies and its customers. The group is also responsible for the creation, development, and support of the bank's e-business services. One of Emfisys®'s* internal consulting divisions is Integrated Business Solutions (IBS), with 15 centers of competence and 200 employees.

The Knowledge Management department is an IBS center of competence. Other IBS competency areas focus on organization design, change management, process design, and information management strategy.

UNDERSTANDING KNOWLEDGE MANAGEMENT AT THE BANK OF MONTREAL

Knowledge management at the Bank of Montreal presents an interesting dynamic, similar to many large, complex, and decentralized organizations. Grounded on one of the Bank of Montreal's stated values— "We share information, learn and innovate to create consistently superior customer experiences"—it is also part of senior management's commitment to improve knowledge sharing, with the bank's chairman and CEO, Tony Comper, being a strong supporter of KM principles.

The mandate of knowledge management is to create value by

- Connecting people looking for knowledge with people who have that knowledge.

---

*Emfisys® is a registered trademark of the Bank of Montreal.

- Connecting people to elements of knowledge that the bank creates as part of its ongoing business.

The development of KM was based on a bottom-up approach to better meet employee needs and directly affect customer satisfaction. A Bank of Montreal goal is to "get it right with customers." Providing employees the right tools and information to provide client satisfaction has been a key priority throughout the bank.

In keeping with Bank of Montreal's collaborative management principles, KM evolved by developing strong "client-supplier" relationships with more than 30 lines of business. The challenge in developing a KM program in a large organization with numerous lines of business is that the KM team has to build consensus among the senior executives (especially when it involves launching organizationwide KM initiatives). However, this decentralized approach helped the Bank of Montreal's KM team avoid overpromising results, and the team was rewarded by working with areas in the bank that were ready or committed to embrace the necessary cultural and process changes related to a successful KM program.

The KM team found that a major role in their service consulting is to communicate the key capabilities they can offer their constituencies and stakeholders: Framing a clear service value proposition and helping define a lexicon were important steps in setting up the KM consulting services.

Given the range of activities, processes, and lines of businesses at the bank, the KM team also relies on a number of KM advocates within its internal clients to promote the benefits of KM. With this in mind, the team fostered the KM community of practice (CoP) to cut across the division and extend beyond the organization to include leading external leaders in the KM program. Bank of Montreal was one of the first members of IBM's Institute of Knowledge Management and continues to maintain close ties to universities doing research on KM in Canada.

The KM team is made up of eight people who provide soft skills related to KM, such as social network analysis, process mapping, and IT competencies (i.e., Web development) used to evaluate and implement emerging technologies and leverage existing technical infrastructure. As a center of competence at the Bank of Montreal, KM is like a startup business with a potential client base that spans across the Bank of Montreal group of companies. Its focus is providing KM tools and processes to line-of-business (LOB) clients who can demonstrate tangible value by using KM.

The KM team strives to understand the ongoing needs of internal clients rather than providing a menu of solutions. Once a specific challenge or ongoing project or initiative is understood, the team usually offers one of two ways to work in partnership with the internal client. The team may

1. Develop a prototype or a new process and technical solution.
2. Provide consulting services to incorporate KM principles as part of other projects (usually IT or organizational redesign projects).

The KM-IBS consulting group currently focuses on:

- *Community of practice development.* This consulting service increases the effectiveness of indiscriminate groups sharing a common strategic focus. It combines the teams' tools, templates, and reuseable information in one place for shared access. With the appropriate technology, the CoP can be supported in diverse physical locations.
- *Knowledge capture and deployment.* By capturing process and knowledge simultaneously, the focus is on reducing the time required to introduce changes, increasing the level of compliance, and reducing the risk of knowledge leaving when employees change jobs.
- *Dissemination of best practices and cross-group collaboration.* This involves organizing specific best practices of certain areas for sharing and reuse by others and brokering "real-time" collaboration of work. This is particularly relevant when different areas pursue the same work and could benefit from joining forces and leveraging each other's resources and initiatives.
- *kCafé design and development.* The kCafé (knowledge Café), located in the Institute for Learning (IFL), a facility dedicated to lifelong learning for employees, promotes the development of an e-literate, knowledge-based workforce. The kCafé is a resource center and a virtual hub that connects learning to practical knowledge. Instead of relying on traditional librarians for help, the students-employees rely on knowledge engineers who can help them learn how to use the latest technologies and collaboration tools and tap into internal and external knowledge sources. The KM team

works in conjunction with the IFL to ensure the kCafé provides leading-edge knowledge tools. Employees attending training courses in the institute can go to the kCafé and start experimenting, learning, and working with tools such as online collaboration, expertise locators, document management, and instant messaging. The kCafé represents an important opportunity to introduce new KM tools and shape the behavior of more than 11,000 employees who attend the institute every year. There are plans to start replicating this environment in other locations of the bank.

To understand the full breadth and scope of KM initiatives within the Bank of Montreal, we asked Richard Livesley, senior manager, knowledge management, and Sasha Zupansky, senior business architect, knowledge management, to clarify which of the following goals was part of the mandate of the Bank of Montreal's KM community (their answers are based on our standard legend: P, primary goal; S, secondary goal; N, not relevant):

Communication tool (top down and bottom up):

(P) Improve communication of vision and knowledge strategy.

(S) Improve communication of company values.

(S) Keep the organization alert.

(N) Engage customers and community at large.

(S) Divulge results more broadly and promote systemic analysis.

(P) Facilitate bottom-up communication.

(P) Make it easy for employees to suggest improvements to management.

Push information and knowledge to employees:

(P) Capture, organize, and distribute codified knowledge (e.g., database access).

(S) Improve access to external sources of information and knowledge.

(S) Improve decision making.

(P) Empower front-line employees.

Improve reuse of knowledge:

(S)   Develop expertise maps (uncover existing knowledge).

(N)   Map and measure intangible assets.

(P)   Facilitate search of previously developed knowledge.

Foster collaboration:

(P)   Increase collaboration among different functions of the organization.

(P)   Increase collaboration among different locations of the organization.

(P)   Improve overall knowledge sharing.

(S)   Support the development of communities of practice.

(S)   Increase connections not related to work.

Improve human capital management:

(S)   Improve hiring.

(S)   Improve internal mobility and deployment of existing employees.

(N)   Integrate temporary and outside human resources and expertise.

(P)   Improve training and acquisition of skills.

(P)   Get new employees up to speed very quickly.

(P)   Reduce time spent on menial activities.

(S)   Improve employee retention.

(N)   Facilitate work and integration of telecommuters.

Improve relationship with external stakeholders and increase information flow:

(S)   Improve information exchange with suppliers, partners, and customers.

(N)   Capture customer information.

(S)   Improve customer satisfaction.

(S)   Reduce sales costs.

(S)   Reduce customer service costs.

our strategic focus is exploit technology and develop organizational readiness

Figure 9-1
Bank of Montreal Strategic Framework for Deployment, Organizational and Technology Readiness

STRATEGIC FRAMEWORK FOR DEPLOYING KNOWLEDGE MANAGEMENT AT THE BANK OF MONTREAL

The vertical axis on Figure 9-1 shows the change stages of the Bank of Montreal's KM journey from the awakening stage to the performing stage. Key initiatives are mapped across the horizontal axis, demonstrating increased value realization as deeper partnership integration occurs. This mapping does not represent all the bank's KM activities. It is an example of how the KM team visualizes and plans its KM projects according to the organizational and technology readiness of the areas involved.

KEY CORPORATE PORTAL INITIATIVES

Like many large organizations, Bank of Montreal faced a proliferation of intranets (over 200 in total) and platforms over the last few years.

In light of its goals of improving access to information and reducing duplication of information, the KM team has been involved in a number of CP initiatives designed to reduce the number of intranets. In some cases, the KM team took the leadership role for the CP effort; in others it joined forces with other areas. Three CP initiatives include My Bank®,* BMO Central, and the IBS community site.

The Bank of Montreal employees have access to information through a number of CPs. An employee's choice of which CP to open depends on whether he or she is looking for local, divisional, product, or general corporate information. It is expected that, by the end of 2002 or beginning of 2003, the bank will move to a more sophisticated CP concept, which will allow employees to truly personalize their experiences and reduce the number of windows required to perform their work. The aggregation, organization, and integration of repositories at the back-end represent a significant step toward helping employees find what they need to be more effective in their jobs.

My Bank®*

In the largest LOB, the personal and commercial client group, the consolidation of intranets is well under way. In mid-2000, a team led by Dave Reddoch, senior manager, Intranet Communication Project, developed a cohesive strategy to streamline the operations, technology, and content of dozens of intranets. This project was the beginning of a CP strategy called My Bank®.* P&CCG's Ontario Division, one of the largest lines of business at the Bank of Montreal, funded the project to support the branch field locations. Approximately 16,000 employees are in the retail bank network, of which 8,000 currently have access to My Bank®.*

My Bank®* is an excellent example of how the KM team at the Bank of Montreal works in partnership with other functional areas. To complete this work the KM team established links to the owners of the website, technical developers, and most important, the staff and leadership of Ontario Division. Three primary strategic goals push this initiative forward:

---

*My Bank® is a registered trademark of the Bank of Montreal.

1. Provide universal, browser-based access to every employee through a common set of tools.
2. Develop standardized job descriptions to help streamline how work is conducted across the bank, including every branch.
3. Define standard processes and procedures for content development to streamline Web-based content publishing.

After addressing basic infrastructure challenges, Dave's team set out to understand what kind of information people really needed to do their jobs. As Dave says, "It's important to focus on what is necessary and not spend time on the latest cool tool." The team analyzed a number of previous employee surveys and, based on this insight, developed three core objectives to meet employees' expressed needs:

1. Provide one place where employees can find all the information they require.
2. Focus on information that is necessary for people to do their jobs.
3. Web-enable applications that are essential for people to do their jobs.

Consolidation of the intranets evolved gradually. Initially, My Bank®'s* basic value proposition was to provide better organization to existing information by aggregating existing sites into logical buckets of information. This first step succeeded in helping employees find information more easily. However, it did not reduce duplicate information. To solve this problem, a central repository for data, processes, ideas, and best practices is being created. Employees will access these shared buckets of information through unique views, based, for example, on their location (division, flagship, community, or local branch). Currently, about 40 intranet sites are integrated into My Bank®* (Figures 9-2 and 9-3) plus a number of separate division and flagship sites. The remaining four retail divisions are expected to follow the P&CCG's Ontario Division integration model.

---

*My Bank® is a registered trademark of the Bank of Montreal.

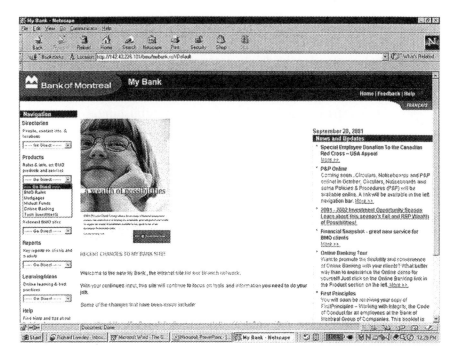

Figure 9-2
Corporate Portal, My Bank®,* Main View
(Source: Bank of Montreal)

---

*My Bank® is a registered trademark of the Bank of Montreal.

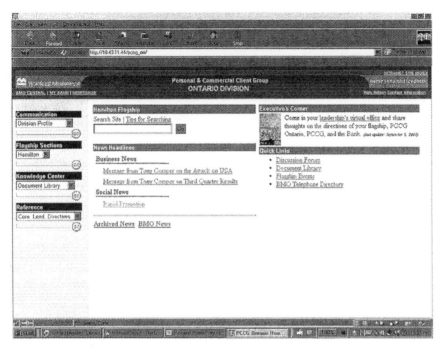

Figure 9-3
Corporate Portal, My Bank®, Branch View*
(Source: Bank of Montreal)

---

*My Bank® is a registered trademark of the Bank of Montreal.

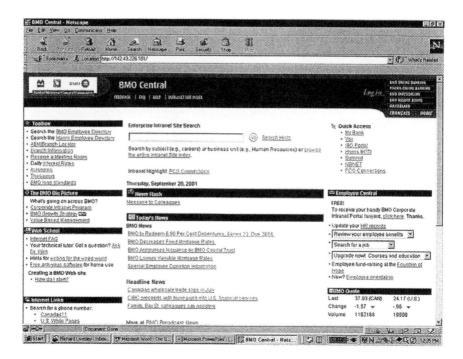

Figure 9-4
Corporate Portal, BMO Central (Source: Bank of Montreal)

BMO Central, Bankwide Intranet Site

BMO Central amalgamates various sources of corporate information and communications relevant for all employees under one intranet site (Figure 9-4). It is the central CP that amalgamates internal communications, Human Resources information, general news about the bank, and a number of productivity, utility, and facilities information and applications.

Integrated Business Solutions Community Site

The Bank of Montreal has a number of functional, divisional, and community-oriented sites. The IBS community site is an example. It hosts the KM community site and several other centers of competence communities.

The IBS community website provides a central communication point for 200 consultants. As seen on the Web page (Figure 9-5), it includes:

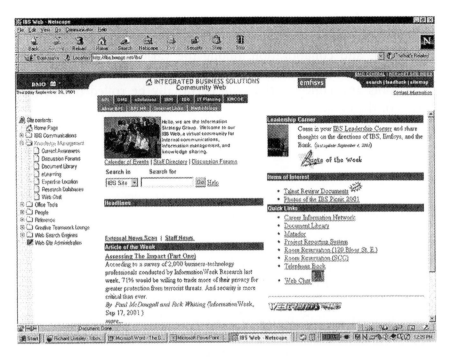

Figure 9-5
Integrated Business Solutions Community Site
(Source: Bank of Montreal)

■ A communications corner to provide key messages to employees, links to e-learning and relevant research databases of value to IBS professionals, and access links to key processes (including project management reporting tracking, appointments, directory access, and chat capabilities).

■ An integrated digital library of documents developed by the various core competence groups provides updated information about each group's mission, team members (with detailed profiles), activities, and projects, providing a much better understanding of what each group is responsible for.

The primary goal of the IBS community is to demonstrate the value of utilizing group portal and KM strategies to improve localized communication processes and integrate various business solutions. This may not appear to be a significant goal, but after the launch of this site, the 200 consultants reported a much better understanding of the activities of other areas within the centers of competence. This CP has been instrumental in fostering a much stronger sense of unity, integration, and collaboration among the various centers of competence. The IBS community site provided a good pilot area to test new KM tools and concepts that will eventually be rolled out to other areas of the bank.

METRICS

The impact of most of the KM team's activities cannot be directly linked to clear bottom-line results. However, there are three distinct ways to measure results that provide meaningful business impact:

1. *Demand for KM Services.* If KM's main goal is to support the business objectives of the bank, its services must be demanded by areas of the bank that have clear strategic and bottom-line objectives. The comparison of 2001 and 2000 budgets shows that LOB units increased their contribution to the KM team's budget by 50%. (The KM team started operating 100% dependent on a central corporate budget in 1998.)

2. *Employee Surveys.* The KM team relies on a number of surveys aimed at evaluating employees' perception about the quality and availability of tools, information, and knowledge to do their jobs. Sometimes, the KM team directly requests the surveys, and other times, it piggybacks on surveys conducted by other areas. Results remain consistently positive.

3. *Proxies of Specific Projects.* In many projects there are a number of quantifiable proxies that support the view that business and KM goals are aligned and being achieved. For instance, in the case of My Bank®,* the traffic on this site went up very rapidly—with at least 80% of the user base accessing it daily—and the usage pattern changed from strong peaks in the morning and afternoon to a more distributed traffic volume throughout the day. This change in traffic and usage suggests employees are increasingly using it as part of their daily work.

---

*My Bank® is a registered trademark of the Bank of Montreal.

KEY LESSONS LEARNED

Lesson 1. Focus Knowledge Management Initiatives in Strategically Important Areas

The KM team at the Bank of Montreal was able to identify strategic areas where KM tools and concepts produced tangible results. Some of these areas for the 2000–2001 period were (1) the need to codify the process for acquisitions, (2) standardized processes across the organization to leverage best practices, and (3) standardized integration of data, ideas, and best practices in a single repository. This strategic focus produces results that make KM more visible in the organization by delivering tangible value. In Richard Livesley's words, "We are a bank that is based on creating shareholder value. The key to deciding which projects to participate in is to what degree knowledge management's involvement will increase shareholder value—either by increasing revenues or decreasing costs." By clearly linking knowledge management to initiatives to value creation, knowledge management's contribution to the organization is more clearly identifiable.

Lesson 2. Knowledge Management Teams Need to Be Highly Skilled at Forming Strong Partnerships with Other Stakeholders

The most interesting and successful projects were developed in areas of the bank where the team was able to form strong alliances with key stakeholders. These alliances usually started through informal networks and eventually became more formalized as KM got "plugged in" to the area's initiatives. A KM community of practice is an important initiative that can foster strong partnerships and, consequently, leverage the reach and depth of KM projects. The KM team considers the ability to "broker alignment" and leverage work and intellectual assets from different areas as an important goal to the KM team's success.

Lesson 3. Knowledge Management Is Effective Only in Areas Where People Are Ready to Share Their Knowledge and Work Collaboratively

It makes no sense to implement KM initiatives in areas without at least a minimum level of readiness to share knowledge and form strong partnerships, as discovered in lesson 2. The KM team will not force "partnerships" in areas where key stakeholders are not committed to KM principles.

Lesson 4. It Is Important to Embed Knowledge Flow within Organizational Processes

Codification efforts (for instance, Best Practices in Mortgage Securitization) need to become actionable platforms. Employees who want to reuse the codified knowledge now have automated links to people, information, and templates at each step of the process. This is a tremendous improvement over the "manual or handbook approach": The KM team develops actionable and knowledge-rich work flow.

Lesson 5. Ask Employees What Kind of Information They Need to Do Their Jobs

Before engaging in a broader portal initiative, the bank conducted a number of surveys with employees to understand what kind of information they actually need to perform their jobs. A significant number of people in large organizations, especially those highly dependent on structured processes, are not necessarily concerned about high-level strategic information; they need and want information and knowledge to be better at their current jobs.

Lesson 6. People Want One "Easy Place" Where They Can Find the Information They Need

Closely related to lesson 5 is the notion that a portal should respond to a pressing need of most employees: Access to a single digital place where all the information and applications they require can be found.

Lesson 7. Link Corporate Portal Initiatives to Learning Strategies

As an increasing proportion of the Bank of Montreal's knowledge is integrated into the CP platform (including access to people and information), it is evident that CPs can become a powerful tool in providing training. Not only can CPs provide employees with the most up-to-date information and processes, they can also facilitate training with the same tools that will be available to them in their jobs. Closely related to integrating training and on-the-job learning through CPs is direct collaboration among people in training and other professionals on the job through the kCafé.

Lesson 8. Whenever Possible, Leverage Existing Technical Platforms to Achieve Quick Wins

Although Bank of Montreal's KM team continually monitors the environment for emerging platforms and concepts, it also tries to leverage existing infrastructure as much as possible. Frequently, the KM team discovers opportunities to further leverage existing applications for improved collaboration and knowledge sharing. For example, the full capability of powerful applications were not being utilized by the majority of the Bank of Montreal employees. A simple example of this is the way in which many staff use Lotus Notes only for mail. The KM team selectively expanded the use of Lotus Notes as a relevant tool to fulfill its client initiatives.

Lesson 9. In Knowledge Management-Related Efforts, Rapid Development and Proof of Concept Are More Effective than "Big Picture" Projects

The Internet environment, with its underlying open architecture and standards, allows the rapid development of proof of concepts and implementation of modular solutions. This, in turn, allows for fast tangible results and increased support and visibility for KM initiatives. While the KM team believes that infrastructure and carefully designed solutions are critical to long-term sustainability, their primary focus is on generating enterprise value and speed to market.

Lesson 10. Market and Leverage Successes

Collaboration is the key to a successful KM program. Through the kCafé, the KM team showcases examples where KM approaches have been used successfully in various areas of the bank.

FUTURE DIRECTIONS

To date, the bank has combined a number of intranets (more than 200) into less than 10 CPs. The next phase will likely see these different CPs further amalgamate under one unique platform that enables personalization by each employee. This will help the bank reduce duplication of content and effort, clearly leverage the best practices, and standardize key processes (such as sales management, strategic planning, and evaluating new technologies).

As more KM digital solutions are integrated into the day-to-day activities of employees, these solutions will foster a closer link between offsite and on-the-job training tools and new collaboration paradigms. The bank is promoting e-literacy and devoting significant resources to train its workforce. The KM team plays an active role in achieving this effort, since this target is a fundamental building block for a collaborative and innovative organization.

The KM team also anticipates increasingly close links between its activities and those of the Human Resources department. Currently, the value of knowledge sharing is not integrated into core competencies of the bank. Increasing awareness of this requirement, as seen by many other multinationals, and integrating these behavioral expectations as part of the Human Resource planning process will result in more effective change leverage.

There is also increasing awareness at the Bank of Montreal that knowledge management should become a more strategic issue. As such, the KM leadership team is exploring its strategic value proposition under a broader intellectual asset umbrella. It is also prepared to demonstrate the implications of not creating, harvesting, and leveraging knowledge production more aggressively. The argument for pursuing KM more intensely is particularly compelling, due to the changing demographic composition of its employees and the high percentage of employees expected to retire in the next few years. The KM team and senior management recognize they must ensure the knowledge, knowhow, and best practices of future retirees are retained to help support the future workforce more effectively.

CLOSING PERSPECTIVES

The KM team at the Bank of Montreal shows that, to achieve results in large and complex organizations, such as a large bank, it is necessary to form a number of alliances and focus on strategic issues that create value. It also shows that there is no single KM solution. The experience at the Bank of Montreal clearly demonstrates the importance of understanding that KM represents a major paradigm shift for an organization and a series of coherent projects is necessary to support significant cultural changes.

An integral component of KM is the bank's central knowledge portals. Substantial portal modifications (from 200 to 10 CPs) have required numerous areas in the organization to work more closely together (and, to a certain extent, relinquish control) to avoid duplication, improve knowledge sharing, and develop a common set of standards and processes. Thus, the portal, in itself, is just the more tangible aspect, a visible end product. The most interesting challenges, however, and the ones that are likely to bear more fruit, are

- The required stakeholders' alignment that had to happen to move the CP projects forward.
- The ongoing support for broader e-literacy and increased virtual collaboration among different areas and locations of the bank.

10

CONTEXT
INTEGRATION

CP/KM EXPERTS

Bruce Strong, chief people officer
Chuck McCann, director of strategic services

BACKGROUND

Context Integration (CI) is a leading integrator of e-business solutions. The company was founded in 1992 and has its headquarters in Burlington, Massachusetts. Its service line includes the integrated delivery of business, creative, and technology design primarily for the financial and media-communications sectors. The company has around 300 employees in six offices across the United States. Despite the recent tough business environment and shortage of funding in its sector, in March 2001, CI announced that it was able to secure $25 million in additional funding from investors including Capital Resource Partners, GE Equity, Atlas Ventures, and Sigma Partners.

THE CATALYST, GOALS, AND DRIVING FACTORS

Bruce Strong, one of the founders of CI, explained that its knowledge management system is a natural outcome of the core values of the company and of a clear, explicit three-pronged pursuit of value creation in every activity.

- The core values of CI are:
  Deliver outstanding client value with integrity.
  Invest in employee growth.
  Balance work and personal life.
  Commit to teamwork.
  Embrace innovation.
- Value creation at CI includes the perspective of the client, the employee, and the investor:
  Client and employee value delivery are often gauged through third-party surveys.
  Value for investors (shareholders) is delivered through a combination of profitable projects and the proactive capture of knowledge developed during the course of projects.

In founding CI, Bruce and the other partners set out on a journey to build intellectual capital and have fun along the way. As the company grew and expanded geographically, with the frantic need to tap into the latest technological know-how to compete successfully, Bruce recognized that CI needed more than just smart individuals and a knowledge-sharing culture. It needed a supporting KM platform that would better connect the minds of the organization.

The Intellectual Assets Network (IAN) filled that need. Over the 6 months beginning in late 1997, CI invested just over $500,000 in the initial development of IAN. Although IAN leveraged CI's initial investment in Lotus Notes collaborative software, a great deal of in-house development was necessary to customize IAN's functionalities to fit the way CI conducts its business. According to Bruce, to be useful, IAN needed to capture knowledge as it was being created and disseminate that knowledge in real ime. IAN was also designed to help CI better serve its customers. As Bruce highlighted, "Although we [at CI] rely extensively on technology, we are not a scientific company, we are a services company."

Since its inception, the basic goal of sharing knowledge vertically and horizontally within CI and within and outside the walls of the organization (especially with clients and occasionally with partners) has been the key driver of the continued development of the architecture of IAN. Other specific objectives have also been incorporated in IAN over time. Bruce and Chuck evaluated IAN's objectives against our standard list of CP/KM objectives and the current inventory of goals follows (as before, P, primary goal; S, secondary goal; N, not relevant):

Communication tool (top down and bottom up):

(S) Improve communication of vision and knowledge strategy.

(S) Improve communication of company values.

(P) Keep the organization alert.

(P) Engage customers and community at large.

(P) Divulge results more broadly and promote systemic analysis.

(P) Facilitate bottom-up communication.

(P) Make it easy for employees to make improvement suggestions to management.

Push information and knowledge to employees:

(P) Capture, organize, and distribute codified knowledge (e.g., database access).

(S) Improve access to external sources of information and knowledge.

(S) Improve decision making.

(P) Empower front-line employees.

Improve reuse of knowledge:

(P) Develop expertise maps (uncover existing knowledge).

(S) Map and measure intangible assets.

(P) Facilitate search of previously developed knowledge.

Foster collaboration:

(P) Increase collaboration among different functions of the organization.

(P) Increase collaboration among different locations of the organization.

(P) Improve overall knowledge sharing.

(P) Support the development of communities of practice.

(N) Increase connections not related to work.

Improve human capital management:

(N) Improve hiring.

(S) Improve internal mobility and deployment of existing employees.

(N) Integrate temporary and outside human resources and expertise.

(P) Improve training and acquisition of skills.

(P) Get new employees up to speed very quickly.

(N) Reduce time spent on menial activities.

(P) Improve employee retention.

(S) Facilitate work and integration of telecommuters.

Improve relationships with external stakeholders and increase information flow:

(S) Improve information exchange with suppliers, partners, and customers.

(P) Capture customer information.

(P) Improve customer satisfaction.

(P) Reduce sales costs.

(P) Reduce customer service costs.

CUSTOMER VALUE

Bruce and Chuck believe that IAN allows CI to win more business, deliver better work, and solve emergencies more quickly. The need for even deeper levels of collaboration with clients has led CI to develop PETE (Project Enablement Team Environment), a natural extension of IAN. PETE takes collaboration and knowledge sharing beyond CI's internal community. It provides CI's clients full access to the evolution of their own projects in a password-protected environment.

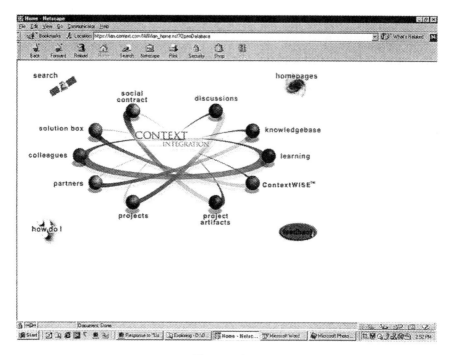

Figure 10-1
Context Integration Project Home Page (Source: Context Integration)

Not only can the clients see the evolution of a number of project elements in real time, such as project plan, key deliverables, and other account management documents, they can easily make suggestions and participate in online discussion boards (see a sample of a project home page in Figure 10-1). It is no wonder that clients seem very satisfied with the results provided by CI. According to a survey commissioned by CI and conducted by Gantz Wiley Research, 93% of CI's clients were either satisfied or very satisfied with the overall results of projects and were particularly impressed (88% Very Satisfied) with how CI employees were able work as a unified team with client team members.

IMPLEMENTATION JOURNEY

1997: Planning and initial development.

1998: IAN roll-out.

1999: Implementation of Good IAN Citizen, metric system to evaluate employees' contribution.

2000: Rollout of PETE.

2001: Integration of IAN and PETE, IAN's upgrades.

CURRENT CORPORATE PORTAL ENVIRONMENT

IAN was developed on a Lotus/Domino platform and uses a Verity search engine. Since the initial rollout, IAN evolved slowly but constantly. CI has only one full-time developer dedicated to improving and maintaining IAN. IAN connects employees from six offices and allows them to share ideas. Employees have access to IAN from anywhere and at anytime: from client sites, home, or anywhere else they can get an Internet connection. To access certain areas or databases of IAN, employees need not even be connected to the Internet, since parts of IAN can be downloaded to the hard drives of employees' laptops (the light version is just under 700 MB and the heavy version is 2 GB). IAN can also direct urgent questions to experts via a pager or other wireless devices (such as a cell phone, Blackberry, or Palm).

IAN is organized into the following key areas, which are as depicted on its home page (Figure 10-2): search, discussions, knowledge base, learning, ContextWISE,™ project artifacts, projects, partners, colleagues, solution box, and social contract.

- *Search.* The Verity engine allows the user to target the search according to a number of parameters including author, date, language, project, technology domain, and topic.
- *Discussions.* This area includes all the ongoing discussion databases, representing a variety of topics related to CI business. The topics are based on either technology, sales category, or some other category—the metadata are constantly evolving to meet the changing needs of the consultants as they capture and search for information. Employees can subscribe to receive notification every time a new posting has a topic of interest to them or has been posted by selected individuals (usually other employees working in similar knowledge fields or projects). They also use the discussion area to post documents, tips, links, and questions. The questions are automatically directed by IAN to be answered by "gurus" via e-mail and pager. Questions are classified by users into one of the following categories according to their urgency:
  - Immediate requires response in less than 1 hour.
  - Urgent requires response in less than 4 hours.

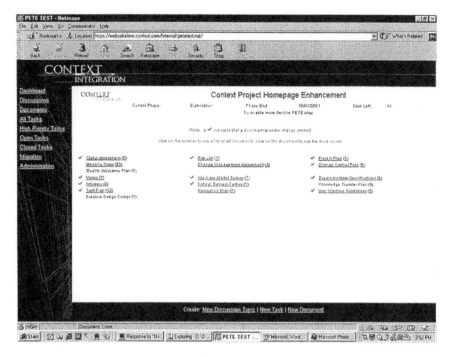

Figure 10-2
IAN Home Page (Source: Context Integration)

- Routine requires response in less than 1 business day;
- Not time sensitive responses can be given within 1 week.

Recently, CI developed an automated work flow to make sure only relevant and updated data are available in the Discussions area. The work flow follows traditional content management system processes: After a predetermined time, authors are notified that their document is up for review. The author may decide whether to maintain existing content on IAN as is, update it, or send it to the archive.

■ *Knowledge base.* This area includes a set of documents or discussion threads that have been reviewed by experts in their field and deemed to be of high value for reuse. Only domain experts can post or upload directly to this collection of documents. Documents called *roadmaps* are posted here. These documents are written by domain experts or practice leaders and serve as a comprehensive introduction for new employees or novices who need to get quickly acquainted with a specific domain.

- *Learning.* This area contains all information related to the learning process at CI. Documents include Curriculum Paths (a set of skills needed to achieve competency in a particular area, including methods for attaining the skills), pointers to internal and external class descriptions and schedules, and previously recorded training sessions available for playback. The playbacks are developed by Presentonline (parent company Intercall) and include audio and slides.

- *ContextWISE.* This area contains all information related to CI's core methodology. Descriptions of all tasks in the methodology (including best practices and pointers to sample deliverables) are contained here. Custom tools are also included here—these are released quarterly for download to consultant's laptops. At this point, the ContextWISE Workbench includes the Word Kit (a series of automation macros and document templates for most ContextWISE deliverables), the Estimating Toolkit (an automated Excel workbook to assist in estimating projects), and the Project Planning Toolkit (a series of Microsoft project templates for each phase in the methodology).

- *Solution box.* This allows employees to enter suggestions around any aspect of the business. The suggestions are forwarded to the senior management team, which needs to respond within a week. The company logs one suggestion per month. Because of the importance and consideration given to this, the suggestions tend to be of high quality.

- *Project artifacts.* This is where employees upload all information (artifacts) related to specific projects at certain predetermined milestones. Artifacts encompass a broad range of intellectual assets, from sales presentations to software codes. Project managers and quality assurance professionals have specific responsibilities related to this area. They have the mandate to make sure that knowledge developed within individual projects is properly captured, packaged, and shared with the rest of the firm. As consultants upload objects to PETE, they have the option to let the system automatically migrate these objects to the Project Artifacts area. If they are unsure, they can mark the documents "undecided," for later review by or with the project manager.

- *Projects.* This work-in-progress area has specific folders for each project. All employees have access to all projects and documents unless otherwise stated. The links to PETE are located here.

- *Partners.* A list of contacts for each important CI partner is listed here. Contacts are usually domain experts in a specific technology.
- *Colleagues.* The firm is adamant that employees keep their profiles up-to-date (see Figure 10-3 with Chuck's profile). A digital photo is taken of employees on their first day with CI, so that their initial profile can be set up immediately. As soon as their profiles are entered in IAN, employees interested in the profiles of new hires are immediately notified. At each major project milestone or training, employees are requested to update their technical and non-technical profiles (see Figure 10-4 for the form). If they fail to keep their profiles current, employees are reminded by project managers and quality assurance personnel of the importance of doing so. Employees are also "incentivized" to keep their profiles current through the opportunity to earn points towards Good IAN Citizenship (discussed under "Organizational Support").

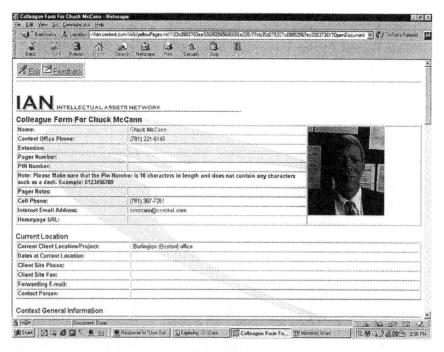

Figure 10-3

IAN Colleague's Profile, Chuck (Source: Context Integration)

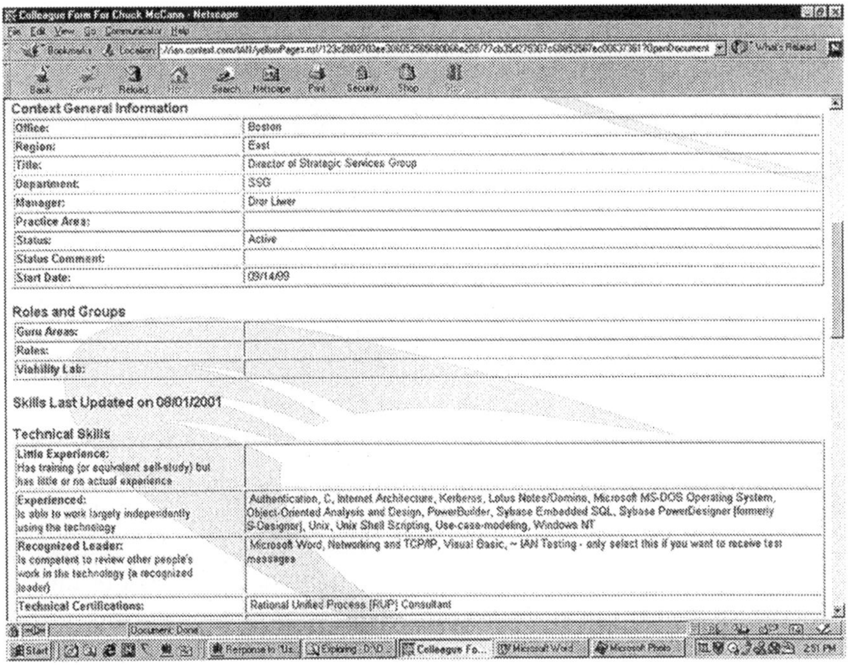

Figure 10-4
IAN Colleagues' Profile Form (Source: Context Integration)

ORGANIZATIONAL SUPPORT

The fundamental role IAN plays in CI's success becomes apparent when one understands the degree to which IAN is integrated into CI's work. This level of success is the result of not only a well-designed system but the strong support offered by management in many areas. In addition to being the brainchild of one of the founders (so no lack of senior management here), five other aspects illustrate the organizational commitment for IAN: the dedicated role of the moderator for IAN, the role of "gurus," the commitment to a knowledge-sharing culture, the CI social contract; and the reward program, Good IAN Citizen.

The Dedicated Role of a Moderator for IAN

The moderator plays a very important role in the ongoing success of IAN. This full-time professional is the "bug behind the ears of the experts" and the "keeper of IAN." The main responsibilities of the moderator include

- Ensuring that the categories of discussions, roadmaps, and navigation elements match CI's business needs.
- Identifying which knowledge domain areas are most and least active. These strategic questions are brought up to senior management, practice, and knowledge domain leaders.
- Ensuring that documents are updated as needed, discarded when no longer accurate, and archived when they become superseded or irrelevant for CI's business. This function is executed together with CI's "gurus" (next item) and practice leaders.
- Monitoring activities within IAN and verifying that requests for help do not go unanswered.
- Evaluating employees' contributions to IAN and tracking employees' point accumulations for Good IAN Citizen awards.
- Always "listening" to users; making an ongoing effort to identify the things they like and do not like about IAN.
- Leading the Advisory Committee (discussed in more detail later).
- Managing new development projects.

The Role of Guru

Knowledge domain leaders at CI are called *gurus*. All employees can apply to become "guru." Most applications are accepted since employees tend to apply only once they feel they have enough expertise in a certain field. "Gurus" play an important role in keeping IAN functioning and delivering high-quality knowledge at the point of need. Not only are they called to help organize, categorize, and update documents in their domain, they are the ones IAN will notify by pager in case other consultants ask for help. As discussed already, some questions may require immediate response. So becoming a "guru" leads to internal prestige but added responsibilities and availability.

The Commitment to a Knowledge-Sharing Culture

The value CI places on building a knowledge-sharing culture is reflected in the profile of people the company seeks to hire. They actively look for SWANs (smart, hard working, ambitious, and nice). Recruiting firms and interviewers are asked to explicitly write down why they think candidates are or are not SWANs. Candidates and employees who do not demonstrate this profile (especially the "nice" aspect) are quickly rejected by management and other employees.

Our conversations with a number of employees at CI revealed that, in addition to helping employees solve specific problems and find valuable knowledge, IAN helps build social capital. Meg Salgado, a project manager, highlighted that "IAN helps us feel part of the company even at client sites." Karl Kutschke, a client manager, explained that, from his point of view, the best aspect of the system was that it helped him develop relationships and get input from other employees across the company: "It is a habit almost everyone follows; whenever you have a free moment, you check your e-mail and IAN."

The importance of sharing knowledge and the role of IAN are highlighted as soon as new employees join the firm. All employees must complete a 2-week orientation program where they receive hands-on training on IAN. They soon discover how IAN is ingrained in every day's work process and is a key source of CI's collective intelligence. Whenever a work-related question among employees at CI emerges, the first response is usually, "Have you already asked or checked at IAN?" Novices who send broadcast e-mail with questions or requests are quickly (and firmly) reminded that they should consult IAN first.

CI also supports projects and ad hoc exchanges of knowledge outside the IAN online environment. For example, teleconferences are a regular occurrence within the company. Employee participation in these events usually depends on the person's practice or specific function affiliation (project management, creative, technology architecture, business analysis). Typical outcomes of these meetings include decisions to write "white papers," review methodologies, investigate specific technologies, and embark on market research projects.

Finally, the direct and visible commitment to IAN and knowledge sharing is also clearly demonstrated by the actions of senior management. Senior managers are active participants in the discussions on IAN, and they make sure that the leading contributors to IAN get public recognition (in addition to monetary bonuses). Every quarter, when Stephen Sharp, CI's CEO, receives the metrics of IAN participation collected by the moderator, he delivers an enterprisewide conference call and acknowledges leading contributors to IAN. These conference calls are another visible sign of support for knowledge sharing: During the calls, everyone is allowed to (and encouraged to) ask questions to the CEO. The whole conference call is also recorded and made available for further listening.

The CI Social Contract

One of the most distinctive and prominent links on IAN's home page is the Social Contract. The company and, particularly, Bruce give great importance to this section. The Social Contract is introduced to new employees as soon as they join the company. It spells out the "rules of engagement" for using IAN and how employees should "operate" in the CI environment:

> Context Integration asks that users of its systems be aware of, and adhere to, these principles of good business practice, courtesy and security. Please read these policy statements. If you have any questions about any of these policies, please contact the IAN Moderator for more information (use IAN Feedback to do this). Violation of these policies may lead to suspension of system privileges and dismissal.

> 1. Being a thoughtful IAN user:
>   - *Searching the Knowledgebase before starting a discussion.* Before starting a new discussion, look to see if there is already a posting in the Knowledgebase. (IAN has many search facilities available to aid you in this process.) Starting "new" discussions when the thread already exists is a waste of time and resources for everyone.
>   - *Priorities in the Discussion area.* Only use priority "Urgent" when you absolutely need an answer quickly. Expect your credibility to drop and to be flamed if you "cry wolf."
>   - *Large documents.* Zip any file larger than 100 K to minimize network traffic and replication times.
>   - *Summarize what you learn from your colleagues for your colleagues.* If you ask for help in IAN, you are expected to summarize your findings and results to share with your colleagues. This means that you post the answer (or combination of answers) that addressed your question. You can do this by adding to the original posting of the question, or by creating a separate response posting. If it's a Discussion posting, you should mark it "closed" at the same time. Please provide enough detail that another person could follow the

steps. If you were unable to resolve your question, or only partially so, that is useful information too, and should be shared.

2. The following is specifically prohibited:
   - *Being abusive or foul.* Communications, internal and external, that are inflammatory, harassing, defamatory, disruptive to others' operations, or otherwise reflect poorly on CI's reputation or image.
   - *Compromising the security of the system.* You may not give any outside body (including clients, partners, or friends) access to IAN. IAN contains vital business information—this information is strictly proprietary to CI. If you should demonstrate the system to anyone outside *Context* on a Web browser, be sure to completely close the browser to ensure that the session with IAN is ended.
   - *Posting client proprietary information.* Please use discretion when asking your questions and posting client information to IAN. Some of what we deal with is considered proprietary information by our clients and they would not appreciate seeing this information broadcast out to a public forum. This could include information such as addressing schemes, network diagrams, etc. If you're not sure, please check with your manager or the client before posting the information. In many cases you can overcome this problem by eliminating references to the client from the posting.

3. The reward program for "Good IAN Citizens." CI has always fostered a nonhierarchical culture, praised knowledge sharing, and rewarded employees who become specialists (gurus) in certain knowledge areas. Despite all of these efforts, the introduction of direct recognition and financial rewards to people who contribute to the knowledge base of IAN did lead to significant increase in the usage of the system. This demonstrates the power and importance of giving explicit and visible rewards for knowledge sharing.

In January 1999, the company included participation in IAN as an objective in every employee's job description. Employees become "Good IAN Citizens" if they actively use the system. In practice, participation is measured by activities such as maintaining an up-to-date personal profile, uploading project artifacts or documents, posting links, answering questions, posing questions, and making suggestions about how to improve the system. IAN tallies the results of these measurements every quarter based on rules defined by management, such as one point for asking a question, five points for uploading a project artifact, etc. Employees with more than 15 points are considered "Good IAN Citizens."

METRICS AND USER SATISFACTION

IAN's moderator tracks a number of items, such as number of postings, number of questions, most active categories, least active categories, and most active employees and offices. This tracking system is not as sophisticated as the measurement systems available for the most advanced Web-based systems, which allow various ways to analyze and display log data, but at least it is closely monitored, well focused on strategic knowledge domains, and serves as the basis for rewards and for the company to gauge activity around knowledge-creating processes.

The company tracks the aggregate number of documents that have been uploaded or sent to archive (negative value). For example, according to an October 2000 spreadsheet, the net results then were:

- 239 new documents were added to the discussion forums.
- 59 to the knowledge base.
- The total number of employees was reduced by 4.
- The project area gained 10 documents.
- 75 new projects or proposals records (metadata) were entered.
- 55 new project objects were added.
- The number of templates in the solution box jumped from three to nine.

IAN's moderator also keeps tight control on the number of postings and questions being asked and how fast and satisfactorily IAN's community responds. According to another report we saw, during July 2001, the average response per question was 1.59 and the average number of days for the first answer was 2.25 days.

Ensuring that IAN continues to meet CI's needs requires the active participation of an advisory board that includes leaders from different practices and locations. The board meets regularly to discuss improvements to the system and set priorities for the development pipeline.

Chuck, who is responsible for all internal services, also completes walk-around surveys periodically with a cross-section of users. He continually looks for employee-IAN success stories and different opinions on what is and is not working in the system.

KEY LESSONS LEARNED

Lesson 1. Customize the Knowledge Management System to Your Specific Business Needs

IAN was developed to suit the specific needs of the projects conducted by CI. It is not only a repository of knowledge, it is each employee's friend, helping him or her through the many phases of a project. Every step of they way, from proposal development to project closing, IAN is there to provide advice in the form of templates, connections to others, access to previously developed work, and the like.

Lesson 2. The Knowledge Management System Has to Reduce Information Overload

Information overload is a huge problem in almost every organization. Yet, despite its vast collection of documents and databases, IAN makes life much simpler for employees. For example, it lets employees preselect the newsletters or notices that they are really interested in and reduces e-mail broadcasting (employees' self-defense mechanism of copying as many people as possible on e-mail). By posting information or questions via IAN, employees receive feedback or responses according to other people's expertise, interest, and availability. It is all about context.

Lesson 3. Timing Adds Value to Knowledge

CI realizes that, to win bids in a highly competitive environment and better serve its customers, its consultants need answers delivered on a timely basis. In some cases, it might be a matter of hours; in other circumstances, the requests may be treated as routine learning. This might be a straightforward concept, but most companies do not pay as much attention as CI did to how perfect timing adds value to knowledge.

Lesson 4. Provide a Risk-Free Environment for the Discussion of Work in Progress

In organizations with a knowledge-hoarding culture, employees are afraid to pose questions that may show their lack of knowledge in specific areas. They also tend to not share work in progress. At CI, senior management sends clear signals that this is not appropriate behavior. In fact, people are rewarded for asking questions, and everyone has access to every project as it develops. The same logic applies in interactions with clients. CI does not want clients to be surprised but to contribute to the success of projects. It wants trust-based relationships internally and externally: Consultants not only spend most of their time at clients' sites, they also share their working in progress through PETE.

Lesson 5. Knowledge Management Systems Require a Combination of Technology and Dedicated Personnel

IAN would certainly not have achieved its current level of success without the full-time dedication of a moderator, gurus who provide needed expertise, and the contribution of each employee toward, for example, maintaining profiles and contributing tips, white papers, links, questions, and answers.

Lesson 6. If You Are Serious about Knowledge Management, You Need to Measure It

Since its inception, IAN's design has included metrics to help management "measure" the usage of the system (for example, growth in traffic, contributions, questions). These metrics do not reveal the quality of the knowledge exchanges, but they certainly provide clues that an attentive and astute management team can use to further investigate and evaluate more qualitative results. The metrics also provide important signals to employees about the kind of behavior that the company expects of them.

FUTURE DIRECTIONS

CI and its employees seem to be very happy with the results delivered by IAN. CI is not a very large organization yet, with tremendous resources to invest in information technology. It works to improve IAN constantly but incrementally. Budget and scale allowing, says Chuck McCann, the next logical step for CI would be to implement My IAN, a personalized Web-based view of IAN for each employee.

Closing Thoughts

IAN has proven a valuable component of CI's trajectory. It is the digital glue that keeps employees connected and part of the whole. Its level of success is due to a number of factors:

- The vision and active involvement of CI's leadership.
- Close attention to the knowledge needed to run the business.
- Adequate operational resources to maintain and constantly improve the system.
- Proactive (and visible) efforts to shape a knowledge-sharing organizational culture.

11

ELI LILLY

CP/KM EXPERT

Aaron Schacht, managing director, Lilly University

BACKGROUND

Eli Lilly and Company marked its 125th anniversary in 2001. The global research-based company was founded by Colonel Eli Lilly in 1876 in Indianapolis, in the U.S. Midwest. Lilly is a leader in the pharmaceutical industry. The company employs more than 35,000 people worldwide (50% outside the United States) and markets its medicines in 159 countries. In 2000, it reported revenues of approximately $11 billion and a net income of $3 billion. The company spends about $2.0 billion in Research and Development and almost 7000 employees are engaged in this knowledge-creating activity. Despite these impressive numbers, Lilly recognizes that it is increasingly hard to create knowledge alone. It has, therefore, entered into dozens of research alliances worldwide to gain access to new research capabilities.

UNDERSTANDING KNOWLEDGE MANAGEMENT AT ELI LILLY

Back in 1999, Eli Lilly's CIO, Roy Dunbar, hired Ernst & Young (E&Y) to help the company quickly shape its e-business and knowledge management strategy. A number of senior executives participated in a series of intensive workshops organized by E&Y. Out of this hyperlearning environment came a leadership commitment for KM at Eli Lilly. Despite being commissioned by the CIO, it soon became clear that KM was not simply an issue of information management. It certainly involved a seamless integration of hard and soft issues that would be better handled under the leadership of a newly appointed chief learning officer (CLO), Sharon Sillivan, former VP of Human Resources. In February 2000, Aaron Schacht became Eli Lilly's first KM director. Aaron came from the business side of Eli Lilly. He used to work at the drug discovery strategy area of the organization.

Aaron's team, from the start, included four individuals with a strong Web development background, two members originally from the Human Resources department with experience in training and organizational effectiveness, and a leading content manager (from the Library and Information Services group but working part time). This initial combination of skills is still at the core of the KM team. The complete team, however, is much larger today, almost 50 people. The higher number of employees is not only the result of the increase in the breadth and depth of projects but a realization, in April 2000, that the existing large team of Library and Information Services needed to work more closely with the KM team. These people became part of the content management team (the change in nomenclature reflects the required Web orientation that the whole team developed). The current configuration of the KM team is as follows:

- Web development, 12 members.
- Process design, 6 members (focusing on the development of communities of practice).
- Content management, about 30 members devoted to external content and 7 members devoted to the architecting and classification of internal content.

The responsibilities for training at Eli Lilly came under Aaron's leadership in May 2001. He is now the managing director of Lilly University. We do not cover these activities but highlight that this change represents a strong view at Eli Lilly that learning requires a seamless integrated approach, including

- Offline and online learning.
- Offsite and on-the-job learning.

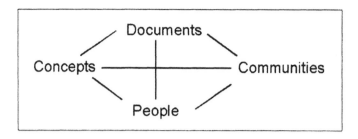

Figure 11-1
Knowledge Management at Lilly, Establishing Meaningful Connections

■ External and internal learning.

An interesting additional perspective that Aaron has is about the role of the KM department: "Our job is to connect people, communities, documents, concepts in meaningful ways." This is explained in Figure 11-1.

To sum up the current scope of KM activities at Eli Lilly, we asked Aaron to respond to our standard questionnaire (as before, P, primary goal; S, secondary goal; N, not relevant):

Communication tool (top-down and bottom-up):

(S) Improve communication of vision and knowledge strategy.

(S) Improve communication of company values.

(S) Keep the organization alert.

(S) Engage customers and community at large.

(S) Divulge results more broadly and promote systemic analysis.

(S) Facilitate bottom-up communication.

(S) Make it easy for employees to suggest improvements to management.

Push information and knowledge to employees:

(P) Capture, organize, and distribute codified knowledge (e.g., database access).

(P) Improve access to external sources of information and knowledge.

(P) Improve decision making.

(P) Empower front-line employees.

Improve reuse of knowledge:

(P) Develop expertise maps (uncover existing knowledge).
(S) Map and measure intangible assets.
(P) Facilitate search of previously developed knowledge.

Foster collaboration:

(P) Increase collaboration among different functions of the organization.
(S) Increase collaboration among different locations of the organization.
(P) Improve overall knowledge sharing.
(P) Support the development of communities of practice.
(P) Increase connections not related to work.

Improve human capital management:

(S) Improve hiring.
(S) Improve internal mobility and deployment of existing employees.
(S) Integrate temporary and outside human resources and expertise.
(S) Improve training and acquisition of skills.
(P) Get new employees up to speed very quickly.
(P) Reduce time spent on menial activities.
(S) Improve employee retention.
(S) Facilitate work and integration of telecommuters.

Improve relationship with external stakeholders and increase information flow:

(S) Improve information exchange with suppliers, partners, and customers.
(S) Capture customer information.
(S) Improve customer satisfaction.
(S) Reduce sales costs.
(S) Reduce customer service costs.

Corporate Portals Project

Aaron's team engaged in the selection of a CP platform in the fall of 2000. His team scanned the vendors' market and studied four companies' offerings in much greater depth, including the development of prototypes. Five key criteria were used to select the winning platform:

1. *Personalization.* How easy and intuitive is it for users to personalize their working space?
2. *Speed.* How long does it take to deploy the platform?
3. *Robustness.* Which release of the software is available, and how many large deployments have used the software?
4. *Catalogue management.* How easy is it to develop a strong content directory?
5. *Application program interfaces.* How many are available and how relevant are they to the applications that the company wanted to integrate into the portal? Leading platforms should be completely modular, allowing organizations to build and integrate new applications gradually.

In the end, Eli Lilly opted for a combination of a Plumtree (CP) and Semio (Taxonomy) solution. Semio was selected for its robust automatic classification engine and its ability to support deeper classification structures.

It must be said, however, that Eli Lilly already had a fairly robust home-built portal, My ELVIS (Eli Lilly virtual information services). This initial solution already provided a central point for information access and included a few customizable applications (such as weather, stock listings, and calendar) and a self-service intranet cataloguing application. Aaron and his team learned that it paid to ask vendors to provide prototypes. Vendors were asked to replicate the experience of the existing portal using their platforms. This quickly separated the winners from the losers: Some vendors developed the prototype in a week, while others never got it running.

After deciding on a platform in December 2000, the KM team was able to launch the new My ELVIS for all worldwide operations of Eli Lilly on April 4, 2001. Four servers were able to balance the added load (one failed but the other three had no problem maintaining the service level). The team wanted to make the experience as user-friendly as possible, so users worldwide could make a seamless transition. Aaron summarizes this goal with the following statement: "Our goal was for users to become self-sufficient when operating in the portal. We wanted to create a complete online environment." Consequently, users needed no initial training. Instead, the new portal relied on Online Help features for each new application and an easier online feedback mechanism.

The total budget, including licenses, limited external consultants, and the KM team salaries, was well under $5 million. Eli Lilly's small Web development team (three to five individuals) did most of the creative work in developing the portal gadgets in a relatively short period of time (90 days). Other teams focused on development of content taxonomies and the integration of Semio software with the portal, while Lilly's IT infrastructure group developed the architecture and support mechanisms. Since the initial launch, the CP is evolving gradually through time-compressed development cycles. The current focus is to enable a more detailed personal profile, support communities of practice and other personal productivity tools, and offer greater access to external information.

At the same time as the KM team worked on the launch of the new My ELVIS, it developed a set of guidelines for the development of intranets. My ELVIS and all the centrally created applications actually represent only a portion of the Internet content being accessed by Eli Lilly employees. Decentralized intranets continue to exist to support specific areas' needs. However, content creators now have to adhere to much stricter format guidelines and standard content classification rules. In fact, in many communities, a two-tier publication model is being established with documents published only after being approved by a "community steward."

CORPORATE PORTAL ENVIRONMENT

My ELVIS's home page (Figure 11-2) includes standard corporate news, links to Eli Lilly's extensive directory and library of internal documents. Like many other pharmaceutical companies, Eli Lilly has a very large library of internally produced documents, numbering in the hundreds of thousands, a direct link to My Workplace (a SAP portal focused on employees' transactions, such as vacation time reporting, expenses reporting), and a number of interesting applications to foster people connections:

- A personal calendar integrated into the home page.
- View a Calendar, which allows employees to view other users' calendars.

Figure 11-2
Corporate Portal, My ELVIS's Home Page (Source: Eli Lilly)

- World Clock, an important feature for global companies.
- Pager, it automatically sends a note to other employees' pagers.
- Contact List, which allows employees to easily customize their contact list right into the browser; it includes phone numbers and direct e-mail and pager links.

In keeping with its focus on fostering meaningful connections, Eli Lilly is building powerful personal profile and communities of practice (CoP) applications. Both were developed through intensive interaction between the Web developers and process design professionals working in the KM department.

The full-text searchable Personal Profile application includes three main areas for each employee (Figures 11-3 through 11-5):

1. *Overview.* This includes basic business card information and a summary of expertise, job description, education, and previous jobs.

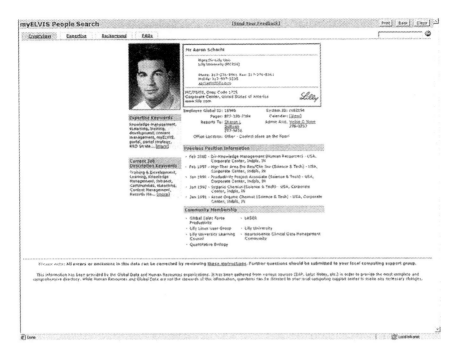

Figure 11-3
Corporate Portal, Personal Profile, Overview (Source: Eli Lilly)

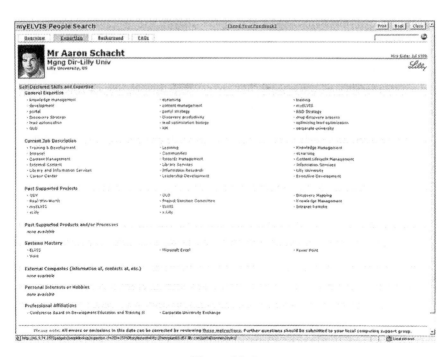

Figure 11-4
Corporate Portal, Personal Profile, Expertise (Source: Eli Lilly)

275

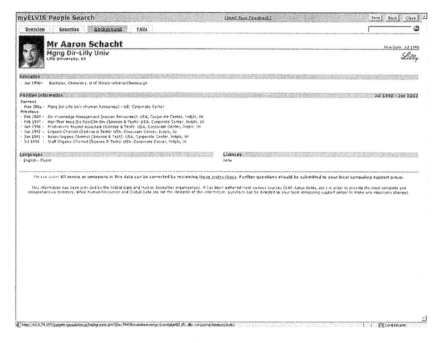

Figure 11-5
Corporate Portal, Personal Profile, Background (Source: Eli Lilly)

2. *Expertise.* This expands on details about the expertise of the employee. It includes the following fields: self-declared skills and expertise, current job description, past supported projects, past supported products or processes, system mastery, external companies (information of contacts), personal interests, professional affiliations.

3. *Background.* This is automatically generated from other company databases and highlights education, position information, languages, licenses.

Eli Lilly's KM team has been researching and supporting CoPs well before the development of the current CP. Among its many activities, we highlight the following:

- Identifying the shared goal of communities.
- Identifying the knowledge needs of community members.
- Establishing key roles for communities such as leaders and knowledge stewards.

Consequently, when it came to developing detailed requirements for the development and integration of a CoP application into the portal, the KM team was able to clearly communicate the core features required to support CoPs online. This is reflected in the core features shown in the "CommunitySpace" of the gadget developers CoP (Figures 11-6 and 11-7):

- Links to other communities.
- Community Overview (What We Are All About, Who We Are, Role Owners).
- Expertise Locator.
- Community Search.
- Feedback/Information.
- Subscription/Notification.
- Events Calendar.
- Upcoming Events.
- Broadcast Message.
- Discussion Forum.

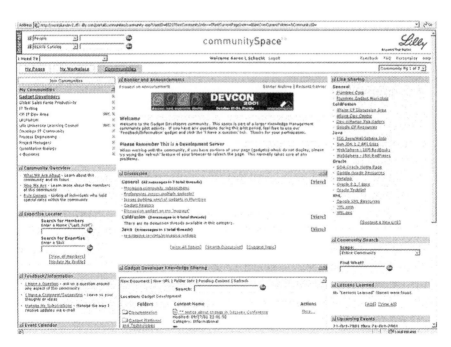

Figure 11-6
Corporate Portal, CommunitySpace (Source: Eli Lilly)

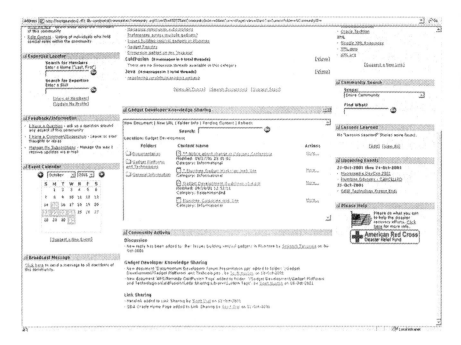

Figure 11-7

Corporate Portal, CommunitySpace, continued (Source: Eli Lilly)

- Best Practice Area.
- Community Activity.

Employees are also able to personalize their pages, My Pages, with the applications and content they require to do their jobs, keep them informed, and address their personal needs (with applications such as Classifieds and Weather). Aaron is of the opinion that it is OK to include applications that are not directly related to work. He understands that, in today's Knowledge Era, people's motivation defines what attracts one's attention and energy. By integrating fun and personal applications, he actually believes people can be even more productive—it just makes it easier to get errands done. In Figure 11-8, it must be noted that Aaron chose to integrate, in his My Page, an application from Moreover.com that allows direct integration of external news feeds into the Plumtree portal.

It is clear that CPs can be designed to include a number of well-organized buckets of competitive information. This was one of the KM team's key taxonomy goals when organizing Eli Lilly's directory.

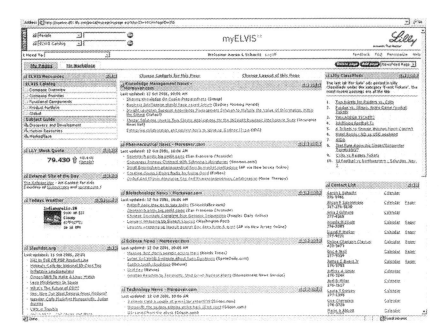

Figure 11-8
Corporate Portal, My Pages

Browsing alone sometimes can be very time-consuming. So, the integrated search helps users get quickly to the information they need by allowing selective full text search (including different file formats) of specific folders or subcategories of information (Figure 11-9).

METRICS

The rapid growth in the number of unique visitors and spike in the frequency of visits per week are the most evident signs that the efforts to develop My ELVIS 2.0 are paying off:

- The number of unique visitors increased almost 20% in just 6 months, as compared to approximately 5% growth in the employee base over the same period of time (Figure 11-10).
- More important, employees are visiting My ELVIS a lot more often, a good sign that the CP is providing more meaningful connections to relevant documents, links, and other people (Figure 11-11).

Figure 11-9
Corporate Portal, Competitive Intelligence (Source: Eli Lilly)

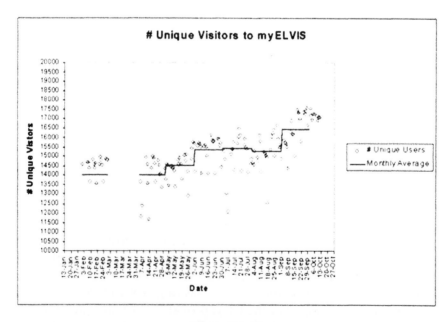

Figure 11-10
Evolution in the Number of Unique Visitors to My ELVIS
(Source: Eli Lilly)

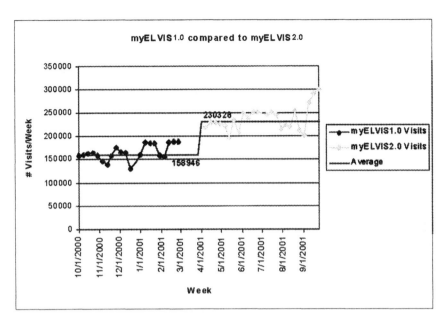

Figure 11-11
Evolution in the Frequency of Visitors to My ELVIS (Source: Eli Lilly)

KEY LESSONS LEARNED

Lesson 1. Knowledge Management Starts with a Strong Value Foundation from the Top

Eli Lilly's CEO, Sydney Taurel, recently gave Eli Lilly's KM team an important, if indirect, sign of support. He has communicated seven key behaviors that he expects of all Eli Lilly's employees. The most relevant for KM is the need for employees to share their key learning. This has become such an important issue that this kind of behavior is now linked to employees' performance reviews.

Lesson 2. A Primary Goal of Knowledge Management Is to Provide Continuous Learning

At Eli Lilly, there is a strong conviction that KM should be instrumental in providing employees continuous learning opportunities. Not only is KM operating under a chief learning officer, it includes most of the functions related to the structuring of internal and external information. That the KM leadership is also responsible for overall training and leadership development is another indicator of the strong convergence among training, learning, and information management. Finally, the CP was clearly developed to be both an individual and a social learning tool.

Lesson 3. Make It Very Easy for Employees to Find Other People and Build Their Own Personal Networks

By having a clear understanding that learning relies heavily on meaningful connections with other individuals, the KM team developed innovative gadgets that make it easy for employees to find other employees with relevant knowledge and to save their contact information right on the CP.

Lesson 4. Develop Web-Based Knowledge Management Applications in Short Development Cycles

After a few successful experiences, Aaron is convinced that short development cycles provide, at the same time, quick tangible results and a strong learning environment for the development team. The development team can easily gauge users' reactions through prototyping, piloting, and surveys. The "time-boxed" approach also gets the development team and key stakeholders a lot more focused on functions that users really care about and that deliver business results. Aaron's key advice is, "Don't let the perfect be the enemy of the good."

Lesson 5. Leverage Solutions That Users Find Useful and Deliver Business Value

The new CP at Eli Lilly leverages a number of existing applications that users care about. It also includes a number of new applications that the KM team thought would draw initial traffic, such as personal productivity tools (calendar, contact list) and personal applications (such as Weather and Classifieds). Most important, though, was that the development of the CP was a joint responsibility of technical (Web developers) and nontechnical (users and key stakeholders) employees. The KM team worked with the assumption that business unit leaders have to make decisions about their KM requirements.

Lesson 6. Choose Platforms That Provide Good Integration and Migration Paths from Your Existing Platforms

Large organizations have important legacy systems. Consequently, the selected CP platform should provide a good integration and migration paths to the existing systems. This becomes quite evident when different vendors are asked to develop pilots and prototypes. Integration efforts can vary widely depending on the chosen platform.

Lesson 7. Use Subject Matter Experts to Develop Taxonomies and Create Parallel Paths to Find Information

As much as automated categorization tools and external public structures can help expedite the development of an organization's taxonomy, in the end, subject matter experts need to be involved. At Eli Lilly, this means the KM's content managers engage in a series of in-depth validation sessions with experts from each relevant business area of Eli Lilly. This is not to say that there is "one right way" to classify information. In large organizations, different people have different ways of looking for information. For instance, some may have a process orientation, while others may have a discipline or a line of business orientation. Redundant or parallel paths to information are, therefore, an important requirement to help users find what they want in the minimal amount of time.

Lesson 8. Large Organizations Need to Combine the Benefits of Centralized and Decentralized Content and Web Development Strategies

It is clear that, in large and diversified organizations with many different offices, it is impossible to centralize content creation and Web development. This would hinder the pace of business, innovation, and the overall speed of information flow. Eli Lilly has not restricted the grassroots' ability to create; it has, however, developed clear publication guidelines for each community or functional area of the organization and still relies to a great extent on self-cataloging of content.

FUTURE DIRECTIONS

Aaron feels that he and his team have built a strong KM foundation with My ELVIS 2.0. However, much work is still to be done. Eli Lilly has a vast document and content library that needs to be "cleaned up." New important applications still need to be integrated (e-mail and business intelligence applications, for example) into the CP. Very much like the Internet itself, Aaron sees that My ELVIS's current challenge is to become an essential tool for collaboration and not only for content access and transaction (as provided by SAP's Workplace).

Eli Lilly also seems to be well plugged into one of the most advanced concepts: collaboration commerce. A stated vision is that the internal CP will provide the content management infrastructure and collaboration tools required for the organization to engage internal, external, and mixed communities into unprecedented levels of collaboration. According to Aaron, "We cannot do e-business externally without learning how to do it internally first." A physicians community is a good example of the kind of community that can easily emerge from this vision. This community could link physicians to their peers, Lilly's experts, and selected content from Lilly's own internal communities. Another example would be the emergence of research alliance communities linked via the CP. From a leadership perspective, this all seems to make sense and come together. The KM team built the CP under the CLO leadership but with the budget provided by the e-Business Division.

CLOSING PERSPECTIVES

There is no question that the pharmaceutical industry is one of the most knowledge-intensive economic sectors and that managing knowledge explicitly and efficiently is a question of survival. Eli Lilly, like many other organizations in this sector, has always managed knowledge, their most important raw material. Recently, however, Eli Lilly, like other leading organizations, embraced KM as a focused discipline. This means a more acute understanding of the impact of the intersection of a number of different business concepts, which is well represented in this case. To the distracted observer, the CP at Eli Lilly is just a tool to provide a centralized point of access to information. A careful analysis of the organizational structure and support, the evolution of the portal features, and the long-term vision show a much more interesting story. Eli Lilly is building a digital framework to provide accelerated innovation, continuous learning opportunities, and deeper relationships within its many internal and external communities and, finally, to leverage its intellectual assets to increase revenues and reduce costs.

12

HILL & KNOWLTON

CP/KM EXPERTS

Ted Graham, worldwide knowledge management director
Nicole Doyle, Canadian knowledge management director

BACKGROUND

Hill & Knowlton (H&K) is the second largest public relations firm in the world and a subsidiary of the WPP Group, a $22 billion U.S. company. H&K has a significant global reach, with 2000 employees operating in 67 offices located in 34 countries. The company strives to leverage the intellectual capital of all these offices while operating in a decentralized culture with a razor-sharp focus on client needs.

Since 1999, H&K has been deploying its knowledge management programs to clients with innovative solutions via the Web, as well as developing an employee portal capability to share internal knowledge and best practices.

THE CATALYST

Every innovative change brings a change agent who has a far-reaching vision. At H&K, this person was Tony Burgess-Webb, a member of H&K's worldwide executive committee and of the NetComs practice, a practice within H&K providing clients with cutting-edge interactive communications via innovative technology: Internet, intranets, and extranets.

In early 1999, Tony assessed H&K's current approach to KM and existing intranet infrastructure and support processes. Employee surveys confirmed the intranet was functionally limited, as the knowledge sourced was irrelevant, outdated, and inaccurate. In addition, the value of the knowledge-based initiatives did not have strong executive alignment, as current users were discontented with the value and performance of the KM infrastructure.

Hence, Tony proposed a new and bold vision to "Build something totally new." He began a leadership quest to share a compelling vision, goals, and project requirements with senior management. In early 1999, in a general management meeting where all global practice leaders assembled, about 60 executives, Tony shared his vision for a more robust and pervasive knowledge ecosystem at H&K. At this meeting, he communicated his rationale and told where H&K's competitors were via intranet and Web-based solutions. He spoke passionately about his beliefs that the focus on knowledge would benefit clients in developing stronger products and services and deliver consistent service across the company. He believed further investment in the KM infrastructure would help improve H&K globalization processes and leverage strategic knowledge into high-margin, repeatable activities. Tony is known for his use of metaphors and he used the analogy that when a horse is dead you do not drag it along, you get a new horse. The outcome of this meeting was unified executive support to invest in a more robust KM organization and initiate an investment process to help realize his dream.

ORGANIZATIONAL SUPPORT

Once the leadership team had aligned on Tony's vision, a worldwide knowledge management director, Ted Graham, was hired to oversee the KM organization and be accountable to bringing Tony's vision to life. Unlike many organizations pursuing corporate knowledge portal initiatives, Ted reports directly to H&K's chief executive officer, Howard Paster.

The organizational structure has a modest centralized operating structure and invested only $250,000 for the initial portal software licenses and development. The central KM organization includes Ted Graham, plus a global intranet content editor, an IT manager, and 50% of an additional information technology manager, who provides site customization services.

The balance of the KM organizational support is distributed as part of a broader community of practice. Each business unit has a KM coordinator and five regional executives are in charge of KM. Approximately 67 employees are engaged worldwide (full time or part time, depending on the size of the office). The majority of these roles are not full-time positions.

GOALS AND DRIVING FACTORS

The overall goals and mandate for H&K's KM initiative are to focus on areas that will benefit H&K clients and result in new products and services, provide consistent services across the globe, and leverage strategic thinking into high-margin, repeatable activities.

According to Ted Graham, the portal provides a guide to public work spaces, strives to meet the needs of different stakeholders and their unique personal interests, and provides strong value to the H&K business community. It has to produce benefits to the customers but also to H&K and its employees.

The company expects to link the portal efforts to faster revenue growth, increased productivity, greater leverage of existing knowledge, and to reduce the impact of turnover of employees. With respect to this last objective, it is important to note that the company realized that a large portion of each employee's contribution to the company's intellectual capital was being registered in e-mail exchanges. It was being registered but not necessarily organized or leveraged by other employees. Worse still, when employees left the company most of this source of intellectual capital was available only to a limited group.

Indeed, a major driver supporting migration to unified knowledge collaboration resulted from a tremendous explosion in electronic mail. The volume of e-mail messages in H&K went from 5000 units per day to 5000 per hour in the year 2000. This explosion resulted in significant organizational problems, as the ability to manage both structured and unstructured information became more acute.

In addition to these requirements, a number of primary and secondary goals were identified to further support H&K's corporate knowledge portal initiative priorities (as before, P, primary goal; S, secondary goal; N, not relevant):

Communication tool (top-down and bottom-up):

(S) Improve communication of vision and knowledge strategy.

(S) Improve communication of company values.

(S) Keep the organization alert.

(P) Engage customers and community at large.

(P) Divulge results more broadly and promote systemic analysis.

(S) Facilitate bottom-up communication.

(N) Make it easy for employees to make improvement suggestions to management.

Push information and knowledge to employees:

(S) Capture, organize, and distribute codified knowledge (e.g., database access).

(S) Improve access to external sources of information and knowledge.

(S) Improve decision making.

(S) Empower front-line employees.

Improve reuse of knowledge:

(P) Develop expertise maps (uncover existing knowledge).

(P) Map and measure intangible assets.

(P) Facilitate search of previously developed knowledge.

Foster collaboration:

(P) Increase collaboration among different functions of the organization.

(P) Increase collaboration among different locations of the organization.

(P) Improve overall knowledge sharing.

(P) Support the development of communities of practice.

(S) Increase connections not related to work.

Improve human capital management:

(N) Improve hiring.

(S) Improve internal mobility and deployment of existing employees.

(N) Integrate temporary and outside human resources and expertise.

(S) Improve training and acquisition of skills.

(P) Get new employees up to speed very quickly.

(P) Reduce time spent on menial activities.

(S) Improve employee retention.

(S) Facilitate work and integration of telecommuters.

Improve relationships with external stakeholders and increase information flow:

(P) Improve information exchange with suppliers, partners, and customers.

(P) Capture customer information.

(P) Improve customer satisfaction.

(S) Reduce sales costs.

(S) Reduce customer service costs.

IMPLEMENTATION JOURNEY

Program Sponsorship and Hiring of a Global Knowledge Management Director

1999: Establishment of KM support organization to support program and communication cascade.

1999: Training and content management processes deployed.

January 2000: Intraspect formally launched.

2000: Rewards and recognition programs deployed.

2000: Extranet: Customer collaboration centers established (e.g., Compaq, Motorola).

2000: Personalized portals deployed.

2001: Marketing of CP in client proposals.

Starting in 2001: CP integration with legacy applications (functional priorities; i.e., accounting, contact management, CRM, extranets, calendaring, instant messaging, Web gallery, etc.).

CURRENT CORPORATE PORTAL ENVIRONMENT

Overview

The evolution of value contributions of H&K's knowledge portal is seen as the collective brains of H&K's people. In everyday management practice, senior management helps set the tone of knowledge sharing and provides insights by including in their e-mail active links to the CP environment. This everyday behavior sets an example to employees worldwide that they should be familiar with the wealth of content available in the CP environment and, when they contribute or find best practices, to actively promote and share content. An organic evolution rapidly occurred; as content value increased, so did the promotion and support of the platform.

Even with the significant progress of the H&K knowledge management team since 1999, the team still describes its portal as a "poor man's portal" compared to some of the higher-end technical solutions, perhaps reflecting the limited budget it works with. Strategically, for content creation and content submissions, H&K adopted the view of giving people the power to add content versus controlling what is added. Everyone can contribute and participate in the process instead of having a centralized categorizing process. Recently added content is frequently monitored and any frequently requested documents are linked into a library for a special search area to highlight value content. End-user training is conducted on a regular basis to ensure that employees are trained to conduct the search properly and use their tools effectively.

H&K's knowledge portal is at the stage where the volume of knowledge has increased significantly and requires people to edit and weed—the maintenance continuum is an area for management attention to improve the sustainability capabilities.

Collaboration Platform

H&K uses the Intraspect platform to support its worldwide knowledge community. Intraspect solutions provide Web-based workspaces to capture information as it is created; many-to-many collaboration technology to share intellectual capital across employees, customers, partners, and suppliers; and an enterprise knowledge base that grows with the company. Over 300 companies and over 150,000 users use Intraspect solutions; it is one of the market leaders for enterprise collaboration management services.

The HK.NET is the company portal (Figure 12-1) that provides immediate access to a number of information sources and people. It includes access to customized portals according to regions of the world, a number of links to find expertise within the firm (directories, case studies, biographies, global client leaders, and organized documentation about key sectors) and several external news feeds that are relevant for H&K business. As part of its effort to create corporate alignment, shared value, and goals, the portal also maintains a prominent link to letters from its CEO, Howard Paster.

Intraspect provides a portal environment to facilitate the ease of content use and publishing. Alerts can be set up easily (Figure 12-2) and directed to a person's inbox or personal pager. Documents can be submitted in a wide range of document formats (office documents, e-mail, news feeds, etc.).

The portal's process capabilities are enhanced by the inclusion of a Verity search engine (Figure 12-3), which allows documents to be

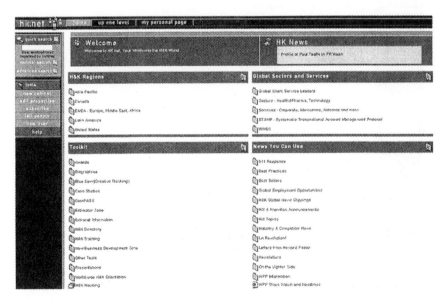

Figure 12-1
The portal: HK.NET (Source: Hill & Knowlton)

Figure 12-2
HK.NET Alert Services (Source: Hill & Knowlton)

Figure 12-3
HK.NET Search Engine (Source: Hill & Knowlton)

searched according to many different criteria (e.g., contextual results, best match searches, recency rankings, authors). Employees can use the search to look for projects, news feeds, topics, or people. Verity supports contextual search results, so one can see things easily categorized. It also allows narrowing the scope of search as it determines the types of documents that meet user requirements.

CUSTOMER VALUE

One capability of this knowledge collaboration environment attractive to H&K is the ability to integrate the company intranet and extranet and share selected information with clients via a password-protected site. An important attribute of H&K's CP is the support it provides their global accounts. The value of H&K's CP environment is actively promoted in business proposals and has helped secure clients such as Ernst & Young and Motorola. These clients, both knowledge-centric in their business approaches, were attracted to H&K's CP capability to access in a password-protected area H&K knowledge with external knowledge from targeted news sources and account activity (including ongoing and scheduled interviews, plans, work in progress documents, etc.). All e-mails related to a specific account are automatically stored in this client folder, so anyone joining the project can easily follow all the major milestones, decisions, and communications related to the project. Clients can also post information easily. The customer environment can be visually customized for each client, to facilitate unique branding.

Customer access capabilities were launched in late 1999 for three practice groups and subsequently launched corporationwide in early 2000. The overall portal implementation helps H&K generate better proposals much faster. Ted and Nicole estimate that the portal has helped H&K win a number of important new accounts.

OTHER METRICS

H&K is currently evolving its benchmarking metrics. The system today tracks standard visits and what information or areas of the Web are frequently used. Since the implementation of the new portal, the Internet traffic increased by 500% (over a period of less than 18 months).

Ted Graham also estimates that H&K's new acquisitions are being integrated much faster (50% of the usual time) and new employees are learning about the H&K culture, scope, activities, and sources of intellectual capital much faster. Ted estimates that the initial time to have them up to speed has been reduced to about one-third of what it used to take.

Currently most metrics are related to standard traffic measurements and occasional local surveys. In the future, the company hopes to evaluate the quality of the contributions and link the reward system to real-time contributions. Measuring what people have *not* found in the system (through structured analysis of search results) is also a desired goal, as this points to the demands of employees that are not being met by the CP.

REWARDS FOR SHARING KNOWLEDGE

According to Ted Graham, "Rewards are one of the toughest things to get right." A number of reward and recognition approaches have been explored at H&K. All senior managers in their performance incentive system have knowledge-sharing leadership behaviors as part of their bonus compensation. Management reports each operating unit's knowledge collaboration, and usage metrics are prepared annually to help frame management activity usage. In addition, employees are recognized for their contributions to the CP environment's best-sellers lists that highlight the contributions that were used most.

KEY LESSONS LEARNED

Lesson 1. Identify the Key Knowledge Sources Important for the Business

The H&K team recognized early on that the most important sources of intellectual capital for its business were tacit and unstructured documents. It resided in the heads of its consultants across the globe and the e-mail exchanged with clients and internal teams. Therefore, the focus of the initial applications within the portal was to make these sources easily identifiable, organized, and distributed. As the initial results proved valuable, the company gradually introduces new features and applications. This approach is important because it does not overwhelm users, fosters personal connections, and most important, produces rapid business results.

Lesson 2. Develop Knowledge Management Efforts with a Clear Client Focus

Ted and Nicole believe HK.NET's clear focus on the needs of clients has been very important for its success. Everyone, from senior management to new hires, can immediately see the benefits of the portal and how it would help the company win more business and better serve existing clients. It is predicated on the idea that knowledge sharing can be directly linked to business results.

Lesson 3. Highlight Success Stories

Many of the interesting stories that have a business impact are not captured by standard usage metrics. This is something Ted Graham captures through the anecdotes shared by his global network of KM supporters. He makes sure, through regular e-mail and postings in the portals, that these successful stories do not go unnoticed. He believes they help foster the attitudes and motivations required to make the most of the HK.NET tools.

Lesson 4. Getting Reward and Recognition Right Is Hard

Getting a reward and recognition (R&R) program in place is one of the hardest things to get right. Recognizing people for the right behavior reinforces that knowledge is valuable. People have very busy schedules and ask themselves, "Why should I contribute? I am already having difficulty finding time focusing on client demands, and time is very precious."

According to Ted Graham, the company is working toward including knowledge sharing and collaboration in the performance appraisals but has difficulty in easily accessing good performance information on employee contributions levels. It experimented on a number of fronts, with identifying employees for their frequently used contributions, like a "best sellers" list, as McKinsey does.

Lesson 5. Fostering Collaboration Requires "Human Connections"

H&K learned that, because it has over 2000 professionals worldwide, providing employees with an opportunity to share their unique identity and specific capabilities is key. For example, fostering electronic exchange of personal information (e.g., photos) helps build social capital that leads to more job-related exchanges. H&K's experience has been that, "Once people personalize their experience, usage increases exponentially."

Lesson 6. Simplicity of Usage Is Fundamental to Success

According to Ted Graham and Nicole Doyle, the simplicity of the CP environment for user traction is fundamental to success. A number of simplification initiatives were undertaken in the CP program. Examples include making posting information very easy (from a technical and process perspective), setting up quality controls and categorization to be completed automatically, setting up environments for people to establish rules for the handling of each posted document (who can read, edit, etc.), and providing tools such as efficient and targeted e-mail alerts linked to public folders and other news feeds to prompt real-time learning, which is critical in the PR/crisis management business.

Lesson 7. Foster Ongoing Collaboration and Sharing Forums for Learning

Fundamental to human growth is continued learning and collaboration. The H&K CP program has a continuous approach to learning, as H&K offers frequent training sessions for employees on how to make best use of the system by explaining the basics of Internet surfing and effective searching. According to Nicole Doyle, a knowledge management director for the Canadian operation, "In Canada, one of our goals is continuous learning, so having an attitude of learning is healthy for all of us. We have learned that established training delivered through 'lunch and learn' initiatives for all employees has had a positive impact on the usage of the CP system." At H&K, all new employees go through specific training sessions to familiarize them with the wealth of knowledge that can help them be more successful in navigating H&K worldwide. Each country and region has a KM director, so ongoing dialogue and inquiries are an evergreen learning process.

Lesson 8. Corporate Portals Increase Customer Intimacy and Create Value

The organization of knowledge and sharing it with H&K clients in real time provides a competitive edge for the organization, especially with global clients.

H&K's CP combines external and internal customer information sources and leverages on the established habits of people. The design of the system can benefit from a deep understanding of the existing paths and patterns people use to gather information and knowledge and provides a real-time window to the client's needs. This type of customer intimacy and stickiness only opens up new possibilities for H&K.

FUTURE DIRECTIONS

Many interesting challenges lie ahead for the global CP implementation team. The continuous evolution of content management to meet local and personalized requirements with local taxonomies is an ongoing challenge.

As usage continues, requirements for further integration of other legacy and business systems (accounting, billing) increase. The company plans the implementation of a Web calendar, new business workflow tools, real-time news feeds, online training, inclusion of a best-sellers list (most checked documents), and Web cams.

Like most systems, there is migration to more robust server environments as H&K's CP migrates from replicated servers to one central server and increased support requirements to download selected public servers to allow offline access to content and keep archives of e-mail and other posted documents in public folders well organized, categorized, and relevant.

Other future projects include

- Developing a pricing model to specify codified knowledge shared with clients.
- Designing the right mix of incentives for knowledge codification and sharing.
- Developing a mapping process to track the qualitative value of individual contributions.
- Improving the metrics used to measure the success of the CP initiative.

13

NORTEL NETWORKS

CP/KM EXPERTS

Danny Murdock, VP eBusiness

Greg Kowal, director eBusiness

Richard Martin, strategy development for eBusiness

Micky Verma, director eBusiness portfolio development, information services

BACKGROUND

Established more than a century ago, Nortel Networks participated in many of the major developments that have shaped the evolution of today's global communications network technology. Nortel Networks is an industry leader focused on transforming how the world communicates and exchanges information. The company supplies its service provider and enterprise customers with communication technology and infrastructure to enable value-added Internet protocol (IP) data, voice, and multimedia services spanning Metro and Enterprise Networks, Wireless Networks, and Optical Long Haul Networks. Nortel

Networks serves the emerging and existing needs of service providers, carriers, dot-coms, small- and medium-sized businesses, and large corporations in more than 150 countries and territories around the world. The company is headquartered in Brampton, Ontario (near Toronto), and has offices and facilities in Canada, Europe, Asia-Pacific, Caribbean and Latin America, the Middle East, Africa, and the United States.

THE CATALYST

Significant turning points in history often begin with insight but are fueled by personal experience and belief. Such is the history of corporate portals at Nortel Networks. In the mid-1990s, John Roth, CEO of Nortel Networks, understood that the world's telecommunication networks increasingly were carrying data traffic and such traffic would soon overtake the volume of voice traffic that had dominated for many years. He knew that his company, a powerhouse in the voice telecommunications marketplace, needed to respond to this trend. A personal experience helped cement this belief.

John has a passion for antique sports cars. One day he began a search for a replacement glove compartment for one of his cars. He searched through his regular dealers and parts suppliers, with no luck. After quite a bit of time and frustration John went to the Web. To his surprise he immediately found what he was looking for in a small store in England. You can imagine his sense of relief in finding the part, but more important, John experienced firsthand how useful a tool and how powerful a business enabler the Internet could be.

This experience helped John internalize how the Internet would provide a powerful new infrastructure on which a new economy would be based. He initiated a number of actions, referred to as *the right angle turn*, to steer the company toward a future in which Nortel became a leader in the creation of the world's Internet infrastructure. The actions included the acquisition of several firms in the Internet/data business, the redesign of internal product development processes, the restructuring of the organization, and the outsourcing of noncore activities, such as line card manufacturing. With the power of the Internet, Nortel could integrate itself with its suppliers and component manufacturers, effectively becoming a virtually connected enterprise rather than a vertically integrated organization.

Through this transition, John recognized that Nortel itself could and should use the Internet to conduct its own business. In late 1998, John began to invest in eBusiness with the objective of electronically integrating and optimizing the common supply chain that connected the company with its customers and its suppliers. He envisioned a Web-based capability that would allow customers, channel partners, suppliers, and Nortel employees to easily share information and establish a more efficient, responsive, and integrated supply chain. This Web portal (Figure 13-1) would be a place where customers came to do business and employees came to find critical information and services.

A few key business objectives guided the initial investment in this corporate portal:

1. *Focus on the customer.* First and foremost, any investment in the extranet (external portal) must benefit the customer and improve the way it does business with Nortel.
2. *Employee effectiveness.* Any investment in the intranet (internal portal) should deliver information and services to employees that

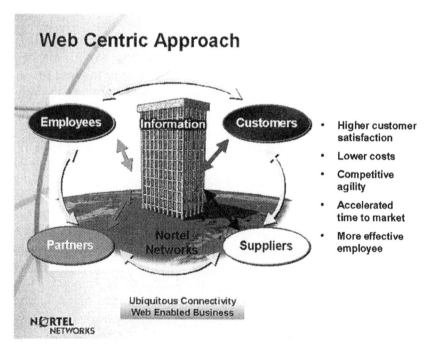

Figure 13-1
Nortel's Web-Centric Portal Approach (Source: Nortel Networks)

enable them to respond more quickly and effectively to customer needs.
3. *Shared services.* Investments leverage a common technology infrastructure and architecture.
4. *Brand identity.* Content on the corporate portal demonstrates a consistent company identity and strengthens the Nortel brand.

In late 1998, a strategy was created that outlined the proposed evolution of Nortel's eBusiness capability (Figure 13-2). As with many other organizations building eBusiness capability early in the Internet economy, the site was to begin by providing product and marketing information, move to a business transaction platform, and then evolve into a site that integrated Nortel into a unified supply chain with its customers and suppliers. The eBusiness strategy took over 2 years to complete. The corporate website, NortelNetworks.com, was the single portal through which all customers and suppliers reached these evolving eBusiness capabilities.

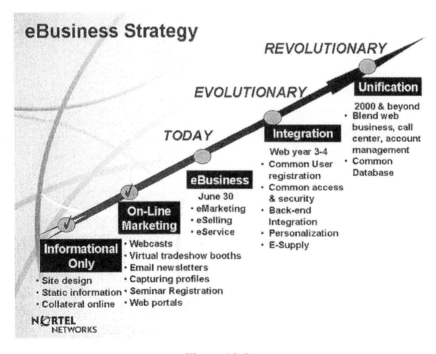

Figure 13-2
eBusiness Evolution Strategy (Source: Nortel Networks)

CORPORATE PORTAL, HIGH-LEVEL GOALS

While the high-level business objectives guided investment, the portal program sought to achieve a number of other goals (as before, P, primary goal; S, secondary goal; N, not relevant):

Communication tool (top-down and bottom-up):

(S) Improve communication of vision and knowledge strategy.

(P) Improve communication of company values.

(P) Keep the organization alert.

(P) Engage customers and community at large.

(P) Divulge results more broadly and promote systemic analysis.

(S) Facilitate bottom-up communication.

(S) Make it easy for employees to suggest improvements to management.

Push information and knowledge to employees:

(S) Capture, organize, and distribute codified knowledge (e.g., database access).

(P) Improve access to external sources of information and knowledge.

(P) Improve decision making.

(P) Empower front-line employees.

Improve reuse of knowledge:

(S) Develop expertise maps (uncover existing knowledge).

(S) Map and measure intangible assets.

(P) Facilitate search of previously developed knowledge.

Foster collaboration:

(P) Increase collaboration among different functions of the organization.

(P) Increase collaboration among different locations of the organization.

(P) Improve overall knowledge sharing.

(P) Support the development of communities of practice.

(N) Increase connections not related to work.

Improve human capital management:

(N) Improve hiring.

(S) Improve internal mobility and deployment of existing employees.

(N) Integrate temporary and outside human resources and expertise.

(S) Improve training and acquisition of skills.

(P) Get new employees up to speed very quickly.

(P) Reduce time spent on menial activities.

(N) Improve employee retention.

(N) Facilitate work and integration of telecommuters.

Improve relationship with external stakeholders and increase information flow:

(P) Improve information exchange with suppliers, partners, and customers.

(P) Capture customer information.

(P) Improve customer satisfaction.

(P) Reduce sales costs.

(P) Reduce customer service costs.

Corporate Portal Implementation

Implementation of the NortelNetworks.com portal and accompanying eBusiness capability progressed through three major segments: the initiation phase, construction of the extranet portal, and construction of the intranet portal.

Initiation

Getting started in late 1998 was a challenge. At this point in the evolution of the Internet, levels of eBusiness awareness varied within the executive ranks. Many operational executives understood that there could be value in developing an extranet and intranet portal but needed to have the business value outlined in terms they were familiar with. In many presentations, business unit leaders had the opportunity to review the portal plans, have their questions answered, and come away with a much improved understanding of the intended strategy, investment, and return. These sessions created the necessary understanding and commitment to initiate the corporate portal program.

Senior executives of the company had arranged to meet on an ongoing basis in what was referred to as the Corporate Process Council, to set direction with respect to critical common process initiatives that affected the entire corporation. The corporate portal was added to the list of key initiatives championed by the Corporate Process Council, which provided a common executive voice in support of the corporate portal effort. John commented at one of these meetings that he would be willing to intervene personally if necessary to help address any organizational roadblocks in the portal program. An eBusiness organization was created, reporting directly to the CIO, with the mandate to create the external portal first and then the internal portal. The eBusiness organization had a dotted line reporting relationship to the chief marketing officer and strong connections to the account teams, the order management group, and the customer service group.

External Portal

The executive team felt that the customer was the first priority for any portal or eBusiness development (Figure 13-3). Design and development of the portal was begun with four key objectives in mind:

1. Make it easier for the customer to do business with Nortel.
2. Enhance the customer relationship.
3. Streamline and integrate business processes to reduce cost and improve time to market.
4. Showcase Nortel Networks products in the operation of the site.

Nortel has always had a brilliant technical research and engineering staff. These people were already aware of the power of the Internet and had been creating websites to serve customer needs. While they were delivering valuable information and capability to the customers, there was no consistency in this approach and customers might need to access several Nortel sites, with several passwords, to accomplish their tasks. Multiple servers and applications supported these sites. As you would expect, there was no full end-to-end support of the customer's business cycle.

Figure 13-3
Customer eBusiness Cycle (Source: Nortel Networks)

The initial external portal (Figure 13-4) addressed these issues. It delivered (1) a consistent customer experience with the appropriate navigation, personalization, and branding; (2) end-to-end coverage of the customer's business cycle from planning, through configuration and ordering to ongoing service, including specific capabilities for channel partners; (3) global reach with local languages; and (4) a shared technology infrastructure using Nortel equipment, with a common application, registration, and security platform.

Over time, this platform evolved to meet the needs of all of Nortel's customers. The smaller customers, without an extensive systems infrastructure of their own, directly utilize many of the Web-based capabilities provided, such as configuration tools, ordering and status tools, and self-service tools. Larger customers have a much more complicated relationship with Nortel, ranging from collaborating on product development requirements and the design, configuration, and installation of complex networks to the electronic delivery of software to customer sites. For these large customers, Nortel extended the portal and is developing standard business-to-business (B-to-B) collaboration

Figure 13-4
External Portal (Source: Nortel Networks)

solutions based on industry standard formats and technology. These solutions allow the larger customer to utilize its extensive internal systems but easily integrate with Nortel's eBusiness capabilities when desired. For example, a customer could be using its corporate purchasing application, link to Nortel's configurator to create a network solution, and transfer that seamlessly back to its purchasing system for processing. This allows the customer to leverage Nortel's product knowledge and tools without making the systems and administrative investment themselves.

In the future, Nortel's B-to-B solutions will integrate the supply chain systems of Nortel, its customers, and its suppliers to provide all stakeholders with real-time access to demand, forecasts, orders, and fulfillment status.

Internal Portal

The internal portal was designed to provide the information and services that would make employees more responsive and effective. It provides up-to-date news; organizational information (dynamic organization charts); functional community services (e.g., Sales, Marketing, Engineering, Customer Service, IS); document sharing; video, audio, and Web conferencing; e-learning and training; customer information; marketing intelligence; administrative services; travel and expense services; and much more (Figure 13-5). It is the single portal and home page for all employees, enabling access to all key applications and services, with a single user ID and password, and a consistent user experience. Today, the internal portal has become part of Nortel's everyday culture. It is part of employees' daily work routines—the following quote from an employee illustrates this point: "I could get around not having access to GlobalWeb for a few hours or so, but after that it would be really difficult to get much work done."

Figure 13-5
Internal Portal (Source: Nortel Networks)

Shared Services

The concept of shared services was an important one in the creation of an effective external and internal portal. It was exhibited in two key areas, the technology platform and the content management process.

Many of the services and much of the information provided to customers through the external portal are also of great value to employees accessing the internal portal. It was important that this information was not re-created for each audience and the technology infrastructure investment was not re-created to deliver it. To ensure this, the eBusiness organization was given the mandate to be the "editor in chief" for the website, and the executive team agreed that no external Web presence would be allowed other than the single company external portal. In this way, the eBusiness team could ensure that the content on the site was timely, consistent in format and brand image, and of high quality. The team was also able to ensure that no other infrastructure was built in competition with the company portal. This meant extensive savings in terms of infrastructure, application, and administrative costs.

The editorial staff in the eBusiness group consists of approximately 30 people, 20 for the external portal and 10 for the internal one. They are closely connected to the Marketing and Product Line Management groups. They ensure that information flows from the product group, through the Marketing team, to themselves, and onto the site. While they do not create the content, they are responsible for ensuring that what is on the site provides the value the customer demands. The product and marketing content is created only once but put to many uses, including both the internal and external portals (Figure 13-6).

According to Danny Murdock, VP of eBusiness, "the strategy for developing our corporate portal was strongly rooted in the recognition that we needed one unified content management infrastructure for supporting our intranet and extranet capabilities." With strong leadership support, Nortel Networks was able to develop corporate portal processes and a technology infrastructure that are world class.

The technology platform is shared as well (Figure 13-7). The same foundation of servers, networks, applications, and databases is used for both the internal and external portals. For example, Nortel uses Broadvision as a personalization engine to allow its customers and employees to personalize their Web page for their particular role. They use Teamsite as the content management engine. Both platforms are shared by the internal and external portals. Access is controlled by

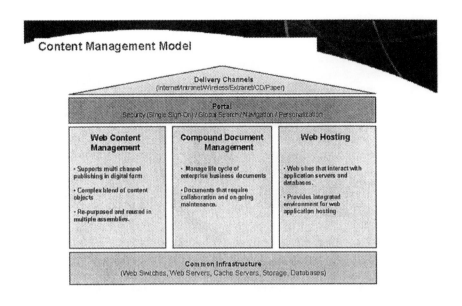

Figure 13-6
Content Management Model (Source: Nortel Networks)

a custom-built shared security platform that registers and authorizes all users, customers and employees alike.

METRICS

Doing eBusiness is IT "heavy lifting." It is not simply creating a few Web pages. It involves significant architecture, infrastructure, application, data, and security work that is constantly visible to customers. You need to plan, execute, and measure your performance to be successful. Portal usage and performance metrics allow Nortel to continually monitor those sites most relevant to its employees and customers. This also helps it determine where its investment dollars would provide the most value as it enhances the portal and its features. Business process metrics are also collected. For example, in one case, a wireless customer that connected with Nortel electronically reduced lead times from 9 weeks to 3 weeks and reduced inventory levels by 40%. Capturing these stories is an ongoing focus that helps reinforce the value of the corporate portal infrastructure.

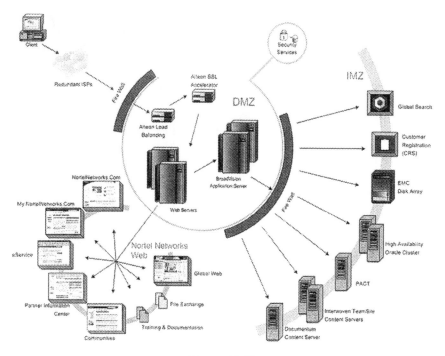

Figure 13-7
Portal Technology Platform (Source: Nortel Networks)

ORGANIZATIONAL STRUCTURE

The eBusiness organization is responsible for the support and evolution of the corporate portals. This organization is well connected to the product line business units, the sales team, the operations team, and the customer service team. It is organized into three main segments:

1. *eBusiness operations.* Approximately 60 employees provide site operations and content management support for the Nortel portal infrastructure. This group ensures that the user experience is positive, by handling areas such as navigation, site management, content management, look and feel standards, and interfacing with content generation groups or communities.
2. *Portfolio development.* This group is responsible for the ongoing technology support, design, and ongoing development required to support the CP and the needs of the customers.

3. *Customer implementation.* This group works closely with the customer, the sales account teams, order management, customer service, and information systems to create joint eBusiness plans and subsequently is accountable to implement the approved projects.

Ongoing investment decisions for the portals are recommended by the eBusiness organization and require the approval of the appropriate product line business unit, the sales and marketing organization, and the IT organization. The customer implementation team is accountable for bringing the priorities of the customer to the portfolio development team and ensuring successful deployment of new functionality.

Future

Nortel sees a continuing evolution toward a more integrated supply chain, more powerful personalization, and extending the portal services to other delivery channels such as wireless and PDA devices.

In its end state, the integrated supply chain promises a level of collaboration between Nortel and its partners that could yield significant benefits. This would mean collaboration in all facets of the communications network life cycle, including market demand forecasting, joint network design, product demand forecasting, configuration, quotation, availability to promise through to component suppliers, procurement, project management, installation, service, and performance management. The challenge is that this type of collaboration would require not only more powerful tools but significant business process change.

Personalization in the future would allow a customer to have immediate access to all business transactions and information automatically when entering the portal. Rather than having to search for information relevant to its functional role or obtain access to systems it is entitled to, in some cases contractually, these would be part of the default privileges and website view from the start.

KEY LESSONS LEARNED

Lesson 1. Ensure Executive Commitment

Line executives must understand the value of corporate portals in terms they can appreciate. A key role of the leader of the corporate portal program is to connect with these executives and ensure they

312 REALIZING THE PROMISE OF CORPORATE PORTALS

understand the intended investment and support the effort in terms of the process changes required to realize the benefit of the new technology implementation. Consistently reporting on progress, including the realization of these benefits, is critical to sustain momentum.

Lesson 2. Focus on the Customer

This was the primary value driver for Nortel's corporate portal strategy and continues to be the main focus for ongoing evolution. Nortel recognizes that, if it is easier to do business with Nortel than any of its competitors, if it supplies superior product information and services, and if it provides ways to easily integrate the supply chain with customers, then those customers, given comparable products, would choose to do business with Nortel.

Each customer has a specific set of needs that must be understood. Large customers, especially, have existing processes and systems that need to be acknowledged and linked into any eBusiness portal. It is not enough to build a site and hope they will come. You must first understand why and how they will come, then build the portal.

Lesson 3. Create a Shared Services Platform

The shared services model enables the portal group to both ensure a consistent, high-quality site and significantly reduce infrastructure and operating costs. The centralized technology platform enables single user ID and password access to all services and ensures a consistent navigation look and feel. The centralized content management group enables the enterprise to truly leverage its content by creating it once but repurposing it for different audiences and delivering it through different channels. The editorial staff model keeps the content fresh and relevant.

Lesson 4. Plan for Business Process Change

The value of a corporate portal and eBusiness services provided to customers and employees lies in their ability to perform their roles differently and potentially perform altogether different roles. If things remain the same, no benefit will be realized. Recognize this up front. Nortel had a Corporate Process Council to champion key initiatives. When implementing a corporate portal, understand what organizations and roles will be affected and ensure the executives in those units understand the changes they must see in their organizations and their processes for the program to be successful. As in any change management effort, this entails up-front process analysis, ensuring those affected understand the need for change and how they fit into the new operating environment.

CONCLUDING COMMENTS

The Nortel corporate portal initiative delivered on its major objectives. It improved the way the customer does business with Nortel, it provided information and services to its employees that enable them to be more effective, and it presented a consistent, high-quality electronic image of Nortel over the Web.

The company continues to evolve its strategy of increased collaboration with its customers and suppliers. In the telecommunications industry, with its complex products, no down-time expectations, and ever-changing technology, increased collaboration can yield benefits to all stakeholders in the value chain. As portal technology improves, Nortel will no doubt be on the forefront, implementing new capabilities in search of new levels of collaboration.

14

SERPRO, INFORMATION SERVICES AGENCY FROM THE BRAZILIAN FEDERAL GOVERNMENT

CP/KM EXPERTS

José Alberto Cadais, chief knowledge officer
Sylvio Bari Filho, technology project leader

BACKGROUND

SERPRO (Serviço Federal de Processamento de Dados) is a federal agency linked to the Finance Ministry of the Brazilian government. It is the largest IT government services agency in Brazil with close to 9000 employees in 330 cities around the country. It provides its services in a competitive environment (private enterprises compete on many of the same projects) to government agencies at all levels that need robust, enterprise-level, mission-critical IT applications. The various systems it implemented over the years register over 1 billion transactions per year. The agency is well known for being at the forefront of technology adoption. One of its most notable accomplishments is the development and management of Brazil's system for income tax return via the Internet in 1996. The system is very user-friendly, fast, and operates at high levels of security and efficiency. This led to a rapid adoption rate. Indeed, 92% of Brazilians' income tax returns were filed via the Internet in 2000: a world record.

THE CATALYST, GOALS, AND DRIVING FACTORS

The corporate portal at SERPRO is part of a broad KM corporate strategy. The corporate portal is the result of a well-articulated, planned process to uncover, leverage, and create intellectual capital. A remarkable thing about KM at SERPRO is the widespread commitment from the highest hierarchical level of the organization to all management levels and divisions and especially from senior management.

Despite its high-tech-oriented organization, the agency clearly understood that IT tools are only one component of KM. It did not invest any resources in IT tools for KM before it was able to develop a comprehensive KM strategy. This strategy included, among other things, the following items:

- A plan to foster changes in the company's values and culture.
- A training plan for the company leadership.
- Creation of a formal organization to support ongoing KM initiatives.
- A plan for the identification and detailed mapping of the company's core processes and associated knowledge domains.
- A method to evaluate the intellectual capital created in projects related to customer services.
- An IT strategy.

Ultimately, senior management of SERPRO, including the president, Wolney Martins, placed KM as a core activity for the agency's survival. The company realizes that other government agencies are increasingly being asked to contract with the "best-of-the-breed" vendors and consultants. That means that SERPRO is facing increasing competition.

SERPRO's CP is part of this broader KM agenda and expected to help deliver the following goals (as before, P, primary goal; S, secondary goal; N, not relevant):

Communication tool (top-down and bottom-up):

(P) Improve communication of vision and knowledge strategy.

(P) Improve communication of company values.

(P) Keep the organization alert.

(P) Engage customers and community at large.

(P) Divulge results more broadly and promote systemic analysis.

(P) Facilitate bottom-up communication.

(P) Make it easy for employees to make improvement suggestions to management.

Push information and knowledge to employees:

(P) Capture, organize, and distribute codified knowledge (e.g., database access).

(S) Improve access to external sources of information and knowledge.

(P) Improve decision making.

(P) Empower front-line employees.

Improve reuse of knowledge:

(P) Develop expertise maps (uncover existing knowledge).

(P) Map and measure intangible assets.

(P) Facilitate search of previously developed knowledge.

Foster collaboration:

(P) Increase collaboration among different functions of the organization.

(P) Increase collaboration among different locations of the organization.

(P) Improve overall knowledge sharing.

(P) Support the development of communities of practice.

(S) Increase connections not related to work.

Improve human capital management:

(P) Improve hiring.

(P) Improve internal mobility and deployment of existing employees.

(P) Integrate temporary and outside human resources and expertise.

(P) Improve training and acquisition of skills.

(P) Get new employees up to speed very quickly.

(P) Reduce time spent on menial activities.

(P) Improve employee retention.

(P) Facilitate work and integration of telecommuters.

Improve relationships with external stakeholders and increase information flow:

(P) Improve information exchange with suppliers, partners, and customers.

(P) Capture customer information.

(P) Improve customer satisfaction.

(P) Reduce sales costs.

(P) Reduce customer service costs.

IMPLEMENTATION JOURNEY

1997: Initial discussions about knowledge management at SERPRO at senior management levels.

1998: Senior management starts developing a comprehensive KM strategy; after looking at some organizational models for the KM function (as part of IT, HR, etc.), the agency decides to create a corporate KM function and the CKO position.

1999: The KM community is formally created (supported) by senior management and starts its initial tasks by publishing KM concepts into the company and developing IT tools for that.

2000: The company decides to invest heavily in training. It contracts for a tailor-made MBA program focused on KM and competitive intelligence with a leading Brazilian university. Almost 26 senior executives from many divisions and functions attended this year and a half long part-time program. Other professionals also attended short-term courses on KM.

March 2000: A formal policy stating goals and principles related to KM is approved.

2000: The mapping of SERPRO's core processes and related knowledge domains starts.

2000: The development of the corporate portal starts.

2000: Digital certification for access control begins.

2001: Corporate portal launched in the first semester.

2001: The integration of intranet information within the CP begins.

2001: Integration of applications within the CP begins.

ORGANIZATIONAL SUPPORT

KM has become a formal strategic corporate-level initiative. The company has had a CKO since mid-2000, who operates at the highest hierarchical level of the organization. His mandate, as per the description of the goals related to the rollout of the CP, is very broad and directly linked to supporting the competitive edge SERPRO wants to maintain. The agency realizes that, without the active and very visible identification and support of its core competencies, it will not remain competitive.

The CKO team (a small corporate team of 41 people and around 25 part-time representatives at the divisional level) has the following responsibilities:

- Develop and keep (with the business units) SERPRO's knowledge tree up-to-date. Knowledge mapping at SERPRO links high-level business goals to specific knowledge domains and disciplines. The initial mapping process was both a very strategic exercise and the basis for the CP's core taxonomy.
- Develop and maintain SERPRO's corporate portal infrastructure.

- Promote CP use and provide employees with the necessary support to make the best use of the tools available in the CP.
- Develop and support training programs aligned with the strategic mapping of core institutional and individual competencies.
- Measure SERPRO's intellectual capital for its internal use and to develop better pricing models for services rendered.
- Promote activities and communication opportunities that reinforce required behavior changes toward more knowledge sharing.

MAPPING OF ORGANIZATIONAL PROCESSES AND KNOWLEDGE CATEGORIES

Many organizations talk about core competencies, but very few actually undertake a systematic and detailed self-examination with an eye to the needs of customers. SERPRO did, and the results of the self-examination became the foundation for its KM strategy and for the design of its corporate portal.

The KM team, working with all internal divisions and business units, developed a comprehensive understanding of the macro processes that support SERPRO's business. Then, a number of supporting "business themes" were linked to each process. Likewise, "knowledge domains" were linked to each "business theme" and "subjects" to "knowledge domains." Sylvio Bari, the technology project leader, gives a simple example to illustrate the overall approach:

Level 1. Macro process: sales.

Level 2. Business theme: systems development.

Level 3. Knowledge domain: databases.

Level 4. Subject: Oracle database.

To be sure, a knowledge domain may support various subjects, a business theme may support many knowledge domains, and business themes can be linked to one macro process. These few categories help explain the thoroughness with which this task was conducted. The first complete knowledge mapping took about 2 months and involved about 30 internal consultants. This first mapping identified

3 macro processes.

25 business themes.

148 knowledge domains.
1280 subjects.

CORPORATE PORTAL ENVIRONMENT

SERPRO's CP was custom developed with the help of Microsoft. A joint team of Microsoft and SERPRO developers took just over 6 months to develop the first release of the portal, using a three-layer design approach (Tier 1, client; Tier 2, IIS server, ASP, components; Tier 3, databases). The underlying platforms were existing Microsoft servers: Windows 2000, SQL Server 2000, IIS 5.0 and Exchange Server 2000. The development team had the goal of leveraging existing, but disparate, online applications. It did this by linking all required applications via XML in a high-security encryption environment, as required by SERPRO. The result of the first release is described next.

SERPRO's CP includes a number of integrated publishing, collaboration, self-service, and e-learning applications. It both links data, information, and people to support knowledge management processes and automates and simplifies menial activities such as applying for vacation time or making travel arrangements. It includes a personalized interface, My SERPRO, and already recognizes each user and provides links to other personalized areas, such as My Contents (Meus Conteúdos) and My Services (Meus Serviços Web).

The home page in Figure 14-1 highlights the links to all the applications that had been integrated into the portal environment by October 2001. They include, but are not limited to, advanced search (pesquisa avançada), Lotus Notes e-mail, forums, chats, community areas, document management applications, an integrated search engine for the physical library, employees' profile database, and a number of HR self-service applications.

Employees' Profile Database

As with many KM digital initiatives, SERPRO's CP allows employees to enter their skill levels into a profile database. The system is designed to allow the input of only skills considered relevant to SERPRO's business (according to the knowledge map). Employees check off their level of a particular skill according to preregistered categories. If they do not find a relevant category, they may suggest the creation of a new knowledge or skill domain in the profile database.

Figure 14-1
SERPRO's CP Home Page (Source: SERPRO)

KM managers and knowledge experts evaluate the request and, if deemed relevant to SERPRO business, create the category and update the knowledge map.

Knowledge Repository

A distinctive, custom-developed application for the portal is its knowledge repository. The knowledge repository is fed by documents (in all formats, including images, sound, videos, ppt presentations) and URLs submitted by employees. Submissions enter the knowledge repository only after being approved by KM managers or domain experts. Through a specific link on the home page, employees can easily check, revise, and update all their submissions to the knowledge repository. The structured submission process includes the following fields:

1. Author or contributor. The employee submitting the document may not be the author.
2. Date. The date of completion and date of submission are separately recorded.

3. Title.
4. Summary.
5. Type (articles, project, paper, photograph, etc.).
6. Keywords. The authors may suggest keywords to facilitate retrieval of the document by others.
7. Community of interest. The contributor identifies specific communities that may be interested in the document. Members of identified communities are automatically notified of the inclusion.
8. Expiration date. On this date, the author is notified that the document needs to be reviewed for validation, updating, or archiving.
9. Classification. Each submission needs to be classified within one macro process, business theme, knowledge domain, or subject area. The level under which it is classified depends on the scope of the contribution.

Advanced Search Page

The advanced search application, in a way, complements the knowledge contribution application. The search functionality of SERPRO's CKO allows users to determine the scope searches (for example, by type of document, author, knowledge domain, date). It also permits full-text or field-based searches. The parameters used for searching correspond to the fields of the Contribution Form. This complementary approach to contributions and searches is not unusual in high-end KM-focused solutions. However, one aspect of SERPRO's CP is particularly innovative: the integration of results from the document's database, employees' profile database, and the physical library catalogue. This integration means that, when searching, for instance, for the word *Oracle*, the user will find not only a list of documents related to this topic that matches the search criteria, but also a list of employees with different Oracle skill levels and a list of all physical publications available in the libraries of SERPRO.

Metrics

The metrics for SERPRO's CP are linked to the knowledge mapping effort. For example, the company measures how its knowledge tree is being fed by tracking contributions and activity in its search engine. Ideally, the core strategic knowledge domains and subjects should be the ones where the KM team will find the most activity: more documents and links being posted and searched, more employees updating their skills, and so forth. This focus on evaluating actual usage of the CP and its relation to the knowledge map is another example of how the CP is directly linked to the corporate strategy.

The company is also experimenting with an innovative measurement tool. Based on the well-known Sveiby's categorization of sources of intellectual capital (client capital, structure capital, and human capital), SERPRO has developed a proprietary solution to measure the contribution of each project or solution to the growth of each aspect of its intellectual capital. When this case was written, the company was making studies to introduce this methodology. Consequently, the KM team felt it could not yet reveal the detailed underpinnings of this new approach. However, the ongoing concern of the KM team for appropriate measurement shows that the company has a strong sense of the need to create, maintain, and measure intellectual capital as it is created. In SERPRO's environment, knowledge is usually created during the custom development projects for its clients.

KEY LESSONS LEARNED

Lesson 1. Communicate the Benefits of Corporate Portals to Employees: What Is in It for Me?

José Alberto Cadais, SERPRO's CKO, realizes that most of SERPRO's early internal communications about the KM and CP initiatives focused on the benefits to SERPRO, not the employees. This, he feels, was not the effective approach to introducing the CP and KM in general. He believes that the KM and CP initiatives also have important benefits for participating employees and his office should promote these benefits more heavily. In his opinion, the CP helps employees better execute their jobs and find new opportunities for personal and professional growth. By strongly participating in knowledge exchange activities, employees are rewarded with better and more visible recognition within the company, new learning and networking opportunities, and ultimately, more opportunities to participate in interesting projects that rely on their accumulated knowledge.

Lesson 2. Employees at All Levels Need to Embrace Knowledge Management Concepts

Unlike many other IT initiatives, CPs cannot be successful without the "buy-in" of many levels of management and various different divisions. SERPRO took this advice to heart and provided substantive training for many layers of its management team. The rollout of the CP was also preceded by significant internal communication, including posters, newsletters, local training sessions, and gatherings (with the presence of senior management). José Alberto Cadais feels that the general concepts and goals of KM are now clear across the organization, from the president to the most junior employees. This is critical, he believes, to ensuring widespread use and ongoing support for KM initiatives.

Lesson 3. Align Every Knowledge Management and Corporate Portal Initiative to the Corporate Strategy

By deeply aligning KM and CP initiatives with the corporate strategy, such initiatives more easily garner support from all levels of management. Broad support not only helps ensure the success of the CP, it also ensures that the projects are not seen as isolated tasks that can be easily discarded during "tougher budget periods."

Lesson 4. Knowledge Management Can Provide the Strategic Foundation for Human Resources Policies

SERPRO uses the strategic knowledge mapping process as a means to evaluate its human capital. By comparing the anticipated demand for particular skills with its existing supply of skills (as per employees profile database), the HR department develops more precise requirements for new hires and more strategic training programs. The CP helps both HR personnel and employees to more clearly see the skills needed by SERPRO and develop collective and individual learning strategies.

Lesson 5. Serious Knowledge Management Initiatives Can Fundamentally Change the Way an Organization Operates

José Alberto Cadais, a true enthusiast of KM, believes that the principles behind the CP reflect more profound transformations within SERPRO. He remembers the time when SERPRO's main activity was to process truckloads of Income Tax Return forms—a time he characterizes as the Data Era—and gazes into the future of the Knowledge Era. He believes that, by digitally linking information and employees across their more traditional functional and divisional clusters, the KM initiatives play an important role in the ultimate survival of SERPRO.

FUTURE DIRECTIONS

By the end of 2001, many corporate intranets could still be found at SERPRO. However, plans were in place to have all intranets completely integrated within the CP by the end of 2002. Single sign-on (or only one password for all applications) was implemented in the first release of the portal. Given the high-security environment of SERPRO's transactions, this occurred by using a digital certification process with public and private keys fully implemented.

One of the most interesting new developments planned for the end of 2002 is the complete replacement of the existing Windows desktop for the portal. In this new environment, when each employee turns on the computer, he or she will be immediately defaulted to his or her My SERPRO and not the usual Windows desktop. With this initiative, SERPRO hopes to achieve a complete change of paradigm from the desktop, individual-oriented environment to the portal, collaborative-oriented environment.

Plans are well advanced to better align the KM efforts with Human Resources policies and practices. For instance, the company plans to introduce a mileage program, which will give incentives to employees based on their "digital behavior." Employees will earn points for their contributions to the knowledge base and participation in other virtual knowledge exchanges through the CP. These points will be then redeemed for incentives and prizes. The value and monetary significance were still being debated at the end of 2001.

CLOSING PERSPECTIVES

SERPRO developed a robust, cohesive KM strategy, supported by the development of a sophisticated CP. The company expects that, when the CP is fully implemented, it will completely change how employees receive and process information, learn, connect with others, and contribute to the company's success. Given this level of ambition, it is too early to evaluate the ultimate business impact. It is clear, however, that neither the KM nor the CP is being taken lightly at SERPRO.

15

SIEMENS

CP/KM EXPERTS

Michael Wagner, vice president knowledge management ShareNet
Beatriz Eguiluz Moreno, ShareNet consultant for Central and South
America, South Africa, and several European countries
Monika Sengberg, ShareNet's manager in the Brazilian office
Loraine Ricino, ShareNet's moderator in the Brazilian office

BACKGROUND

Siemens is one of the oldest and largest companies in the world. The company was founded in 1847 in Germany but now has offices in more than 190 countries. The company had around 450,000 employees and revenues of €87.0 billion (euros), approximately $80 billion, in 2001. It invests circa €6.8 billion in R&D. Its business lines include a wide range of products and services related to electrical engineering: information and communication, industrial automation, electrical power, transport, medical, lighting, semiconductors, and also turnkey real-estate and factory projects.

UNDERSTANDING KNOWLEDGE MANAGEMENT AT SIEMENS

Although the long history of Siemens has always been associated with important innovations, over the last few years the company has been making a huge effort to transform itself into an e-business, knowledge-based enterprise. This means a focus beyond product innovation and sales: It means aligning the whole organization to provide comprehensive knowledge-based solutions for its clients. The transformation demands a complete revision of communications infrastructure, mindset, organizational structures, and rewards. Employees and managers need to think more broadly and reach across the many divisions within Siemens and to external partners (including competitors) that can provide a piece of product, knowledge, or solution that is often customized for each client.

These business goals reflect a new set of core values, which have been promoted over the last few years. Among the most relevant for KM initiatives, two stand out: "Our cooperation has no limits" and "Learning is the key to continuous improvement." The one about cooperation, in particular, seems to reflect the new mantra across Siemens. Indeed, in a recent presentation, the KM leadership at Siemens stated that, "The orchestration of global knowledge networks is becoming the crucial competitive advantage."

It is interesting to observe that KM at Siemens had emerged as a series of uncoordinated, grassroots initiatives in the mid-1990s. These included a number of IT applications and formal and informal communities of practice. Senior management eventually sponsored a formal KM community of practice in 1998 and created a corporate knowledge management office in July 1999. The office is directly linked to the CIO office, which changed its designation in April 2000 to IK (information and knowledge management). The leading officers involved with the corporate support and formalization of the KM initiatives were Peter Heinold, from the Corporate Planning and Development Department; Dr. Josef Hofer-Alfeis, from Corporate Technology Department; Peter Vieser, from the Corporate Human Resources Department; and finally Chittur Ramakrishnan, the chief information officer.

Since the formalization of the KM corporate initiative, the company has hosted a number of KM internal events. During these events, hundreds of employees from different parts of the globe meet to present their own initiatives and, when possible, develop coordinated global efforts. The company supports both localized and divisional initiatives and global, companywide KM efforts and platforms.

To understand the breadth and scope of KM initiatives within Siemens, we asked Michael Wagner, one of the leaders of Siemens' worldwide KM community, to clarify which of the following goals were part of the mandate of the KM community (as before, P, primary goal; S, secondary goal; N, not relevant):

Communication tool (top-down and bottom-up):

(S) Improve communication of vision and knowledge strategy.

(S) Improve communication of company values.

(N) Keep the organization alert.

(S) Engage customers and community at large.

(P) Divulge results more broadly and promote systemic analysis.

(P) Facilitate bottom-up communication.

(S) Make it easy for employees to suggest improvements to management.

Push information and knowledge to employees:

(S) Capture, organize, and distribute codified knowledge (e.g., database access).

(N) Improve access to external sources of information and knowledge.

(S) Improve decision making.

(P) Empower front-line employees.

Improve reuse of knowledge:

(S) Develop expertise maps (uncover existing knowledge).

(N) Map and measure intangible assets.

(P) Facilitate search of previously developed knowledge.

Foster collaboration:

(P) Increase collaboration among different functions of the organization.

(P) Increase collaboration among different locations of the organization.

(P) Improve overall knowledge sharing.

(P) Support the development of communities of practice.

(S) Increase connections not related to work.

Improve human capital management:

(N) Improve hiring.

(S) Improve internal mobility and deployment of existing employees.

(N) Integrate temporary and outside human resources and expertise.

(P) Improve training and acquisition of skills.

(P) Get new employees up to speed very quickly.

(N) Reduce time spent on menial activities.

(S) Improve employee retention.

(S) Facilitate work and integration of telecommuters.

Improve relationship with external stakeholders and increase information flow:

(S) Improve information exchange with suppliers, partners, and customers.

(P) Capture customer information.

(P) Improve customer satisfaction.

(P) Reduce sales costs.

(P) Reduce customer service costs.

SHARENET: THE CATALYST, GOALS, AND DRIVING FACTORS

ShareNet is a KM initiative developed at Siemens' Information and Communication Networks (ICN) division. One of the most successful initiaves, it now has corporatewide sponsorship. From the start, it relied on the support of ICN's board members and the activities of a core team led by Michael Wagner, ShareNet's worldwide champion.

By the end of 1998, this team decided that the existing intranet could not serve as the ideal platform. So, it resolved to develop a new system "from scratch." Siemens employed its own development team.

The first pilots (China, Malaysia, Portugal, and Australia) started development in mid-1999 and rolled out at the beginning of 2000. By the end of 2000, employees from approximately 60 countries had joined the ShareNet community. The number of users evolved from 3000 by the end 1999 to 11,000 by the end of 2000 and 18,000 by September 2001. The impact of ShareNet on the bottom-line was $146 million in 2000 and the company estimates it will reach $330 million in 2001.

It is important to say that ShareNet is a technological enabler of a much broader effort at Siemens to rethink how the company could better serve its customers. The team that eventually developed Share-Net was heavily involved in a number of change management and reorganization projects that aimed to improve Siemens' sales and marketing effectiveness. These efforts preceded deployment of any IT or Web solution.

ShareNet was developed to help sales teams across the globe to improve their ability to sell solutions. It is now available to any employee within the ICN and ICM (Information and Communication Mobile) division. To design a system that would work, ShareNet was developed in a collaborative setting. A steering team was formed, with close to 40 sales representatives and marketing professionals working with different countries and types of customers. This team started with what some managers at Siemens consider to be the foundation of KM: "Know your processes well."

In this case, the selected team developed detailed maps of the sales processes (defined as a core process) and linked each step or aspect of the process to specific "buckets" of knowledge. These buckets of knowledge were derived after extensive interviews with sales and marketing professionals. These professionals were asked directed questions, such as

How does your process work?

What are the important sources of knowledge that you need to do your job?

Why have you been successful in your projects?

After the interviews, the ShareNet central team clustered the relevant sources of knowledge into specific "knowledge objects" such as Technical Solutions, Functional Solutions, and Customer Knowledge. Once agreement was reached, the ShareNet team developed a series of prototypes while periodically asking future users how they would like the information and knowledge buckets to be presented. In Michael's words, "It was a very interactive process."

ORGANIZATIONAL SUPPORT FOR SHARENET

The ShareNet community is supported by a team of 15 dedicated individuals, working full time in Germany, and one ShareNet manager and a number of moderators and representatives in other countries (the number varies according to the size of the operations in each country). These ShareNet managers and representatives may be fully dedicated to ShareNet or work with ShareNet only part time, as they usually have other responsibilities within the organization.

The participation of employees on ShareNet is completely voluntary. The rapid growth of the number of users is the result of strong support from corporate headquarters and each region's management. Although ShareNet's central team provides support to local offices, the local office is responsible for promoting ShareNet locally and supporting its users with training and ongoing help.

Michael and his team have always believed that the success of ShareNet depends heavily on the committed support of local offices and local "knowledge evangelists." With this in mind, a key activity involved in the rollout of ShareNet was a "boot camp" in Munich in July–August 1999 with the participation of about 50 ShareNet managers from 15 countries. During the boot camp, these managers learned not only the operational side of ShareNet but also the "soft side" of the KM principles being introduced at Siemens. Each manager was coached on how to develop a plan for the rollout of ShareNet in his or her office. Everyone left the boot camp with a detailed job description, a rollout plan, and, maybe most important, with a trusted network of knowledge evangelists (many activities were geared initially at building trust among this core group and team building). Since then, there was a ShareNet Manager Conference in December 2000, where all the knowledge evangelists came together for team- and trust-building activities on top of lots of work.

SHARENET'S ENVIRONMENT

ShareNet is easily accessible through Siemens' corporate intranet. Its home page includes the links shown in Figure 15-1.

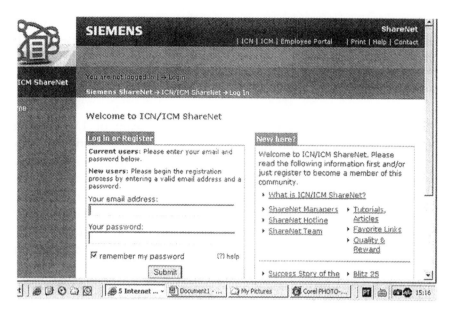

Figure 15-1
ShareNet's Home Page (Source: Siemens)

In addition to the typical frequently asked questions (FAQs) and other links with instructions for users, it is interesting to highlight that ShareNet's team places a lot of effort on promoting the "Success Story of the Month." These add the engaging power of storytelling to promote the benefits of the ShareNet's community. This practice helps create the history and myths that are so important for the growth of any community.

Immediately after checking his or her e-mail, an employee enters ShareNet's main workspace area (Figures 15-2 and 15-3). ShareNet's workspace includes the following core areas:

1. *Urgent requests.* This is the area where employees can post questions they think need an urgent response. These are usually technical, sales, and client-related issues and questions. The questions may or may not be directly linked to specific forums or communities to receive more targeted responses. The authors are immediately notified if anyone responds to their requests. Many ShareNet users check this list of requests daily, as part of their routine. Some moderators also play a proactive role in finding people who can answer specific questions. These questions and

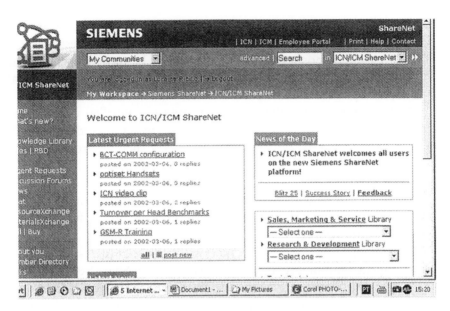

Figure 15-2
ShareNet's Workspace (Source: Siemens)

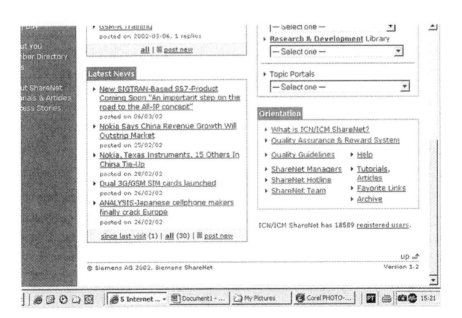

Figure 15-3
ShareNet's Workspace, Continued (Source: Siemens)

the corresponding answers are then archived in another area of the site, discussion forums, where they are always accessible.

2. *News.* The postings in this area tend to be more informational in nature and require no specific action or response. Typical postings here include press articles and links to other sites.

3. *E-mail alerts.* Employees can choose to be notified when a new posting is added to specific areas of ShareNet, including forums, urgent requests, and knowledge objects such as projects, functional solutions, and technologies.

4. *My saved items.* This area is similar to the "Favorites" areas of any browser, where employees keep direct links to any object or document they think they might consult again or find particularly interesting.

5. *My objects.* This is where employees can check the list of the documents and objects that they have added to ShareNet. These objects can be private or made public at the employee's discretion. After 6 months a notification is sent with a request to keep the knowledge updated. The employees decide whether to change or update the content.

6. *Knowledge browsing.* This is where employees can browse different categories of information. The taxonomy here is decided and revised frequently by ShareNet's maintenance team in Germany.

7. *Knowledge input.* Siemens's focus is on the quality of the documents and the information that describes them. Consequently, employees are requested to think carefully before uploading documents or links to ShareNet. Once they decide that the information might be of relevance to a colleague, they are required to respond to seven questions about the document and preferably a number of other additional questions (the list of mandatory and optional questions follows). According to Loraine, "It is not enough to just upload documents; employees need to clearly explain why the information is useful and the real-life circumstances related to the documents." This detailed questionnaire is very important to help other employees to quickly find relevant information and documents.

Mandatory fields:
Name: What is the name of this project? Overview: What are the key highlights of this project?

Reasons for success or failure: Why was this project successful or unsuccessful?
Type: What type of project is this?
Knowledge source: What is your information source concerning this project?
Location: Which geographic location is this project best associated with?
Key words: What key words would enable other users to quickly find this contribution?
Optional fields:
Customers: Who is (are) the customer(s) of this project?
Dealing with customers: How did you approach and develop business with the customer(s) of this project?
List of contacts: Who can provide more information about this project?
Markets: Which markets best relate to this project?
Analyzing the market: How did you analyze this (these) market(s) while developing the project?
Opportunity: What is your knowledge about this opportunity?
Competitors: With whom did we compete on this project?
Identifying competitors: How did you learn more about the competitors on this project?
Technical solutions and services: Which technical solutions and services did you create or reuse for this project?
Preparing the technical solution: How did you prepare technical solutions and services for this project?
Technologies: Which technologies were used in this project?
Functional solution components: Which functional solution components did you create or reuse for this project?
Preparing the functional solution: How did you prepare the functional solution components for this project?
Creating the contract: How did you develop contracts for this project?
Preparing key selling arguments: How did you prepare key selling arguments and your negotiation strategy for this project?
Complementors and partners: Which partners did we work with in this project?
Uploaded documents: Which uploaded documents relate to this project?
Status and time frame: What is the project's status and time frame?
Related projects: Which other projects relate to this contribution?
Relevant files: Which file(s) or document(s) contain(s) more information concerning this project?

8. *ShareNet community portals.* In this area, employees find information especially organized for predetermined communities of practice. It differs from the kind of information that employees would find in the "knowledge browsing" area, because the information here consists mainly of Internet links preselected and organized by the ShareNet team.

9. *Chats.* This application has rarely been used by employees. ShareNet's team is changing that by hosting "special events" with Siemens' leaders and experts. During these events, employees can ask questions from experts in different fields.

10. *ResourceXchange.* This is an internal job market area within ShareNet, where job postings are placed and employees can apply to work on any project or function around the globe. Beyond that, it is clear that, via more one-to-one connections formed through ShareNet, employees are being offered new career and project opportunities within Siemens.

11. *Quality guidelines.* As discussed before, ShareNet's goal is to have only objects of high quality. The quality guidelines that follow reflect that:
   - Contribute in English language only.
   - Contribute only knowledge that is relevant to a large community or has an important impact on business.
   - Focus on your analysis and personal information as well as on your experience and your learning.
   - Focus on the reusability of the knowledge provided (e.g., valuable, innovative, best practices).
   - Focus on reliable, up-to-date, and valuable information—review your contributions regularly for aspects of relevance.
   - Give your contribution a self-explanatory name. Be as specific as possible.
   - Your answers in the object questionnaire should be as precise as possible. Note that it is not necessary to answer all questions of an object.
   - Describe all your objects with key words. This is essential for others to find and reuse your knowledge.
   - Do not provide redundant information, already stored in ShareNet. Check for identical information, before you contribute.
   - Do not provide information easily accessible on the Internet to the ShareNet Knowledge Library.

- Contribute press articles only to the ShareNet News section and not as knowledge objects. There, use links to the original sources (e.g., Internet).
- Make feedback comments on other contributions (discussion threads or knowledge objects) whenever you have additional knowledge about the subject.
- Do not delete "global" objects (named "xx—Global," in bold letters) because you then delete all links pointing to this object.
- Uploading empty documents in ShareNet is regarded as a severe violation of policy.
- When sharing knowledge about products, please consider that information about versions or country variations is important for a global community.
- When referring from ShareNet to other information sites with login using a hyperlink, make sure there is public access to that knowledge.
- When linking between ShareNet objects, check for internal consistency and logic of the compound of linked objects. Please describe in the "Reason for Linking," why you made this link and why this linked compound might be important for other colleagues.

METRICS

Michael applied the "big bang" theory to ShareNet. To draw attention to the new "supported corporate metrics" of knowledge sharing, the ShareNet team invited the top 50 contributors to ShareNet in the first year to a meeting of minds in New York. Each contributor could invite a significant other to this event, which was a mix of work and fun. Siemens no longer does that, but Michael believes that this was important to promote ShareNet within the Siemens organization.

Since then, Siemens has developed its own "mileage program" to track employees' contributions to ShareNet. Employees can check their accumulated "shares" at anytime (Figures 15-4 and 15-5). They are rewarded "shares" toward their individual accounts if they do the following:

- Respond to urgent requests.
- Participate in discussion boards.

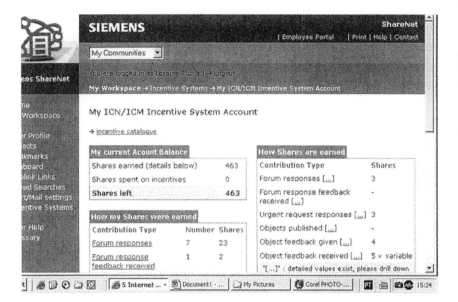

Figure 15-4
ShareNet's Incentive Program (Source: Siemens)

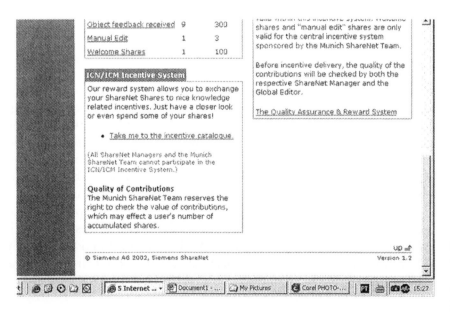

Figure 15-5
ShareNet's Incentive Program, Continued (Source: Siemens)

- Publish knowledge objects (projects, technologies, functional solutions, etc.).
- Receive feedback about published objects (it shows others were interested).
- Provide feedback to other employees' documents (it not only serves to measure the relevance of published objects but adds value to published objects by corroborating them, updating them, or adding other individual contexts).
- Receive feedback to urgent request answers (it shows the relevance of their answers).

Based on the number of accumulated shares, employees are entitled to knowledge-creating opportunities, which are prizes given by the ShareNet program. From time to time, local offices may also give prizes to their employees and even link part of regular bonuses to ShareNet participation. Some of the prizes are a visit to a conference, individual training of their choice, or international travel to another location to help employees that collaborate online to meet face to face, thereby, increasing Siemens's social capital. Of the 18,000 Share-Net participants worldwide, almost 2500 have already collected "shares" and almost 1000 received some sort of incentive or prize.

Because of its focus on the quality of input, employees' contributions are validated by expert committees when they claim their prizes. The total number of shares accumulated by employees is actually reduced if they do not follow ShareNet's quality guidelines.

Michael Wagner has a vision that one day people at Siemens will have "personal knowledge-sharing targets" in the same fashion that they currently have the specific business targets (e.g., sales targets).

Key Lessons Learned

Lesson 1. Feedback Is as Important as Posting Information

The ShareNet team realized early on that knowledge grows as it is applied or reused. Consequently, they wanted employees to add comments to posted information on ShareNet. By doing this, users add value to the original documents. Sometimes, they disagree with the conclusions or tips of existing documents; sometimes they add new context or simply confirm its usefulness. Anyhow, after a number of iterations, the original documents usually have their intellectual capital enhanced by the contributions of others. Employees are rewarded with "shares" when they post valuable feedback. *Valuable* means that they have explained how the information was used and whether and why it was useful for a specific business purpose.

Lesson 2. Hands-on Training and Coaching Are Very Important

Loraine explained that part of the success of ShareNet is related to the great attention given to user training. Initially, training focused on the procedures and rules to participate. Now it has evolved as much as possible to a hands-on approach. During the introduction of Share-Net to new users, employees are asked to bring documents and information that they think would be valuable to other employees. Thus, the training session becomes their first opportunity to collaborate. In addition to this initial training session, employees can rely on the direct support of local moderators and, in some cases, official coaches who help them make the best use of the system (e.g., how and where to upload files). The "coach concept" started in Australia and is being adopted in many countries. By mid-2001, the Brazilian office, for instance, relied on 15 official coaches.

Lesson 3. Quality Is More Important than Quantity

A remarkable thing about the strategy behind ShareNet is its stringent quality focus. In as large an organization as Siemens, any collaborative portal like ShareNet could easily become a "dump" and quickly lose credibility if people did not trust the information available in the system. The ShareNet team realized this and developed a number of policies focused on keeping only high-quality references in the system:

- Employees are asked a number of questions whenever they upload content to ShareNet.
- Detailed feedback improves the quality of existing knowledge objects and helps quickly exclude references with little value.
- Training is taken very seriously. Users rely both on local and headquarter's support.
- Employees can have part of their "shares" taken away if some of their contributions are judged not to add value to the community.

- ShareNet has a centrally dedicated team constantly monitoring usage and interviewing users and local moderators to find ways to improve the system.

Lesson 4. Local Support and Promotion Are Very Important

The offices where ShareNet has been most widely accepted rely on the strong support of local senior management. Senior management at these offices helps promote the behaviors necessary for ShareNet to work. They do this by constantly reminding employees about the importance of ShareNet in their companywide e-mail, speeches, and smaller gatherings of management and employees in general.

Lesson 5. Detailed Metrics Should Be Available for Users and Moderators

ShareNet strives to create a healthy competitive environment for ideas. Employees can easily check out why and how many shares they have accumulated. The rewards can be significant for the heavy contributors. Most employees, however, can earn symbolic prizes and learn about the behavior valued by the company. ShareNet administrators, on the other hand, can gauge the usage of the system. This allows the team to coordinate offline training and promotions to engage users or rethink the value of specific applications and areas of ShareNet.

Lesson 6. Success Stories Create Myths That Help Change Behavior

One of the most prominent links on ShareNet is the "Success Story of the Month." The ShareNet team believes that highlighting stories of how different offices around the world collaborated to deliver value to clients reinforces one of the new core values at Siemens: "Our collaboration has no limits." This action also responds to a pressing need of creative people and knowledge workers in general: recognition. The ShareNet team clearly understood that, in an increasingly faceless world, wide recognition can be the ultimate reward.

Lesson 7. In Large Organizations, Voluntary Participation Does Not Happen Easily

The positive evolution of ShareNet is the result of close attention to many details that foster participation: technology, usability, quality of materials, reward system, and local promotion and support. In such a large organization as Siemens, which not too long ago was strongly organized around division and products, the idea of vertical, horizontal, and geographical collaboration could not happen without a cohesive thrust in the areas that influence behavior. The reported stories tell us that ShareNet users usually start out a little bit skeptical, but once they start receiving answers to their questions in a matter of hours, they get "converted" and contribute and help others participate.

Lesson 8. In Large Organizations, It Is Important to Find "Knowledge Evangelists" and Get People Involved

ShareNet's worldwide success stems, to a large extent, from the granular, day-to-day work of many ShareNet managers who provide local support, training, and promotion. These people really "got it." Michael's central team in Germany made sure that ShareNet managers were individuals who truly believed in the concepts and principles of KM and ShareNet and were in tune with local operations. In a few cases, individuals were replaced as ShareNet managers, especially in the beginning, because success requires very enthusiastic change agents. In addition to these knowledge evangelists, many other people were needed from the start. The ShareNet team made sure that users and field personnel were involved very early on in the development of the concept, designing, prototyping, and rollout of the system. User inputs are constantly taken into consideration through simple feedback mechanism within ShareNet's site and surveys, specific meetings, and information collected by local ShareNet managers.

Lesson 9: Knowledge Management Is 80% About Change Management

In line with lessons 7 and 8, Michael Wagner believes that ShareNet's success relies on a team with a strong change management background.

Even 2 years after the rollout of ShareNet, most of the dedicated staff that supports ShareNet (with the help of local managers) stills spends most of its time on issues related to change management, such as internal communications, training, coaching, organizing workshops, and building internal alliances. In Michael's words, "You gotta push it every day."

Lesson 10. Corporate Portals Shorten Distance and Avoid Vertical, Centralized Communication

A huge benefit of ShareNet is that offices around the world communicate more directly, instead of using the large German office as the connecting point. In a way, ShareNet helps shape Siemens into a "networked" organization as opposed to a "hub-and-spoke" organization.

Lesson 11. ShareNet Strengthens Siemens' Social Fabric around the Globe

An interesting benefit of ShareNet for an organization such as Siemens is that it forges new connections across geographies and cultures. Fernando Stefano, a leading engineer in the hot area of IP Routing at the Brazilian office and a heavy contributor to ShareNet, for instance, told us that, "ShareNet is helping me to overcome some of my own preconceived notions about how people behaved in other cultures. Before ShareNet, I did not know that people in country XYZ could be so cooperative. Now, we even exchange information about things that are more personal, such as travel information, study opportunities, hobbies, etc."

Lesson 12. Develop Detailed Business Cases for Knowledge Management Projects

Even though a number of benefits of KM initiatives may be hard to quantify, it is important to develop coherent business cases. At Siemens, although KM has been embraced as a core thrust by the worldwide board, many KM projects have specific and quantifiable targets. For example, a number of assumptions about the number of knowledge objects that would be uploaded, visited, and reapplied were made to justify the investments in the tool and operations budget. After more than 2 years, the ShareNet team is completely convinced that Siemens is getting a large return on its investments. Both on the cost side (reduction in wasted time looking for information) and, especially, on the revenue side (additional sales that include reused ShareNet's knowledge objects), the numbers show the tremendous impact of ShareNet.

FUTURE DIRECTIONS

ShareNet will eventually be rolled out to all Siemens divisions. This means that it could be accessible by all 450,000 Siemens employees worldwide. As of mid-2001, it was potentially accessible by 75,000 employees (with 18,000 registered users). This is, of course, a major step for the ShareNet team and Siemens. It also means new requirements and opportunities for cross-divisional knowledge sharing and cooperation as well as managing information overload, personalization, and community affiliation.

As Siemens also embarks on a corporatewide employee portal initiative that will provide much more sophisticated personalization capabilities, ShareNet's different applications will be seamlessly integrated into this portal. Employees will be able to configure their portal and select which ShareNet applications and communities they want to be affiliated with.

CLOSING PERSPECTIVES

The ShareNet project at Siemens shows the tremendous benefits a CP project can have on large global organizations. It also reinforces the idea that KM initiatives are more likely to succeed if they grow organically and through careful planning and deployment of the technical infrastructure and local support.

Top management support is of paramount importance. Most of the success of KM at Siemens can be attributed to the visible support (speeches, budget, and vision) from the most senior management team to knowledge management. Senior management is striving, on many fronts, to help employees around the world to understand that Siemens is moving from being a product-based company to becoming a solutions-based company. KM initiatives such as ShareNet are at the core of the kind of new organization Siemens is trying to build.

To build a world-class knowledge enterprise, Siemens applies a sociotechnical approach that aligns knowledge and business strategies. This is achieved through a combination of actions that demand focus on core value-adding processes, standardization of platforms, deployment of sophisticated portal architectures, e-learning systems, and clear support for knowledge communities (or communities of practice) that cross local, divisional, and even company boundaries (to include customers, suppliers, and partners). In a large organization such as Siemens, this can be achieved only through intense corporate alignment coming from the very top of the organization.

SOFIA

Another interesting KM initiative at Siemens is the SOFIA project, "a solution for managing R&D knowledge." This project, which started in early 2001, was led by Filipe Cassapo, a French engineer, and developed by a small R&D team under the leadership of Sandro Melhoreto, in one of the Brazilian offices. Since then, it has been rolled out to a number of other offices around the world (Germany, Argentina, Austria, Belgium, and Portugal as of end of 2001). Although not fully implemented by late 2001, SOFIA, in particular the Athena module, was already receiving strong corporate support from the Siemens worldwide KM corporate office. In the words of Peter Heinold, program manager, corporate knowledge management, "The Athena tool has already shown interesting results. We are looking forward to following closely its future, and we are interested to see how it could be integrated into the Siemens knowledge sharing and competence mapping activities." According to Sandro Melhoreto, various parts of it are expected to be increasingly integrated into the ShareNet system.

This specific KM portal for R&D at Siemens includes a number of knowledge assets individuals can tap into to better do their jobs. As with most KM systems, employees are also supposed to contribute to this knowledge base. Before we discuss each component of SOFIA in detail, it is important to understand some of the core principles behind the design of this system:

- Valuable knowledge for the organization needs to be linked to organizational processes. We will see how all codified knowledge is categorized in a "knowledge tree" and "certified."
- Knowledge cannot be separated from where it can be applied. It is important to link human capabilities to organizational processes.

- "One does not manage what one does not measure." This means that, from the start, the project was designed in a way to allow the measurement of the "proxies" of the knowledge evolution.
- The system can play an important role in reducing organizational "silos."

The components of SOFIA are

1. *Athena (R&D competence networking).* This was the only system functioning by the end of 2001. It includes a typical profiling system that helps Siemens and its employees to find out "Who knows what?" Employees voluntarily update their skill levels according to a knowledge map already registered in the system. This knowledge map includes sets of skills, certificates or diplomas, events, and languages (very important to be singled out as a separate area in a global organization such as Siemens). If employees do not find a match for their skills, they can then suggest new ones to be registered in the system. Some of the interesting features of this system include
   – It allows grouping employees with similar profiles.
   – It allows the "measurement" (data mining) of available skills by tracking details (how many?) about employees included in their profiles.
   At the end of 2001, the Athena system and Siemens valley learning, a community of practice tool developed out of Belgium, were being closely integrated.
2. *Hestia (R&D e-learning).* This is where employees will create (the platform is incorporating easy-to-create virtual courses) and receive online e-training and find information about training opportunities. This module, which will include multimedia features, was expected to be launched sometime in 2002. It also integrates with Athena, since Athena's competence model is an important reference for setting priorities for course development and content validation (through the list of accredited experts).
3. *Apollo (R&D infrastructure control).* This is basically a reservation system where employees can find available information about existing equipment and book it for their research projects. The module was expected to be launched sometime in 2002.

4. *Poseidon (R&D best practices sharing).* Here, project best practices are filed electronically. Best practices are published here only after they have been approved (certified) by senior expert committees. This is considered the most important explicit knowledge base of R&D projects. The module was scheduled to be launched in 2002.
5. *Hephaestus (R&D projects).* Here, employees will find information about all R&D projects happening at Siemens. This module was still in the planning phase in late 2001.

16

TEXACO

CP/KM EXPERTS

John Old, director of information management
James Hughes, leader of the "Know-How Leverage Team"
John Gazouleas, corporate collaboration tools

BACKGROUND

Texaco (now part of ChevronTexaco) is one of the oldest oil companies in the world. It currently has approximately 18,000 employees and operations in more than 150 countries. It performs a wide range of activities and business along the value chain of the oil industry. It explores, produces, and commercializes oil and natural gas; manufactures fuels and lubricant products; operates a number of transportation and distribution facilities; and produces alternate forms of energy for power, manufacturing, and chemicals. In 2000, it produced 1.15 million barrels of oil per day, collected over $51.1 billion in revenue, and achieved a net income of $2.5 billion. Texaco has recently merged with Chevron (the final legal merger approval happened in the second semester of 2001). Teams formed of employees of both companies are already in the advanced stage of planning the operations of the new organization. In this case, we report primarily Texaco's KM initiatives.

UNDERSTANDING KNOWLEDGE MANAGEMENT AT TEXACO

KM at Texaco relies on initiatives and projects led by a number of departments and business units. Funding and support for the projects and operational budgets come from or are approved at the highest levels of organization. Greg Vesey, the senior VP for e-business, and Jim Metzger, Texaco's CTO, are leading supporters at the senior executive level. The senior leadership of the global exploration and production business provide support for the KM projects via the Knowledge Highway Project.

Instead of focusing on a large KM organization, Texaco relies on a strong and enthusiastic KM community, "The Networking People Team." It includes members from Corporate IT (particularly the Collaboration Tools Team), Information Management Department, Human Resources, Organizational Effectiveness, business units representatives, discipline leaders, program leaders (e.g., Quality Movement), and so forth. About 10–15 members meet regularly (a couple of times a month) to discuss joint projects, exchange experiences and knowledge about the field, and support one another's projects. Regardless of the department of origin, all tend to be technologically literate. James Hughes, leader of the Know-How Leverage Team, played a key role in providing support and energizing this community.

According to John Old, an important milestone linked to the beginning of "formalized" KM at Texaco is the Knowledge Highway Project. This project, which started in early 1999, marked a strong commitment from KM leaders to (1) standardize data, information, and software across business units and (2) foster stronger professional connections among people within Texaco.

Despite the more obvious benefits of standardization, the implementation of this initiative encountered a few pockets of resistance, because Texaco's employees pride themselves on their strong sense of freedom, independence, and creativity. Eventually, through the strong support of very senior executives, the standardization project moved ahead and achieved its objectives (making it easier for people to work together was the primary goal; standardization was one means to that end; sensitizing employees to the soft issues around people collaborating was a second means to that end). The PeopleNet project is the leading result of the initial focus on connecting people. It is a highly detailed mapping of personal skills, experiences, personal networks, and personal information. According to John, despite being an application that depends on voluntary participation, it already has the participation of a significant number of the knowledge professionals at Texaco. We discuss this application in more detail later in this case study.

Many facets of KM initiatives are discussed in this chapter by the Networking People Team. According to John Old, the projects and concerns of this community are the following (as before, P, primary goal; S, secondary goal; N, not relevant):

Communication tool (top-down and bottom-up):

(P) Improve communication of the vision and knowledge strategy.

(N) Improve communication of company values.

(S) Keep the organization alert.

(P) Engage customers and community at large.

(P) Divulge results more broadly and promote systemic analysis.

(S) Facilitate bottom-up communication.

(N) Make it easy for employees to suggest improvements to management.

Push information and knowledge to employees:

(S) Capture, organize, and distribute codified knowledge (e.g., database access).

(S) Improve access to external sources of information and knowledge.

(P) Improve decision making.

(P) Empower front-line employees.

Improve reuse of knowledge:

(P) Develop expertise maps (uncover existing knowledge).

(S) Map and measure intangible assets.

(S) Facilitate search of previously developed knowledge.

Foster collaboration:

(P) Increase collaboration among different functions of the organization.

(P) Increase collaboration among different locations of the organization.

(P) Improve overall knowledge sharing.

(P) Support the development of communities of practice.

(S) Increase connections not related to work.

Improve human capital management:

(N) Improve hiring.

(P) Improve internal mobility and deployment of existing employees.

(S) Integrate temporary and outside human resources and expertise.

(S) Improve training and acquisition of skills.

(S) Get new employees up to speed very quickly.

(P) Reduce time spent on menial activities.

(S) Improve employee retention.

(S) Facilitate work and integration of telecommuters.

Improve relationship with external stakeholders and increase information flow:

(P) Improve information exchange with suppliers, partners, and customers.

(N) Capture customer information.

(N) Improve customer satisfaction.

(N) Reduce sales costs.

(N) Reduce customer service costs.

MAIN WEB-BASED KNOWLEDGE MANAGEMENT APPLICATIONS

Texaco deploys a number of Web-based applications that can be linked to KM efforts or are managed by members of the Networking People Team. We describe three core groups: PeopleNet, team tools, and best practices.

PeopleNet

PeopleNet is a core KM application developed internally about 2 years ago. Of the 8000 employees that John believes should be uploading their information in the system, almost 5000 have already done so. The system also played an important role during the merger of Texaco and Chevron. It is used as one of the pieces of information to help merger teams to select employees who stayed with the merged company. (There were workforce reductions as result of this merger.)

Although in the same category as many other employees' profiling systems, it evolved to include a number of innovative elements.

- Employees can match their skill set against a number of preregistered skills on PeopleNet. Employees are prompted not only to say whether they have a skill but their specific level (e.g., working knowledge, extensive knowledge). Each main skill category has two other lower levels that provide more precise fields to describe the specific skill of the employee. Employees can also add as much detail as they want to their profiles.

- Employees' personal profiles (Figures 16-1 and 16-2) include a number of interesting pieces of information that go beyond their personal knowledge (such as areas of expertise, résumé, and documents they wrote and uploaded). It also includes personal information not related to work (hobbies, photos, interests) and tries to capture part of the social network related to knowledge domain areas: personal network of experts in the same field, interesting Internet links, and list of formalized communities to which the employee belongs. The idea behind this application is that, if employees have a specific question, they may more easily find a number of people with similar knowledge. The names in an individual's network may also serve as validation of his or her expertise in a particular area.

Here's a shot of a profile showing the listed expertise areas and the network connections around those areas.

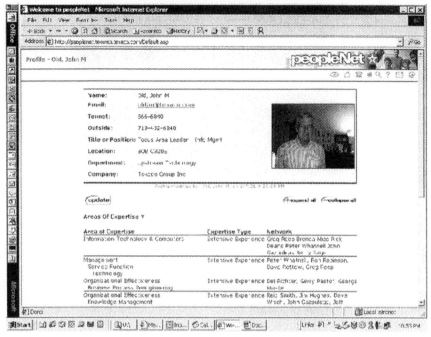

Figure 16-1
PeopleNet: Employee Profile (Source: Texaco)

The resume section of a profile

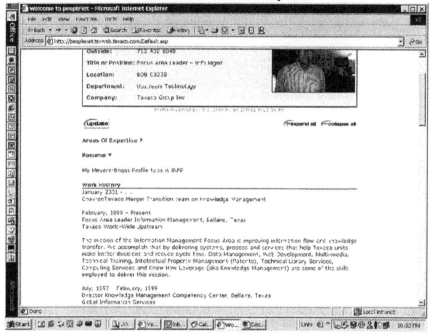

Figure 16-2
PeopleNet: Employee Profile, Continued (Source: Texaco)

PeopleNet Home Page...note PeopleNet for Networks

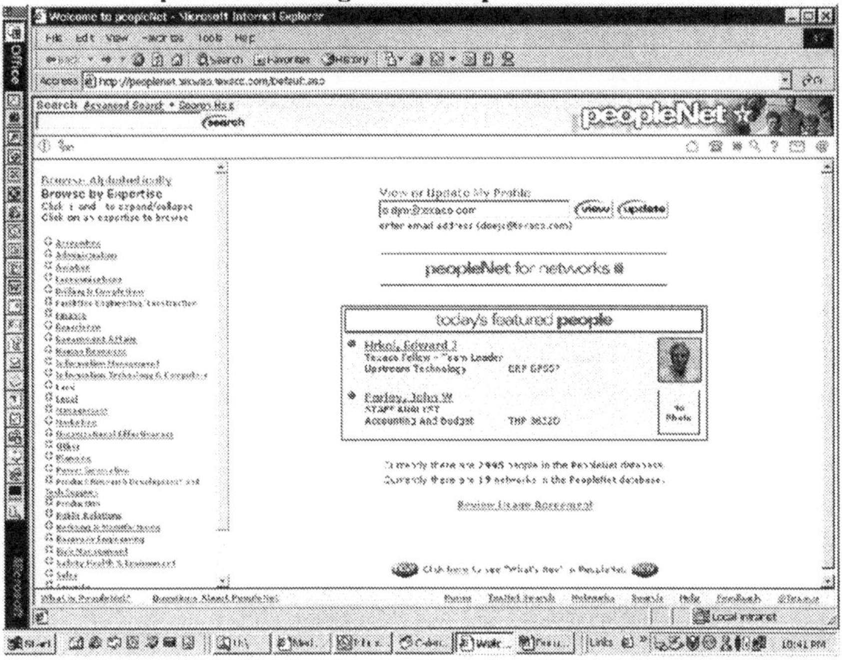

Figure 16-3
PeopleNet Home Page and "Today's Featured People" (Source: Texaco)

- The "Today's Featured People" on the home page of PeopleNet (Figure 16-3) is innovative. Two individuals are selected every day, showing their photos, a brief description of their locations, positions, and so on. This quick summary is linked to the person's complete PeopleNet profile. It is an application John believes helps people meet virtually by chance and fosters meaningful connections within Texaco.

Click on the Skills Tree and get a list of people with those skills

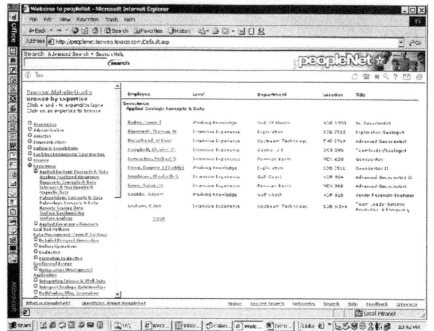

Figure 16-4
PeopleNet: Finding Employees with Specific Skills (Source: Texaco)

■ Any Texaco employee can search for experts and specific communities through PeopleNet by browsing this application via the skills tree or the PeopleNet for networks. Also, an advanced search engine allows very targeted searches based on a number of narrowing criteria such as expertise areas and Boolean expressions. The search results or browsing leads to a page where employees find a detailed list of all employees with that specific skill, their knowledge level in that skill, their department, location, title, and most important, a link to each individual detailed profile (Figure 16-4).

■ PeopleNet also helps locate experts and employees in general, even if employees did not register and upload their personal information. It includes a general and searchable directory application with the location and telephone of all Texaco employees and an application called KnowledgeMail. KnowledgeMail is a search engine (provided by Tacit) that mines Texaco's e-mail repository to reveal and link employees' latest communications with specific subjects or key words. In John words, "it adds a time component to PeopleNet" by tapping into very recent exchanges or areas of focus that have not yet been captured by the more detailed employee's profile.

■ PeopleNet for networks allows employees to create and join specific communities. These communities can be open to everyone or only selected members. They can also be internal or external (including individuals who do not work for Texaco). Almost 40 different communities were active in September 2001.

■ Another interesting feature is PeopleNet's Statement, which reminds employees of the expected appropriate behavior when using PeopleNet.

Team Tools

In addition to PeopleNet, a number of other applications are extensively deployed at Texaco to foster online collaboration and make it easier for virtual teams to work together. The Networking People Team, and in particular the leaders of the Know-How Leverage Team and the Corporate Collaboration Tools Team, led the selection and deployment of these tools. They also provided the necessary internal communications and training of users across the enterprise. For an organization with employees in many parts of the globe, this is a mandatory solution. Indeed, these tools have been widely embraced at Texaco. Here are the top two tools:

■ *MeetingPlace.* This Web conferencing tool is used extensively by Texaco's employees (the system had registered 93,302 conferencing minutes by September 2001). A rather simple application, it allows employees to use their Web browsers to view all sorts of applications and documents and collaborate in real time.

■ *QuiCPlace.* This application allows teams to create their own virtual team space, where they can upload in an organized way all kinds of project documents and participate in targeted discussion forums. It not only helps the teams keep track of project tasks and exchange valuable information, it also allows Texaco to capture, to a great extent, the historical evolution of projects and some of the more informal and valuable exchanges among team members. It may include external parties as well. In September 2001, Texaco's system registered 1528 QuiCPlace users from Texaco and another 714 non-Texaco employees.

Other tools being deployed include instant messaging, audio conferencing, video conferencing, net meeting, and IPTV (a technology for video recording and video streaming).

According to John Gazouleas, one of the most interesting lessons learned introducing these tools is that, if there are no champions within a team or community environment, people tend to fall back to the old ways of doing things. That means that people tend to easily forget to use these more advanced tools that register the interactions and keep everyone in the loop. His team finds and works with early adopters and internal champions. Training and demonstrations are critical to a massive rollout. He also concedes that most of these tools are immature and not very integrated, making life somewhat harder for many non-IT users.

Best Practices

Texaco's engineering department has been publishing "best practices" stories since 1998. These stories can be very technical or nontechnical. It evolved from a realization of the engineering team leadership that the company was not fully leveraging the ingenuity and creativity of employees from different divisions. Publishing the stories started small, with a low level of technical sophistication (e-mail distribution lists, bulletin boards, newsletters, internal magazines). The number of interested parties grew fast though (due, to a great extent, to the active "animation" and internal marketing led by the leadership team: quarterly meetings to discuss specific engineering topics, t-shirts), and by 1999, the existing intranet solution was launched.

The current database has close to 300 stories. Based on recent estimates, the knowledge exchanges that occurred due to this application have already had a bottom-line impact of around $100 million. Any employee can submit a story. A central team examines the story, gets it validated by experts, and publishes it in the best practices site. Employees submitting a story are prompted to answer four key questions:

- Where has the best practice been implemented?
- What are the estimated dollar savings associated with the best practice?
- Background information (people involved, required investments) can you supply?

■ Can you suggest other situations and locations where the best practice can be reapplied?

The idea is not to provide very detailed stories, but short, concise, enticing stories that allow any employee to understand its application, general benefits, and potential dollar savings. By including contact information to employees who submitted the best practice, other interested employees can obtain all the detailed information needed for reuse.

The site also tracks how many times a best practice has been seen and, more important, how often it has been reapplied by other Texaco employees. By mid-2001, about 160 stories of best practices were being reapplied. This last point is particularly interesting, as it lends further validation and credibility to the story.

KEY LESSONS LEARNED

Lesson 1. Keep Knowledge Management out of the Spotlight

At Texaco, despite a few more focused activities and functions such as the Know-How Leverage Team, KM efforts are distributed efforts led by a number of different individuals from all areas that embrace KM concepts. It relies strongly on a KM community of practice. By using this strategy, Texaco can leverage the personal networks of a number of different agents of change and budget and personal contributions from relevant senior executive sponsors and key relevant stakeholders.

Lesson 2. Divulge and Celebrate Knowledge-Management-Related Initiatives, Behaviors, and Results

At the same time that Texaco avoids putting the spotlight on KM as a central, overhead-laden function, it uses many different communication tools to highlight achievements and projects that have a strong KM component. Since KM depends heavily on each individual's motivation and desire to share knowledge, it is clear, particularly in large organizations, that KM initiatives need to use all means of internal communications, such as intranet stories, newsletters, video streaming, leaflets, and brochures.

Lesson 3. Successful Knowledge Management Strategies Foster Meaningful Connections

Many of Texaco's KM strategies aim to help individuals and teams to work together and more effectively. Even when knowledge artifacts, databases, and best practices documents are employed, they work as "pointers" to carriers of knowledge, other employees and even external parties. Supporting this strategy is a strong belief that Texaco's key intellectual capital is its ability to leverage, in meaningful ways, the minds, brains, and commitment of its employees.

Lesson 4. Personal Information Humanizes Knowledge Management Applications and Helps Reduce Communication Obstacles

Texaco espouses many concepts of social learning theory. John Old reminded us that, in a global organization such as Texaco, with offices spread over 150 countries, it is important to "humanize" relationships. Small tokens, such as photos and lists of personal interests and hobbies, help reduce communication barriers. In a number of reported cases, employees called experts in a distant office only after finding some "human" characteristics that helped them overcome some preconceived notions about people in other offices.

Lesson 5. Personal and Trusted Networks Are Valuable Assets for Knowledge Management

Knowledge in organizational settings is rarely held by single individuals. This is not to say that individuals do not hold unique, specific, and valuable know-how. However, learning is essentially a social activity, so knowledge holders or experts are well positioned to point to others who have similar expertise or have participated in joint learning experiences. Texaco pays attention to this fact and solicits this information from employees who fill out their personal profiles in the PeopleNet application.

Lesson 6. Senior Executives Play Very Symbolic Roles in Promoting Knowledge-Management-Friendly Cultures

Very large organizations contain many subcultures. This is no different in the case of KM. The level of acceptance, adoption, and fostering of KM activities can vary widely. At Texaco, the KM leaders and senior executives that sponsor KM activities wisely acknowledge this. So, instead of trying to change the whole organization at once with a number of "empty" speeches, they work on one-to-one coaching, value-laden projects, and other symbolic acts (such as sending strong letters of support or granting awards to employees who engage in valuable knowledge-sharing activities).

Lesson 7. To Be Successful, Knowledge-Sharing Communities Need to Create Value for the Organization and Employees

According to John, Texaco did a survey for a Lessons Learned summit in which they asked people questions about the personal value they got from a community and the business value that community generated. A very strong positive correlation was found between the business and personal value communities generated. If community members felt they got little personal value from the community, those communities generated little business value. Or, maybe only communities that generated business value were interesting enough to hold members' attention.

Lesson 8. Build Processes and Apply Project Management Techniques That Include Reflection Time

Since a lot of new knowledge is created in project environments, it is important to build reflection time to capture knowledge as it is created. John tells of this being applied in projects across Texaco. For instance, project management business processes at Texaco now include explicit steps for peer consultation and review activities.

Lesson 9. Develop Proxies to Measure the Value of Knowledge Artifacts

At Texaco, a number of proxies measure how often a "best practice" document has been seen and reapplied. While most organizations have digital metrics about only CP traffic, uploads, downloads, and the like, Texaco tries to capture how often specific "knowledge artifacts" are reused and the profit benefit it brings to the organization.

Lesson 10. Knowledge Quickly Gets Outdated: Develop Knowledge Management Applications That Capture Proxies of the Most Recent Knowledge Activity

As much as PeopleNet provides interesting and detailed background on individuals' skills and experiences (the carriers of knowledge), John and his team realized that this application could be complemented by a tool provided by Tacit that data mines e-mail communications. At Texaco, the tool, called KnowledgeMail, helps employees to find others discussing some of the same issues in more recent times. This tool is particularly important because some employees do not keep their profiles on PeopleNet up-to-date.

Lesson 11. Too Much Personalization Reduces Important Shared Contexts

As Texaco starts its journey toward the implementation of its high-end portal, John Old alerts that too much personalization can be harmful. Although recognizing that personalization can reduce information overload, he points to two counterproductive factors. First, not all employees are ready to properly select and organize the most valuable sources of information and applications. Second, if everyone starts building a personal view of the world, the organization may suffer from lack of sufficient corporate or even departmental alignment and shared contexts that foster dialogue.

Lesson 12. Portal Solutions Need to Take into Account That Employees Play Several Different Roles

This lesson is closely related to the personalization issue. As Texaco plans to deploy a sophisticated corporate portal application, John's key concern is to have the portal deployed in a way that helps people find the right context or content environment for the many roles that individuals play in the organization. Individuals can see themselves, for instance, according to their profession, organizational level, division, location, community of practice, projects, and so forth.

Lesson 13. Invite People to Tell Success Stories about Knowledge Management

The KM leaders at Texaco understand the power of stories from the field. There is strong internal marketing to capture and tell these stories. John Old's and Tom Lionetti's teams constantly solicit stories through one-to-one conversations, the company's intranet and internal magazine, leaflets distributed to all employees, and even running contests (employees can win gift certificates). Some of the communications channels are also used to promote the selected stories. Recently, they even employed IPTV to record and video stream some of the most interesting anecdotes.

Lesson 14. Knowledge Management Applications May Produce High Returns on Investment

One of the most interesting aspects of KM applications is that they can provide very high financial returns to organizations. First of all, Web-based KM applications are easier, faster, and cheaper to deploy than more traditional IT applications. Most important, though, is that, when important human connections are made and significant knowledge is reused, the increase in profit can be very large. At Texaco, for instance, the "best practice" application alone is estimated to have had an impact of about $100 million so far (well beyond any development and maintenance costs).

Lesson 15. Leverage Existing Awards for Outstanding Behavior or Achievements

Knowledge sharing should not be seen as belonging to a different category of outstanding performance. At Texaco, senior managers can nominate employees for cash rewards for outstanding behavior or performance that has an important business impact. John and other KM leaders believe that KM activities should become ingrained in the working practices of Texaco's employees. Consequently, they should not be seen and rewarded separately.

Lesson 16. New Communications Tools Help Change Established Communication Behavior

As many new collaboration Web-based applications are deployed at Texaco, John expects that new behavior will emerge that changes existing communication and relationship patterns. Without making many predictions about the future, he recalls that even the introduction of e-mail at Texaco made communication a lot more informal and a lot more open. Before e-mail, written communications, particularly between different businesses units, had to be formally approved at senior levels before being sent.

Lesson 17. New Communication and Knowledge Management Tools Require Important Behavior Changes and Dedicated Champions

Thousands of employees now use Web-collaboration tools and avoid saving documents on their hard disks. A significant number of employees now understand that collaboration requires a proactive effort. This current level of success at Texaco in deploying Web-based KM and team tools results from the concerted effort of a number of professionals from different areas who formed the Networked People Team.

They worked together not only to develop the infrastructure but also to publicize, train, and motivate people throughout the organization. They worked with employees in general, but also with a number of early adopters that helped disseminate concepts and remind other employees.

FUTURE DIRECTIONS

John Old is a strong believer in the power of human connections, lines of trust, and the ability of people to be innovative if the right conditions are there. KM, in his mind, is less about the systems and more about working with people and communities. In his words, "One day some company will recognize the untapped potential laying dormant on their doorstep. . . . the network of people in the company . . . instead of building systems that enslave the workforce and keep the company from changing, that company will create an atmosphere of high trust, clear purpose and principles freeing the employees to do great things."

At this point, it is hard to say exactly how KM will evolve in the merged organization. Chevron is also an organization with a strong tradition in KM. According to James Hughes, one of the key initial goals is to build a larger KM community that includes members from the two previously independent companies. The concept of communities and a number of Web-based collaboration tools have already shown their value during the activities leading to the official merger. They are expected to continue to do so as people find it easier to connect with others with similar learning and personal growth goals.

CLOSING PERSPECTIVES

As James Hughes said in one interview, "There's no individual that can say: I did that alone. It was indeed a team effort." This is a case where we can see a strong people-oriented KM strategy. This is not to say that the many KM leaders do not try to keep up-to-date on the latest KM-friendly technologies. Indeed, as shown here, they have experimented and deployed a number of the latest Web-based solutions. The focus on establishing and facilitating meaningful connections permeates almost every KM initiative at Texaco.

The merged company, ChevronTexaco, will certainly apply new technical solutions and reshape some of the fundamental principles of KM applied so far at Texaco. For instance, there is an emerging vision that the implementation of a corporate portal that integrates tools for KM, internal communications, and business development will be one of the key priorities for the new organization. Time will tell how these different and successful KM leaders are able to merge and exchange some best practices in KM.

17

XEROX, THE DOCUMENT COMPANY

CP/KM EXPERTS

Daniel G. Bobrow, research fellow, systems and practices, The Palo Alto Research Center (PARC)

Michel Boucher, Eureka World Wide database quality coordinator; service technician

John Burgess, VP, customer services, Xerox

Pricilla Douglas, prior principle, Xerox Professional Services

Gary Lee, manager, service systems, Xerox

Thomas Ruddy, prior manager, organization design and development, Xerox

Jack Whalen, research scientist, The Palo Alto Research Center (PARC)

BACKGROUND

Founded in 1961 in Rochester, New York, the Document Company, Xerox, is a leader in the global document management market, providing document solutions (hardware, software, and services) that enhance business productivity and knowledge sharing. Headquartered in Stamford, Connecticut, the company has revenues exceeding $18.7 billion and has over 72,000 employees worldwide. Since the company's inception, six core values have guided its business:

1. We succeed through satisfied customers.
2. We value and empower employees.
3. We deliver quality and excellence in all we do.
4. We provide superior return to our shareholders.
5. We use technology to deliver market leadership.
6. We behave responsibly as a corporate citizen.

The company has a long history and commitment to Total Quality and knowledge sharing to improve business practices, and has been recognized internationally for its leadership in knowledge management. One of the most published projects demonstrating knowledge sharing is the Eureka project, which over time, became a Web-browser-based portal solution. Its application of cultural anthropological underpinnings make this a unique case, demonstrating the value of storytelling and virtual teams to rapidly create and share knowledge worldwide to improve business performance and empower employees.

KNOWLEDGE SHARING PORTAL, EUREKA

Xerox has gone to great lengths to tailor its knowledge management initiatives to people by understanding how they do their jobs and the social dynamics behind knowledge sharing. For some time, Xerox's Palo Alto Research Center (PARC) research scientists have focused on capturing the tacit knowledge locked in employees' heads for richer insight. One knowledge management initiative recognized for its success in tapping into both explicit and tacit forms of knowledge is the Eureka project.

Eureka was originally developed as a grassroots effort out of PARC in 1994 to help service technicians share their knowledge through the collaborative assembly of a searchable database of tips and best practices. Eureka's purpose was to capture knowledge about equipment fixes and new problems encountered on the job and to share this knowledge across field service organizations. Driving the need for Eureka was that service technician manuals were continually out of date, almost as soon as they were printed, and failed to include many of the creative solutions repair technicians naturally improvised in the field.

Examples of this type of know-how include problems that resulted from aging machines, intermittent faults, different environments, network interaction, or the quirks presented by new machines. This often left technicians with no easily accessible solutions, requiring them to escalate the call to a technical hotline or their buddies. These environmental and social factors became the foundation for Eureka.

In partnership with PARC, Eureka was further developed in the mid-1990s as a grassroots effort in Xerox France under the vision of PARC technology guru, Olivier Raiman, a member of the PARC Eureka team. However, widespread distribution of the Eureka toolset within support centers began only in June 1998, after Eureka was further developed jointly by PARC scientists and Xerox World Wide Customer Services.

Eureka's purpose has been to capture knowledge about equipment fixes and new problems encountered on the job and share this knowledge across the field service organizations. The field service organization is composed of more than 23,000 service technicians worldwide, handling a million repair visits to customer sites per month.

Eureka reinforces the value of conversations and knowledge sharing via stories, as anthropologists at PARC found that Xerox engineers all tell similar war stories to each other about diagnosing and fixing machines. This is how they brag but also how they instruct each other. Xerox recognizes that manuals and training programs cannot keep up with the fast-paced change of hardware or the current know-how in the heads and hands of their service technicians.

Anthropologists who analyzed the behaviors of the service technicians saw that they made it a point to spend time not with customers but each other.[1] They would gather in common areas, like the local parts warehouse, hang around the coffeepot, and swap stories from the field. Some managers or people would see this socialization as an immediate opportunity for productivity gain. Cut out the conversation, eliminate the dead time, and pocket the savings. The anthropologists saw just the opposite. The time at the warehouse was anything but dead. The tech reps were not slacking off; they were instead doing some of their most valuable work. Field service, it turns out, is no job for lone wolves but a strong social activity. Like most work, it involves a community of professionals. The tech reps were not just repairing machines, they were coproducing insights about how to repair machines better. Through these conversations at the warehouse, tacit knowledge was transferred.

For Xerox and the Eureka project, the challenge was to capture and transform such knowledge into a shareable form. Many of the solutions to repairing the copier reside only in the heads of the most experienced technicians, who can solve complex problems faster and more efficiently than less experienced ones. By drawing on the tacit knowledge they accumulated over the years, these technicians save time and costs, reduce customer aggravation, and increase customer loyalty—a significant foundation for business growth.

Guiding Collaboration and Knowledge Management Values and Principles

Xerox created its knowledge management strategy in an overall cultural focus on knowledge sharing. Programs that were funded were viewed as enablers that allow Xerox employees to share their knowledge. Chairman Paul Allaire says that,[2]

Aligning knowledge management and its related technologies with the way people function in the workplace is key. Fundamentally, the way we work is changing, and we have to look at ways to help share the workplace of the future technology. Because work has become much more cooperative in nature, technology must support this distributed sharing of knowledge.

A complete knowledge management strategy (knowledge link) was created for the global customer services community. The strategy consisted of several guiding principles for Xerox:

- Never create the same solution twice. If a solution already exists, it should be used rather than re-create a new solution. In addition, focus should be on continuously improving existing solutions.

- Make knowledge easily accessible in real time to employees, customers, and partners. Solutions should be made available to everyone as soon as they are created.
- Create an environment where the organization highly values continuous learning and development for the future.
- Recognize and reward people who benefit the organization by creating, sharing, and reusing knowledge rather than reinventing known solutions.

These strategic operating principles helped align executive and front-line managers as the organizational strategy and cultural values reinforced knowledge sharing as a growth strategy for the company. Hence, Eureka had a strong strategic foundation to work from.

OVERALL GOALS AND DRIVING FACTORS OF EUREKA

As before, P, primary goal; S, secondary goal; N, not relevant:

Communication tool (top-down and bottom-up):

(S) Improve communication of vision and knowledge strategy.
(S) Improve communication of company values.
(S) Keep the organization alert.
(S) Engage customers and community at large.
(S) Divulge results more broadly and promote systemic analysis.
(P) Facilitate bottom-up communication.
(P) Make it easy for employees to suggest improvements to management.

Push information and knowledge to employees:

(P) Capture, organize, and distribute codified knowledge (e.g., database access).
(P) Improve access to external sources of information and knowledge.
(P) Improve decision making.
(P) Empower front-line employees.

Improve reuse of knowledge:

(S) Develop expertise maps (uncover existing knowledge).

(S) Map and measure intangible assets.

(P) Facilitate search of previously developed knowledge.

Foster collaboration:

(P) Increase collaboration among different functions of the organization.

(P) Increase collaboration among different locations of the organization.

(P) Improve overall knowledge sharing.

(P) Support the development of communities of practice.

(N) Increase connections not related to work.

Improve human capital management:

(N) Improve hiring.

(S) Improve internal mobility and deployment of existing employees.

(S) Integrate temporary and outside human resources and expertise.

(P) Improve training and acquisition of skills.

(P) Get new employees up to speed very quickly.

(S) Reduce time spent on menial activities.

(S) Improve employee retention.

(N) Facilitate work and integration of telecommuters.

Improve relationship with external stakeholders and increase information flow:

(N) Improve information exchange with suppliers, partners, and customers.

(P) Capture customer information.

(P) Improve customer satisfaction.

(S) Reduce sales costs.

(P) Reduce customer service costs.

The Eureka Solution

The Eureka initiative is based on the concept of knowledge sharing through the collaborative assembly of a searchable database of tips and best practices. With Eureka, the goal was to develop a system that would suit field technicians and a database they would populate with content. "Eureka is a robust toolset which enables authoring, validation, subscription, and distribution of hardware and software solutions," said Tom Ruddy, manager of service knowledge programs for Xerox worldwide.[3]

The original (French) Eureka technology was based on a centralized database on a mainframe tied to a Minitel, with a simple protocol for capturing tips and processes for validating and distributing them. The version of the Eureka program currently deployed involves a number of key technologies, including laptops for more than 90% of service technicians, CD-ROMs of service manuals, a mechanism that incrementally updates the database on the laptop to ensure it is synchronized with the central database, and interfaces that allow authors to easily find author tips whether or not they are connected to the server. All these components are critical in creating a system that effectively supports a mobile service workforce.

Inherent in the Eureka design is an understanding of how community practices and technology work. The Eureka system used a four-step design process:[4]

1. *Authoring tips.* Xerox factored in the different ways people express themselves. Although the process was kept simple for the end-user, it was made flexible and creative. An author can attach diagrams and sound with the written suggestions. His or her name is listed on the tip form. This assures credit and ensures the seriousness of the entry. The entry is uploaded from a laptop computer when the technician connects to the Internet. It is then fed into a pending knowledge base for review.

2. *Validating tips.* The tips are reviewed by respected, trusted local experts with which the tip authors typically collaborate. The validators analyze the pending tips by downloading them from the server to their laptop computers. Then the author is notified, the validator's name is added to the tip, and the result is uploaded to the server. Once on the server, the validated tips are placed in the community knowledge base for use by everyone.

3. *Sharing tips.* An understanding of community includes telling anecdotes and sharing cheat sheets, while confirmed solutions are shared within and sometimes outside the work group. The technology making this feasible downloads the new solutions from the knowledge base to server to laptop, with notification and subscription service.

4. *Using tips.* It is crucial for the user to have a simple process to seek out and implement solutions. The solutions are made accessible, and the advice is practical. The technology used to attain this includes a Xerox SearchLite search engine and customizable search engines.

BUSINESS RESULTS

To date, more than 20,000 tips have been entered by Xerox technicians, and all are available via their ubiquitous laptops. Dozens of tips are entered daily, and most are validated and put online within 5 days. Once a solution has been validated, it is also distributed back to service personnel, using push technology. As the solutions are used, a success rate is developed for each. The success rate helps find the most common problems and solutions. Over 15,000 hits are received monthly. The screen shot in Figure 17-1 provides an example of the structure of the tips entered by service technicians into the Eureka knowledge base.

The Eureka project allows Xerox's support organizations to create and reuse its intellectual capital on a wide scale throughout the world, but more important, it improves service to customers and enhances the financial performance of the business. The system was built on the service technicians' work practices by creating a knowledge-sharing environment that improves customer service.

As time progressed utilizing the Eureka database, a decision was made to migrate Eureka into a Microsoft Internet Explorer and Web-based browser environment. The following screen shot reflects the current environment and design of Eureka.

The success of Eureka is measured through many metrics, including the number of solutions available in the database, the number of tips created, the time it takes to validate new solutions, and the number of problems solved. More specifically, the rollout of Eureka has led to

1. A reduction of the average time to repair machines of 5–10%.

Figure 17-1
Example of Tip Entered By Service Technician

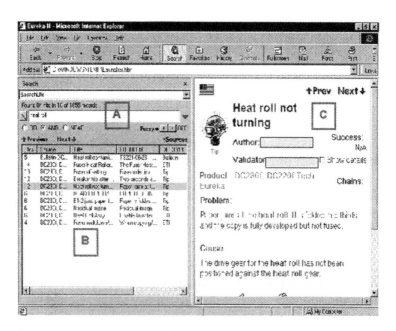

Figure 17-2
Current Environment and Design of Eureka

374

2. A 5–10% cost savings in the cost of parts used in repairs and engineer's time.
3. Dozens of tips entered per day by technicians.
4. Validated tips generated by over 10 percent of the service representatives.
5. Access of tips by 85% of the technicians.
6. Environmental benefits, such as reduction in customer visits and, therefore, vehicle emissions by service engineers and reduction in paper-based best practices sharing.
7. Enhanced customer service by increasing the Xerox service team's ability to diagnose, solve, and prevent equipment problems in the field all over the world.
8. Cost savings to Xerox of over $11 million annually.

After initial support just from PARC for the first four years, funding for Eureka has steadily increased in the range of 60% year over year. The sources of funding have also increased as new geographic communities became involved in Eureka. Return on investment has been in the range of tenfold, but most important, management has supported Eureka at all levels in the organization.

As a good example of the value, in Brazil, a customer had problems with a Xerox DocuColor 40 production color copier-printer to the point where the technicians were going to replace the $40,000 machine. Using Eureka, the technicians in São Paulo discovered a tip from Canada that suggested replacing a 90 cent connector. The technicians replaced the connector and fixed the machine. That tip was sent back to manufacturing, and the problem could be remedied at the source. A little knowledge, insight, and experience went a long way toward the bottom line and customer satisfaction.

The major impact of the Eureka program has been to create global work groups, where employees from different countries around the world can share their technical knowledge. It has broken down the barriers between numerous technical communities that, in the past, shared knowledge only when it was requested of them.

Reasons for Success

The success of the Eureka project can be attributed to a combination of approaches used to develop the solutions: A social-technical approach, the "trust" foundation, the empowerment philosophy and user-based solutions, and the leveraging of communities of practice.

Sociotechnical Approach

The user interface for Eureka is based on a sociotechnical approach that values human factors such as behavior, learning, and process as critical components of an integrated knowledge support system. The social interactions are what make Eureka work. First, a Xerox technician must reflect on his or her performance and decide there is a tip to share. Then, he or she writes it up (making it explicit) and submits it to the review team. The tip, with the technician's name, is certified and broadcast on the company intranet. Xerox found that, for the program to work, the review board had to be made up of people whom the technicians respected, or no one would bother to submit tips. Xerox also learned that name recognition (having the technician's name associated with the tip) was more motivating than any cash incentive.

The company discovered that the technicians were happy to add tips to the database, because they received credit for their contributions, which enhanced their standing among colleagues. Indeed, when management suggesting attaching financial incentives to the tips, the technicians resisted the idea. They felt this would diminish the value of their contributions.

The Eureka project is a good example of a sociotechnical solution, in that it recognizes that both the value of distributing information and sharing it are two distinct processes, one is technical and the other human. Being sociotechnical, Eureka is easily customized to communicate to several work communities in different kinds of entities, not just a Xerox service setting. Being a flexible solution is at the heart of the design of this project, and the organic, adaptive, and free-flowing attributes are the social glue that holds this project together.

Eureka operates as a free-flowing democracy, much like the natural and informal collaborations among tech reps. It relies on voluntary information exchange. Any tech rep, regardless of rank, can submit a tip but is neither required to nor explicitly rewarded. In Eureka, the financial rewards for the service representative are the incentive to be a good colleague, contribute, and receive knowledge as a member of a community.

Xerox recognizes that manuals and training programs cannot keep up with the fast-paced change of hardware, and the really current know-how is in the heads and hands of the service technicians. It realizes the value of sharing war stories as another way they learn to diagnose and fix machines. The technology supported a natural social interaction process, which was the real glue to making Eureka work. Eureka is a good example of converting individual knowledge into collective knowledge and converting tacit into explicit knowledge. The Eureka project also is a good example of applications of both Eastern and Western approaches to knowledge sharing. Eastern cultures value conversation, dialogue, and storytelling as an effective vehicle for learning and collaboration to improve business performance. Western cultures value explicit knowledge—the quantifiable, definable information that supports effective action. Eureka recognizes the tremendous value and richness of tacit knowledge in informal conversations and combines effective technology solutions to support the natural and pervasive knowledge-sharing processes already in practice.

The Trust Foundation

Perhaps the most significant factor in the success of the Eureka project in which individual knowledge was converted to organizational knowledge was "trust." Just as the participant of an outdoor survival course must trust the competence and integrity of the facilitator, a technician, before sharing his or her knowledge, must trust that the organization will use it for his or her own good as well as the common good. Social trust is also evident as service technicians are supported actively in their commitment to a unifying purpose and shared reward. As the Eureka project scaled globally, the service technicians increased the trust and value they placed on the information they received and their information channels.

The Empowerment Philosophy and User-Based Solutions

Mr. Raiman, a Xerox technology visionary in the Eureka project, says,[3]

Implementing an intranet takes courage, because it is more than a technology fix. Eureka was about a commitment to constant listening and adaptation. . . . In fact, it requires an acceptance of what many companies consider a radical concept—the person who does the job is in the best position to know how it can and should be done. This is a scary proposition for middle managers because it fundamentally changes their job description and takes away their role as the residential expert on operational functions.

Eureka is a great example of what might be called *vernacular knowledge sharing*; that is, harvesting, organizing, and passing around insights that come from the grassroots of an organization. Most support organizations report that some 60–75% of issues reported by customers are problems previously resolved. Technical support organizations, therefore, benefit by storing support issue resolutions, creating an ever-growing knowledge base that streamlines the support process.

Perhaps the most disturbing reality in Eureka was that management could not see the depth of knowledge actively shared in the informal settings by their service technicians. The value of informal dialogues or storytelling was viewed in a productivity- or time-wasting context initially. Even a detailed examination of the social behavior and value by an anthropologist did not convince Xerox management. Only when there were quantifiable results did the managers look carefully and gain insight about what was really occurring. What this confirms is that knowledge fields (lenses or filters) of perceptual reality can be rigid and potentially punitive in terms of systems dynamics.

The service organization at Xerox consistently held a strong sense of identity, socialization processes for orientating and training employees were augmented by knowledge management processes, and most important, the Eureka project strived for empowerment and reducing power and organizational hierarchies to enhance organizational effectiveness and business productivity.

In summary, the Xerox Eureka system successfully marries technology with community practices and creates a unique and virtual community distant-learning environment. The socialization attributes of the project are what create the stickiness culturally. The success of this project depends highly on engaged practitioners helping develop the work practices, processes, and underlying support technologies. By participating in the design process, the technicians possess ownership in the system and a stake in its overall success.

The Leveraging of Communities of Practice

In the Eureka project, Xerox social scientists and computer scientists teamed up with the service technicians to create a system that would grow community knowledge through a knowledge-sharing process. Within each stage of the process, it was important to understand the community of practice and design a system that honors the practice and makes sharing knowledge an intuitive part of the normal work process.

Eureka focuses on extending this shared sense making and distributed understanding by augmenting an existing community of practice's know-how through a toolset that would support the ongoing practice of knowledge sharing. There is an apparent relationship between the service technicians' community of practice and Xerox's corporate interest in organizing the knowledge flow across its global and likely hybrid communities. The results of Eureka are a flexible and self-organizing system to support the social knowledge flow of Xerox service technicians.

Due to its social origins, knowledge moves differently within communities than it does between them. Within the Eureka community, knowledge is continually embedded in practice and thus circulates easily. Members of the service community implicitly share a sense of what practice is and set up their own standards of judgment to support the spread of quality-vetted knowledge. The Eureka technology solution includes different degrees of formality and trust to support the community. Recognizing employees by name for their high-quality contributions reinforces the individual propensity and willingness to share and gains trust by the recipients when the knowledge captured is accurate, coherent, and executable. The Eureka system was designed as an interactive learning system so the service technicians could continue to foster knowledge sharing and learning in real time and, more important, transfer this collective knowledge know-how globally.

REFERENCES

1. Brown, J. S., Gray, E. S. The people are the company. *Fast Company*. 1995:90–111.
2. Hickins, M. Xerox's knowledge sharing culture has enabled the company to emerge as a leader in KM practices. *Management Review*. 88(1999):40–47.
3. Xerox announces adoption of customer support consortium standards. *Business Wire* [New York]. May 24, 1999:1–2.
4. Kettler, V. Eureka. A distance learning project. Available at: http://www.cdlr.tamu.edu/dec/papers/kettler/kettler.htm (2000).

Appendix A

Leading Vendors

In the wake of the recent growth of interest in corporate portals, many software vendors have claimed to have a CP software solution. Some of the current leaders in this space are startups such as Plumtree, Viador, Autonomy, InfoImage, Epicentric, and TopTierSoftware (bought by SAP and now SAP Portals). Since middle to late 2000, they have been joined by very large players coming from various fields:

- Work-flow and document management.
- Content management systems.
- Data warehouse.
- Collaboration software.
- Business intelligence.
- Enterprise resource planning and customer relationship management.
- E-mail management.
- Portal business.
- Search and retrieval engines.
- Enterprise application integration solutions.
- Platform suppliers.

Most players in this market (and there are lots of them) recently launched integrated CP solutions that combine in browser-friendly interfaces many of the functions just mentioned, through either a native application or a seamless integration, depending on the roots of the software company. The trend is definitely for consolidation, easier integration, and interoperability of the many different tools under a single platform based on open-architecture standards. In the end, although the different products are at different stages of development, all point to similar visions. The winners are likely to be those who can, in the shortest period of time,

- Integrate as many knowledge-management-related applications and back-end systems as possible.
- Provide the easiest and fastest setups.
- Develop a very scalable architecture.
- Make personalization (including personalized alerts) a very user-friendly task.
- Develop interesting alliances with other software companies in the collaboration space.
- Pay enough attention to performance (speed of download, up-time, etc.).
- Develop interesting and flexible pricing models.

As discussed before, the CP platform market is still growing fast. This is reflected in the large number of players. One finds everything from very small vendors providing hosted solutions to very large software companies providing enterprise-class solutions. In a situation like this, one can easily forecast some sort of shakeout in the near future.

Many vendors provide solutions relevant for KM that can be integrated into a CP platform. We believe the following are the most relevant categories and list the most important vendors in the cited tables:

- CP platforms (Table A-1).
- Search, retrieval, and categorization systems (Table A-2).
- Web-based discussion, communication, and community tools (Table A-3).
- Document and content management systems (Table A-4).

Table A-1 *Vendors of Corporate Portal Platforms*

Vendor	Product	URL
2 Bridge Software	2 Share	www.2bridge.com
Abilizer	Dynamic Web Engine	www.abilizer.com
ActiveIntranet	Active K*OS Workplace	www.activeintranet.com
Adenin Technologies	Enterprise Portal	www.adenin.com
Allegis Corp.	Allegin ebusiness Suite	www.allegis.com
Alvea Inc.	Alvea Portal	www.alvea.com
Arisem	OpenPortal4U Enterprise Edition	www.arisem.com
AskMe Corporation	AskMe Enterprise	www.askmecorp.com
Autonomy	Portal-in-a-Box	www.autonomy.com
Baan	iBaan Portal	www.baan.com
Backweb	Backweb	www.backweb.com
BCN Ltd	IV5 Knowledge Portal	www.bcnintraview.com
Bowstreet	Business Web Portal	www.bowstreet.com
BrainRanger	Brain Ranger Portal	www.brainranger.com
Brio Technologies	Brio One	www.brio.com
Broadvision	InfoExchange Portal	www.broadvision.com
Citrix Systems	Nfuse and XPS	www.citrix.com
CivicLife.com	Interprise	www.civiclife.com
Cognos	Cognos Portal	www.cognos.com
Comintell	Knowledge Xchanger	www.comintell.com
Computer Associates	Jasmine ii Portal	www.ca.com
Corechange	Coreport 3g	www.corechange.com
Covia	InfoPortal	www.covia.com
Data Channel	DataChannel Server	www.datachannel
Data Mirror	Enterprise Administrator and others	www.datamirror.com
Enformia	Enformia EIP	www.enformia.com
Epicentric	Epicentric Foundation Server	www.epicentric.com
IBM	WebSphere and K-Station	www.ibm.com
InfoImage	Decision Portal	www.infoimage.com
Informu	KnowledgeControl	www.informu.com
Gauss	VIP PortaManager	www.gaussinterprise.com
Hummingbird	Hummingbird EIP	www.hummingbird.com

continues

Table A-1   *Vendors of Corporate Portal Platforms (continued)*

Vendor	Product	URL
Hyperwave	Hyperwave Information Portal	www.hyperwave.com
InfoImage	InfoImage Decision Portal	www.infoimage.com
Intraspect	Intraspect4	www.intraspect.com
Iona Technologies	iPortal Application Server	www.iona.com
KnowledgeTrack	KnowledgeTrack Enterprise	www.knowledgetrack.com
Linq	Linq Portal	www.linqportal.com
Lotus	Lotus K-Station Portal	www.lotus.com
M3ksolutions	Beemer	www.m3ksolutions.com
Mediapps	Net.portal	www.mediapps.com
Microsoft	Share Point	www.microsoft.com
Mobius Management Systems	ViewDirect	www.mobius.com
Mondas	My IntraLink	www.mondas.com
Mongoose Technology	PortalStudio	www.mongoosetech.com
MultiSource	iWebWizard Portal Builder	www.multisource.com
Netegrity	Netegrity Interaction Server	www.netegrity.com
Objexis	TeamPortals	www.objexis.com
OnePage	Content Connect	www.onepage.com
Open Text	Livelink	www.opentext.com
Oracle	Oracle Portal	www.oracle.com/portals
Plumtree	Plumtree Corporate Portal	www.plumtree.com
PeopleSoft	PeopleSoft Portal	www.peoplesoft.com
Portalwave	Enterprise Application Portal	www.portalwave.com
Radium Systems	C-Portal	www.radiumsystems.com.br
Q Media Group Network	q	www.qmgn.com
Sagemaker	Sagewave	www.sagemaker.com
SAP	SAPPortals	www.sapportals.com

Table A-1 *Vendors of Corporate Portal Platforms (continued)*

Vendor	Product	URL
Siebel	Siebel Employee Relationship Manager	www.siebel.com
Silverpeas	Silverpeas	www.silverpeas.com
Silverstream	eXtend	www.silverstream.com
Sopheon	Worker Information Network (WIN)	www.sopheon.com
Snippets	Snippets	www.snippets.com
Sun Microsystems	iPlanet Portal Server	www.iplanet.com
SurfMap	Portal Author	www.portalauthor.com
Sybase	Sybase Enterprise Portal	www.sybase.com
Tibco Software	TIBCO ActivePortal	www.tibco.com
Tomoye	Simplify	www.tomoye.com
Verity	Verity Portal One	www.verity.com
Viador	Viador E-Portal Express	www.viador.com
Xerox	DocuShare	www.xerox.com
Yahoo	Corporate Yahoo	http://corporate.yahoo.com
Workaday	Hosted Intranet Portal	www.workaday.com
webMethods	Business Integrator	www.webmethods.com

Table A-2 *Vendors of Search, Retrieval, and Categorization Systems*

Vendor	Product	URL
Abuzz	Beehive	www.abuzz.com
ActiveNavigation	Portal Maximizer	www.activenavigation.com
AltaVista	Enterprise Search Engine	solutions.altavista.com
Applied Semantics	CIRCA	www.appliedsemantics.com
Antartic.ca	VisualNet	www.antartic.ca
AskJeeves	Answers	business.ask.com/home.asp
Autonomy	Dynamic Reasoning Engine	www.autonomy.com
Biap Systems	Gotrieve	www.biap.com
Cerebyte	Infino Systems	www.cerebyte.com
Cipher Systems	Knowledge Works	www.cipher-sys.com
Cognos	PowerPlay, Query, Visualizer, Impromptu	www.cognos.com

continues

Table A-2 *Vendors of Search, Retrieval, and Categorization Systems (continued)*

Vendor	Product	URL
Copernic Technologies Inc.	Copernic Family	www.copernic.com
Convera	RetrievalWare Suite	www.convera.com
Conversagent	Utiliza 1.0	www.conversagent.com
Dragon Systems	Naturally Speaking	www.dragonsys.com
EasyAsk	EasyAsk	www.easyask.com
Empolis	Orenge	www.empolis.com/englisch/home.htm
Freedom Intelligence	Freedom Intelligence	www.jointtechnology.com
Gavagai Technology	Gavagator line of products	www.gavagai.net
GlobalWisdom	Bravo Engine	www.globalwisdom.com
Gnutella	P2P search engine—Gnutella	www.gnutella.wego.com
Google	WebSearch	www.google.com
Hummingbird	Fulcrum SearchServer	www.hummingbird.com
IBM	Intelligent Miner	www.ibm.com
Inktomi	Search/Enterprise	www.inktomi.com
Insight Software	InXight	www.insight.com
Invention Machine	Knowledgist	www.invention-machine.com
First Light Communications	Cornerstone Solutions Knowledgebase	www.firstlight.com
Knowledge Manag. Software	Deskartes	www.kmsoftware.com
Kamoon	Enterprise Expertise Management	www.kamoon.com
Lotus	Lotus Discovery Server and Extended Search	www.lotus.com
Mobula Technologies	Mobular engine	www.mobular.com
Moreover Technologies	CI-Watch and CI-Database	www.moreover.com
Microsoft	Sharepoint Search Engine and Index Server	www.microsoft.com
Net Perceptions	Net Perceptions for Knowledge Management	www.netperceptions.com
Netscape	Compass Server	home.netscape.com

Table A-2 *Vendors of Search, Retrieval, and Categorization Systems (continued)*

Vendor	Product	URL
NextPage	NX T3	www.nextpage.com
Northern Light	Search ToolKit	www.northernlight.com
OpenCola	OpenCola Folders	www.opencola.com
Open Text	Knowledge Query Server	www.opentext.com
Oracle	Ultra Search	www.oracle.com
Orbital plc	Organik	www.orbitalsw.com
PurpleYogi	Discovery System	www.purpleyogi.com
Quiver Inc	Quiver Knowledge Suite	www.quiver.com
Semio	SemioTagger and SemioSkyline	www.semio.com
Semantix	Intelligent Information Retrieval	www.semantix.com
SER Systems	SERbrainware	www.ser.com
ServiceWare Technologies	SmartMiner	www.serviceware.com
Smartlogik Group plc	Muscat product line	www.smartlogik.com
Sun Microsystems	iPS Compass Server	www.sun.com
Tacit Knowledge Systems	Tacit ESP (Expertise Search for Portals)	www.tacit.com
Tikal Knowledge	H-Sphere	www.tikalknowledge.com
The Brain	WebBrain	www.thebrain.com
The Learning Trust	Geneva Solutions	www.learningtrust.com
Thinkstream	Distributed information/ commerce engine	www.thinkstream.com
Trivium	Gingo, SEE-K, Umap	www.trivium.fr
Verilytics	Alert & Text Engine	www.verilytics.com
Verity	Verity Information Server and others	www.verity.com
Webmind	Webmind Search	www.webmind.com

Table A-3   *Vendors of Web-Based Discussion, Communication, and Community Tools*

Vendor	Product	URL
B2bScene	The Collaborative Platform	www.b2bscene.com
Bungo	Connected Workspaces	www.bungo.com
Buzzpower	Buzzpower	www.buzzpower.com
Cassiopeia	The Cassiopeia Community	www.cassiopeia.com
Communiscape	Communiscape	www.communiscape.com
Centor	Interaction Server	www.centor.com
Centra	CentraOne	www.centra.com
Centrinity	FirstClass	www.centrinity.com
Copernus	WebSpace	www.copernus.com
Corel	NetPerfect	www.corel.com
Correlate	Personal and K-Map	www.correlate.com
Consilient	Consilient Process Collaboration	www.consilient.com
Divine	Mindalign, Opinionware, Athena	www.divine.com
DWL	DWL Collaboration	www.dwl.com
eGain	E3	www.egain.com
Engenia	B2B Collaboration	www.engenia.com
Engineering Animation	e-Vis	www.eai.com
eProject	eProject Enterprise & Express	www.eproject.com
eRoom Technology	eRoom	www.eroom.com
eZ Communications	EZ P2P Live Internet Meetings	www.ezmeeting.com
Ezenia	Encounter Family & Infoworkspace	www.ezenia.com
First Light Communications	Cornerstone Solutions Knowledgebase	www.firstlight.com
Flypaper	TeamSpace	www.flypaper.com
Genesys Conferencing	Astound	www.genesys.com
Groove Networks	Groove 1.0	www.groovenetworks.com
GroupServe	GroupPort	www.groupserve.com
Ikimbo	Omniprise	www.ikimbo.com

Table A-3 *Vendors of Web-Based Discussion, Communication, and Community Tools (continued)*

Vendor	Product	URL
iMeet	iMeet Corporate Meeting Center	www.imeet.com
Inovie Software	TeamCenter	www.inovie.com
Lotus	Many products (QuickPlace, Teamroom, Notes)	www.lotus.com
Matrixone	Team Central	www.matrixone.com
Microsoft	Exchange Server, NetMeeting, and others	www.microsoft.com
Netscape	Collabra Server	http://home.netscape.com/collabra
NextPage	NXT 3	www.nextpage.com
Novell	GroupWise and Messaging System	www.novell.com
Outhink	ThinkDesk	www.outhink.com
OpenAir	Workspace	www.openair.com
PeopleLink	eCommunity Solutions	www.peoplelink.com
Placeware	Placeware	www.placeware.com
PowerMeeting	PowerMeeting Services	www.powermeeting.com
QUIQ	QUIQ	www.quiq.com
Raindance	Raindance Web Conference	www.raindance.com
Real Communities	CiviServer	www.realcommunities.com
SiteScape	Forum and WebWorkZone	www.sitescape.com
Tomoye	Simplify	www.tomoye.com
Tridion	DialogServer	www.tridion.com
Virtualteams	Team Workplace	www.virtualteams.com
Web Crossing	Web Crossing	www.webcrossing.com
WebEx	WebEx Services	www.webex.com

Table A-4   *Vendors of Document and Content Management Systems*

Vendor	Product	URL
ArsDigita	ArsDigita Community System	www.arsdigita.com
Broadvision	One-to-One Publishing	www.broadvision.com
Chrystal Software	Astoria	www.chrystal.com
Communiscape	Communiscape	www.communiscape.com
Convera	Convera Screening Room	www.convera.com
Cypress	Cypress.Web	www.cypress.com
DeskNet	ContentWelder	www.desknetinc.com
Documentum	ITeam and 4i	www.documentum.com
eBT	entrepid and engenda	www.ebt.com
Eprise	Participant Server	www.eprise.com
Enigma	Enigma 3C	www.enigma.com
Fabrica Digital	Publique	www.fabricadigital.com.br
FatWire	UpdateEngine	www.fatwire.com
FileNET	Panagon	www.filenet.com
Gauss	VIP	www.gaussinterprise.com
Hummingbird	DOCSFusion	www.hummingbird.com
InStranet	InStranet 2000	www.instranet.com
Interwoven	TeamSite	www.interwoven.com
JetForm	InTempo	www.jetform.com
Lotus	Many products (Notes, iNotes)	www.lotus.com
Mediasurface	Mediasurface	www.mediasurface.com
Mondas	IntraLink ST	www.mondas.com
Ncompass Labs	Resolution	www.ncompass.com
Open Market	Content Server	www.openmarket.com
Open Text	Livelink	www.opentext.com
Oracle	iContent	www.oracle.com
Percussion	Rythmyx	www.percussion.com
Showcase-SPSS	Web Content Management	www.showcasecorp.com
Starbase	eXpressroom	www.starbase.com
SurfMap	Portal Author	www.surfmap.com
Terra-Axis	Terra Portal	www.terra-axis.com
Vignette	V/5 Suite	www.vignette.com
Vioma	Vioma Content Manager	www.vioma.com
Xerox	Docushare	www.xerox.com

APPENDIX B

TECHNICAL CRITERIA TO SELECT A CORPORATE PORTAL PLATFORM

The criteria used here are based on review of the software market at the end of 2001. The questions are organized around the following six categories: integration of applications and components; development environment; management, maintenance, and monitoring; systems architecture; performance; security; and vendor's future and platform evolution.

Integration of Applications and Components

- Does it provide application program interfaces (APIs) that make it easy to integrate all sorts of legacy systems, package applications, and different data sources?
- Are the specific applications of the organization easily integrated into the portal?
- Does it include rendering or viewing facilities for non-HTML documents (so the user does not need the applications installed in his or her desktop)?
- What kinds of prebuilt objects are included in the platform library?
- How many predefined connectors (gadgets, portlets, Web parts, modules, adapters, etc.) does it include? Are they those most relevant to the applications in your company?
- Does it allow easy customization of connectors, according to the attributes of the end-users?
- Does it provide easy integration of external content feeds (e.g., HTML and XML)?
- Are there any integration problems with other systems?
- Is it compliant with most Internet standards and protocols?
- Do the applications run on a Web server or an application server (for performance considerations)?
- Can applications be integrated beyond the interface layer? Does the portal provide true integration of data sources?

Development Environment

- What is the philosophy behind the platform? Is it to provide a hassle-free turnkey solution or the tools for IT departments to build, "with lots of coding," a custom portal?
- Does it leverage the organization's existing skill base, technical infrastructure, and package applications?
- How much customization does it require for the specific needs of the organization?
- How good are the development environment and tools provided for the client's own developers?
- What kinds of restrictions does the CP solution impose on interface development?
- Does it support object-oriented software development?
- Does it support most of the standard programming tools?
- How fast and easy is the deployment of the platform?

Management, Maintenance, and Monitoring

- Does it require a separate database to install?
- Does it provide graphical wizards to help set up and manage it? Are these wizards intuitive?
- How easy it is for Web managers to view and edit the content, hierarchy, and presentation of the CKP?
- How easy is it to add, delete, and change the status and profile of users and groups?
- How easy is it to set up default components based on users' profiles?
- Can content be managed at different levels (pages, group of pages, connectors, etc.)?
- Does it provide good analytical tools that allow easy monitoring of system usage?
- Does it allow administrators to remotely address problems in the system?
- Does it provide prebuilt features to analyze the behavior of each user?
- Does it keep a log of all events processed within the portal?
- Does it include real-time notification of failures or problems in the system?
- Does it include self-fixing tools that are triggered when problems emerge?
- Does it provide one centralized, completely Web-based interface for management?
- Does it allow decentralized administration? Does is allow for different combinations of centralized and decentralized management of various portals within the enterprise?
- Does it come with a large number of preset measurement tools to help monitor usage, volume, and contributions?
- Does it make it easy for companies that want to set up their own metrics (including qualitative ones; e.g., popularity tools)?

Systems Architecture

- Is it a flexible platform?
- Is it based on a multitiered architecture?
- Is it based on an open architecture and common e-business standards?

- Does it allow for easy separation and integration of many different components from different vendors?
- Is the presentation layer clearly separated from the applications layer?
- Does it allow experimenting with new applications, without hampering the performance of the entire system?
- Will failures in one component or application shut down the whole system?
- Does the architecture support fault tolerance and high availability?
- Does it support XML-based plug-in architecture and systems integration?
- Does the system architecture provide a robust solution for the buildup of various different roles and applications, such as B-to-E, B-to-C, B-to-B?
- To which databases does it connect (Oracle, SQL, Sybase, DB2, etc.)?
- On which Web servers (Apache, iPlanet, Microsoft IIS, etc.), applications servers (WebSphere and WebLogic), and operating systems (Windows, Solaris, Linux, etc.) does it run?

Performance

- How scalable is the platform?
- Does it scale up by working seamlessly with powerful databases (Oracle, SQL, etc.)?
- Can it be deployed and perform equally well in Windows, UNIX, or AIX platforms?
- Does it allow caching? Does the caching include automatic refresh?
- How is the performance affected by a large number of concurrent users?
- Does it allow load balancing through use of multiple servers?
- How many people can reach the server concurrently?
- Does it allow the development of distributed architecture implementations?
- Does it support multiple servers to improve performance?
- Does it include session management capabilities?
- Do the APIs run on a separate server?

SECURITY

- Does it support standard authentication and security protocols? Are they provided out of the box? Is the authentication server native or external?
- Does it allow global definition of users, groups, and roles (e.g., via n-tier LDAP)?
- Does it provide single sign-on for users?
- Does it include both permission levels (owners, groups, individual users) and permission types (read, write, execute)?
- Does it block password reuse?
- Does it provide automated log-off after a time-out?
- Does it allow high-level encryption solutions?
- Does it support the organization's existing security infrastructure?
- Does it provide additional layers of security?
- Does it allow the development of customized security features?
- What network, platform, and security issues affect integration?
- Does it allow users outside the company's firewall to safely use the portal?

VENDOR'S FUTURE AND PLATFORM EVOLUTION

- What is the vendor strategy? Is it going to focus on a specific industry, platform, or company size?
- Will the vendor provide onsite support for all offices of the organization?
- Does it offer a low-cost entry-level version that provides a seamless path for future upgrades?
- Is there a community of software developers working in tandem and helping shape the evolution of the CP platform?
- Does the CP vendor have a good service unit or system integrator community skilled at implementing the portal and at developing specific APIs? Who is capable of implementing the platform?
- Who already uses the vendor's platform?
- Is a user group in place?
- Does the vendor provide a structured training program for developers and administrators?

BIBLIOGRAPHY

Amabile, T. M. How to kill creativity. *Harvard Business Review.* September–October 1998.

Anders, G. Interview with Steve Ballmer: "Steve Ballmer's Big Moves." *Fast Company.* March 2001.

Aneja, A., Rowan, C., Brooksby, B. Corporate portal framework for transforming content chaos on intranets. *Intel Technology Journal.* 2000. White paper available at: www.intel.com.

Angus, Reid. Information overload: What is it doing to physicians? *Report.* 6;3 (May–June 2001).

Argyris, C. Double loop learning in organizations. *Harvard Business Review.* September–October 1977.

A survey of the world economy: The hitchhiker's guide to cybernomics. *The Economist.* September 28, 1996.

Axelrod, B., Handfield, H., Welsh, T. *War for Talent.* Boston: Harvard Business School Press, 2001.

Bank site offers e-training 24/7. *Globe and Mail.* January 17, 2001.

Barron, T. A smarter Frankenstein: The merging of e-learning and knowledge management. Learning Circuits—ASTD at: www.learningcircuits.org/aug2000/barron.html.

Best practices: Eureka discovers ways to grow community knowledge and customer satisfaction. *KMWorld.* 7(2001):1.

Bidault, F., Nihitila, J. ESI and the role of trust in the information age. FP Mastering. *National Post.* June 26, 2001.

Brown, J. S., Duguid, P. Organizational learning and communities-of-practice: Toward a unified view of working, learning and innovation. *Organization Science.* 2(1991).

Brown, J. S., Duguid, P. *The Social Life of Information.* Boston: Harvard Business School Press, 2000.

Brown, J. S., Gray, E. S. The people are the company. *Fast Company.* 1995.

Brown, S., Tilton, A., Woodside, D. The case for on-line communities. *The McKinsey Quarterly.* 2002, Number 1. Web exclusive at: http://www.mckinseyquarterly.com.

Castells, M. *The Internet Galaxy: Reflections on the Internet, Business and Society.* New York: Oxford University Press, 2001.

Chandler, A. D. Jr., Cortada, J. W. *A Nation Transformed by Information: How Information Has Shaped the United States from Colonial Times to the Present.* New York: Oxford University Press, 2000.

Chavez, J. E-mail blamed for wasted work time. Rogen International, research results reported in the *Globe and Mail.* June 21, 2001.

Clark, K., Serfon, M. The sequential prisoner's dilemma: Evidence on reciprocation. *Economic Journal.* January 2000.

The Conference Board, Bureau of Economic Analysis. iBiz. *PC Magazine.* July 21, 2001.

Content for dollars. *PC Magazine.* August 2001.

Cusumano, M. A., Selby, R.W. *MICROSOFT secrets.* New York: The Free Press, 1995.

Davenport, T. Attention: The next information frontier, FP Mastering. *Financial Post.* May 29, 2001.

Davenport, T. Putting the "I" in information technology, FP Mastering. *National Post.* May 15, 2001.

Davenport, T. H., Prusak, L. *Working Knowledge: How Organizations Manage What They Know.* Boston: Harvard Business School Press, 1999.

Davenport, T., Harris, J., DeLong, D., Jacobson, A. Data to knowledge to results. *California Management Review.* 43(Winter 2001).

David H. Wiring the labor market. *Journal of Economic Perspectives.* 15;1(Winter 2001).

Davis, B. e-Knowledge markets—The $ trillion opportunity. White paper, the Kaieteur Institute for Knowledge Management. Available at: www.kikm.org, 2000.

Detlor, B. *Web Work: Information Seeking and Knowledge Work on the World Wide Web.* Waltham, MA: Kluwer Academic Press, 2000.

Digital doorways. *PC Magazine.* June 12, 2001.

Earl, M. Every business is an IT business, FP Mastering. *National Post.* May 15, 2001.

E-strategy brief: GE. *The Economist.* May 19, 2001.

Eurostat; World Bank; CSO; BEA. *The Economist.* March 31, 2001.

Fukuyama, F. *Trust: The Social Virtues and the Creation of Prosperity.* New York: The Free Press, 1996.

GartnerGroup. Communities: Broad-reaching business value. Publication N. COM-13-9032, July 3, 2001.

Gates, W. H. (with C. Hemingway). *Business @ the Speed of Thought: Using a Digital Nervous System.* New York: Warner Books, 1999.

Glaeser, E., Laibson, D., Scheinkman, J., Soutler, C. Measuring trust. *Quarterly Journal of Economics.* August 2000.

GM offers on-line business courses. *Globe and Mail.* April 11, 2001.

Gordon, R. J. Does the "New Economy" measure up to the great inventions of the past? Working paper 7833, National Bureau of Economic Research, 2000.

Grant, R. Shifts in the world economy: The drivers of knowledge management. In: C. Despres and D. Chauvel, eds. *Knowledge Horizons.* Boston: Butterworth-Heinemann, 2000.

Häcki, R., Lighton, J. The future of the networked company. *McKinsey Quarterly.* Number 3(2001):26–39.

Hamel, G., Prahalad, C. K. *Competing for the Future.* Boston: Harvard Business School Press, 1994.

Hickins, M. Xerox's knowledge sharing culture has enabled the company to emerge as a leader in KM practices. *Management Review.* 88(1999).

iBiZ STATS. *PC Magazine.* July 2001.

iLogos Research. *CMA Management*. October 2001.

Interbrand/Citibank. In: *WPP Group plc Annual Report and Accounts*, 2000.

Ipsos-NPD Grocery Digest. U.K.: Sainsbury to develop new food products on the Internet, bringing NPD to shelves quicker. January 24, 2002.

Kanter, R. M., Kao, J., Wiersema, F. *Innovation: Breakthrough Thinking at 3M, Du Pont, GE, Pfizer, and Rubbermaid*. New York: HarperBusiness, 1997.

Kaplan S. Calling all workers. *CIO Magazine*. December 1, 2001.

Kettler, V. Eureka. A distance learning project. Available at: http://www.cdlr.tamu.edu/dec/papers/kettler/kettler.htm, 2000.

Kluge, J., Stein, W., Licht, T. *Knowledge Unplugged*. New York: Palgrave, 2001.

Kuitenbrouwer, P., ed. Egads, we've got e-mail. *Financial Post*. October 18, 2001:1.

Lamont, J. KM and e-learning: A growing partnership. *KMWorld*. July–August 2001.

Landes, D. S. *The Wealth and Poverty of Nations: Why Some Are Rich and Some Are Poor*. New York: W.W. Norton & Company, 1998.

Leonard-Barton, D. *Wellsprings of Knowledge: Building and Sustaining the Sources of Innovation*. Boston: Harvard Business School Press, 1995.

Lyman, P., Varian, H. How much information? In: Castells, M., *The Internet Galaxy: Reflections on the Internet, Business and Society*. New York: Oxford University Press, 2001.

Malone, T. W., Laubacher, R. J. All change for the e-lance economy, FP Mastering, *National Post*. July 10, 2001.

Malone, T. W., Laubacher, R. J. The dawn of the e-lance economy. *Harvard Business Review*. September–October 1998.

Marquis, D. G., Myers, S. *Successful Industrial Innovations*. Washington, DC: National Science Foundation, 1969.

Maskus, K. *Intellectual Property Rights in the Global Economy*. Washington, DC: Institute for International Economics, 2000.

McDermott, R. Why information technology inspired but cannot deliver knowledge management. *California Management Review*. 41; 4(Summer 1999).

McGee, M. K., Murphy, C. Collaboration is more than squeezing out supply-chain costs. Available at: www.informationweek.com, December 10, 2001.

Morgan Stanley Capital International World Index. In: K. E. Sveiby. *The New Organizational Wealth: Managing and Measuring Knowledge-Based Assets.* San Francisco: Berrett-Koehler Publishers, 1997.

Nasscom. *Financial Times.* February 21, 2001.

Neilson, G. L., Pasternack, B., Viscio, A. Up the (e) organization! A seven-dimension model for the centerless enterprise. *Strategy & Business* [Booz-Allen & Hamilton]. 18(2000, first quarter).

The new workforce. *The Economist.* November 1, 2001.

Nonaka, I., Takeuchi, H. *The Knowledge-Creating Company: How Japanese Companies Create the Dynamics of Innovation.* New York: Oxford University Press, 1995.

O'Reilly, C. Corporations, culture and commitment: Motivation and social control in organizations. *California Management Review.* Summer 1999.

Pinchot, E., Pinchot, G. The end of bureaucracy and the rise of intelligent organization. In: P. S. Myers, ed. *Knowledge Management and Organizational Design.* Boston: Butterworth-Heinemann, 1996.

Polanyi, M. The tacit dimension. In: L. Prusak, ed. *Knowledge in Organizations.* Boston: Butterworth-Heinemann, 1997.

Powell, W. W. Learning from collaboration: Knowledge and networks in the biotechnology and pharmaceutical industries. *California Management Review.* 40;3(Spring 1998).

Psacharaopoulos, G. The contribution of education to economic growth. In J. W. Kendrick, ed. *International Comparisons of Productivity and Causes of Slowdown.* Cambridge, MA: Ballinger Publishing, 1984.

Reichheld, F. The loyalty effect. *Harvard Business Review.* 1996.

Rosenberg, M. *E-Learning: Strategies for Delivering Knowledge in the Digital Age.* New York: McGraw-Hill, 2001.

Saxenian, A. *Regional Advantage: Culture and Competition in Silicon Valley and Route 128.* Cambridge, MA: Harvard University Press, 1996.

Skyrme, D. New metrics: Does it all add up? In: C. Despres and D. Chauvel, eds. *Knowledge Horizons.* Boston: Butterworth-Heinemann, 2000, p. 308.

Skyrme, D. J. *Capitalizing on Knowledge: From e-Business to k-Business*. Boston: Butterworth-Heinemann, 2001.

Snowden, D. The social ecology of knowledge management. In: C. Despres and D. Chauvel, eds. *Knowledge Horizons*. Boston: Butterworth-Heinemann, 2000.

Stevens, C. From bland to blend: Intellectual capital development and blended learning. Presentation at the Fifth World Congress on Intellectual Capital, Hamilton, Ontario, Canada, January 16–18, 2002.

Stewart, T. The smartest U.S. companies. *Fortune*. April 16, 2001.

A survey of the pharmaceutical industry. *The Economist*. February 2, 1998.

Tapscott, D. *Digital Economy: Promise and Peril in the Age of Networked Intelligence*. New York: McGraw-Hill, 1996.

Tapscott, T., Lowey Digital Capital. *Harnessing the Power of Business Webs*. Boston: Harvard Business School Press, 2000.

Terra, J. C. *Gestão do Conhecimento: O Grande Desafio Empresarial*, 2nd ed. São Paulo: Negocio Editora, 2001.

Thurow, L. *The Future of Capitalism: How Today's Economic Forces Shape Tomorrow's World*. New York: Penguin USA, 1997.

Venkatraman, N., Henderson, J. C. Business platforms for the 21st century. In: D. Marchand, T. Davenport, eds. *Mastering Information Management: Complete MBA Companion in Information Management*. London: Financial Times—Prentice-Hall, 2000.

Welch, J. Administração depois da Internet, interview. *HSM Management*. 22(September–October 2000).

Wenger, E. C., Snyder, W. M. Communities of practice: The organizational frontier. *Harvard Business Review*. January–February 2000.

Wensley, A., Verwijk-O'Sullivan, A. Tools for knowledge management. In: C. Despres and D. Chauvel, eds. *Knowledge Horizons*. Boston: Butterworth-Heinemann, 2000.

Why high-tech firms can't afford to ignore patents. The Knowledge@Wharton Newsletter. At: http://knowledge.wharton.upenn.edu, December 19, 2001–January 15, 2002.

Will the corporation survive? *The Economist*. November 1, 2001.

Withers, P. *CMA Management*. October 2001.

Xerox announces adoption of customer support consortium standards. *Business Wire*. May 24, 1999.

Zack, M. H. Developing a knowledge strategy. *California Management Review*. 41;3(Spring 1999).

Zarifian, P. *Travail et Communication: Essai sociologique sur le travail dans la grande entreprise industrielle*. Paris: PUF, 1996.

INDEX

405

tacit, case study on, 3–5
knowledge artifacts, 362
knowledge-base repositories,
118–119
knowledgebase searches, 105
knowledge brokers, 158–159
at Bain, 220–221, 227
Knowledge-Creating Company,
The (Nonaka, Takeuchi), 70
knowledge directors, 155–157
knowledge evangelists, 342
knowledge exchanges
role of, 33–35
knowledge management, 12, 56–94
agenda for, 87–91
at Bain, 205–219
communities of practice and,
72–76
connectivity and, 22
definition of, 58–59
e-learning and, 83–86
financial impact of, 58
goals of, 140–142
history of, 57
human capital and, 82–91
information management
compared with, 59–65
leaders in, 155–157
online communities and, 76–81
organizational culture and, 65–72
personal contact in, 63–65
reengineering fad and, 60–62
return on investment from,
137–138, 363
stand-alone application
integration for, 119–124
strategic level, 88–89
tactical level, 89–91
at Texaco, 349–351
trust building and, 69–71
validation methods and, 60
knowledge managers, 155–157
knowledge practice leaders,
157–158

knowledge sharing
case studies on, 6–7
in collaboration, 26–27
communities of practice and,
72–76
encouraging, 146–148
online communities and, 76–81
organizational culture and,
65–72
rewarding, 146–148
storytelling as, 150–151
vernacular, 377–378
knowledge workers
growth in numbers of, 25–26
mobility of, 82
rewarding knowledge
contributions of, 32
social interaction of, 18–19, 21
tools for, 49
Kowal, Greg, 45, 46
K-Portals, 9–10

L
Landes, David, 27, 65, 66
Laubacher, R.J., 36
leadership, 180, 181. *See also*
management
capital, 120–121
cultural changes and, 66–67
implementation and, 147
knowledge practice, 157–158
in online communities, 169
trust building and, 68–69
learning. *See also* e-learning;
training
communities, 8–9
continuous, 281–283
Lev, Baruch, 24
Levitt, Theodore, 179–180
Libert, Barry, 24
librarians, 160–161, 228
licenses, 25
Lippert, Marty, 47–48, 126
listening, 151–152

José Cláudio Terra is Vice President of Balance Consulting, a technology and knowledge management consulting firm. Over the course of his career, Dr. Terra has served clients in Brazil, Canada, and the United States, working extensively with strategy development and e-business-related projects. He has held senior executive and consulting positions with McKinsey & Company, Organic, Excite Canada, Globo, and Abril.

The current focus of Dr. Terra's research and practical business involvement is the development of knowledge management initiatives and systems that are concurrently based on the learning and action needs of the knowledge-worker and clearly linked to corporate strategy.

A popular speaker at academic and industry events, he also lectures at numerous MBA programs. A prolific author, Dr. Terra has published over 40 articles in academic journals, trade publications, and conferences. His first book, *Knowledge Management: The Great Business Challenge*, is currently in its second edition (Elsevier Brazil). He has also contributed articles to two other books about knowledge management and has several new publications in the works. He has a Ph.D. in Knowledge Management, a M.Sc. in Business Administration, and holds undergraduate degrees in both Economics and Production Engineering.

Dr. Terra lives in Toronto with his wife, Janine Dodge. Both love to go for long walks on the beach, learn languages, and explore different cultures and places. He can be contacted at jcterra@yahoo.com.

Cindy Gordon is currently the CEO of Helix Commerce International Inc., a company specializing in collaboration commerce to accelerate growth (www.helixcommerce.com). Prior to starting Helix, she was a Partner in XDLI, a tier-one Canadian Venture Capital technology fund. She also has senior executive experience with Accenture, Xerox, Nortel Networks, and Citicorp. Cindy is currently a Board Director/ Advisor of a number of early-stage technology companies, including Bianix, Got Marketing, TrueContext, Jive Media Technologies, CQUAY, Mongoose Technologies, The Milestone Group, and Tomoye.

Ms. Gordon is a published author of numerous publications on the new economy, knowledge management and eCommerce. She has collaborated on three other published books: *Chief Knowledge Officers in the New eEconomy, Knowledge: The Great Business Challenge* (Negócio Editora), and *Knowledge Management: Classic and Contemporary Works.*

Cindy has recently been recognized by the University of Western Business School for her business, community, and board leadership in a new book entitled *Women in the Lead.*

She has a master's of Information and Administration specializing in Information Systems and Business Strategy, a bachelor's of Education, and has recently completed her doctorate specializing in Knowledge Management and eCommerce.

Cindy is married with two children, and in her spare time she enjoys classical piano, weight training, squash, skiing, reading, and writing. She can be contacted at cindy@helixcommerce.com.

*For Product Safety Concerns and Information please contact
our EU representative GPSR@taylorandfrancis.com Taylor & Francis
Verlag GmbH, Kaufingerstraße 24, 80331 München, Germany*

T - #0050 - 230425 - C0 - 229/152/24 - PB - 9780750675932 - Gloss Lamination